100 MAGIC MILES
OF THE GREAT BARRIER REEF
The Whitsunday Islands

100 MAGIC MILES
OF THE GREAT BARRIER REEF
The Whitsunday Islands

by David Colfelt

Illustrations by Carolyn Colfelt

Windward
PUBLICATIONS

Published by:
Windward Publications Pty Ltd
464 Woodhill Mountain Road
Woodhill Mountain, via Berry, NSW 2535

National Library of Australia
    Cataloguing-in-Publication entry

Colfelt, David, 1939–.
    100 magic miles of the Great Barrier Reef: the Whitsunday Islands.

    5th ed.
    Includes index.
    ISBN 0 9586989 0 2.
    1. Pilot guides – Queensland – Whitsunday Group.
    2. Whitsunday Group (Qld.) – Description and travel.
    I. Colfelt, Carolyn, 1941–. II. Title. III. Title: One hundred magic
    miles of the Great Barrier Reef.

623.89299436

Printed by Dai Nippon Printing Company (Hong Kong)

First Published 1985
Second Edition 1987
Third Edition 1990
Fourth Edition 1993
Fifth Edition 1997

Credits

Illustrations

All of the illustrations are by Carolyn Colfelt. The original sketch maps were also by Carolyn Colfelt; these have been digitised.

Photographic contributions

Australian Survey Office (Crown Copyright Reserved); Carolyn Colfelt; David Colfelt; Department of Natural Resources, Queensland; Kerry Cox; Tony Fontes; Great Barrier Reef Marine Park Authority; Hamilton Island Charters; Robert Hartwick; Sandy Peacock; Queensland Tourist and Travel Corporation; Richard Timperley.

Acknowledgements

The Fifth Edition of *100 Magic Miles* represents an accumulation of knowledge about the Whitsunday islands, gathered with a very long, wide net over a period of several decades. The contributors of each bit of information are too numerous to mention individually. All can take some satisfaction from the fact that they are in some measure responsible for this book, which makes it so much easier to get around the Whitsundays than it used to be, with some confidence that there are probably no unpleasant surprises in store.

Thanks are due the following, whose contributions have been especially valuable at one time or another: Tony and Denise Allsop; Ansett Airlines; Greg Andrews; Avis; Ray Blackwood; Kevin Bowe; Nigel and Lisa Brown; Mel Day; Corrie de Waard; Terry Done; Cmdr Joe Doyle, RAN; Tony Fontes and the members of OUCH; Hamilton Island Enterprises; Hayman Island; Martin Hindle; Peter Holland; Rob Hughes; David Hutchen; Artie Jacobson; Yvonne and Bernie Katchor; Tony Kelly; Donald Kinsey; John Latchford; Dr Peter Lavarack; Phil and Rhada Luks; Kim McClymont; Leon O'Donahue; Peter Phillips; Bob Porter; Maureen Prior; Queensland Tourist and Travel Corporation; Des Ward; Doug White; Leon Zann; Len Zell.

A few people deserve extra-special thanks: Harry and Anne Smith; Ray Blackwood; Wendy Craik; Margie and David Allsopp; Carlo Grossman; David Bradley; the Great Barrier Reef Marine Park Authority; the Queensland Department of Environment; Ella Martin.

David and Carolyn Colfelt
Woodhill, NSW. 1997

Above:
Continental islands of the Whitsunday Group, with their sometimes massive
fringing coral reefs: Bird Island (foreground right); Langford Island
(foreground left); Hayman Island (upper left); Black Island (centre
midground); Hook Island (background).
Opposite:
Pinnacle Bay, north Hook Island.

THE 100 MAGIC MILES

In the distance the islands rise majestically, their dark silhouettes like pyramids on the shimmering horizon. Along their rocky shores, patches of brilliant white sand merge with the sea turning at first aquamarine, then emerald, their fringing coral reefs iridescent beneath the surface, their voluptuous hills becoming yellow-green in tropical sunlight. The Cumberland Islands span almost one degree of latitude on the eastern coast of Australia. They lie close to Queensland and the heart of that State's 'sugar belt', their limits marked on the mainland by the coastal towns of Mackay in the south (about latitude 21° south) and Bowen in the north (latitude 20° south).

The route north takes one from Scawfell Island, the southern gateway, along a vibrant blue passage through some one hundred islands and islets on the way to Bowen. Brisk trade winds fan a passing landscape which was, until geologically recent times, the preserve of eagles – yesterday's mountain tops, which rise steeply out of coral waters that are now some one hundred metres deeper than when the Aboriginal people probably first came here. It is about one hundred nautical miles by the shortest course to the quiet little town of Bowen through a tropical island paradise in the heart of Australia's Great Barrier Reef Marine Park. The magic of these islands has been appreciated since they were first recorded in the history books of the 18th century, by Lieutenant James Cook – during his first voyage of discovery – on Whit Sunday, in the year 1770.

Drowned mountain ranges
The Cumberlands, or Whitsundays as they are more often referred to these days, are actually two drowned mountain ranges cut off from the mainland by past geologic events.

The islands have, since Cook, been divided, for the convenience of the map makers, into smaller groups – the Whitsunday Group, the Lindeman Group, the Anchor Islands, and the Sir James Smith Group. The Whitsunday Group drew the first attention of the pioneers who came to this part of the mainland coast in the mid-1800s, and this group's name is now generalised to refer to any of the Cumberlands.

Opposite above:
A view from Hamilton Island looking
east over the southern side of
Whitsunday Island. When the trade
winds are still, the sea is a brilliant blue,
and those aboard yachts in the
Whitsundays seize the opportunity to
visit beautiful anchorages, on the
exposed southern sides of the islands,
that are untenable during
the trade winds season.

Opposite below:
Shades of fading day in
the Whitsunday Passage.

The Whitsundays are called 'continental islands' because they are composed of the same rock and have generally the same flora and fauna as the adjacent mainland. Their colourful fringing coral reefs pulsating with marine life are generally absent on the mainland. Some twenty-five nautical miles further north-east is the nearest of the platform reefs that are usually associated with the Great Barrier Reef, and these are referred to locally as the 'outer reefs'.

Since the earliest days of this maritime nation when it was discovered that there was a route up the Australian east coast inside the Great Barrier Reef, vessels have been using the Whitsunday Passage as part of the shortest route north. At one time the government planted coconut palms on some of the islands to provide an energy-rich food for the shipwrecked, and the passing sailors went one better and turned pigs and goats loose to run wild. The more than one hundred islands and islets offer scores of sheltered anchorages, and it isn't surprising that they became the favourite of yachtsmen because of these hundreds of hideaways all within easy sailing distance of each other. Later exploration proved that the mainland coast, too, between Bowen and Airlie Beach, is studded with anchorages, almost all protected from the prevailing south-east trade winds. In these sheltered bays mangrove communities are often found, the primeval nurseries, so typical of the northern Queensland coast, which make for fascinating exploring and good fishing.

Pioneer settlers on the adjacent mainland in the mid-19th century needed timber to build their houses, and their land was both difficult to fence and subject to visitation by large salt-water crocodiles. They sought out the islands for their tall pines and for safe paddocks on which to graze sheep and cattle. By the 1920s, half a dozen or so of the islands had full-time residents, some of whom started up small resorts, with huts made out of corrugated iron, floors of coral fragments. The Whitsundays were to become popular island retreats after World War II. The resorts were generally homely and very much a product of post-war Queensland. Seasoned sailors with time on their hands knew that the islands offered excellent cruising. But the Whitsundays were, even so, a relatively well-kept secret.

The 1970s brought great change. Cyclone Ada, in 1972, devastated the area, levelling trees and extensively damaging several of the resorts. This was the beginning of a period of historic development. The creation of the Hamilton Island resort in the 1980s started a chain reaction that saw redevelopment of each and every island resort, four of them razed and begun again from scratch. Hayman, always a magic name in Australia, closed its doors for more than two years to undergo a complete metamorphosis, emerging a brilliantly coloured butterfly, stunning in form and style. Lindeman was rebuilt virtually from the bottom up, as was the resort at Happy Bay, Long Island, and the resort on Daydream Island. Brampton has been extensively refurbished. The ownership and financial base of the resorts is no longer a family matter but is the business of major corporations, which has brought an injection of capital to bring the resorts into line with contemporary standards for resorts.

Airlie Beach is the adjacent mainland holiday centre, and it has expanded west towards Cannonvale. There are a number of mainland resorts now, from smart hotels to backpackers accommodation. There are new motels and holiday flats. The marina at Abell Point has become a major point of embarkation for the islands; other marinas are planned.

The Whitsundays have the largest bareboat charter fleet in the South Pacific. The islands offer all manner of adventure holidays – diving, camping, cruising among unspoilt national park islands. Every day hundreds of day-trippers get a taste of the islands or catch a first glimpse of the Great Barrier Reef from the deck of one of many vessels that ply the Whitsunday Passage and beyond. For those who want resort comfort combined with a holiday afloat, there are charter yachts taking week-long cruises among the islands and to the Barrier Reef.

Above:
Stopping off at Whitehaven,
Whitsunday Island.

Left:
The most spectacular beach in all the
Whitsundays, Whitehaven stretches for
some three nautical miles up the eastern
side of the largest of the Cumberland
islands. The Aboriginal name for it meant
'whispering sands'. It is composed of
virtually pure, white silica, a bountiful gift
from the geologic past.

Above:
Blue Pearl Bay, Hayman Island, is a popular daytime anchorage with very good coral viewing for divers and snorkellers. It is also a favourite beach of guests at the resort on Hayman Island.

Right:
Nara Inlet, on the southern side of Hook Island, is a deep, fjord-like indentation that provides good protection from all winds and is thus popular with those cruising in the Whitsundays.

Above:
Sunset over Plum Pudding Island and
the Whitsunday Passage.
Right:
Daydream Island, living up to its name.
Below:
The beckoning profile of Hayman Island seen from
the sand spit at Langford Island.

Left:
A mother humpback whale beats the water with her tail, her calf (right) like a 'ditto' mark beside her. Humpbacks migrate from their Antarctic feeding grounds to breed in tropical and subtropical waters, favouring the continental shores as they travel. They are now a common sight in the Whitsundays from July through September. Those pictured were photographed just south of Whitsunday Island, early on a September morning; the mother put on a spectacular five-minute display of 'breaching' – leaping completely out of the water – before she and her calf went on their way.

Below:
The Whitsundays are among the finest cruising grounds in the world, and the area is visited by hundreds of itinerant yachts each winter. The area also has a large bareboat (sail-it-yourself-yacht) charter fleet.

Above:
Continental island fringing coral reefs at low tide resemble a moonscape and can provide endless diversion for fossickers. This massive expanse of reef between Haslewood and Lupton islands is alive with crabs and shells at low tide. When the tide comes in, a rush of marine life returns to feed on the reef.

Left:
Most of the Cumberland Islands are unspoilt national parks, and they allow indulgence in a feeling of real escape. The landscape is extremely varied, producing a wide range of natural habitats.

Above and right:
Airlie Beach surveys a brilliant blue expanse of water, and the islands to the north sit up majestically, breaking the line of the horizon. The town is a mainland holiday centre, with resorts, holiday apartments, shops and restaurants. In winter it is common to see many itinerant yachts at anchor in the bay.

Below:
Shute Harbour is a centre for island cruises and charter boat activities. It is the finest mainland harbour for many miles.

Before the dawn of man

How the islands arose

Looking at a globe you can't help but notice a remarkable, if rough, 'fit' between the west coast of Africa and the east coast of South America. Analysis of offshore depths allows Africa and South America to be fitted together, very snugly, at the 100-metre contour. The same is true of North America and Europe, and of Africa, Australia, South America and Antarctica.

Scientists believe that all of the earth's present land masses were, about two hundred million years ago, part of a supercontinent, 'Pangaea' ('all earth'), named by Alfred Wegener, the German inventor of the theory of continental drift. Nobody believed him at first, because existing knowledge made drifting continents unlikely. But in the 1960s the theory of plate tectonics provided an explanation which gave Wegener's theory more or less the same degree of scientific acceptability as Darwin's theory of evolution by natural selection.

Plate tectonics says that the continents 'float', like logs on water, on denser but plastic basaltic crustal rock 'plates'. The plates fit together around the globe like pieces in a giant jigsaw puzzle. Throughout the history of the earth great blocks of continental crust have been moved by expanding suboceanic plates. These plates are being enlarged by a spreading process that takes place in a direction away from great mid-ocean rift areas. In parts of the world some of the plates are tearing apart, or sliding past each other. When plates collide, one slides beneath the other (is subducted). Fractured blocks of continental rock accumulate and others are folded in these areas of contact. Mountains are formed. The plates dipping and plunging deep down (subducting) heat and become viscous. This hot, viscous material, being of lighter, siliceous rock, begins to rise towards the surface. If it cools and crystallises below the surface it is granite. If it breaks through, volcanoes form and basalt flows. People have noticed for ages that earthquakes recur at the same places around the globe. Definite earthquake belts are identified and mainly lie where the crustal plates are colliding.

About sixty-five million years ago Australia began to detach itself from Antarctica. At that time the whole of the continent was south of latitude 40° south. India was advancing on the Asian continent (the ultimate catastrophic collision would form the Himalayas). The advancing 'active' edges of moving continents are where mountain ranges are thrown up. The Rocky Mountain chain in western USA is at the 'leading' edge of the North American continent. Queensland's volcanic eastern coastal ranges are near its leading edge, but some also occur where the drifting Australia has passed over a deep 'hot spot'.

You can safely assume that the continents will continue to move in geologic time; Australia is heading north-east, at about five centimetres a year, into the Pacific which is itself shrinking. The Mediterranean Sea will, one day, close up completely as Africa completes its collision with southern Europe.

Two hundred million years ago all of the earth's continents were united in a single land mass dubbed Pangaea ('all earth') by a German meteorologist, Alfred Wegener. Gondwana began to break up about a hundred and eighty million years ago. Australia started to separate from Antarctica some sixty-five million years ago and became an island continent about forty-five million years ago, moving north-eastwards into the Pacific.

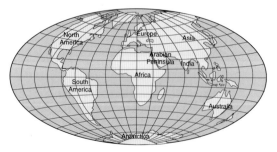

The position of the continents is explained today in terms of the theory of plate tectonics, which suggests that the continents are carried on rigid plates that 'float' around the globe driven by the thermal dynamics of the planet's interior. Today Australia continues its north-easterly movement into the Pacific, moving about five centimetres a year.

How the mountains were drowned

Throughout most of the earth's four and a half thousand million year history there was little or no ice, and the climate was warmer than during the last one million years. The breaking up of the land mass, and the movement of continents across the earth's surface, caused new heat transfer patterns to be established, and cooling probably began when North America and Europe reached their present positions several tens of millions of years ago.

Glacial ice began to form on Antarctica about thirty million years ago, after it had separated from South America and was cut off from the circulation of warm equatorial waters, and colder southern ocean waters were able to circle the earth, especially after Australia moved clear of the Antarctic.

Present knowledge suggests that the build-up of ice on earth has to do with the amount of solar radiation that reaches the large land masses that now lie in the northern latitudes. This, in turn, is controlled by periodic variations in the earth's tilt on its axis and the shape of its orbit around the sun. The cycle takes about one hundred thousand years.

Eighteen thousand years ago ice was several kilometres thick over most of Canada and much of northern USA. Two-thirds of the earth's land was covered with it. So much water was locked up in the ice that sea level was about one hundred metres lower than it is today. This glaciation was the most recent of ten ice ages during the past million years.

About eighteen thousand years ago the earth entered a new orbital cycle that caused the northern latitude land masses to receive a net increase in heat from the sun. Ice began to melt. During the next twelve thousand or so years the sea rose some one hundred metres, isolating two mountain ridges from the Queensland central coast, cutting off Tasmania from the mainland and flooding all of the current natural harbours around the Australian coast. During this period the corals of today's Great Barrier Reef grew upwards, on top of the ancient remains of earlier reefs, matching the advance of the sea. Today, if all global ice melted, the sea level would rise by eighty-five metres; in recent times it has been rising about one millimetre a year, but this rate is accelerating due to the 'greenhouse effect' caused by man-made gases in the atmosphere.

The Whitsundays are drowned mountains, cut off from the Queensland mainland when the last great thaw began to flood the continental shelf about ten thousand years ago. Hook Island (background) is the loftiest of these mountain peaks of yesterday. It is seen here from Hayman Island, whose expansive fringing coral reef flat dries extensively at low tide.

The discovery of the Whitsundays

Dreams of South Pacific isles have infected the minds of European men since the day in September 1513 that Vasco de Balboa scrambled up a hill on the isthmus of Panama and saw that there was water beyond. The fever really took hold in the 17th and 18th centuries as the Spanish, French, Dutch and English successively rediscovered the many islands, flung across the vast Pacific Ocean, that the Melanesians and Polynesians had made their homes some four and a half thousand years earlier – when sailors in Europe and Asia barely dared to go out of sight of land.

The first remarks by a white man about the great quality of the Cumberland Islands were made by James Cook and, like many of his observations, they have stood up to modern critical appraisal. He was not the first to appreciate the islands, however; Aboriginal people have been in Australia for at least forty thousand years, and they were in the Whitsundays for thousands of years before Cook sailed up the Passage.

Cook was a lieutenant in His Majesty George III's Navy, promoted from the rank of master in May 1768. He was nearly forty years old, and his rise from the lower deck since joining the Navy as a seaman in 1755 was an indication of the talent that was ultimately to bring him world recognition.

The 18th century was an age of science and reason – and one of aggressive economic imperialism. While Great Britain's North American empire was cracking, she was thinking about laying the first bricks of another. Cook had attracted the favourable attention of his superiors for his meticulous charting of Newfoundland, and he had been noted in scientific circles for his observations on the eclipse of the sun in 1766.

An event of immense scientific importance was to take place in June 1769 – the phenomenon of the transit of Venus with the Sun. The British nation was not to be left behind in the quest for scientific discovery and the Crown agreed, at the behest of the Royal Society, to pay the expenses of an exhibition to observe this once-in-a-lifetime astronomical occurrence from Tahiti, where southern hemisphere observations could be related to those made at various positions on the northern half of the globe to help determine the distance of the earth from the sun. The Admiralty was to provide a ship, and James Cook got the job.

Some five years before the Americans dumped tea into Boston Harbour, Cook was given the 368-tonne *Endeavour Bark* (the 'Bark' in the name was included because there was already another *Endeavour* in the Royal Navy). The ship was cat rigged, roomy and seaworthy. After making his observations of Venus, Cook was to proceed to latitude 40° south to try to find the supposed great southern continent. He left Plymouth in August 1768.

Early mainland settlers sought out tall pines from the islands for timber to build their houses. A mill was operated on Whitsunday Island, at Cid Harbour, from 1888 to 1904.

Whit Sunday, 1770

Almost two event-filled years and many discoveries later, on Whit Sunday June 3, 1770 (as the time was reckoned then – it was actually Monday, June 4 in Australia), he was sailing up the central coast of what is today Queensland, and at noon on that day he was in the entrance of a passage between the mainland and a group of lofty islands to the east, with 'Everywhere good anchorages … Indeed the whole passage is one continued safe harbour'. He named the passage 'Whitsundays Passage' after the day of its discovery, and the islands the Cumberlands, after Henry Frederick, Duke of Cumberland, the younger brother of King George III, the reigning monarch. Cook put a number of names on the map as he made his way through the Passage, and some of these that remain today are Cape Hillsborough[1], at the southern extremity of Repulse Bay[2], Cape Conway[3], Cape Gloucester[4], Holburne Island[5] and Edgecumbe Bay[6].

Australian Aboriginal people in strength roamed all of the coast between Mackay and Bowen long before pioneer explorer George Dalrymple founded the settlement at Bowen in 1861. Evidence suggests that Aboriginal people from the mainland visited the islands seasonally in search of available foods rather than that there were permanent settlements on the islands.

European man's early encounters with natives of the South Pacific were frequently troubled, and there is little doubt that the coming of the white man was extremely unsettling. In many encounters it is difficult to decide who did what to whom first. Some white historians have noted that the 'natives' of the Whitsunday area were unpredictable and belligerent. No doubt if there were any recorded notes of the Aboriginal people's thoughts on the coming of the white man, these would also reflect considerable misgivings.

After Cook the next white visitor to the area was Lieutenant Phillip Parker King, in 1819, on the Mermaid. His party found Aboriginal huts and the remains of a canoe on the northern side of Conway Peninsula. Throughout the 19th century a series of British naval surveys were undertaken among the islands during which the presence of Aboriginal people was noted on some islands.

In 1878 *Louisa Maria* called in at Whitsunday Island for water; it is not clear what provocation was or was not given, but the ship was scuttled and burned by the tribesmen there; three of her four crew were picked up later by a schooner and taken to Bowen, but the cook was never found. Aboriginal people, according to some reports, were still on the island when in 1888 James Withnall set up his sawmill there. Withnall employed some of them in building a dam for the mill and in gathering timber.

The lure of the islands

There is no doubt that James Cook's favourable impressions of the Whitsunday area were echoed by many who followed him. The botanist Jukes, aboard *Fly* when Captain Blackwood surveyed the area, noted: 'Shores rise in a very steep slope, with occasional precipices to a height of several hundred feet and are completely covered by a magnificent forest, the greater part of which is pine tree … if it should be desirable to push settlements of N.S.W. further to the north, I think this part of the coast has greater natural advantage than any other we have seen'.

After the settlement of Bowen and Proserpine, the islands were sought out. Timber from Whitsunday and Hook islands was used extensively in early buildings at Bowen. Some of the islands were leased for grazing cattle and sheep or for breeding goats.

By the end of the 1920s there were fledgling resorts on a number of the islands, although the ensuing world depression, and then the war, held back any extensive development for another fifteen years.

In years past, trochus shells (used in making mother-of-pearl buttons) were taken in commercial quantities from the east side of Lupton Island.

1. Hillsborough was named after Wills Hill, the first Viscount Hillsborough, who was Secretary of State for the Colonies.
2. Cook, at first, thought that Repulse Bay might be the way north along the coast. He anchored in the mouth of the bay until sunrise, but then he noted that the flood of the tide came in from seawards, and his first assumption was wrong. His intended route thus 'repulsed', he so named the bay.
3. Henry Seymour Conway, Secretary of State from 1765 to 1768.
4. William Henry, Duke of Gloucester, second younger brother of George III.
5. Francis Holburne, Commander of the North American fleet in which Cook served in 1757, and Lord of the Admiralty, 1770–71.
6. George Edgecumbe, Naval Commander-in-Chief at Plymouth, 1766 –70.

Above:
Anemone and clown fish, one of many intriguing
arrangements of nature on the reef.

Opposite:
A deep channel separates the mid-shelf reefs, Hook and Hardy,
which are the nearest ocean reefs to the Whitsundays, some
twenty-five nautical miles north-east of Hayman Island.

THE WHITSUNDAYS AND THE GREAT BARRIER REEF

The Great Barrier Reef is said to be the largest structure on earth ever created by living creatures. It is a submarine chain of small limestone hills that stretches some two thousand kilometres along the eastern coast of Australia from above Cape York (latitude 10°41' south) to Fraser Island (24° south) and covers some three hundred and fifty thousand square kilometres on the Australian continental shelf. The limestone has been created in part by tiny colonising animals which absorb calcium and oxygen dissolved in sea water and, with some help from tiny plants that live in their tissues, secrete calcium carbonate (limestone) skeletons which become massive reefs.

In spite of its name, the Great Barrier Reef is not a single reef, nor is it a 'barrier reef' in the sense that Charles Darwin used the term. 'Barrier reef' was first used by Darwin in his attempts to classify coral reefs, and they were reefs seen at mid-ocean islands around which they formed a close offshore barrier. This type of reef began life as a fringing reef, skirting the shores of an island that was slowly sinking into the ocean as a result of the tectonic movements of the earth's crust. Eventually, when the island submerged, only a ring of coral with a central lagoon was left at the surface – an atoll. There are no atolls in Australia's reef system, which sits on our relatively stable continental shelf, although the term is used by some tourist promoters who are ignorant of its true meaning but knowledgeable about the promotional magic of the word!

'Barrier' was probably first used to describe Australia's system of reefs by Matthew Flinders when he explored the coast in the early 1800s. The term had a certain logic, especially in the northern sections of the Reef Region, where the reefs form almost a continuous rampart, and in other parts, such as the Hard Line Reefs east of Mackay, are an almost impenetrable maze perforated by intricate channels. Throughout the Region the reef structures bar the incursion of huge oceanic swells from the east, rendering the waters behind them smooth in comparison with the ocean. And they certainly constitute a barrier to easy navigation even today.

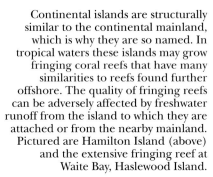

Continental islands are structurally similar to the continental mainland, which is why they are so named. In tropical waters these islands may grow fringing coral reefs that have many similarities to reefs found further offshore. The quality of fringing reefs can be adversely affected by freshwater runoff from the island to which they are attached or from the nearby mainland. Pictured are Hamilton Island (above) and the extensive fringing reef at Waite Bay, Haslewood Island.

The Great Barrier Reef Region

After years of growing concern about how oil and mineral exploration might affect this magnificent living structure and marine habitat, the *Great Barrier Reef Marine Park Act 1975* was passed by Federal Parliament. The Act defined a Region which incorporates roughly all of the Queensland coast from the shoreline to the edge of the continental shelf, from the tip of Cape York to just north of Bundaberg. Within it are approximately three thousand individual coral reefs (including some three hundred cays, about seventy of which are vegetated) as well as a host of other islands which lie closer to the mainland and which are referred to as 'continental islands' because they are geologically similar to the continental mainland. Many of these have their own fringing coral reefs with associated reef life similar to that of the offshore reefs.

All places where reefs form in the Pacific are located on major oceanic rises or on the continental shelf. Greatest development is near the shelf edges next to deep water. Reef development declines as the distance from deep water increases, because water pooled in lagoonal or shelf environments does not favour good reef growth. Corals, moreover, do not like fresh water or sediment found close to larger mainland rivers. Reefs tend to reflect the range of physical and biological possibilities; the direction and extent of their growth closely reflects the bottom that they grow on and the influences of currents and the contents of the water around them.

In the northern section of the Great Barrier Reef Region, where the continental shelf is narrow, the 'typical' reef is a long, linear 'ribbon' close to the shelf edge and running parallel to it. These are separated by narrow passes. The shelf slopes off steeply east of the reefs to depths of about two thousand metres. Inshore are oval platform reefs and low wooded coral islands.

In the central Region the continental shelf is wider. Opposite the Whitsundays it is about seventy-two nautical miles wide, and it expands rapidly to reach maximum width just south of Mackay (21°south), where its edge is almost two hundred nautical miles from the mainland. Continental islands with fringing reefs lie close to the mainland – Hinchinbrook, Orpheus, the Palms, Magnetic, the Whitsundays. Beyond them out towards the shelf edge are platform reefs.

The southern Region is a vast wilderness of patch reefs separated by open water or narrow winding channels. Further south the continental shelf narrows again, and east of Gladstone close to the shelf edge there is a series of well-developed lagoonal platform reefs and vegetated cays, the best known of which is probably Heron Island.

A modern veneer over ancient animal ruins

The individual reefs of the Region are composed of a cemented base of accumulated plant and animal calcium carbonate skeletons upon which

grows a veneer of living coral animals and plants. In the Region there are some three hundred cays, islands which have in a sense lifted themselves out of the ocean, when enough reef debris – broken bits of corals, shells and the skeletal remains of other marine life – has been piled up by currents and storms to remain above water even at high tide. Sea birds then provide the organic matter to form a soil base.

The Great Barrier Reef is the world's largest and most complex expanse of living coral reefs, supporting many unique forms of marine life. There are over fifteen hundred species of fish, about four hundred species of coral animals, and a host of sponges, anemones, worms, crustaceans, shells, sea stars, urchins, and so forth. The cays are nesting places for around two hundred and forty-two species of birds, and six species of turtle (it is one of the world's significant turtle-breeding areas). Whales, dolphins and dugong are found in the area.

The great diversity of life forms makes the Great Barrier Reef an area of immense scientific importance. It has been included in the World Heritage List, a list of world assets of such importance that they warrant special protection under international scrutiny.

'The Reef'

Today anything that lies within the Region is often referred to by the all-encompassing term, 'the Reef', which is confusing as it can refer to an outlying shelf-edge reef, a near-shore platform reef, a coral cay or (sometimes) a continental island with its fringing reef. However, 'the Reef' seems to communicate an idea of the locality with a certain economy of words, and although less than precise, it satisfies the desire to express a sense of magic that most visitors feel about the area.

What are corals?

Corals baffled men for ages. The ancient poet Ovid referred to them as organisms that were soft underwater but hardened on contact with air (the soft living animal, of course, dies out of water, leaving behind the calcium carbonate skeleton). Because they were attached and didn't move about, it's perhaps easy to understand how even scientists of old declared these underwater 'shrubs' to be plants, although credulity must have waned after they'd picked one and taken it home to Mum. Even today, no one has figured out a way to prevent dead corals from losing colour or, more significantly, smelling like last month's prawns.

Back in 1723 a French scientist dared to challenge this herbal notion of coral. Jean Peysonnel put it to the French Académie des Sciences that corals were, in fact, animals! Many colleagues thought Peysonnel had momentarily taken leave of his senses, and they tried to persuade him not to publish his findings lest he ruin his reputation.

Above:
Continental island fringing reefs can produce beaches of a very similar nature to the beaches of true coral islands (cays). Langford Island, for example, has an expansive reef on which a small sand cay has formed, giving the island a somewhat 'dual' character – part continental island, part cay.

Above left:
True coral islands, such as North West Island in the Capricorn Group off Gladstone, have grown up on top of coral reefs and are composed entirely of calcareous sands. Their beach vegetation is distinctive and is made up of plants that can tolerate a salty environment.

Above:
Soft corals take a variety of forms –
branched, delicate flowers, fans. Those
which have skeletons contain internal
crystalline structures of limestone.

Above left and centre:
Feather stars (crinoids) are delicate,
colourful inhabitants of the reef.

Today with hindsight and more study we know that the truth lies in
both camps. Coral polyps are carnivorous; they are relatives of jellyfish,
the link being that they are armed with stinging cells – nematocysts –
which are a devastating weapon for immobilising their animal prey. But
living within their tissues they have microscopic algae called zooxanthellae which provide a substantial proportion of their total food energy. Reef-
building corals can lay down hard skeleton far more quickly due to the
energy provided by their resident algae.

How a coral reef is formed

The reef begins when, after drifting in the plankton community for several weeks, a coral planula (the larval stage which results when a coral
egg and sperm get together) settles, attaches itself to a clean piece of shallow ocean floor and secretes a cup-like calcium carbonate skeleton, thus
insuring its survival. Now a 'polyp', the individual coral animal proceeds
to reproduce itself simply by growing another. When this process has occurred enough times to produce a structure, other organisms join the
project for protection.

Corals are the initiators and the visually dominant organisms, but algae and all of the animal life associated with the fledgling reef contribute
to its success. As already noted, corals have living in their tissues single-
celled plants, algae, called zooxanthellae, which, like all plants, have the
ability to create food by a process called photosynthesis. Given the energy
of sunlight to drive their factory, the algae turn basic nutrients (nitrogen,
phosphorus, carbon dioxide) into chemical energy in the form of carbo-
hydrates and amino acids (the building blocks of protein and fats). Like
all plants, they also produce oxygen, helping to keep the reef water well
oxygenated. These resident algae get their own needs – nitrogen and
CO_2 – from the by-products that corals create in digesting their tiny animal food and by their respiration. It has been estimated that somewhere
between 30 and 90% of the corals' food requirements are provided by
these symbiotic algae, and the corals are thus free to concentrate on building skeleton and dividing into more polyps.

The reef has begun, and little fishes and other creatures have sought
protection among the corals' branches and intricate folds. Algae have
grown here and there, various planktonic animals have sought protection, and soon bigger fishes have come around looking for algae to graze
on or for little creatures to eat. Some of the zooplankton have grown up
into shells and crabs and fishes. And so on and on.

The reef grows upwards seeking maximum light for the benefit of the
corals' resident algae. It continues until it reaches the surface, where it
can grow up no more, so it continues outwards. The best growth is on the

Opposite page:
Acropora is the most prolific genus of
corals, and its species assume a
number of diffent forms, from delicate
antlers found in lagoons, to robust
staghorns on the reef front, to tabloid
structures that maximise their
exposure to light on the reef slope.
Reef-building corals, or stony corals,
have hard calcium carbonate
skeletons. They are nocturnal animals,
and in the daylight the observer
usually sees only the skeleton with a
trace of colour.

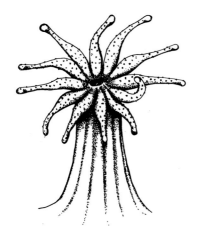

A single coral polyp.

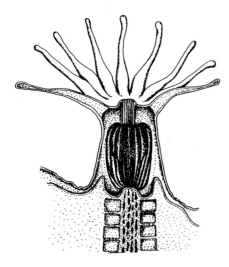

Polyp in cross-section.

The individual coral polyp is a sac with a hole surrounded by multiples of six waving tentacles, each armed with batteries of stinging cells which immobilise planktonic prey. From the mouth a muscular gullet descends into the central digestive cavity which is connected to the body by vertical partitions. The cells lining the digestive cavity have symbiotic algae which live and divide in them and which contribute greatly to the efficiency of the coral as a reef builder. The polyps secrete a protective limestone cup, consisting of radiating vertical plates, which interleaf with the partitions.

seaward/windward side of the reef, subjected to the clean ocean water and high turbulence. However, most of this growth is not realised.

Having reached the surface the reef begins to reflect the physical factors that now impinge upon it. The pounding of the waves soon breaks bits of coral away from the exposed surface and tosses the debris back away from the weather side. When coral dies, algae grows on the dead reef, and in the very punishing surf zone a species of tough, calcareous algae thrives. It cements-over the abraded surface forming a durable pavement called the 'algal rim', or reef crest, behind which, the wave energy having been dissipated, corals can again survive and grow. Debris consisting of dead coral skeletons, pulverised calcareous algae, shells and the skeletal remains of other animals eventually accumulates behind the crest and the living coral zone, creating another kind of physical zone – a sand flat – which in turn provides another biological environment. Nothing succeeds like success, and the mature reef becomes a marine habitat.

The Great Barrier Reef Region has been described as a watery desert, a vast expanse of clear, warm tropical waters that are low in nutrients, its reefs oases, marvels of evolution. It is now considered questionable whether the tropical ocean is necessarily a watery desert, and in fact reefs occur in waters with quite a wide range of nutrient levels. Nevertheless the reef is certainly a finely tuned complex, creating and consuming much of its own food supply, and it maintains the delicate balance of production and consumption. Every member of the community has some part in the equation. This critical balance of species is important for human reef visitors to remember; spear fishing, excessive line fishing, shell collecting or even just inconsiderate viewing can, theoretically, upset normal predation patterns and thereby the balance of the reef, which would threaten its survival.

There are many ways to enjoy coral reefs – diving over the unearthly landscape of a reef slope, or snorkelling in the coral pools of a lagoon while a fantasia is acted out for you by the local inhabitants, or walking on the reef rubble at low tide watching crabs skitter and shells going about their business.

There are many different types of reef to enjoy, from oceanic platforms to continental island fringing reefs. Although there are differences between them, certain fundamental characteristics are always present. As reefs expand, they have an influence on the water circulation around them. Different sorts of conditions are created which suit different sorts of marine life and, with this in mind, some sort of order emerges from the chaos that confronts the novice reef explorer. Pages 40–41 provide a brief glimpse of the life that is associated with the coral reef. In 'Tips for tropical holidays', some words of advice are offered on how to get the best out of your day on a reef.

The Great Barrier Reef Marine Park Authority

The Federal authority charged with overall responsibility for planning and management of the Great Barrier Reef Marine Park, GBRMPA (as it is usually referred to) had a monumental task in creating the first zoning plans for the Reef. From its inception this organisation attracted a motivated and well-informed group of officers who had to work out a means of protecting the Barrier Reef for future generations while 'allowing life to go on' at the same time. Zoning has often been a balancing act and has been accomplished with imagination and a remarkable lack of conflict, considering the widely varying interest groups that use Queensland's coastal waters. GBRMPA is responsible for examining all proposals that might affect the Barrier Reef and for issuing permits for all commercial operations and for those who wish to undertake collecting within the Marine Park.

The Marine Park

The Great Barrier Reef Marine Park covers most of Australia's north-eastern continental shelf, and it is quite different from a 'park' as in 'national park', where everything is totally protected. The Marine Park incorporates a vast area of water and islands, with a 'town plan' superimposed; it has various zones that cater for the equivalent of a town's residential, commercial, light-industrial, and recreational areas, along with areas that are off limits (which are usually for wildlife preservation). The Marine Park provides the framework for managing and preserving the Reef.

Within the boundaries, everything from low water mark to the edge of the continental shelf is under Marine Park jurisdiction; it is complemented and overlapped by a system of Queensland State Marine Parks which protect from high water out to 3 miles offshore. Above high water mark the islands are either Queensland national parks or are covered by State or Federal Government lease or, in a few cases, by freehold title.

In zoning the Marine Park, GBRMPA had to consider pre-existing activities on the continental shelf; for example, commercial fishing, amateur fishing, tourist resorts, shipping. It was apparent that a model much more flexible than a national park was needed. A zoning scheme was devised allowing different uses of the park to coexist without undue interference between them. It took about ten years to zone the entire Reef, section by section, a process completed not long ago. A review of each section is undertaken every five years, with public involvement at all stages.

The Marine Park is managed on a day-to-day basis by the Queensland Department of Environment. Queensland's Boating and Fisheries Patrol also has a role. Whitsunday visitors can obtain extensive information about the Reef, the Marine Park and the Whitsunday area, including some excellent publications which outline the various zones and explain the types of activities permitted, from the Whitsunday Information Centre, corner

The Great Barrier Reef is really a maze of thousands of individual reefs separated, in some cases, by only narrow channels.

The Marine Park has been divided into sections with separate management plans and zones worked out according to the desires of users and the dictates of conservation. The Whitsunday islands fall in the Central Section (yellow infill). The other sections are (north to south): Far Northern; Cairns (including Cormorant Passsage); Mackay–Capricorn.

Mandalay Road and Shute Harbour Road (about one and a half kilometres from the centre of town), Airlie Beach, Qld 4802, telephone (079) 467 022.

In conjunction with zoning, GBRMPA has devised a permit system controlling collecting, research, and tourist activities in zoned sections of the Park. Permits are a simple way to keep a reasonable check without the need for total prohibition. Unlike national parks, where *nothing* may be taken, in certain Marine Park areas you may fish, and in some areas you may collect a small number of shells without a permit. In still others you may be granted a permit to collect, if you have formally requested and received permission to do so. The desirability of permits is easier to understand when one reflects on the delicately balanced ecology of coral reefs.

Crown-of-thorns starfish

The crown-of-thorns starfish (*Acanthaster planci*) has become a major worry for the Reef because in the past three decades it has swarmed over reefs (primarily from Lizard Island to Bowen) in plague proportions causing a significant amount of damage to corals. Minor (controllable) outbreaks have occurred in the Whitsunday area in recent years, principally at Butterfly Bay, northern Hook Island, and at Blue Pearl Bay, north-western Hayman Island. The crown-of-thorns is a normal part of the Reef community and is but one of a number of coral predators and parasites, which include a variety of fishes, crabs, nudibranch and gastropod molluscs, worms, an encrusting sponge and one other starfish. However, it is the only one that is known to cause physical damage on such a large scale.

Population explosions of the crown-of-thorns may have occurred periodically throughout history and in recent times throughout the Indo-Pacific region. The first of recent outbreaks on the Barrier Reef was noticed in the 1960s. It began at Green Island, off Cairns, where there is a tourist resort and where thousands of people get their first look at a coral reef. Green Island's reef was devastated. *Acanthaster* attacks particularly staghorn corals, the fastest growing and most plentiful species. These starfishes have no table manners; they lie on top of the corals, turn their stomach out through their mouth, release digestive juices all over the corals, and then slurp up the 'polyp soup'. One starfish can wipe out an area the size of a dinner plate a day, leaving nothing but a bleached white skeleton. In aggregations of millions, they can devastate an entire reef in a matter of months.

The crown-of-thorns starfish (*Acanthaster planci*) is a predator of corals and has caused extensive damage to some reefs. There is a question whether the starfish represents a real threat to the future wellbeing of the Reef or whether it is just an occasional phenomenon. Another question is whether the activities of man have started to alter the pattern of nature to the detriment of the Reef.

By 1976 the crown-of-thorns started to disappear as suddenly as they came, and an advisory committee concluded that there wasn't sufficient evidence to suggest that the starfish posed a real threat to the Reef. In 1979 the crown-of-thorns returned with a vengeance, and some people began predicting the end for the Reef, that it would crumble and be destroyed by the sea (which wouldn't happen, as the living corals of any reef form only a thin veneer, the rest being limestone). The media created an atmosphere of panic, there were loud calls of 'somebody do something' – although, without understanding the cause of the phenomenon, it is difficult to see just what anyone could do. Practical field work suggested that the cost of killing the starfish wholesale would soon bankrupt the country. One reef may have starfish in the millions, and estimates put the cost (at the time) at about ten dollars per starfish killed. Small-scale eradication on parts of reefs used for coral viewing – done by injecting starfish with small amounts of copper sulphate, a poison – have proved more feasible but still expensive and time-consuming. Other methods of control suggested so far, such as dusting reefs with lime, are neither ecologically sound nor feasible.

The reasons for population explosions are not yet known. The starfish is extremely fecund, one female producing up to one hundred million eggs per year. That sort of population economy is known in other animals, such as giant clams, and it is one characterised by the survival of only a few offspring. Anything that tips the balance in favour of survival of the larvae, which are produced in such great numbers, even if the survival rate is increased only by a minute percentage, can result in a plague.

Several theories have been advanced. One is that human beings are responsible, because they have removed in great numbers one or more natural enemies of the crown-of-thorns, particularly the triton shell and some species of fishes. Some scientists haven't given the triton theory much credit and say that this mollusc would not be a significant factor in controlling plagues. On the other hand, some feel that normal starfish populations may have been kept sufficiently thinned out by predators such as the triton that their blitz-spawning strategy has not resulted in plagues. Man has also been implicated by his activities on the land – clearing and agriculture – which have increased runoff of nutrients which have, in turn, fertilised the phytoplankton upon which the crown-of-thorns starfish larvae survive. Another argument holds that starfish plagues are a natural phenomenon that recurs from time to time, a caprice of nature.

Researchers now mostly agree that the crown-of-thorns phenomenon is not a simple cause-and-effect relationship. There may be many reasons for the outbreaks, perhaps even a combination of natural and man-induced factors. The managers of the Marine Park feel that, until most crown-of-thorns experts can agree that the infestations are unnatural, measures to control them should be limited to areas of scientific importance or importance to tourists. As noted above, there's not much that can be done anyway.

Skeletal remains of the crown-of-thorns have been found in core samples taken from reefs, yielding sediments dating back thousands of years and suggesting that outbreaks may not be just a recent phenomenon. This evidence may indicate that nature is taking its course, but it is also subject to a number of doubts.

Since the effect of humans on nature is now being felt more regularly, what used to be an infrequent natural disaster may have become a more frequent unnatural one. The earth and oceans are becoming warmer. Science is, by definition, conservative, so the final proof may not be available until after the truth is apparent to all.

The Reef Authority continues to follow the situation closely. Significant new sightings of crown-of-thorns should be reported to GBRMPA, PO Box 1379, Townsville Qld 4810. The Authority is also interested in *negative* reports from reefs off the beaten track, where it is difficult to maintain up-to-date data.

Sunset on a coral cay in Capricornia (southern Great Barrier Reef). Enjoyment of the Reef is the privilege of the current generation, which has the responsibility to preserve it for future generations.

A jungle in the sea

A coral reef could be said to be a 'jungle in the sea' with an amazing quantity and diversity of life, so diverse that a whole book scarcely provides an introduction. Detailed discussion is beyond the scope of this author, and those interested should obtain one of several good general books about the Reef, such as Isobel Bennett's The Great Barrier Reef *or the* Reader's Digest Book of the Great Barrier Reef, *and read more about it. The following is a superficial smattering of facts about some of the more obvious forms of life encountered on a coral reef.*

Corals

For simplification, reef-building corals can be grouped into categories based upon their general appearance: branching; digitate; massive; tabulate (table-like); encrusting; foliaceous (leaf-like); free-living. Simplifying further, these are often described using words such as staghorn, brain, plate, mushroom, slipper, microatoll, 'bommie'. The most prolific coral growth usually takes place at the windward edge on the slope of the reef, and this is where to look for greatest variety of, and the most colourful, coral, although it is also possible to find excellent coral on protected leeward sides of islands in the Whitsundays. Staghorn and plate forms are the most abundant; staghorns are the fastest growing and they are great contributors to the debris of the reef. On continental islands the sand beaches usually begin as piles of coral fingers, the broken tips of staghorns.

In the coral zone you will see beautiful blue-tipped antlers; massive rounded corals with intricate patterns on their surface that resemble brains; 'microatolls', circular formations of smoother massive corals so called because they have a depression in the top that holds water like the lagoon of an atoll (typically these have purple coral around the sides and are found in the coral and sand flats); encrusting corals; corals that have soft leathery bodies and look as if they have been 'plopped' on the reef; mushrooms, or slipper corals, which have slits like mushroom gills and resemble a fluffy slipper (these corals are not colonies but individual polyps).

Coral reproduction

The economy of life in the sea is as flamboyant as the handling of money in a Monte Carlo casino; heaps of it is thrown around, most of it disappears.

Corals reproduce by budding (like having your own do-it-yourself clone kit), or when individual polyps 'bail out' of the colony and re-establish themselves. Corals also reproduce sexually. Reef-building corals usually contain both male and female sex cells. The cells mature rapidly in spring; eggs coloured pink, red, orange, blue, green, or purple will attract sperm with long wiggly tails.

When the corals of the Barrier Reef mate, they do it in one great orgy a few nights after the full moon in late spring. Marine biologists have wondered at this mass spawning of corals which has been described as an 'upside-down snow storm' that goes on for perhaps a week, reaching a peak just after 'mid-week'. Mass spawning – which other forms of reef life, such as clams, do also – increases the chances of survival of these immobile animals which cannot move into sexual contact and which live in an environment of continuous water movement. The behaviour may also serve to 'overwhelm' predators by giving them a plethora of targets, a strategy employed by schools of fish which distract predators by presenting a blur of prospective meals, rendering a decision about 'which one' very difficult and reducing the chance that any one will be caught.

The food of the reef

Plankton on which many of the reef community feed is of two basic types, animal (zooplankton) and vegetable (phytoplankton).

The zooplankton has representatives from all the major divisions of the marine community. They consist of small animal organisms, some which always remain plankton, and some which are temporary, larval stages of animals that will grow up to be fishes, lobsters, crabs, snails, and corals. Phytoplankton is a principal food source for all sea life, especially small larval life forms. Because plants actually *create* food by photosynthesis, they are the fundamental element of the reef food web. Filamentous algae are the most significant source of plant food on the reef.

All plankton generally live in the upper, sunlit part of the oceans, although upwards and downwards migration of zooplankton takes place. In daylight zooplankton go well below the surface, some burrowing (in shallow water) in the sand. After dark they rise. This behaviour helps them to avoid being eaten. It is the reason that corals have learned that night-time is the best time to feed (night-time, of course, also renders the corals less subject to *being* eaten). It is also why many visitors to a reef never see coral at its most beautiful, in 'full bloom'.

The reef economy thus goes around and around. All other members of the reef contribute to the zooplankton – the fish, the snails, the slugs, the bivalves, and the corals themselves. The waste products of consumption and digestion of zooplankton create a source of nitrogen for the algae to assimilate and convert back to food.

The role of algae as food of the reef should not be underestimated. The corals' resident algae (zooxanthellae) produce a significant proportion of their total food requirements, and many reef dwellers are vegetarian and depend upon algae for their food. Many others are detritus feeders and consume the animal and plant debris that abounds in the reef environment.

Molluscs

One of the most populous divisions of the animal kingdom, molluscs include all shells, plus a few shell-less types, squids and octopuses. Molluscs are important in the reef ecology as food (zooplankton) producers and algae mowers. The dead skeletons are also converted into actual reef structure by cementing algae.

These animals have a soft body with a flap of skin called a mantle which secretes the shell. All (except bivalves, e.g. clams) have a 'tongue' coated with teeth (called a radula) with which they rasp algae from the reef or with which they bore through other shells. They have eyes sensitive to light but which don't form images; some eyes are on stalks, some are on the surface of the shell, and some are deep in the skin.

The vast majority of molluscs live in the intertidal zone.

Clams. Large clams lie on the top of the reef, with brilliant, fleshy lips (the colour is caused by microscopic layers of crystalline, colourless pigments – the purpose of which is unknown). They filter water for phytoplankton. Clams are primarily photosynthetic and have in their mantle tissues zoox-

High water

Low water

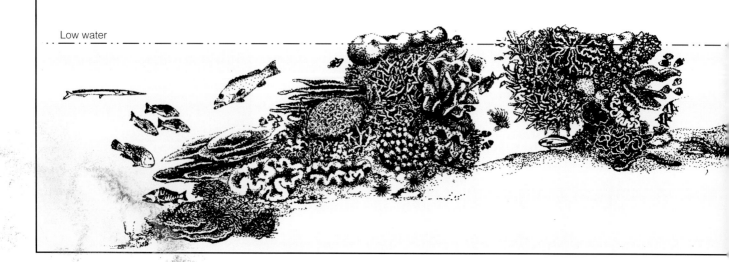

anthellae similar to those in corals. Clams close their shells when a reef-walker's shadow falls on them, and they occasionally squirt fossickers up the pants leg. They are quite harmless, even the giants, in spite of B-grade movie images of giant clams entrapping divers who were silly enough to insert a foot in them. Some burrowing clams actually dig their way into coral boulders, so that all you can see is their 'smile'.

Snails. There is a large variety of snails, all with an acute sense of smell. They have a specialised organ in their mantle cavity which senses chemicals in the water. Many carnivorous snails have a long siphon which they wave around, sensing the direction of smells.

Cowries. These beautiful, smooth shiny shells have always been attractive to man and used to be employed as money in some of the Pacific islands. They are active at night, when they crawl out from under their boulders with their mantle completely covering their shell.

Spider shells are among the most graceful, with long curved projections on one side. They are grazers and have a long green 'foot' with an eyeball on the end. Usually difficult to see because of brown slime which covers the top, their undershells are shiny and delicate reddish-pink. They often hang around in pairs.

Helmet shells. Helmets, or Cassids, are found on reefs in inter-tidal sand flats. They are beautiful shells whose name comes from their similarity to the headgear worn by early Roman soldiers. Helmets eat sea urchins, including (believe it or not) those with the long poisonous black spines.

Tritons are among the most spectacular (if not common) shells which grow to almost sixty centimetres; they are totally protected and are an enemy of

the crown-of-thorns which somehow they manage to eat.

Cone shells are plentiful each with a distinctive colour pattern which is usually obscured by a horny browny-green slime, or periostracum. Their radular teeth have become tubes through which they can eject poisonous harpoons. These species can be venomous and therefore dangerous to your health; don't pick them up in your bare hands.

Sea slugs. These shell-less animals, called nudibranchs, come in a variety of vivid colours and shapes. Many have bad-tasting poisonous skins, their bright colour being a warning to predators. They eat coelenterates (corals, jellyfish, anemones); some have projections on their backs in which they can store the stinging cells of the animals they've eaten and re-use them for their own defence.

Echinoderms. This ancient group includes stars, cucumbers, sea urchins. They have been around for some five hundred million years and are a mixture of the primitive and of ultra-sophisticated engineering. Their space-age skeleton is light, strong and self-repairing and replacing. They have a water vascular system with a diversity of form and function, including 'tube feet' which serve as legs, suckers, chemical sensors, breathers and execretors. Some are carnivorous but most are algae eaters.

Stars come in a variety of colours and forms, including the blue linckia commonly seen on reef flats and the brittle stars – (they look like a cross between a tarantula and a starfish and are able to shed a limb if molested (hence 'brittle'). Starfish limbs can regrow a body, and vice versa. The crown-of-thorns, currently notorious because it eats corals and causes extensive reef damage, has spines

covered with toxin which inflict a painful wound. (Triton shells eat them, and trigger fish flip them upside down and attack them from underneath.)

Sea urchins are common on the reef. They are algae grazers. Watch out for their long black spines which cause a painful wound if trodden on.

Sea cucumbers are sedentary detritus feeders. The Chinese, in the past, for some reason decided that they could make one virile if taken in soup. A burgeoning industry existed for 'bêche-de-mer', so-called by the French, who misunderstood the Portuguese fishermen's name for them – 'bicho da mar' or sea worm/slug. Sea slugs are also called 'trepang' which is an English corruption of the Malay teripang, a term used by the hoards of Macassan fishermen who used to descend on northern Australian shores for the cucumbers; at one time this was Australia's largest export industry. They come in all sizes and colours and when spawning assume a posture that resembles a rampant penis in the act of ejaculating, which may have been what gave the Chinese the idea of eating them in soup. When frightened, sea slugs can 'ejaculate' sticky, milky threads that entrap their antagonists.

Fishes

More species of fishes may be found on coral reefs than anywhere else. Every conceivable size and shape and lifestyle is represented. They have specific feeding habits and locations. There are algae grazers and carnivores.

Fishes have evolved from sea squirts and have made a number of changes, including the development of jaws and paired fins. Some left the bottom to become mid-water predators.

Bony fishes are the most successful of water animals, with more than twenty thousand known species. Their success lies in their bony structure and

their 'buoyancy tank' which enables them to control their ascent and descent without having to swim forward, a big evolutionary step ahead of the cartilaginous fishes such as sharks and rays. They have achieved vertical flattening which facilitates lateral movement, and they are capable of very subtle movements and apparently effortless swimming.

It is common among reef fishes to be sexually ambidextrous; some start life as male, some as female, and change over as they grow older. They are territorial; a dominant male patrols his area, which contains a number of females; if he gets killed, the dominant female in the group changes sex in a few days and takes over the male role.

Reef fishes have adopted some fascinating habits. The clown fish, or anemone fish, for example, lives with impunity among the poisonous tentacles of the anemone. Another, the little cleaner fish, swims boldly inside the mouths of larger fishes which permit him to do so because he rids them of parasites. As always, life throws up its opportunists, and there is also a *false* cleaner fish; you can imagine the mischief he gets up to. (As the clown fish says, with friends like that, who needs anemone?)

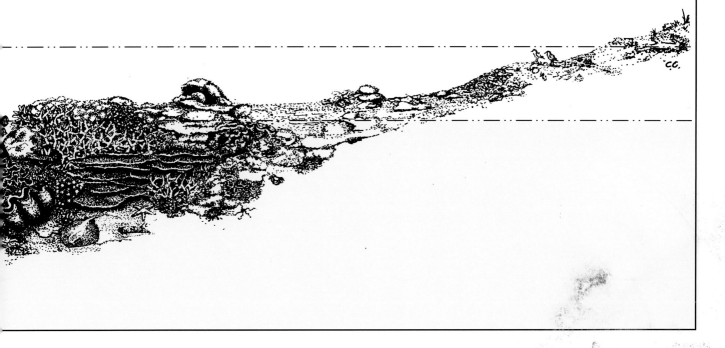

Hayman Island's swimming pool is elegantly set against the
backdrop of Hook Island's lofty peaks that in a previous era were
a coastal mountain range.

ISLAND RESORTS OF THE WHITSUNDAYS

The islands of the Whitsundays were first sought out, around the turn of the century, for timber to build houses for the mainland settlements and for grazing land. By the 1920s a number of leases were held, and the first families began to establish permanent residence. In 1923 a family called Nicolson was living on Lindeman Island, and the first manifestations of tourism began when the Nicolsons first dabbled at having the occasional paying guests.

By the late 1920s groups of enchanted holidaymakers were beginning to carry tales of adventures on 'Robinson Crusoe' islands back to their home states throughout Australia. The resort accommodation was pretty primitive; in some cases it was tents, and guests were expected to supply their own plate, cutlery, linen and lamp. But in surroundings like the Whitsundays, this just added to the magic.

By the mid-1930s resorts were operating on Lindeman, South Molle, Long, Daydream and Hayman islands. Guests arrived by coastal passenger vessels which plied between Melbourne, Sydney, Brisbane, Townsville and Cairns. It was then that the concept of 'package' tours, so widely employed today, was first established. The resorts were, with one or two exceptions, very much family affairs. They were homely and informal, a pleasant quality they shared with many Queensland resorts which later, in some cases, became a fault; 'informality' became an excuse for not keeping up with the times.

During the war the resorts were, for the most part closed; they re-opened in 1946. Flying boats later replaced the coastal passenger vessels, and what a romantic way to arrive that was!

Today the islands and the adjacent mainland have some of the most up-to-date resort accommodation found anywhere. They are served by two jet airports, one at Proserpine and one at Hamilton Island.

Above, right:
Hayman's West Wing is constructed in three tiers, and each of its present eighty-four units and six suites has a balcony overlooking the pool. The rooms are luxuriously furnished, with bathrooms in marble, TV and video playback, and multiple telephones. The watercolours on the walls are all originals. Each wing has a *Lanai*, an indoor-outdoor area where guests can relax and meals are available. The resort offers round-the-clock room service.

Above, top:
A man-made boat harbour carved out of Hayman's fringing coral reef has a floating marina and a jetty for the island's motor vessels that transport guests in style from Hamilton Island airport. The marina provides berths for the resort-based dive boat, game-fishing boat and day-cruise vessels. Casual visitors may tie up at the marina provided that arrangements are made in advance.

Above, bottom:
The gigantic salt water lagoon, five times the size of an Olympic pool, has a uniform depth of 1.3 metres. It surrounds a deep freshwater pool. Timber walkways with palms and pots create a number of individual pool areas, where waiter service is available.

Hayman

The view south from the horseshoe of Hayman Island looks out to the majestic blue-green peaks of Hook Island, which thrust skywards, the highest mountains of the Whitsunday islands. Only a nautical mile or so away, these lofty hills provide Hayman both protection from the blustery trade winds and a very handsome vista. The sheltered waters between Hayman's wide sand beach and the northern shores of Hook are, in effect, one large lagoon – Hayman's playground – and on the adjacent Hook Island is some of the best coral growth to be found on any of Australia's near-shore islands. The scenery is vaguely reminiscent of Hawaii. Perhaps this is why Sir Reginald Ansett fell in love with Hayman; in the mid-1940s he purchased the island and set about building his own version of the Royal Hawaiian there. The resort was to be finished in time for a visit from King George VI and Queen Elizabeth, and Ansett obtained a Royal Charter for it. The royal visit never eventuated, but from the time the resort opened on July 4th, 1950, Hayman has been an enchanted name in Australian tourism.

In 1985 Royal Hayman Resort was closed for demolition and the re-building of a $300 million resort complex. The old and new resorts might be likened to a caterpillar and a butterfly; the Hayman that has emerged is elegant. It is a member of the prestigious Leading Hotels of the World, a group that nominates only the world's most eminent establishments.

Hayman has a European flavour, a hint of the south of France, with dusty pinks and architecture faintly suggestive of a town on a hillside at the edge of the Mediterranean. The atmosphere is that of a stately residence rather than a hotel; guests are visitors in a private mansion with profusely planted gardens that are adorned with huge Grecian urns, statues and fountains. The lobby and passages are furnished with vases and antiques, the walls hung with original art by some of Australia's best known artists. No effort has been spared to create a grand style, an elegant, civilised 'place of good living'.

The resort rooms, restaurants and other public areas are in two wings – East and West – which are linked by scenic walks and gardens. There is a total of over two hundred rooms and eleven penthouses. The West Wing overlooks the gigantic pool complex; Palm Garden View and Beachfront units extend between the two main wings; the East Wing is set amongst

palms and ornamental ponds. Its penthouse suites each have a different decorative theme – Greek, Japanese, Italian, Moroccan, English, Art Deco, French Provincial, north Queensland, and others. The island caters for over four hundred guests and, being a five-star resort, has round-the-clock room service.

Hayman has six *à la carte* restaurants: La Fontaine, French and formal with Louis XVI reproduction furnishings and a connoisseur's wine list; Trattoria, casual, with rustic atmosphere and Italian regional cooking; the Oriental Seafood restaurant with Japanese decor and cuisine of China, Malaysia, Thailand and Japan; Planters, a Polynesian restaurant; the Coffee House, by the beachfront, for buffet breakfasts, lunches, pastries, snacks, ice cream and chocolates made in Hayman's international kitchen; and the Beach Pavilion, which features blackboard specials, barbecues, snacks and drinks.

The resort has six day/night tennis courts, a sports centre with two squash courts, ping pong tables, a golf target range, eighteen-hole putting green, a health club, a PADI diver training facility and water sports centre, and three swimming pools. Dinghies and outboards are available for hire. Water skiing and para-sailing are available. The island has some good walking tracks.

Scuba diving is well catered for. The island dive boat, *Reef Goddess*, is a purpose-built vessel, very well equipped with every possible consideration for the diver. *Reef Goddess* does day trips to the Barrier Reef for divers and snorkellers (it takes less than one hour to get there) as well as trips to local island reefs. Hayman has its own game-fishing boat and experienced local skippers. Other yachts based at Hayman's marina do casual day and sunset cruises.

Visitors are checked into the resort while travelling to the island on a luxury cruiser that meets flights arriving at Hamilton airport. The island has a helipad, and amphibious aircraft regularly taxi through the boat harbour and up the ramp to pick up passengers for trips to the outer reefs. The marina has floating berths for about twenty-five yachts; casual visitors are welcome provided they make arrangements well in advance. Those wishing to stay overnight are not permitted to stay aboard the yacht.

Above, left:
The design of the main lobby, with marble concierge desk at one end and marble main desk at the other, is reminiscent of a Moorish courtyard. The clear skylight dome admits a shaft of light which moves with the sun across the pink marble columns and floor. Beneath the dome is a reclining nude, one of the world's first sculptures in acrylic, by German artist Fleischmann, who took nine years to complete the work in the 1930s.

Above, top:
The Coffee House, one of six *à la carte* restaurants on the island, serves buffet breakfast, lunch and snacks all day, including continental pastries, ice cream and chocolates made in Hayman's international kitchen. The decor is cheerful and bright, with cane furniture, and the restaurant looks out through tropical gardens to Hayman's lagoon.

Above, bottom:
Hayman has the atmosphere of a residence as much as a hotel. It is cosmopolitan. Pictured is the lounge, a 'London club' – rich, warm and plushy.

Hamilton Island

Hamilton Island was a catalyst for resort redevelopment in the Whitsundays in the 1980s. When it opened in 1984 it gave a clear signal to other resorts that 'homely informality' was no longer an acceptable euphemism for aging facilities.

Hamilton resort (it is really more an island town) was created by Keith Williams, a self-made entrepreneur and proponent of free enterprise who turned an island pastoral lease into a hustling, bustling community. Many of the services on the island are run by concessionaires, and the resort doesn't have the typical 'village' atmosphere that some associate with an island resort. Everything is *à la carte*. Accommodation ranges from individual buré units to a nineteen-storey hotel, Hamilton Towers, where guests travel to their rooms by transparent capsules (lifts) that run up the outside.

Hamilton has everything. With a jet airport only a minute or so from the harbour, it is a major trans-shipment point for the Whitsundays. The harbour side of the island is a major yachting centre and a busy community, with bakery, fish and chips shop, restaurants, take-aways, and Trader Pete's island store. There are several bareboat charter operators on the island, as well as crewed charter and game-fishing charter boats.

The island has eight restaurants, a night club/disco, fauna park with native Australian animals, gym and spa, tennis courts, squash courts, golf driving range, putt putt golf, and convention centre. Electric buggies are available – a great way to get up One Tree Hill to watch the sunset.

Hamilton offers trips to the Barrier Reef on a wave piercer catamaran, and there are also regular helicopter flights to the Reef. Cruises around the islands are available on a number of craft.

Catseye Bay, onto which the resort faces, has a yawning expanse of sand for sunbaking, windsurfing, sailing, waterskiing, parasailing, parachuting, snorkelling, fishfeeding, or just watching a glorious sunrise. There are several walks to elevated points on the island with spectacular views of the Whitsunday Passage and surrounding islands.

Scuba diving tuition is available, from full certificate courses or a 'resort course' which offers an opportunity to dive on the Reef with just a couple hours of instruction and a minimal investment.

Above, right:
Hamilton Harbour is a principal yachting centre in the Whitsunday region with facilities not matched at some mainland marinas. Accessibility by air solves many logistical problems for yachtspeople, and the marina offers a complete range of services – fuels, power, water, showers, toilets, laundry and supplies. There are travel lift, engineering and refrigeration services. Visitors pay a mooring fee and then have complete access to island amenities, including all restaurants and sports facilities.

Above, top:
The resort has a range of accommodation, from individual burés set amongst handsome old gum trees to high-rise hotel rooms (*see opposite*).

Above, bottom:
Cruises to the Barrier Reef are offered aboard a fast catamaran.

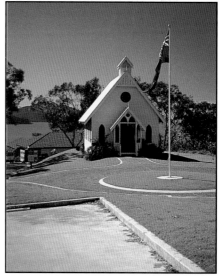

Left, top:
Hamilton is both an island resort and a resort town. It features high-rise accommodation with magnificent views over Catseye Bay.

Left, middle:
Guests at the Hamilton Towers enjoy a swim in their pool.

Left, bottom:
Catseye Beach is the centre for water sports, fishfeeding and snorkelling.

Above, top:
The Hamilton community has its own church where, over the years, many visitors have been married.

Above, bottom:
The turban shell (*Turbo petholatus* – the 'cat's eye' for which Catseye Bay is named, because these shells have been found there) has a thick, glassy, rounded operculum with a green centre resembling an eye. It is used by shell jewellery makers in necklaces and rings.

Far left, top:
Palm Bay, Long Island, a low-key
hideaway, with lagoon anchorage.

Far left, middle:
Sunlovers Bay, on the north-west side of
Daydream Island, offers a peaceful escape
for resort guests on that island as well as
idyllic anchorage for those cruising
around the islands on yachts. The bay has
a well-developed fringing coral reef.

Far left, bottom:
Hook Island underwater observatory is
located in the narrow passage between
Whitsunday and Hook islands. There is a
small camping resort there, too.

Centre, top:
Lindeman Island has a Club Med resort
with excellent sporting facilities including
a full-length nine-hole golf course. The
island, most of which is national park,
has been a favourite escape for tourists
since the 1920s when the Nicolsons were
the first to operate a
Whitsunday island resort.

Centre, bottom:
Sunrise over Neck Bay, Shaw Island, as
viewed from the Lindeman Island
golf course.

Above:
Tandem parachute jumping at Catseye
Bay, Hamilton Island.

South Molle

South Molle Island is close to the mainland, and because of its protected anchorage, its beach and its bountiful grasslands, it early attracted the attention of graziers and, later, settlers in search of an idyllic island life. Long before that time Aboriginal people in the area discovered that the island had a natural wealth of basaltic stones that made excellent axes and cutting tools, and they called the island 'Whyrriba' for that reason (the remains of their stone quarry may be seen today on the track to Spion Kop).

The Lamond family lived on South Molle from 1927 to 1937 during which time Henry Lamond, a grazier-turned-author who escaped from western Queensland to this paradise island, had articles published around the world about the idyllic Whitsundays. These, along with stories such as Banfield's tales of paradise on Dunk Island – *Confessions of a Beachcomber* – undoubtedly were a major factor in development of tourism in this part of Queensland.

Lamond swapped his South Molle lease in 1937 with Ernest Bauer, farmer-turned-adventurer, and it was Bauer and his family who, after quite a struggle, established the resort on the island. Old 'Pop' Bauer used to entertain the guests after dinner with an inexhaustible supply of yarns, jokes and tricks, and relaxed informality has always been a popular hall-mark of South Molle. It has changed hands a number of times since then and has been extensively renovated over the years.

South Molle has traditionally catered largely for the family market. Its units are set amongst tropical gardens and along the beach front. Activities are organised every day for those who like to join in, and entertainment is provided nightly, with regular special occasions, such as 'island feast nights', which attract visitors from all around the Whitsundays – a favourite with bareboat charterers.

South Molle has a nine-hole golf course, gym, squash court, two flood-lit tennis courts, and a swimming pool. Scuba diving instruction is available. The beach is crowded with catamarans, water bikes, and other water sports equipment. Trips to the Barrier Reef and to Hook Island under-water observatory are available several days a week.

Most of South Molle is national park, and the island has some excellent tracks which offer spectacular views from its promontories or escape to several secluded beaches around its shores for a picnic lunch.

Daydream Island

Daydream Island is located just across the Molle Channel, about two and a half nautical miles north-east from Shute Harbour. The story is told that in 1930 Major Lee 'Paddy' Murray, with his wife Connie, a deckhand and an Airedale dog called Toby, left Sydney in the yacht *Day Dream* on a world cruise. They got as far as the Whitsundays, where the Murrays fell in love with the islands and particularly with what was then called West Molle Island. They went over to South Molle to meet the owner (well-known author Henry Lamond) and persuaded him to sell them West Molle. Murray renamed it Day Dream after his yacht (it later became Daydream), and he and his wife set about establishing a tourist resort.

The first buildings on Daydream were primitive – of corrugated iron, with coral shingle floors – but they were considered something special at the time. The first visitors in any numbers arrived on tourist ships, such as the *Canberra* and *Kanimbla* and others which cruised the Queensland coast; they anchored off Daydream for one day on their touring schedule. Daydream was thus one of the early forerunners of tourist growth in the Whitsundays. In the early post-war days the island became a setting-down point for the romantic flying boats. It is a small and intimate island, with beautiful views out over the Whitsunday Passage.

In the early 1990s a completely new family resort with over three hundred rooms was built at the northern end of the island, and the old resort at the southern end became a day-visitor facility. The day-visitor facility has a swimming pool and pool bar, tavern, souvenir shop, boutique, restaurant, coffee shop and bakery. An all-tide coral shingle beach on the western side of the island offers all manner of seaside activities. A boardwalk leads from the day-visitor area past a small marina to the new resort (for house guests only), which has a pool and pool bar, spa, gym, shop and two restaurants.

Club Crocodile Long Island Resort

Happy Bay was the original name of the resort situated on Long Island's northern beach facing Port Molle. It opened in the 1930s and it went on for many years. The place had a sense of history about it, with cannonballs and old wrecks found on the beach, testimony that the island and Port Molle used to be a favoured stopover for early ships – including bêche-de-mer fishermen and survey ships, some of the latter probably having had some gunnery practice while at anchor.

In the mid-1980s the Happy Bay Resort was renamed Whitsunday 100, and it was born again as a resort for the young, a place where 'if the pace doesn't flatten you, a falling coconut will', as its advertising promised. In its last days everything at the resort had been pretty much flattened, by marauding, partying youth, and the resort was closed in 1987 and demolished. A new resort reopened a year or so later by a company specialising in adventure tours for the young, and it was alleged to be the first resort in the world exclusively for 18–35-year-olds, a policy that was supposedly strictly enforced (there were, however, numbers of flabby '35-year-olds' with greying temples on the scene, proving once again that prohibition simply challenges the determined). The resort has changed hands once or twice since and is now operated as resort for all ages. It has two swimming pools, tennis courts, and water sports of all varieties – sail, motor, and muscle-powered – may be indulged in.

Long Island is a national park with some tropical vine forest with several good walking tracks that offer tantalising glimpses of The Narrows (between the island and the mainland) and of the Passage to seaward.

Palm Bay Hideaway, Long Island

Palm Bay is a tiny hideaway located just over a kilometre south of Happy Bay. It has a pleasant beach fringed with coconut palms, and a lagoon has been created with an entrance dredged through the fringing reef to allow access for yachts with a draught of up to 2.5 metres. An informal, tranquil place catering for everyone from families to honeymooners, it also offers peaceful anchorage within its lagoon and is a popular 'first night' stopoff for bareboat yacht charterers, who tie their yachts stern-to to a palm tree.

Palm Bay first opened as a resort in 1933, when it was operated by Tim Croft. It was one of the permanent casualties of cyclone Ada in 1970 but was rebuilt and then further upgraded in the late 1980s. It has operated since as a small, friendly affair, a combination of Sleepy Hollow and Gilligan's Island. Accommodation on the lagoon side consists of several cabins and burés, all with private bathroom and kitchen. The Islander restaurant and bar provides informal meals and refreshments. A small shop has basic provisions. Visitors by sea are encouraged to join in the activities in a casual, relaxed atmosphere.

Paradise Bay, Long Island

Paradise Bay is located at the southern end of Long Island and is the home of a small resort consisting of eight cabins (maximum sixteen guests) grouped around a gazebo. Its mission is to provide seclusion for escapists (no day visitors, no children). Access is via the resort's cruiser.

Hook Island (resort and observatory)

The Hook Island underwater observatory, in the narrow passage between Hook Island and Whitsunday Island, is another of the observatories built in the days before it was possible to take day-trips to the Barrier Reef before the advent of coral-viewing 'subs'. It provides an opportunity to see and to photograph fish at very close quarters, and coral-viewing craft

takes sightseers out over the fringing reef. The observatory is in a narrow channel between two islands, and visibility is sometimes reduced, particularly at times of spring tides or strong winds. For those who haven't the time, money or inclination to go to the Barrier Reef, this is one way to get a close look at marine life without travelling too far or getting wet. Immediately north of the observatory is a small resort with camping area and twelve cabins with bunks, a restaurant/coffee shop, kiosk, barbecue facilities and small bar. Snorkelling and coral viewing are available just off the resort beach. Moorings are available for visitors.

Lindeman Island

Located in the centre of the Cumberlands, Lindeman is a little off the beaten track, between the gateways of Shute Harbour to the north and Mackay to the south. Its relative isolation and many natural attributes traditionally fitted it for a role as a quiet, family sort of island, one where day-trippers did not make a daily assault on the resident guests. The resort was virtually demolished and completely rebuilt from 1987 to 1988 and was again extensively modified in 1991 and 1992 before reopening as a Club Med village. The resort is still in the old location, tucked against a hill in a bay on the south-western end of the island. The central complex is a series of open pavilions by the sea which take full advantage of the setting; its buildings, in natural timbers with pyramid-shaped shingled roofs, impart a village atmosphere.

Club Med is well known to many Australians who have visited this international holiday group's villages throughout the Pacific basin – Tahiti, New Caledonia, Thailand – and many others throughout the world. Club Med Lindeman was the company's first holiday village in Australia operated and staffed along the familiar Club Med lines – all-inclusive tariff, guests join in or drop out as they wish, staff (who come from all over the world) blend almost indistinguishably with guests.

Lindeman's grasslands made it an obvious place for a golf course, and the island has a true links, a nine-hole course (definitely not a putt putt course) with some spectacular vistas out to the Passage (and some severe penalties for golfers who slice). There are six day/night tennis courts (one covered). Lindeman has an all-tide beach in front of the resort, a marvellous water sports playground (provided the trade winds are not piping in). A number of other attractive beaches may be found on Lindeman, as well as on the adjacent Seaforth and Shaw Islands, where it is possible to escape with a picnic lunch. Boat Port, on the north-western side of Lindeman, is quite protected if it is windy at Home Beach.

Being a national park, Lindeman has several graded bush tracks, one which meanders through forest and a valley of butterflies until it makes the ascent up a grassy slope to the summit of Mt Oldfield, a spectacular place from which to watch the sunset. A resident national parks ranger is there to interpret the island's natural resources for guests.

Visitors to the resort who arrive in private boats are welcome, provided they book in and spend the night.

Brampton Island

It is said that the scenery in the southern Cumberland Islands resembles the Lake District of north-western England, and certainly the islands today carry many names of that area – St Bees, Keswick, Cockermouth, Wigton, Calder, Skiddaw, Maryport, Helvellyn, Scawfell, Carlisle, Brampton. Bêche-de-mer fishermen of the 19th century found the islands, particularly Brampton, an attractive place to boil and smoke their catch, in the days when the Whitsundays were fished for this 'delicacy' so prized on the tables of Chinese epicures. Because these islands were the closest to the large, cosmopolitan settlement of Mackay, escaped convicts from New Caledonia once or twice used Brampton as a staging ground before going ashore (in Mackay, foreigners were much less noticeable than in the small northern ports).

Opposite above:
View over Bauer Bay, South Molle Island, from Lamond Hill. South Molle is a national park and has a number of graded walking tracks which offer spectacular views over the island and the surrounding waters.

Opposite below:
Brampton Island's northern beach is well suited to water sports, and when the tide rolls back, guests can walk out to the tiny Pelican Island, or even across to neighbouring Carlisle Island.

One of the earliest settlers in the Cumberland Islands was Joseph Busuttin. In 1917 he acquired the pastoral lease for Brampton Island, in addition to those he already held for St Bees and Keswick. His early attempts at breeding chinchilla rabbits on Brampton failed. So he turned to the breeding of the sturdy 'Walers' that were such successful cavalry horses in the wars of the late 19th and early 20th centuries (a few of these horses still run wild on Carlisle Island).

The Busuttins were among the earliest island settlers to take in paying guests, on St Bees, and then, in the early 1930s, they decided to set up a resort on Brampton as this island had more advantages – good anchorage, beautiful beaches, water, abundant wildlife. The first tourists arrived in 1933. The Busuttins sold Brampton in 1959, and in 1962 Tom McLean's Roylen Enterprises bought the lease and ran the resort in conjunction with his cruise business until 1985.

Brampton has traditionally been a romantic retreat for those on their first – or subsequent – honeymoon, an island for quiet relaxation where guests can either enjoy each other or the natural surroundings.

The sand beach directly in front of the resort looks north to the islands of the Sir James Smith Group, which sit majestically on the horizon. This beach, unlike many in the Whitsundays, remains usable for water sports at all tides (the fringing reef does not dry), and the beach is the focal point of the resort. Brampton offers a complete range of water sports. It has a short, 'fun' golf course, tennis courts and an archery range. A full schedule of organised activities is offered. The island is a national park and has a system of graded walking tracks that is regarded by many as the most scenic track system in the Cumberland Group, with many spectacular views, particularly over the southern bays of the island.

Visiting the resorts

Calling in at one of the resort islands can provide a welcome change of pace during a week of cruising, an opportunity to 'make port', to go ashore and enjoy a shower, a meal in a restaurant and perhaps some evening entertainment. There are a few mainland resorts that can provide a similar experience by virtue of their seaside locations, and these are included here along with the island resorts offering facilities for visitors by sea.

Visitors in yachts are generally welcome at the resorts, with a few provisos. Arrangements usually must be made before landing, and once ashore, it is necessary to register with the reception desk or the harbourmaster. Resorts expect visitors to conform to the usual standards of dress 'good Queensland casual' (see 'What to wear', page 57) in the evening and in the formal areas of the resort. Visitors are also expected to behave appropriately (the fact that this bears mentioning at all indicates simply that, in the past, some yachties have behaved like pirates).

Resorts generally charge for use of their facilities, and in most cases this entitles you to a free run, enjoying the same privileges as the in-house guests.

Contacting and making arrangements to land

Brampton Island Resort (079) 51 4499

Anchorage is available off the jetty. The office can be contacted on VHF channel 16; present yourself at reception when you go ashore.

Club Crocodile Long Island Resort (079) 46 9400

Radio ahead on VHF channel 16 and speak to the water sports manager to book one of ten moorings that are available. Payment of the fee entitles you to use of showers and all resort facilities, including barbecues, tennis courts, swimming pools, and nightly entertainment. The jetty is for resort use only; permission may be given to pick up or discharge passengers, but check with the water sports manager before going alongside. Long Island is a national park with good graded walking tracks.

Coral Art, Dent Island

There are two moorings. The western one (towards the mainland) is for use by private and bareboat-charter yachts; the eastern one may be used by private or charter yachts in the afternoon when it is not occupied by commercial vessels. This is a difficult anchorage and use of a mooring is advisable , if one is available. Bill and Leen Wallace, who have lived in the Whitsundays since the early 1950s, operate a shell jewellery shop in a unique falé-style structure

which they built themselves just beyond the top of the beach. The Wallaces are fonts of local lore, and their shop is full of artefacts and Pacificana.

Daydream Island resort (079) 48 8488
The resort has a small man-made harbour (on the north-eastern side of the island) which has two pile berths for use by visitors. Radio ahead on VHF channel 16 for a booking. The jetty on the western side of the island is for commercial traffic only. There is a fee for day or night use of the pile berth which entitles you to use the showers and change rooms in the departure lounge and all resort facilities, including those at the day-visitor area at the southern end of the island.

Earlando resort (079) 45 7133
Anchorage is available just off this small, informal resort with tent and campsites and caravans for hire. The office monitors 27Mhz channel 91. Showers are available at a small charge. The resort operates a fully-licensed restaurant and bar. Limited supples of groceries are available at the kiosk.

Hayman Island (079) 40 1234; Marine Operations (079) 40 1882.
Radio well in advance (or telephone Marine Operations) on VHF channel 16 or HF 2638Khz for a berth in the floating marina in the man-made harbour. It is essential to make prior arrangements because space is very limited (at some busy times no visitors are allowed). Day visitors are permitted to stay on the island between 10.00 am and 3.00 pm. Overnight visitors must book into the resort; no one is allowed to stay on board a yacht in the marina overnight. Dress standards are strictly adhered to.

Hamilton Island (079) 46 9999; marina office (079) 46 8353
Radio ahead on VHF channel 16 or 68 to book a floating berth at the marina in the man-made harbour; moorings are also available. Payment of the fee entitles you to the 'keys to the island' with all its many attractions, including showers, laundry, restaurants, night club, putt putt golf, golf driving range, squash courts, tennis courts, water sports equipment and swimming pools. Hamilton is a complete marine centre in its own right, with all the usual marine facilities.

Hook Island resort and underwater observatory (079) 469 380
Radio ahead on VHF channel 16 to book one of the eight moorings. The anchorage is littered with underwater snags and use of a mooring is preferable to anchoring. The resort itself consists of 12 cabins with bunks, a shared amenities block, restaurant/coffee shop, kiosk, barbecue facilities and a small bar. The observatory operates a coral-viewing 'sub'; scuba diving and snorkelling are available at local reefs.

Laguna Quays (079) 47 7777
Radio ahead (VHF channel 16/9/21, HF 2524kHz or 27Mhz channel 88, 8.00 am to 4.30 pm) for instructions about entering the harbour. Laguna Quays marina has floating berths, and swing moorings are also available. Payment of the fee entitles you to use all facilities at this very attractive resort, including the championship golf course (green fees payable), tennis, and non-motorised water sports equipment. There is a coin-operated laundry and a small kiosk located by the marina.

Lindeman Island (079) 46 9333
Advance bookings are not accepted; radio on VHF channel 16 upon arrival to book one of the three swing moorings available outside the reef. Day visitors are permitted at the resort between 11.00 am and 3.00 pm; overnight visitors may stay between 3.00 pm and 8.00 am or between 11.00 am and 11.00 am the following day. There is a fee for use of the mooring and a per capita charge for meals. Visitors arc permitted to use all facilities, including the full-length nine-hole golf course, tennis courts, a basketball court, archery range. The jetty is a public facility and may be used by anyone for access to the national park, to load/unload passengers and to tie up dinghies.

Monte's Resort (079) 45 7177
Call ahead on VHF channel 16 to book a mooring; the anchorage is free as the wind. Transport ashore is available if you require it. Monte's is a small, relaxed, privately-owned resort in a secluded location on Cape Gloucester (Gloucester Passage, map N4). Facilities include self-contained beachfront bungalows, a public bar and restaurant, toilets, laundry, barbecues and a shop (groceries, ice, bait and tackle are on sale).

Palm Bay Hideaway (079) 46 9233
Radio ahead on VHF channel 16 to book one of the eight moorings within the lagoon (for yachts less than 2.5 metres draught) or one of two moorings outside for larger craft. Do not attempt to enter the lagoon without the Palm Bay guide; negotiating the channel requires local knowledge and knowledge of the tides (there must be a low tide of at least 0.7 metres at Shute Harbour before vessels are permitted in the lagoon). Payment of the fee entitles visitors to use of all facilities at this small, low-key hideaway, including showers, barbecue and a small shop. Long Island is a national park with good graded walking tracks.

South Molle Island (079) 46 9433
At the time this edition goes to press, there are no moorings in Bauer Bay for visitors. Those wishing to visit the resort should radio the office on VHF channel 16 before coming ashore; tie the dinghy at the wharf (the wharf may also be used to tie up the dinghies of those wishing to visit the national park). A small fee entitles visitors to use of all resort facilities, including the nine-hole golf course, squash and tennis courts, swimming pool, showers and laundry. Island feast nights are popular. South Molle has some excellent graded walking tracks in the national park.

TIPS FOR TROPICAL HOLIDAYS

Whitsunday weather

The Whitsundays are located a little over a hundred nautical miles north of the Tropic of Capricorn. From March/April through September the islands and most of the coast of Queensland are fanned by trade winds. During these months the temperature is always equable. In the dead of winter one may be wearing a bathing suit by day and will probably want to put on a jumper when the sun goes down. If you are on the water and the trade winds are piping fresh, warm gear may be the order of the day. For sailors, the winds blow stronger from May through August, tending lighter from then on, although seasons are not clearly defined. The summer months are warm and sultry. July is the coldest month, January the warmest.

Whitsunday weather	Jan.	Apr.	July	Oct.
Av. daily high temp.	31°C	28°C	23°C	28°C
Av. daily low temp.	25°C	23°C	17°C	21°C
Days rain (over 0.2 mm)	13	14	5	5
Normal rainfall	203 mm	115 mm	36 mm	16 mm
Mean sea temp.	27°C	26°C	22°C	24°C
Normal annual rainfall: 1445 mm				

The wet season is January to March. The peak of tourist activity falls between May and October, although holiday times are very busy. Cyclones, if they happen at all, are most likely from February to March, although very occasionally one has come as early as November and as late as May.

What to wear

At night, if out in company, one is expected to conform to a standard of dress known as 'good Queensland casual' – neat, and comfortable for the tropics. For men, this means sports shirt, slacks or shorts with long socks and shoes). Women are expected to wear slacks or dresses, not shorts. Two items not considered good casual, particularly for evening wear, are T-shirts and thongs.

Four simple tips

Sunscreen cream, polarised sunglasses, good solid footwear and a broad-brimmed hat: these are the essentials – not necessarily in that order – for the Whitsundays. A lightweight, long-sleeved shirt may also come in handy.

Polarised sunglasses. Imagine skippering your drive-it-yourself yacht, approaching the night's peaceful anchorage, your heart warming at the sound of your beloved one mixing Mai Tai cocktails in the galley. Because of the reflections on the surface of the water you fail to see the edge of the island's fringing reef. Without as much as a last-minute croak acknowledging imminent doom, you drive-it-yourself right up on the reef. You are now sitting on the floor in the main saloon, next to your love, having catapulted over the wheel and straight down through the companionway. The Mai Tais are dripping from the ceiling onto both of you, and the foredeck hand is flat on his back halfway up the beach.

Polaroids (or any sunglasses with polarised lenses) are invaluable in coral waters because they reduce reflections; you can see into the water rather than just the reflections of the sky on it. Reefs become much more visible. Even if you're not a yachtie, polarised glasses make the sky a deeper blue, the clouds stand out like balls of fluff, and colours become more vivid. (A polarising filter on your camera can yield dramatic results, too.)

Sunscreens. The sun in Queensland is very strong. Even those who can tolerate a lot of sun down south get burned in the Whitsundays. If you arrive looking like you just crawled out from under a rock and try to convert your Melbourne alabaster to Bo Derek brown on the first day, you will give your skin an insult it will never forget. Take along plenty of sunscreen, consider upping your normal grade to one that gives greater protection, and if you plan to be getting wet, use a waterproof type.

Footwear. Good solid footwear can get you off the number one casualty list – those with oyster cuts on their feet – and may also protect you in the unlikely event that 'Thomas the Terrible' toadfish happens to be around when you're wading in Shute Harbour or Pioneer Bay (see page 116). Be sure to take along an old pair of sand shoes that you don't mind getting wet.

Hat. A broad-brimmed hat will provide extra protection from the very strong Queensland sun when your layer of sunscreen cream has been thinned by salt spray, perspiration or wiping your face. It will also protect the shoulders and tops of the ears, which don't always get their full measure of protection. Experienced snorkellers frequently wear a long-sleeved lightweight shirt in the water to provide some protection to those parts of the body which remain exposed when the sunscreen gets washed off. Such a shirt is often welcome when reef walking on a hot afternoon, too.

Tips for enjoying a coral reef

The best way to really appreciate a reef is while in the water yourself, where you have intimate contact with the corals and other living inhabitants. Reefs can also provide hours of entertainment from on top – just fossicking.

First and foremost, wear that pair of old sneakers or running shoes that you brought with you. Decent footwear (the thicker the soles, the better) is essential for reef walking, not only because of all the bits of coral and shells that are there but also because if you tread barefoot on a stonefish lying concealed in the rubble at low tide, you can get a very painful foot. Socks are also a good idea, to protect your ankles and calves from inevitable coral scratches. Thongs are useless on a reef.

Polarised sunglasses can be a great help to sailors because they allow underwater reefs to be seen much more readily. The lens on the left is polarised, the right one isn't. The difference can be even more pronounced than shown by this example.

Right:
All reefs have distinctive physical and biological zones, moulded by the physical factors that impinge upon them.
The offshore platform reefs of the Great Barrier system have grown up on top of ancient sedimentary structures, away from mainland influences such as sediments and freshwater runoff. Depending upon their particular circumstances and their age, some have lagoons, while in others the lagoon has, over time, become filled with sand. Fringing reefs formed on the rocky shores of the continental islands when the sea level rose after the last ice age. They have parallels with offshore reefs, but being adjacent to land masses, are vulnerable to freshwater runoff, which can kill the coral animals. These reefs usually have wide mud/sand flats and expanses of algae-covered coral rubble between the beach and the edge of the reef. They also lack the deep pools or lagoons found in the leeward areas of some platform reefs on the continental shelf. The best coral growth on island fringing reefs is at the edge and on the reef slope.

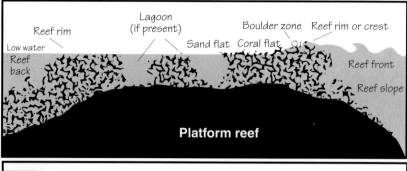

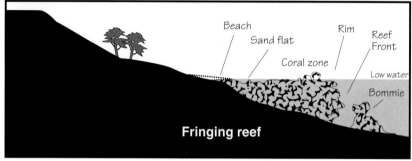

 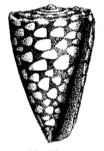

Textile cone
Conus textile

Marble cone
Conus marmoreus

Cone shells are among the more beautifully patterned shells, although they are often covered with a thick greeny-brown slime which hides their beauty. They are more or less straight-sided, with a low pointed spire and straight narrow aperture. A few species are highly venomous and potentially very dangerous to man. Don't pick up any of them in your bare hands.

Many tourists who have heard all about wondrous colourful corals are dumbfounded when they have their first look at a continental island reef, when it is drying at low tide and when, from all appearances, it is a vast expanse of dead, slimy, brown rubble. The part of a fringing reef that you first reach from the beach is 'dead' on the surface (although many animals live there). Reefs grow upwards until the top remains exposed at low tide, whereupon the corals on the surface die and are covered over by the characteristic yellow–brown coat of algae. The reef continues to grow outwards, and it's towards and at the edges that you find the most living coral growth.

Physical factors impinging upon a reef create zones with various physical characteristics, which are preferred by different kinds of marine life. The inter-tidal reef flat (the part that exposes between high and low tide) is the habitat of the shells, crabs, sea cucumbers, starfish, and tiny fishes. Generally, as you get further out towards the growing edge, the reef life becomes more prolific. It is amazing how much there is to see, besides coral, if you are patient and use your eyes.

Naturally, better coral is usually found on the offshore reefs where, away from adverse mainland influences such as silting and freshwater runoff, coral achieves its true potential. Walking and snorkelling in the lagoon of one of these 'mid-ocean' reefs is a magical experience.

When reef walking, either on a continental island fringing reef or on an offshore platform reef, watch where you put your feet. If you step on live coral and break it, it will almost certainly die. Try to walk on the sandy spots in between the patches of coral or on those places that appear 'cemented over'. A walking stick may be useful, especially if you're not good at balancing on one foot while deciding where to put the other.

If you pick up a coral boulder to look underneath, replace it just where you found it after you've had your look. A number of creatures will have made a home under it, and if you leave it upside down their home will be destroyed and they may not survive.

Watch the state of the tide. Reefs are mostly flat with a slightly raised crest out towards the edge. They are often very wide, and you may have wandered a considerable distance from your boat or from the beach. When the tide comes over the crest, the water comes in with a rush, along with the marine traffic jam that has been stuck at a red light for the past six or so hours. You simply cannot walk fast over a reef, and in water that's up to your calves, walking gets even harder.

Keeping safe and well

The following tips are based on the observations of a general practitioner who has been treating patients in Airlie Beach for many years, long enough to gain a very good picture of the problems commonly encountered in tropical waters. Those with a thirst for extra detail may wish to read more in 'Avoiding tropical hazards'.

Oyster cuts and coral grazes are Problem Number One (statistically). To begin with, any cut inflicted below high tide mark in the tropics is guaranteed to be infected within seconds. If not treated properly, it can develop into a major infection. A twofold reaction is caused, first, by marine bacteria, some of which multiply with blinding speed, and second, by the physical presence of slimy gunk which produces an allergic response in some people.

Cleaning oyster wounds in particular is most important; if an injury is more than a graze, and if it's early in the holidays, go to a doctor, have a local anaesthetic, and get the wound cleaned *properly*. Oyster shells disintegrate as they cut; they're like shale, in layers, and they shatter, leaving mica-like slivers in the wound. The incidence of complications is virtually 100 per cent.

If it's the last two days of the holiday and you're catching lots of coral trout, you can probably sweat it out and see the doctor when you get back to the mainland.

Always clean wounds thoroughly and apply a disinfectant (any lingering moisture in the tropics is 'bad', so use a disinfectant with an alcohol or aqueous base (such as Betadine) or one in powder form rather than a cream.

'Tropical ear' (inflammation of the external ear, which doctors call *otitis externa*) spoils more holidays than just about anything on the list. It is caused by too much water in the ears too frequently; the ear gets waterlogged, never dries out, infection (bacterial or fungal) sets in. It occurs most frequently in people who have a tendency to 'waxy ears'.

Before going to the tropics and doing a lot of swimming, those with a tendency to get ear trouble should see a doctor and make sure that their ears are clean. Chemists have ear drops, and mouldable ear plugs that fit comfortably, and one or both of these may help.

Minor barotrauma in divers, a pressure-induced ear problem, is very common in tropical travellers. If you had difficulty with your ears in the plane on the way to the Whitsundays, you will probably have a problem if you go diving. Don't dive if you are having any difficulty equalising the pressure.

Windsurfing. Don't exceed your capabilities. If you're inexperienced, don't sail out of an anchorage on a sailboard into 20 knots of breeze and 3 knots of current. A common problem is falling over in areas where there isn't a sandy bottom, getting badly cut, sometimes a long way from help. Alcohol and sailboarding don't mix.

Sea creatures

Everyone has read about tropical horrors – sharks, stingrays, man-eating clams, giant squid that wrap their arms around you and love you to death. Evil-doing by creatures of the sea is vastly exaggerated and always gets very extensive press. It is unlikely that you will ever have a run-in with any of the following, but some discussion is necessary (for more details, see the section 'Avoiding tropical hazards').

Sharks are a natural feature of all tropical waters. The species most commonly seen in the Whitsundays are timid blacktips, which are reef fossickers, and unaggressive whitetips. Divers sometimes encounter tiger sharks and hammerheads. The Whitsundays are on a broad part of the continental shelf, where everyone in the sea gets plenty to eat. Whenever one is in the water in the tropics, however, it is prudent to avoid attracting unwanted attention, such as by making a huge splash diving into the water from the deck of a yacht, or by doing 'wounded fish' impressions while swimming or snorkelling. Slip quietly into the water. Swimming and fishing are incompatible activities, for obvious reasons. Don't fish near swimmers or swim near those who are fishing. Sharks have excellent vision, but they need light in order to see; don't swim at night, to avoid being mistaken for a fish. Sharks are scavengers; don't throw food scraps into the water. If on a reef, don't pick up a reef shark by the tail (yes, that *did* happen a while ago, and the person got a good bite on the hand, which might have been expected from a neighbour's dog were it so treated.

Stingrays are, biologically, flattened sharks that have taken to the bottom to feed on shellfish. Their teeth are flattened too, for crushing instead of cutting. Most species are very timid and will run away if they have the choice. Stingrays lie on the bottom and flick up sand on their back rendering them better able to feed and to surprise the unsuspecting mollusc on its way to grandmother's house. Stingrays frighten the pants off you when they 'erupt' from the sand half a metre in front of you and skitter away. Problems can occur if, because it is pinned to the sand with a foot, a stingray just cannot skitter away.

Always shuffle the feet when wading in shallow sandy areas. If you encounter one stingray, there are probably more of them about. The wound they inflict with a venomous barb in their tail is painful and will require the attention of a doctor, but unless you get stung on the torso, the wound is seldom serious.

Pressure-immobilisation of stingray wounds is not recommended. Use warm to hot water to relieve pain. Medical attention should be sought as wounds invariably require expert attention. (See 'Avoiding tropical hazards'.)

Stonefish are diabolically ugly creatures that look akin to a warthog that ran into a brick wall at a hundred and sixty kilometres an hour, resulting in (1) much of its bulk being permanently shifted forward on its frame, (2) the pugging of its face, and (3) the accordion-plaiting of its brow. Cover that lot with brown slime and carbuncles, and you have a stonefish, more or less.

At the outset let it be said that you are highly unlikely ever to see one, because they are so perfectly disguised where they lie on algae encrusted coral rubble that they virtually defy detection.

Stonefish have thirteen dorsal spines each attached to a poisonous venom sack, and if you tread on one it can give you an agonisingly painful wound. About one-half of the people treated for stonefish wounds have been wearing nothing on their feet. The moral is, always wear a solid pair of sneakers when reefwalking. Never run on a reef top; walk very gingerly.

Unlike some other types of envenomations, stonefish stings shouldn't be treated by pressure-immobilisation (see 'Avoiding tropical hazards'). Pain is severe and may be alleviated by immersing the wound in warm to hot water (but not scalding). Antivenom is available; always consult a doctor.

Box jellyfish (*Chironex fleckeri*), sometimes inappropriately called the 'sea wasps' because they pack a nasty sting. These creatures have absolutely no resemblance to a wasp, and calling them such trivialises the danger. They can be a hazard to swimmers along much of the Queensland mainland coast from November until May. Box jellyfish almost never get as far as the islands, their home territory being mainland estuaries and rivers and nearby mainland beaches. They are transparent and are therefore difficult to see and, although agile swimmers that avoid contact if they can, they cannot always avoid stinging those who race headlong down the beach into the water. They produce an extremely painful sting and have very adherent tentacles.

Observe warning signs posted on mainland beaches and be aware if a 'jellyfish alert' has been announced on the radio. In the danger months, swim with clothing on, which will protect those parts of you that are covered. In cases of stings, the adhering tentacles should be doused liberally with household vinegar for at least 30 seconds before attempting to remove them (vinegar inactivates the stinger cells preventing further envenomation). Apply compressive bandages if the sting covers more than half of one limb (major sting). Be prepared to give resuscitation. Antivenom is available and should be administered, and medical assistance should be sought in all cases. (See 'Avoiding tropical hazards' for more first-aid information.)

Cone shells are among the most strikingly beautiful shells (although they are frequently covered with a tenacious green slime that hides their beauty). They are common on reefs and are found all along the coastline. A number of species are poisonous and can give a potentially lethal sting.

Don't pick up cone shells in your bare hands, as the animal is capable of harpooning you from anywhere along the cleft entrance to the shell. In the event of a sting, treat with pressure-immobilisation. (See also 'Avoiding tropical hazards'.)

Above:
Coral scene at the Pinnacles, northern Hook Island.

Opposite:
Dive boat at Bait Reef, 16 nautical miles north-east of Hook Island.

DIVING AND SNORKELLING IN THE WHITSUNDAYS

The Whitsundays and the surrounding hundred or so miles of Great Barrier Reef Marine Park offer a wide variety of diving and snorkelling opportunities. The islands are ringed by fringing coral reefs with a high diversity of coral and fish species; the mid-shelf reef complexes of the Great Barrier system some twenty to thirty nautical miles further to the north-east offer the visitor a real taste of what the Barrier Reef is about.

Diving is well catered for in the area. Opportunities range from feet-wetting courses for beginners, in mainland and island resort swimming pools, to full certificate courses, to extended excursions to the outer reefs aboard purpose-oriented dive vessels. Because of the number of dive operators on the mainland and islands, diving can play some part in holidays of various kinds – a diversion from lazy resort life, an interlude in a bareboat charter, an event on an extended island cruise, or just part of a day-trip out of Shute Harbour. If you are bareboating, for example, you might even arrange to have an instructor run a private course for you and your friends right on your yacht. Or you can join up with a dive boat at various locations throughout the islands.

Snorkelling

Snorkelling is one of the most popular pastimes on the Great Barrier Reef and one of the best ways to appreciate it – in shallow water, where the light and colours are brightest. Snorkelling involves a minimum of fuss with equipment and it gives complete freedom to explore and to observe the creatures of a reef in their own environment. If you are venturing for the first time into tropical waters, or if it's been a few years since you donned your face mask and flippers, a few hours practice before you leave for your holiday will be very well spent. You will miss much of the Great Barrier Reef Marine Park if you can't get into the water and be relaxed and confident while you're there.

All of your attention when snorkelling ought to be directed at what you're looking at rather than at keeping yourself watertight, and this is where practice comes in. You should be able to lie face down in the water and breathe through the snorkel in a relaxed, easy way. Floating over the reef of a tropic isle may, to you, be a new world full of strange creatures. If your mask starts to leak, or you inhale a little water through the snorkel, you may find in these unfamiliar surroundings that anxiety will cause your breathing to become erratic and you will tend to gulp water. Just when you have cleared your mask and got the salt water out of your eyes is when you will fancy that you see 'Jaws' coming at you around a bend in the reef. Normally a cool, rational person, in these circumstances you may do a massive twitch, spit out your snorkel, and inhale enough water to make the water level at the reef fall several centimetres. Adrenalin pumping and all senses now ready for a life-and-death struggle, you will notice for the first time that the current has carried you a hundred and fifty metres from the boat, a distance you couldn't swim in your peak of fitness at high school even with a shove off the diving board from your swimming instructor. Your cry for help is a mere gargle that attracts only the attention of a nearby seagull. A number of points are illustrated here.

How to get the most out of snorkelling

First and foremost, have a mask that fits. Even if the holiday brochure said that you would be supplied a face mask and snorkel at no charge, consider buying your own face mask. If you think about what you are paying for your holiday, the cost of a mask is peanuts; not having one that works properly for you can assume un-peanut-like proportions. Go to a good dive shop and make sure that the mask you buy makes a good seal around your face. To check that a mask fits properly, put the strap in front of the faceplate, out of the way, and with one hand hold your hair back away from your face and put the mask into place with your other hand. Holding it lightly against your face with your index finger, breathe in gently through your nose. When you take your finger away, the mask should stay in place by suction, and no air should get in around the seal. Shake your head gently from side to side; the mask should still stay in place. If it does, you've got a good fit.

If you think you might be using the mask for some years, consider spending the extra money for a good one – one made of siliconised rubber rather than just plain rubber. Silicon masks are softer, more comfortable, they seal more readily and they won't crack and develop leaks as soon as rubber ones will. Any good dive shop will have one. If you have a difficult face (not an unpicturesque face, but one that is, for example, narrow at the temples so that it is difficult to get a good seal at that point), you are more likely to overcome this with a supple silicon mask.

Don't forget that the children who are going with you will also need masks that fit. Small masks can be obtained relatively inexpensively. You will be lucky, indeed, if your charter yacht has masks that will fit children's small faces properly. An ill-fitting mask is worse for children because their irritation threshold is usually lower, and if they're unhappy, you probably will be, too!

You may also wish to buy your own snorkel. There are some good ones now available that have several adjustments (mouthpiece angle, for example) which are more comfortable and which may improve your water-tightness. Don't bother with some department-store models, such as extra-long ones or with those with a ball float that seals the end when it goes underwater. While these seem a good idea to the novice, they aren't. The longer the snorkel tube the harder it is to clear, and the ball just gets in the way. In spite of all the natives you have seen on TV breathing through two-metre-long reeds, a two-metre-long snorkel is not a good idea; the volume of 'dead air' you exhale never gets out of the tube. You simply rebreathe bad air until you have extracted the last traces of oxygen, and then you pass out – which may be your last chance to buy a good snorkel.

Mastering the basic technique

The secret of snorkelling is learning how to relax with your face in the water. Breathing *easily* and *normally* is the key; it may take a few moments to overcome the natural anxiety that most people have when their mouth and nose are underwater. Spend a little time in a pool, or in shallow water by the beach, where you can stand up immediately if you feel the need to. Legs and feet should float out straight behind you. Once you can control your breathing you will feel confident to deal with the odd bit of water that gets into your snorkel; for example, when a wave slops

over the top or you put your head in too deep. Small amounts of water in the snorkel will be trapped in the U-bend under the mouthpiece and will gurgle as you breathe in. To clear this, inhale slowly and gently (so as not to draw in this water with the air) until you have a deep breath, then exhale sharply into the mouthpiece. Remember, never inhale sharply through your snorkel – always slowly and gently.

Finning is almost a straight-legged action, with the knees slightly bent. Some people say it helps to imagine having splints on your legs; it may be easier to get the hang of it on your back.

More-advanced technique

When you're happy about snorkelling on the surface, you may wish to try some shallow diving. The first thing to remember about diving is that you will need to equalise the pressure in your ears from the very moment you start to go down. Pressure increases rapidly as you descend. Everyone is familiar with equalising – 'popping' their ears – when landing in a plane; the principal in diving is the same. Divers start equalising from the moment they are beneath the surface, and they keep equalising all the way down. Pinch your nose and exhale gently with your mouth blocked. You shouldn't wait to actually feel the pressure coming onto the eardrums; if you wait until you feel it, you may not be able equalise. If you feel pain, go back up.

'Duck diving', as it is sometimes called, is done from a position flat on the surface with arms by your sides. Take a deep breath and swing your arms straight down and forward, which will force your head and trunk down. As you go head down, point your legs straight up in the air. The weight of your legs above water will force your body down, and you can begin finning downwards.

Snorkelling is an easy skill to learn with a minimal investment in equipment. With a little practice it becomes an effortless way to have intimate contact with a reef. A properly fitting face mask is very important, and to insure this it may be well worth purchasing your own.

The beautiful feather-like fronds of the stinging hydroid can produce a painful sting. These are best admired from a little distance.

Opposite above:
Little wonder corals were for so long considered plants. These are tube corals, with polyps extended.
Opposite below:
Plate corals at 'The Wood Pile' dive, northern Hook Island.

Watch the boat and the time

In spite of the relatively warm water you will experience in the Whitsundays all year round, most people cannot tolerate more than 20–30 minutes without getting chilled (unless they wear a wet suit). The more vigorous your activity the quicker you become chilled. Watch the boat to see that you are not getting too far away. By the time you realise that you are too far away, you may already be cold and tired.

Another hazard of prolonged snorkelling is sunburn. Lying face down on the surface you will not have your usual cue – heat – to tell you that you may be getting burned. A small portion of your back or shoulders usually floats just above the surface. This exposed part may get seriously sunburned.

Many snorkellers actually wear clothes in the water – shirt and trousers. This helps to protect you from the sun, it provides some small degree of 'wet suit' effect, and it also protects you from coral grazes if you get too close to the reef (it's amazing how often people get scratched on reefs through failure to appreciate their own draught).

Visibility in the Whitsundays

Contrast is the principal visual cue by which objects may be distinguished from their background, and the water medium is a greater reducer of contrast. Light is scattered by particles suspended in the water, and it is absorbed by water itself. As a result, even in water of exceptional clarity the greatest distance at which an object of any size may be seen is about two hundred metres. In practice, it is usually much less; scuba divers the

Diving considerately

Reefs are fragile and may be easily damaged. The dive sites throughout the islands are being visited increasingly, and divers need to be conscious of good technique to prevent inadvertent damage to corals. It is the cumulative effect of many small incidents that can lead to degradation of a reef.

The most common causes of coral damage are snagging by spare regulators and instrument consoles; damage caused when divers pull themselves along by grasping corals; crash landings due to improper weight and buoyancy control; damage caused by fins; collisions with corals by underwater photographers intent on what's in front of the viewfinder rather than what's going on behind it.

Divers can help preserve the marine environment by following these simple rules:

- Keep spare regulators and instruments close to the body by tucking them into the buoyancy compensator (BC).
- Maintain neutral buoyancy by using the correct amount of weight and inflating the BC on the way down.
- Don't use live corals for support.
- Watch the fins; avoid downward kicks when near the bottom, which may break corals or stir up sediments that can choke delicate organisms.
- Don't harass marine creatures; let their natural curiosity direct the encounter.
- Don't feed fish things that aren't part of their normal, naturally occurring diet (that is, don't feed them pasta).
- When taking pictures, be mindful of what's going on at your end of the camera.

world over consider visibility of 30–50 metres to be exceptionally good. This sort of visibility is usually available only in waters far away from land masses from which freshwater runoff, laden with sediments, greatly reduces clarity.

The islands of the Whitsundays are high continental islands which create their own freshwater runoff, and they are adjacent to the mainland river systems. Moreover, they are swept by very strong tidal currents, particularly at times of spring tides, that race to and from Broad Sound just south of Mackay, which has the greatest tidal range of anywhere on the Australian east coast. The result is that Whitsunday waters carry, from time to time, a heavy load of suspended sediment particles; these scatter the light and give the water a brilliant turquoise colour, enhancing the view above water but diminishing it underwater.

Visibility among the islands ranges from 15 metres down to as low as 1.5 metres depending upon the winds and the range of the tide; average visibility is perhaps 6 metres. Corals, with their resident algae, are sensitive to (dependent upon) light penetration of the water, and they find the depth that suits them best. This fact gives another side to the coin; there is a greater diversity of corals within a shorter vertical distance in Whitsunday waters than in clearer waters out on the Reef itself – a real bonus for snorkellers and in some ways for divers, too, who have less tendency to rush here and there to the detriment of really seeing what is in any one place.

Beware currents

Reefs require clean new water for optimum growth. The best coral development is found at the outer edges of a reef. The windward slope is where the most virulent growth is taking place. Reef development is also strongly moulded by the flow of currents, and for this reason some of the best reef development in the Whitsundays is adjacent to areas of swift currents. The tide when flooding courses south and is first obstructed by the northern side of Hook Island (map C14/15), and here some of the best diving and snorkelling in the Whitsundays is found. Cateran Bay, on the northern side of Border Island (map C29), sports a rich growth of fringing reef; so does the northern side of Deloraine Islet (map C30). Currents sweeping south around Langford Island (map C12) have fostered a substantial kidney-shaped reef there.

The corollary of all this is important to divers and snorkellers alike: beware strong currents. In certain locations you have no choice but to drift dive (for example, at Bird Island (map C12), and in others great care must be exercised to avoid being swept too far from your boat.

'Never dive by yourself' is especially true in the Whitsundays, and if at all possible, always leave someone tending the dive boat so that you can be assisted if you get into difficulty with currents.

Christmas tree worm.

What about sharks?

The species of sharks most commonly seen in the Whitsundays are the timid blacktip, a reef fossicker, and the whitetip, which is not aggressive. Divers have reported encounters with hammerheads and tiger sharks. As is true of all tropical waters, sharks are a natural part of the scene. You probably have a better chance of losing a toe to a giant toadfish in Shute Harbour than you have of being bitten by a shark (see 'Avoiding tropical hazards' for diabolical tales of terrible toadfish). However, it is prudent when in the water to behave in a manner that will not attract undue attention (see the following discussion). Swimming and fishing are not compatible activities, for obvious reasons. Don't fish near swimmers, and don't swim near those who are fishing. Sharks have excellent vision, but they need light in order to see. Don't swim at night, as this obviously increases your chances of being mistaken for a fish. Sharks are scavengers; don't throw food scraps into the water.

When in the water

When the water, assume the attitude that you are a 'visitor' in a foreign environment. Behave the same way that you would expect a visitor to behave in your home – not to damage your furniture or insult your family and friends. Sea creatures can be as curious about you as you are about them. They will often show little fear, especially if they haven't been mistreated by man before. Don't be deceived by all appearances. A moray eel, for example, peering at you from under a reef ledge, opening and closing its mouth as though practising how it is going to chew you up, is actually gulping water and forcing it over its gills, that is, it is breathing. These reef eels are not aggressive. It takes months to train one to take food from one's hand. In the water, do unto others as you would have them do unto you, not *before they do it unto you*. If you provoke anything enough, it will have a go at you.

Don't dive or jump into the water from the deck or swimming platform of a yacht, creating a large splash and shock wave that will attract the attention of every fish for miles around. Slip quietly into the water. Don't thrash around on the surface making a lot of noise or doing an impersonation of a wounded fish. Marine creatures depend upon a spectrum of low-frequency sounds that might almost be called 'vibrations'. They use these for communication as well as for navigation. For example, some fish attract mates by vibrating certain muscles in their air sacs. The spiny lobster, by vibrating an apparatus at the base of its antennae, makes a sound that you can feel as well as hear if you pick it up.

The lateral line of fishes and sharks is exquisitely sensitive to low frequency sounds. This is one way that fish maintain their perfect formations when schooling and escaping predators. The lateral line is made up of gelatinous canals along their sides which communicate with the external environment through pores in the skin. These canals have millions of tiny hair cells which act like the cells in the ears of land animals; displacement of the hairs by pressure gives the fish information about the direction and speed of an approaching object. Sharks are particularly sensitive to such vibrations. They have additional pores scattered about their head which are connected via jelly-filled tubes to sensory cells called Lorenzini's ampullae.

Sharks are attracted to wounded-fish-like vibrations. This fact has led to incidents on the Great Barrier Reef where sharks have been attracted to divers who have stayed underwater too long with a fish wiggling on the end of a spear.

Sound travels much further in water than light does, so this sense assumes greater importance in water. Whales, for example, communicate with each other near the surface for distances of over forty nautical miles, and further down they use temperature barriers (thermoclines) to make their voices travel even further. Swim smoothly and quietly. You will see very much more if you do. If you spear a fish while snorkelling in a Marine Park General Use zone*, get it to the surface and hold it out of the water until you can get it into the boat.

Diving safely

Among the Whitsunday islands, dives are usually fairly shallow, and decompression is not an issue; out on the reefs there is greater temptation and opportunity to go deeper. The nearest decompression facility is Townsville. The outer reefs are about two and a half hours from the mainland by boat, and Townsville is three and a half hours by road from Shute Harbour or Airlie Beach. After the six hours or so that it will take you to get to Townsville it may either be too late, or you needn't have gone in the first place. So, in the Whitsundays, it's best to remember that decompression is, for practical purposes, not available and prevention is therefore very much better than cure.

* Spear fishing with scuba gear is illegal everywhere in the Marine Park, and spear fishing (with or without scuba) is not permitted in Marine National Park 'A' or 'B' zones.

A polybranch sea slug feeds on algae. Its leaf-like projections emit unpleasant secretions to offend would-be attackers.

Diver training in the Whitsundays

The Whitsundays are now the second largest diver training centre in Australia (Cairns is the largest), and some of Australia's most qualified sports diving professionals work in the area. The Whitsundays are ideal for diver training because it is possible to dive there virtually every day of the year, at a choice of Great Barrier Reef or island sites. The Barrier Reef lies 32 nautical miles north-east of the Whitsunday mainland, about one and a half to two hours by motorised catamaran or fast launch. If it's too windy to go out to the Reef, there will be somewhere amongst the many island fringing reefs that will be sheltered enough to dive in comfort.

The area offers good opportunities to mix diving with other holiday pleasures, too, such as restaurants, night life, sailing, and resort life. Diving is available with a number of dive establishments on the mainland and, on a lesser scale, at all of the island resorts. It may be done on vessels that are specifically designed to cater for divers or those that take sight-seers out to the Barrier Reef or on yachts that cruise around the islands and which offer diving as a sideline. Diving may be done on a day-trip basis or on vessels that spend three, four or seven nights away from the mainland.

In the Whitsundays, if you're not sure if you really want to devote a lot of time to diving, or whether you will even enjoy the sport, it is possible to do a 'resort course', a two-hour introductory session that prepares the student for a shallow (9-metre) dive under the immediate supervision of an instructor. This is a good way to decide whether to go ahead with a certificate course, and it's also a way to sample a bit of the Barrier Reef without any significant investment of time or money.

Above:
The nudibranch, or sea slug, is a shell-less mollusc whose bright colour warns predators that it is unpleasant to the taste.

Left:
Manta rays are among the most graceful creatures of the sea. They startle mariners by erupting from the water and taking momentary flight. Rays are, biologically, flattened sharks that have adopted a bottom-dwelling lifestyle. Mantas are commonly seen by divers at Manta Ray Bay, northern Hook Island.

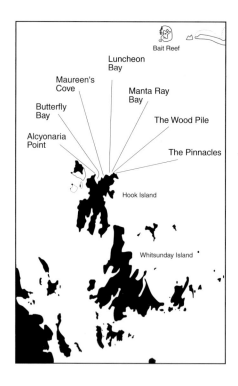

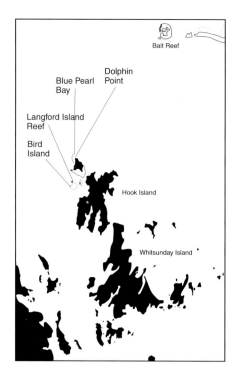

Best diving in the Whitsundays

Island sites

The Pinnacles (Hook Island, map C14/15). Site location: 20°0.3', 148°50'. One of the best dive sites and a very good snorkelling area. Excellent beach for snorkellers. In strong south-east winds anchorage is uncomfortable and visibility adversely affected; in northerlies of more than 5 knots, visibility is adversely affected. Gentle slope from 5 to 21 metres with bommies rising from 9 metres to within 3 metres of the surface. The Pinnacles has the best corals in the Whitsundays, predominantly hard corals with some gorgonians in coves. Parrotfish, coral trout, sweetlip, bream, schools of fusiliers, giant Maori wrasse and manta rays common May–October. Excellent for nudibranchs and for several species of cowries.

The Wood Pile (Hook Island, map C14/15). Site location: 20°03.6', 148°57.6'. An excellent dropoff dive, not for snorkellers. Subject to strong ebb tidal currents which should be considered in selecting dive time. Suitable in south-east winds to 15 knots or very light east-to-north winds. *Tubastraea* are common, other forms not prolific. Fish similar to those at The Pinnacles, with large groper, black- and white-tip sharks.

Manta Ray Bay (Hook Island, map C14/15). Site location: 20°03.7', 148°57.4'. One of the best-protected diving anchorages on Hook Island ('anchoring' is prohibited). Diving and snorkelling over interesting terrain and reef life. Fish can be hand-fed. Best diving is from a boat, although there is access from an attractive beach. Manta Ray Bay slopes gently from the shore to 27 metres with bommies rising from level of 9–12 metres. There are gullies and tunnels. Below 15 metres is mainly sand and rubble. Staghorn coral to 5 metres and alcyonaria lie beyond this depth. Angelfish and butterfly cod are common. Parrotfish, cod, coral trout, sweetlip, bream, batfish, fusiliers, manta rays, feather stars, nudibranchs, Christmas tree worms.

Luncheon Bay (Hook Island, map C14/15). Site location: 20°03.8', 148°57.3'. 'The Bommie' is an exciting dive for experienced divers. Very strong current.

Maureen's Cove (Hook Island, map C14/15). Site location: 20°04.1', 148°56.2'. Maureen's Cove is named after Maureen Prior, a nursing sister theatre supervisor who lost her heart to the Whitsundays, gave up nursing and started, in the mid-1970s, Barrier Reef Diving Services, the first scuba diving company to operate in the Whitsundays. The cove offers good shallow diving; it is not particularly good for snorkelling. It is well protected except in northerlies. Bommies rise from 12 metres with gullies, caves and ledges to 15 metres, after which is sand and debris. Variety of porites and favia, acropora (staghorn and plate). Gorgonians abound in gullies and caves. *Tubastraea* common. Angelfish, butterfly cod, parrotfish, coral trout, sweetlip, bream, batfish, fusiliers.

Butterfly Bay (Hook Island, map C14/15). Site location: 20°04.0', 148°55.4'. Diving in 3–6 metres, dropping vertically to 15 metres. Wall diving with coral outcrops, gullies and small caves. Good hard coral diversity.

Alcyonaria Point (Hook Island, map C14/15). Site location: 20°03.8', 148°55.4'. Alcyonaria Point is an excellent dive site in Butterfly Bay. It is so named because of the abundance of alcyonarians (soft corals) there. Anchorage is difficult because of dropoff. At mid-tide, current can be a problem, particularly on the point. It is somewhat exposed to south-easterly winds but bearable if the wind is not too strong. Again, northerlies more than 5 knots make visibility a problem. There are two types of dive: a shallow 3–4.5 metres shelf with a garden of plate corals; a fairly deep dive (for the islands) of 12–15 metres with vertical cliff and caves, sloping to 27 metres and then dropping to the sea bed at 40 metres. Black coral, fans in the depths, and the wall is a mass of stony corals and alcyonaria. Gullies and caves are covered with gorgonians. Most prolific fish life of the Whitsundays, with large sweetlip, wrasse and cod.

Dolphin Point (Hayman Island, map C13). Site location: 20°03.3', 148°52.8'. This site on the northern tip of Hayman Island offers a spectacular seascape where house-size blocks have fallen. Dive is 6–18 metres on rugged terrain, bommies rising from 15 metres down to 6 metres on an undulating bottom covered with rubble. Excellent diversity of tropical fish including trevally, mackerel and the occasional hammerhead shark. Feather stars are common, as are anemones and clown fish.

Blue Pearl Bay (Hayman Island, map C13). Site location: 20°03.9', 148°52.8'. A lovely bay which offers shallow water snorkelling and diving to 18 metres. It shoals gradually to a vertical wall at 15 metres with gullies, tunnels and overhanging ledges. There is prolific cover of staghorns along shallow sections with occasional large plates. Alcyonaria and millepora (fire coral) line the wall. Parrotfish, cod, coral trout, sweetlip, bream, batfish, fusiliers, butterfly and angelfish are common. Nudibranchs and free-swimming worms.

Langford Reef (Langford Island, map C12). Site location: 20°04.8', 148°52.8'. Langford, although it has had heavy use over the years, still offers excellent diving on the eastern side of the reef. Watch out for current.

Bird Island (map C12). Site location: 20°05.3', 148°52.3'. This is a drift dive sometimes subject to very heavy current, which seems to run south at all times. Similar in character to Blue Pearl Bay.

Hannah Point (North Molle Island, map C8). Site location: 20°12.9', 148°48.4'. Although the visibility is usually not good, the northern tip of North Molle offers an interesting dive, particularly at times of neap tides and moderate to light winds. Sometimes used as a night dive due to its proximity to the mainland. Watch out for current off the point. Trout.

False Nara Inlet (Hook Island, map C11). Site location: 20°09.9', 148°53.2'. This is a difficult anchorage. Conditions for diving and snorkelling are best during neap tides and in light winds. Parrotfish.

Nara and Macona inlets (map C10). Site location: 20°10.2', 148°54.7'. This site is exposed and is best in neap tides and very light winds. It is worth a look, particularly for those with vessels too small to safely go around to the northern side of Hook Island.

East Hayman Island (map C13). Site location: 20°03.6', 148°54.2'. A very beautiful area that is difficult to get at because there is no anchorage and it is very exposed. You need virtually calm conditions. Dropoff dive with lots of turtles and rays.

Mackerel Bay (Hook Island, map C14/15). Site location: 20°05.4', 148°57.2'. Good coral cover in shallow water, dropping off to scattered bommies at 7–12 metres. A dive which is better at some times than at others depending upon visibility. This is a popular dive site during northerlies when most of the more popular sites are untenable. A relatively shallow dive through a maze of coral bommies, which form shallow canyons, ledges and swim-throughs. Exposed to southerly winds.

Saba Bay (Hook Island, map C14/15). Site location: 20°07.2', 148°56.6'. Good coral cover in shallow water, dropping of to scattered bommies at 7–12 metres. As with Mackerel Bay, this is another popular dive site during northerly winds. The northern end of the bay is studded with numerous small bommies in relatively shallow water, dropping down to 15 metres with scattered bommies among coral rubble and sand. Plenty of shallow canyons, ledges and swim-throughs. Best dives during neap tides. Exposed to southerly winds.

Cateran Bay (Border Island, map C29). Site location: 20°09.5', 149°02.0'. Border is one of the outlying islands. Cateran Bay is a relatively shallow dive (coral diminishes below 6 metres). It offers a rich diversity of very colourful corals. Snorkellers can therefore see almost everything. Visibility may be limited in spring tides, and it can be blustery in fresh south-east winds. Accessible from boat only at low tide; from beach at high tide. Be careful not to damage fringing reef if ashore. Off the north-west tip of the bay watch out for current.

Nearest sites at the Barrier Reef

Bait Reef (map R1). Site location: 19°49.2', 149°03.8'. First-rate dives at a number of different types of site ranging from shallow garden coral – beautiful, fragile corals in shallow (3 metres) water – to a wall that drops to 20 metres, with black coral and fans. Deep caves. There is a chimney at 3 metres which opens up at 21 metres . Lots of manta rays.

The Stepping Stones (Bait Reef, map R1). Site location: 19°48.4', 149°03.8'. These are a series of bommies that run from the lagoon right up the north-west side of Bait Reef. Well protected in south-east winds, with very good visibility. To do a 'figure 8' around two bommies requires about one tank of air. Good diving virtually anywhere. Often there is better visibility here than at Hardy Reef.

Sinker Reef (map R1). Site location: 19°43.2, 149°11.8'. Excellent wall dive. Extremely strong currents run between Line Reef and the western side of Sinker Reef.

Line Reef (map R1). Site location: 19°43.4', 149°11.4'. Excellent wall dive. Very strong current.

The Caves (Hardy Reef, map R1). Site location: 19°43.2', 149°12.4'.

The Walls (Hook Reef, map R1). Site location: 19°44.7', 149°10.8'. Subject to very strong current. When you get into the channel the current hits you like a wave and has a tendency to drive you down, and you 'tumble off into space' and travel 100 metres in a matter of minutes. Sometimes back-eddies can be ridden in opposite direction.

The Beach (Hardy Reef, map R1). Site location: 19°43.5', 149°12.0'.

Shark Alley (Hardy Reef, map R1). Site location: 19°43.8', 149°11.1'. Very prone to current. Must be dived at slack water, high tide.

The Canyons (Hook Reef, map R1). Site location: 19°44.0', 149°09.8'. Shallow dive through a maze of coral.

Hardy South (Hardy Reef, map R1). Site location: 19°48.1', 149°15.4'. For diving in northerly winds only. Very strong current.

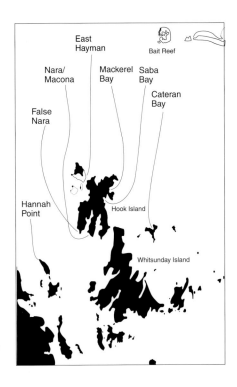

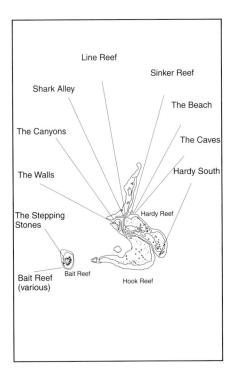

Above:
Sailing in the Whitsunday Passage.

Opposite:
Charter yacht at anchor on a golden
afternoon in the Whitsundays.

BOATING IN THE WHITSUNDAYS

The Cumberland* Islands, now more often referred to as the Whitsundays, are arguably the best cruising grounds found anywhere in Australia, and they rival the best in the world. These wrinkled and indented mountain tops of a bygone era today provide a wide variety of anchorages, one seldom more than ten miles from the next. Of more than one hundred islands and islets in the group, at least fifty offer comfortable anchorage, many of them several anchorages. Almost all of the islands are national parks, covered with trees and bush, creating the impression that they have yet to be discovered and offering visitors the faint smell of adventure.

It used to be so that by the time sailors made their way to the Whitsundays they knew all about trade winds, and coral, and how the big tides of this part of the coast play merry hell with contrary winds. With the advent of the sail-it-yourself yacht, this assumption of experience is no longer always true. This chapter will provide, for the uninitiated, an introduction to the winds and tides of the area, a few tips on cruising in coral, and some suggestions for gettting around happily. The sketch maps and sailing directions later in the book take up the finer points of finding anchorage in the Whitsundays.

The weather and the winds
The Whitsunday islands, at about latitude 20° south, lie between a band of subtropical high pressure and the equatorial low presure belt. These pressure zones shift their positions north and south as the sun moves back and forth across the equator in summer and winter, and the pressure differential between them causes a general movement of air (in the southern hemisphere) from south to north. In 1835, a French physicist, Gaspard de Coriolis, pointed out that any particle moving relative to the earth's surface is deflected to the right (in the northern hemisphere) or left (in the southern hemisphere) when viewed from the respective poles. Although the force of this deflection is only one millionth the magnitude of the gravitational force of the earth, it nevertheless has a significant effect on the horizontal movements of the atmosphere and the oceans, even on water swirling down the drainpipe.

---

*Cumberland was the name that Lieutenant James Cook gave to the islands he discovered on the Whitsunday coast in 1770, and other surveyors and the navy hydrographers later subgrouped the Cumberlands into the Whitsunday Group, Lindeman Group, Sir James Smith Group, the Anchor Islands and the Repulse Islands. The name 'Whitsundays' today is generalised to refer to all of them.

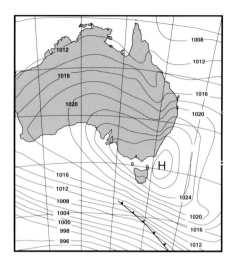

Typical April weather map showing high pressure, well south, ridging up the Queensland coast.

Our weather in Australia is marked by a series of 'highs' which march across the continent from west to east, centred over the mainland at about 30° in winter and at about 35° in summer. They are set spinning in an anti-clockwise direction by the rotational force described by Coriolis, and from autumn to spring, these highs tend to produce ridges of high pressure all up the east coast of Queensland. The winds course around the ridges, producing persistent fresh south-east-to-east trades, their strength varying according to the central pressure of the highs.

It is important for sailors in the Queensland central coast to watch the high pressure systems which are way down south, as remote as they are from the tropics; strong wind warnings for St Lawrence to Double Island Point often have to do with a strong high in Bass Strait, producing on the weather map a spate of isobars across the coast between New South Wales and Queensland. The ridge of the high, where the isobars undergo maximum local curvature, produces acceleration of winds. Keep in mind, too, especially if your eye is trained to anticipate the strength of winds based on the relative spacing of isobars on a weather map, that in the lower latitudes of central Queensland, air is more easily moved than it is at, say, latitude 40° south, and what looks like 10–20 knots to the southerner may in fact produce 20–30 knots in the Whitsundays.

The strongest highs usually occur during March–April, and Whitsunday winds tend to follow suit.

Weather is always capricious, and generalisations frequently leave egg on the face of the generaliser. Seasons have blurry edges, but the 'wet' season in the Whitsundays is January–March, the windiest months are March–May, the driest months are August–September. From late September onwards the trade winds abate, and some say late September to early November is the best cruising weather in the Whitsundays. At any time of year you can almost always be assured of having enough wind for a pleasant sail, with flat calm days occurring less than 5 per cent of the time.

Whitsunday Wind Strength (knots)
Incidence of winds in given range, 1500 hrs, Hayman Island (observations over 15-year period)

Month	0–11	11–16	17–22	22+
Jan.	55%	29%	9%	6%
Feb.	42%	34%	19%	6%
Mar.	47%	29%	16%	8%
Apr.	44%	28%	20%	8%
May	47%	33%	15%	5%
June	64%	25%	9%	1%
July	65%	27%	6%	1%
Aug.	61%	26%	10%	2%
Sept.	63%	22%	12%	3%
Oct.	54%	33%	11%	3%
Nov.	56%	28%	12%	4%
Dec.	54%	30%	12%	5%

This wind strength table shows the per cent incidence of winds of various strengths (knots). Figures add across to 100% (more or less). They confirm T.S. Eliot's observation that 'April is the cruellest month' when, in the Whitsundays, on almost one in three days, the mean wind strength at 3.00 pm is over 16 knots (stronger gusts will, of course, be common). Weather is confounding. All these figures are based on 15 years' statistics, but quite exceptional weather is always on the cards.

Whitsunday Wind Direction
Incidence of winds from given direction, 1500 hrs, Hayman Island (observations over 15-year period)

Month	Calm	N	NE	E	SE	S	SW	W	NW
Jan.	2%	7%	22%	31%	21%	2%	1%	4%	10%
Feb.	2%	5%	11%	32%	33%	6%	1%	2%	8%
Mar.	1%	2%	13%	35%	37%	6%	1%	*	5%
Apr.	3%	1%	6%	30%	46%	7%	*	3%	4%
May	4%	*	4%	24%	46%	18%	1%	2%	1%
June	3%	1%	3%	14%	41%	25%	4%	5%	4%
July	3%	1%	6%	23%	40%	16%	5%	3%	3%
Aug.	3%	4%	13%	26%	35%	5%	1%	4%	9%
Sept.	2%	5%	19%	33%	25%	2%	2%	5%	7%
Oct.	*	6%	20%	32%	21%	2%	*	4%	14%
Nov.	1%	10%	22%	27%	16%	1%	*	5%	18%
Dec.	*	10%	21%	29%	17%	1%	*	5%	16%

*Occurs, but incidence is less than 0.5% ▢ = predominant wind direction

The predominant winds in the Whitsundays are south-east and east; north-east winds occur with increasing frequency from September onwards through January, giving sailors an opportunity to visit some of the south-exposed anchorages.

Buys Ballot's law says that, if you stand (in the southern hemisphere) facing the true wind, the centre of the low pressure will be 8 to 12 points of the compass to your left (one point of the compass is 11.25 degrees, so 8 to 12 points are 90 to 135 degrees). Facing the predominant south-east to east winds in the Whitsundays, your left arm, when extended 90 to 135 degrees, will point to low pressure somewhere north of the islands. The almost total absence of afternoon south-west and west winds confirms the point – that the tropical lows are to the north. South-west winds do occur with thunder squalls and, sometimes, overnight.

The march of the weather systems over Australia results in periodic bursts of trade wind activity throughout the season, which lasts from March or April through September. Winds can spring up from a southerly direction on the spur of the moment, even in the middle of the night. For this reason, local skippers strongly advise against the overnight use of south-exposed anchorages from March through September. Exceptions are Nara and Macona inlets (map C11), which are deeply embayed and are not as exposed, for example, as are the anchorages on the southern side of Whitsunday and Haslewood islands – Turtle Bay, Chance Bay, Waite Bay (White Bay).

Bullets

Gusty winds that joust with the lofty Whitsunday Island profiles increase in velocity as they whistle over the peaks and funnel down into the anchorages, producing what are locally referred to as 'bullets'. Bullets can be almost twice the strength of the ambient wind. Anchorages on the north side of Hook Island – Stonehaven and Butterfly Bay – are particularly bullet-prone, as are some others. Bullets needn't worry you particularly, but it is good practice to get your sails down before you enter the confines of an anchorage, where all your attention should be directed towards locating the fringing reef and any scattered coral heads, not towards retrieving sails or articles of clothing blown overboard by a sudden unexpected gust.

Cyclones

Cyclones, or tropical revolving storms, when they do occur on the Queensland coast, come most often between December and April. It is unfortunate that 'cyclone' is such an innocuous name; it is correct in describing the clockwise circulation of an air mass around a low pressure system but deceptively meek-sounding compared with the hurricanes and typhoons of the Caribbean and South China Sea. A cyclone heads the list of sea experiences to be avoided.

Fortunately Queensland has a very good cyclone warning system, and yachtsmen, particularly those on bareboat charter, are most unlikely ever to have to cope with one. Cyclones breed in low tropical latitudes, and at latitudes 10° to 20° move at an average speed of only 6–12 knots. You will almost always hear of one days before it might pose any threat. Whenever a cyclone is within 434 nautical miles, the Bureau of Meteorology initiates a programme of regular warnings which are broadcast through the media with increasing frequency as danger becomes more imminent. Yacht charterers will be advised by their bases what action to take and when.

Riding out a cyclone

In the unlikely event that you are caught 'with your pants down' while cruising in the Whitsundays, you will need to find an appropriate anchorage and prepare for the worse. Traditionally, one runs the yacht into a sheltered creek and ties or anchors amongst mangroves. Some of the best anchorages in this respect are Trammel Bay (map C5), Funnel Bay (map C2), Woodcutter Bay (map C6), and Upper Gulnare Inlet (map C21). The advent of man-made harbours in the islands and marinas on the mainland has had some affect on traditional behaviour; Hamilton Harbour is now used by many of the island cruise boats as their cyclone anchorage, as is Abel Point Marina on the mainland. How well all of these will stand up to a real cyclone has yet to be proven, and hopefully it never will be.

Traditional cyclone anchorages in creeks are obviously shallow and must be entered with a tide that gives you a little more water than your draught. Among mangroves, there are probably not too many rocks around, and the yacht will settle comfortably in soft mud as the tide goes out. Don't get too close to the shore line; stay amongst the mangroves and allow enough room for the boat to lay over however much it will. A powerful motor left ticking over slowly in reverse will wash out mud from under the boat and may prevent the angle of heel from becoming uncomfortable. If you find a natural 'hole' the boat will hardly lean over at all.

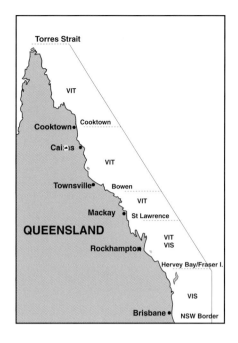

Weather forecasts for the Queensland coast are issued covering five sections: Torres Strait to Cooktown, Cooktown to Bowen, Bowen to St Lawrence, St Lawrence to Hervey Bay, and Fraser Island to Coolangatta (NSW border). The forecast of prime interest for yachting in the Whitsundays is Bowen to St Lawrence.

Weather information

Telstra coast station broadcasts
Townsville Radio VIT broadcasts daily at 0633 and 1633 local standard time on:
  VHF channel 67
  HF 2201, 4426, 6507, 8176, 12365 kHz
and at 0630 and 1630 on:
  VHF Seaphone channels 28, 65, 66 and 86.

Limited coast station broadcasts
Penta Comstat VZX broadcasts weather daily (NSW local time) at 0735, 1335 and 1635 hrs on:
  4483 and 8713 kHz.

Coast Guard and Air Sea Rescue stations broadcast weather on:
  2524 kHz, 27 MHz and on
  VHF channels.

Bareboat charter companies conduct their own schedules on VHF channels.

Weather information may also be heard on commercial and ABC radio stations, from Townsville and Mackay, at various times throughout the day:

  4QN Townsville (630 kHz)
  4QA Mackay (756 kHz)
  4RR Townsville (891 kHz)
  4MK Mackay (1026 kHz; 91.5 MHz FM).

Above:
Wind against tide produces lumpy
sailing in the Passage.

Left:
Exhilarating sailing conditions are
a feature of the
Whitsunday Passage.

Right:
The Whitsunday shower can
reduce visibility for short periods
while winds keep the yacht moving
at speed. Navigate cautiously in
these conditions.

Far right:
The large tidal range of the
Whitsundays must be considered
when cruising, particularly when
going ashore.

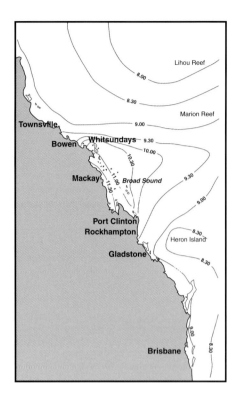

Above:

In this illustration, lines connect equal points in time, and they trace the advance of the tide on the Queensland central coast. Note the convergence around the broad expanse of continental shelf, which reaches its widest point off Broad Sound south of Mackay. Tide range decreases north and south from Broad Sound; at the top of the Whitsundays, the range is about one half that at Mackay.

(After Maxwell, W.G.H., Atlas of the Great Barrier Reef, *Elsevier, 1968.)*

*Tides – a note on tide terminology

Unless defined, the expression 'maximum tide' may mean different things to different people. It may mean 'maximum height of water above the chart datum', or it may mean 'maximum tide range', i.e. the greatest difference between successive high and low tides, or the difference between the highest/lowest astronomical tides.

The tidal range for successive tides says something about how much a yacht will rise and fall in an anchorage, which is important in calculating the amount of scope to pay out when at anchor. It may also have indicate the strength of current that will be encountered, or the size of the seas in the Whitsunday Passage, or how much water will be in the shallow entrance to an inlet. The *Tide Tables* gives clear definitions of all terms used and is well worth perusing.

Remember, heavy rains accompany cyclones, and creeks when flooded will be awash with logs and debris coming down from the land, especially if the particular creek has not flooded for a while. Keep your lines high and tied onto solid mangrove trees. If necessary, run anchors out around trees before dropping them into the mud. Secure several bow lines to keep you headed upstream.

Batten down all hatches, close all ports and deadlights, close skin-fitting valves (except those needed for the engine), board up large windows (if this is not possible, run vertical and horizontal strips of tape across them to prevent flying glass if they fracture), pump the bilges, clear the decks, stow all gear, turn on the radio so that you can hear all about the fun you're about to have, break out the OP rum, and pray!

Tides*

Tides in the Whitsundays rise and fall more than those experienced by many yachtsmen, and they are the single most important consideration in cruising the area. Their effect on sea conditions, particularly when they oppose fresh south-east trade winds causing the sea to 'stand up' a bit, can be important to trip planning, as is their swift ebb and flow through the narrow passages between islands. Spring tides may influence a decision on the use of a few shallow anchorages, for as well as providing more water at high tide, they give less water than normal under the keel at low tide.

The direction of tidal flood (rising tide) is southwards through the Passage, and the ebb (falling tide) sets to the north. This is worth making a note of and remembering.

Broad Sound, south of Mackay, has the highest tides of any place on the east coast of Australia, with a maximum in some estuaries of 10 metres. The magnitude of tides decreases to the north and south of Broad Sound. Mackay Outer Harbour, which is the Standard Port for tidal predictions for some of the islands, has a maximum astronomical tide of about 6.95 metres. As you move north through the islands, the tides decrease until, at Butterfly Bay on the northern side of Hook Island, the range is just half that of Mackay. As a rule of thumb, tide range in the Whitsunday Group is about 60% that at Mackay; further south, in the Lindeman Group for example, the range is about 75%; and still further south, at Brampton Island, the figure is about 90%. Keep this in mind if you sail from Shute Harbour to southern anchorages.

Tidal waves (i.e. standing waves of tide as opposed to *tsunamis*, the latter being monstrous, so-called 'tidal', waves created by undersea earthquakes) approach the Queensland coast in a general easterly direction and converge around the broad eastern expanse of continental shelf east of Mackay. The shape of the shelf accentuates the effects of convergence, and shoaling produces bottom interference, resulting in a tremendous build-up of water, some hundred cubic nautical miles of it. The tide floods south through the Whitsundays on the way to Broad Sound, and these islands form an obstruction to the flow of water. In the restricted passages, currents can be very swift.

Queensland's Official Tide Tables & Boating Guide, a copy of which should be aboard every yacht, is a very useful book with lots of valuable information. Among other things, it provides the means for calculating tides at points throughout the islands, and there are interpolation diagrams for calculating the height of tide at any time (see also the note 'Estimating tide' later in this chapter for the 'rule of twelfths' method).

The *Tide Tables* gives data for the Standard Ports of which there are now four in the Cumberlands – Hay Point, Mackay Outer Harbour, Shute Harbour and Townsville (there used to be only one, Mackay Outer Harbour). Under the Standard Ports are listed various Secondary Places; for example, under Shute Harbour are Airlie Beach, Hamilton Island, Hayman Island, Lindeman Island and Nara Inlet (southern Hook Island). These five localities are grouped under Shute Harbour as their tidal data is similar to that of Shute Harbour. The tidal range various tremendously throughout the islands; for example, at northern Hook Island (Butterfly

Bay) the range is only one half as large as it is at Mackay. That is why one needs to consult the data on the appropriate Standard Port to calculate the tide for a particular anchorage – for example, to determine how much scope to let out on the anchor at Butterfly Bay, or how much water there may be at a given time at the entrance to Gulnare Inlet.

Calculating Whitsunday tidal range and times

The *Tide Tables* gives a series of figures for the various Secondary Places – time difference, ratio, and a constant – which enable exact tide heights to be calculated. The following shows some of the data for Secondary Places listed under the Standard Port Shute Harbour.

Secondary Place	Relative time high (mins)	Relative time low (mins)	Ratio	Constant
Hamilton Island	+2	+2	1.13	+0.07
Hayman Island	+3	+1	0.99	+0.06
Lindeman Island	+6	+8	1.13	+0.05
Nara Inlet	-12	-12	0.97	+0.06

Explanation: At Nara Inlet the time of the high and low tides is twelve minutes earlier than at Shute Harbour (-12 means subtract 12 minutes from the times at Shute Harbour). The ratio 0.97 means the height is about 97% that at Shute Harbour with a constant of +0.06 metres to be applied afterwards, which raises the previously calculated height somewhat. The height of high or low water above the depths shown on the chart at Nara Inlet is calculated by extracting from the *Tide Tables* the figure for high (or low) tide at Shute Harbour, multiplying that figure by 0.97, then applying the constant (in this case, adding 0.06 to the result. (*See the marginal note* 'Calculating scope and tide'.)

Sailing with the tides

When a spring tide is flooding south through the Whitsunday Passage against a fresh south-east trade wind, the tidal current opposes surface drift set up by the wind and the waves stack up into short, steep lumps. Yachts sailing against the wind will take plenty of spray and occasionally a bit of green water over the bow. Some sailors revel in these conditions; some prefer to avoid them.

The first note in the daily log should be the time of high and low tides for the day, and plan all trips accordingly. Spring tides can cause currents to run at several knots in the Passage, and currents in Fitzalan and Solway Passages may attain 4–5 knots. Even in calm conditions this can have significant effect on your travel time, and at times of fresh winds against the tide it may be foolish to even attempt passage.

Navigation

There are so many readily identifiable landmarks throughout the Whitsundays that 'navigating' almost seems unnecessary. There is a temptation not to be formal about it, nor to be scrupulous in recording one's position which, after all, may be obtained at a moment's notice with a hand-held compass and a couple of quick bearings on any of the many prominences.

To revert to the old truths about the necessity of fixing one's position at every opportunity sounds schoolmarmish under such circumstances. There may be something to be gained, therefore, from relating a true story of the chap who was crossing the Passage in fresh breezes and spring tides. He disappeared into one of those 'occasional' Whitsunday showers, only to find that, on this occasion, the shower didn't clear immediately – in fact, not for 45 minutes. He hadn't a clue what he was closing in on, at a rate of 7.5 knots, nor did he really know the precise direction in which he was travelling, as there was 2 knots of tide setting up the Passage and it was on his beam. Under such circumstances the book says you should immediately go into a defensive posture; however, feeling certain that the shower was only momentary, he continued on at speed for an imprudently long time. The story ended happily, the only permanent

---

Calculating scope and tide
Example
Lindeman Island, June 8–9.
The *Tide Tables* shows the following details for the Standard Port, Shute Harbour.

8 0413 3.34
SA 1057 0.55
◑ 1709 2.81
2259 1.00

9 0522 3.24
SU 1158 0.46
1819 3.03

The highest tides in the winter are at night, and the difference beteen the low at 2259 on the 8th and the high at 0522 on the 9th is the greatest, so this one is used to calculate the scope required.
The high on the 9th is 3.24 metres. The range between this and the previous low is 3.24-1.00 = 2.24.
The tables show that Lindeman Island has a ratio of 1.13 and a constant to be applied of +0.05. Applying the ratio and the correction factor:

Tide range 2.24 x 1.13 =	2.53 m
plus constant +	0.05 m
	2.58 m
Chart depth at anchorage ③ =	2.40 m
Add high tide =	2.58 m
Total depth =	4.98 m
Scope factor (because depth < 7 m) =	x 4
Total scope at least 19.92 or	20 m

casualty being the captain's image of infallibility in the eyes of his crew as, in spite of the jaunty angle of his sun visor and the presence of his mirror sunglasses, there was no mistaking that on this occasion he was not totally the master of their destinies. That skipper has gone back to more formal navigating and log-keeping in accordance with the ancient prophets of seamanship.

Currents accelerate around points of land and edges of reefs, and if the skipper is not alert he may find himself careering towards a hazard faster than the yacht's sails are carrying him away from it. It is, of course, just at this moment, his having called for full steam ahead, that the key breaks off in the ignition, or the engineer is doing her nails and can't respond immediately to his request and so avoiding the '*pickle you shouldn't have got yourself into, dear*' (these words flung back in his face on the rescue craft as they proceed back to port to explain to the charter company that the security deposit is all that's left of their ship). Be particularly watchful when negotiating the reef off the southern end of Daydream Island (map C9); 'The Beak' on the northern entrance to Shute Harbour (C3); Roma Point at the south-west end of South Molle Island (C9); Reef Point at the southern entrance of Cid Harbour; and the channel between Cid and Whitsunday islands (C19) – to mention a few potential trouble spots.

Preparing to anchor

The moment of achieving anchorage is a very special one in cruising, signalling the beginning of a whole series of pleasures. Refuge attained, the crew can peel off gear after an exhilarating sail, the galley slave breaks out the drinks and lunch, and everyone languishes in the sun. This is occasionally dampened, however, by the few moments that preceded anchoring.

The anchorages of the Whitsundays are almost invariably surrounded by majestic hills and, along the shorelines, fringing coral reefs. The hills behave like funnels and air foils; they create very disturbed air which makes sailing difficult, with wind coming from all directions, causing the occasional surprise gybe and sometimes even a knockdown. It is advisable to get your sails down and start your motor before you enter an anchorage in order to allow you and your crew to concentrate fully on picking up the fringing reef and sighting scattered coral heads rather than retrieving items of clothing lost in a last-minute battle with flogging sails.

The best way to pick up a reef (with the sun behind you and wearing polarised sunglasses) is with an oblique approach rather than a straight one; you will see the reef merging from the right or left, and you can gently manoeuvre yourself at a respectable distance without violent turns that tend to make the crew depart the deck and the sauce invert over the cabin sole (cabin sole is not, in this instance, a local Queensland fish dish).

It is very important both to have a lookout on the foredeck and to be able to communicate effectively with this person. Establish a set of signals and agree upon their meaning. If you haven't done this you will very likely repeat the drama so frequently re-enacted … the lookout points to one or other side of the bow while yelling a startled instruction which, because the lookout is facing forward, carries away over the bow and the helmsman doesn't hear it. The helmsman responds by turning the yacht in the direction the lookout pointed, thinking this was her meaning, only to run square onto the coral head that was the original cause of the lookout's alarm. 'You idiot!' screams the lookout, saving herself by a few fingernails which she manages to get around the headstay as her inertia propels her over the bow.

'You blind idiot!' the helmsman retorts. He is momentarily at a loss for words, still trying to comprehend why his skippership has suddenly come unstuck.

His wife, who is lying on the galley floor, wearing the drinks and savouries she was preparing in anticipation of at last having attained the evening's peaceful anchorage, yells out, 'You idiot, George, why don't you watch out where you're going?'

The yacht secure in a snug anchorage, the crew can settle down to reliving the day.

This is all easily avoided. The lookout, when communicating with the person on the helm, should always turn his/her head full around so that that person can see his/her face. This way, even if the sound is dissipated by the wind or noise of the motor, the person at the helm has some chance of reading the lips or of getting some message from the expression. Agree on signals for steering right or left, for reversing, and for cutting the engine.

Whitehaven Beach, Whitsunday Island, a favourite with boating visitors to the Whitsundays, has a marvellous stretch of fine white sand to feel between the toes.

Anchoring

There are many yachtsmen these days who sail off marinas or moorings whose anchoring experience is largely gained in rafting up on a mate's anchor for Sunday lunch, or perhaps on Easter weekend, dropping a lunch hook in a sheltered estuary where the maximum wind encountered may be 10 knots, the maximum seas 4 centimetres, and the bottom of muddy clay that would hold the anchor by suction even if it were upside down and the line straight up and down.

The Whitsundays demand good anchoring technique. Many of the most beautiful anchorages are subject to sharp gusts of wind which may be twice the average velocity of the wind, which places extra demands on the ground tackle. There is also a large rise and fall in tide which makes extra demands on scope. The anchorages are surrounded by coral reefs, too.

The recommended ground tackle for most Whitsunday anchoring is all-chain cable with a CQR (plough) anchor. The debate between Danforth and CQR fans about which of the two is best will possibly never be laid to rest, but locals favour the CQR because it cannot be jammed by coral, as sometimes happens when a piece of staghorn lodges in the flukes of a Danforth preventing it from resetting if the yacht has ridden over and dislodged it because of a change in wind or tide.

Chain anchor cable has several advantages. Corals can quickly sever

<table>
<tr><td colspan="2">

Estimating the state of the tide

Tidal ebb and flow is not a linear function, i.e. is not equal over time but is a wave that may be described as a cosine curve. The rise and fall of water is much greater in the middle of the cycle (as the wave builds up) than it is in the first or last hours, for example.

There is a simple, easy-to-remember 'rule of twelfths' for interpolating the state of the tide at various intervals between low and high tide.

Rise/fall during:	Rise/fall by rule of twelfths	% of total rise/fall
1st hour	$1/12$	8%
2nd hour	$2/12$	17%
3rd hour	$3/12$	25%
4th hour	$3/12$	25%
5th hour	$2/12$	17%
6th hour	$1/12$	8%
6 hours	$12/12$	100%

Only a small proportion of tidal movement occurs during the first hour before or after the change of the tide. Twice as much movement occurs in the second hour, and the middle two hours account for fully one-half of the total rise or fall.

Tidal stream, or lateral movement of water, is not the same thing as 'tide' (tidal amplitude), which is the rise and fall in water level. Stream, or tidal current, reflects the constrictions of land and of the bottom. Tidal currents may run swiftly right up until the time of high or low water (and sometimes afterwards), and the rule of twelfths is therefore not necessarily useful in predicting the best time to negotiate a passage, which will, as often as not, be at the turn of the tide. Sea conditions are a more important consideration in the Whitsundays than the direction of set, and state of sea has to do with the net effects of wind and tide.

In the Whitsundays:
- with winds from the south, the water is smoother on a falling tide;
- with winds from the north, the sea is smoother on a rising tide.

</td></tr>
</table>

fibre ropes, and there are patches of coral everywhere. Chain ensures that the pull on the anchor remains horizontal, or nearly so, as long as sufficient scope has been put out; this guarantees that, once set, the anchor stays set. Chain puts extra catenary (sag) in the line, which acts as a shock absorber and prevents tugs and jerks from being transmitted directly to the anchor. Sag also considerably shortens the swinging distance at anchor, a great advantage in deep anchorages where lots of scope is required, or in crowded anchorages. Any yacht in the Whitsundays should carry at least 30 metres of chain.

Holding in the Whitsundays is generally good, the commonest type of ground in these continental island anchorages being a combination of mud and sand or coral and sand. Some anchorages have patches of live coral and coral bommies, which appear as dark patches. Try to drop your anchor over a light, sandy patch and keep your chain away from coral.

Setting the anchor

Having selected a spot which is a sufficient distance from any other yacht not to create a swinging problem or a social problem (see 'Anchoring etiquette'), with the yacht moving slowly backwards, pay out your cable in a straight line to avoid the anchor being fouled by its own chain. With all-chain cable, three times the maximum expected depth should be enough scope if the water at high tide will be 7 metres deep or more; in blustery conditions four times the depth is a good idea. In shallow anchorages (where depth will be less than 7 metres) pay out at least four times the depth (no matter what the wind) to be sure that the angle of pull remains horizontal. Yachts with rope anchor cables should pay out at least six times the depth.

Having let out the required scope, reverse slowly, watching a stationary landmark until the yacht ceases to go backwards, then slowly increase power (to about half cruising revs) until it is clear that the anchor isn't going to budge. When the engine is turned off the yacht will move forward as the chain settles; make a note of your position by taking transits or bearings on stationary landmarks so that if the wind comes up in the night you will know that you're not dragging (and will spare yourself a lot of needless uneasiness). If you follow this routine religiously, you will seldom get into trouble.

There are a couple of anchoring styles that you will see employed which will serve as an example of what not to do: the first is that of the skipper who enters the anchorage, circles around and, with obvious care, picks a spot – not too close to anyone else and with apparent calculation as to how much the yacht will drop back on its line – and then, as the yacht continues moving just perceptibly forward, the loud clatter of the entire predetermined length of chain can be heard exiting the bow, in one fell swoop. It's all over in six seconds. One can imagine either a tidy pile of anchor and chain on the bottom, like a galvanised wedding cake, or equally risky, noodles of chain lying immediately to windward of the anchor waiting to be dragged right over the top of the anchor, fouling the flukes as the yacht settles back.

The other example which works for some but which is not recommended in Whitsunday anchorages is called 'the cruising drop', a technique employed by the salty, round-the-world single-hander type. He steams through the anchorage at a relatively brisk 2 knots, weaving and winding nonchalantly until he has surreptitiously identified his spot, whereupon he wheels around, and steaming downwind, still at 2 knots, drops the anchor and cuts the engine. The momentum of the yacht carries it on until all the chain has been laid down and the yacht snubs up against the end of the scope. The skipper has a drink in his hand and is puffing a cigarette in the cockpit almost before the last ripples cease to radiate from the stationary hull.

This dashing technique has more to recommend it than the previous one, although it leaves a bit to chance – the anchor could initially become fouled with weed or something else that prevents its penetrating the bottom. It at least gets all of the chain laid down in a straight line and in such a way that it doesn't itself foul the anchor. Of course, if the anchor does become fouled and doesn't set, this technique will give everybody else in the anchorage something to laugh about for months to come.

The more conventional technique of anchoring is recommended. Before you start, shorten up on the dinghy painter so that this doesn't get wrapped around the propeller when you are reversing to set the anchor.

Calculating scope

Vertical pull on an anchor stock at an angle of more than about 8° starts to dislodge rather than bury it, even with chain cable, and to maintain an 8° angle you must put down enough scope. Allow for the maximum depth that will occur at high tide, which is simply the depth shown on the chart added to the height of tide you've calculated according to the formula already discussed.

Anchoring etiquette

The Whitsundays are being discovered by more and more sailors, and good anchoring etiquette is important. Enter anchorages quietly (i.e. slowly and being careful not to create more than a few centimetres of wake). If you are dragging half the Pacific Ocean behind you in your large, square-sterned motor vessel, remember that those sailboats with masts sticking up have, in effect, a pendulum above deck, and once set in motion by large waves side-on, they unfailingly set up an action that throws all drinks, bowls of nibbles and perhaps even the baby and its mashed dinner onto the floor in the cockpit. You might as well walk up to strangers in a restaurant and raise the side of their table off the ground.

Observe the basic laws of not violating others' 'space' – by not dropping anchor right next to someone else when it is possible to get further away. In some crowded anchorages even the most seamanlike efforts will sometimes result in one yacht ending up too close to another. If good seamanship doesn't make it immediately clear just how close 'too close' is, then anxious looks from the yacht already anchored should. In such instances the yacht which was anchored first has the right of prior occupancy, and any moving should be done by the latest to arrive and *before* it has become necessary to physically intervene to separate the yachts. Don't wait until a collision has occurred; the worry about whether one is *going to* will spoil everyone's relaxation.

And for those who may love having the comforts of home wherever they are, including microwave ovens, TVs, dishwashers, etc., all of which require that the yacht's engine be run constantly to keep the batteries from being sucked inside out, spare a thought for those who have come to the Whitsundays to enjoy a bit of wilderness, away from the constant reminders of urban civilisation. Use of generators should be restricted to times when they will not interfere unduly with the serenity of the anchorage and the peace of others.

Sailors should remove all halyards and tie them away from the mast to prevent these keeping everyone in the anchorage awake all night. In light and variable winds the dinghy may bump the hull annoyingly at just the moment you have fallen asleep. Either strap it alongside with fenders to cushion it or hold it off by rigging a spinnaker pole.

Anchor noise

Chain dragging over the bottom in some Whitsunday anchorages makes a noise which resonates through a fibreglass hull like a troll rolling boulders around in the cellar. The racket is transmitted right up the chain making sleep impossible for all but the comatose. The noise may be dampened by using a rope 'snubber'. To make a snubber, attach a piece of line to a link in the anchor chain and lead this through the fairlead or over the bow roller and secure it to the sampson post, bollard or cleat, letting it take the strain. Keep the chain secured to the yacht as well (but let it hang loose over the bow) so that if the snubber should part the yacht will not go exploring the anchorage while you sleep.

The importance of swinging circle

The swinging circle of a yacht describes its potential at anchor for interaction with other yachts, fringing reefs, or nearby coral heads. It is a function of the amount of scope paid out on the anchor and is the radius of a circle which the yacht can scribe around the point where the anchor is fixed to the bottom. Theoretically this is the hypotenuse of a right-angled triangle (see diagram), but because of sag in the anchor line it is, in fact, somewhat less. Without going into all the many imponderables, suffice it to say that one should assume that the yacht will swing around the anchor on a radius that is about 80% of the amount of scope paid out.

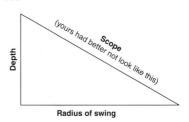

If all boats in an anchorage swing the same way, as usually happens if a steady breeze is blowing and there is no tidal influence, life at anchor remains uncomplicated. When the wind drops and the tide starts to do its capricious tricks, swirling around the anchorage, and where there are yachts with different underwater profiles using different types of anchor cables, that's where the fun begins. As a general rule, try to anchor next to yachts similar to your own and next to those using similar ground tackle – big keel yachts next to big keel yachts, trailer sailers next to trailer sailers, motor vessels with flat bottoms next to motor vessels, and chain warps next to chain warps. If you see rope hanging off the bow of the yacht next to which you are about to anchor, ask how much scope is down. This personal 'intrusion' will not be objected to by a good seaman, rather it will be appreciated for the forethought it demonstrates.

Obviously if the gods have decided to play havoc, and they suck the breath from an anchorage while sending in the tidal clowns, yachts will need more than just one swinging distance between them to avoid collision. In uncrowded anchorages the ideal of maintaining a distance of two swinging radii can be achieved, but it is often impracticable where there is congestion.

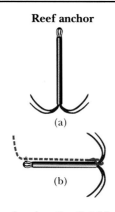

Reef anchor

(a)

(b)

The reef anchor ('reef pick') (a) is a kind of grapnel with multiple flukes (not flattened at the ends) designed for temporary daytime use over coral. This design is intended to hook into coral and to be retrieved doing less damage to coral than is done by a sand type or admiralty pattern anchor. If you must anchor over coral (and for the future good of the Marine Park this should be avoided, if at all possible), always use a reef pick. Attach the anchor line to the crown and lead it back alongside the ring at the end of the shank, as in (b), seizing it loosely to the ring with twine. This method of attaching the anchor insures that, if the anchor gets stuck, a strong vertical pull will break the twine and the anchor will come up crown-first (that's the theory, anyway).

Never leave a yacht hanging from a reef pick unattended.

Stern anchors

There are times, particularly in anchorages open to the sea, when swell may be refracted around points and headlands into the anchorage. Just as a slice of buttered bread falls butter-side down, yachts turn side-on to the swell and roll uncomfortably. Butterfly Bay, Cateran Bay and Whitehaven Beach are notorious for this, and it can happen elsewhere.

A stern anchor may make life more pleasant by keeping the yacht headed into whatever is making it roll. It's sometimes a good idea to buoy a stern anchor with a trip line attached to the crown to make it easier to retrieve, especially if this is done from a dinghy where, if the anchor is set well, you may well pull yourself down to Davy Jones's locker before the anchor starts to dislodge. Keep the buoy line as short as possible or you may find another yacht winding up your stern anchor with its propeller. If a stern anchor has been taken ashore (for example, at Whitehaven) tie something to the line so that others will know it is there.

Getting the anchor up

Getting the anchor up is the time when you are likely to see more of the colour puce than at a flower show – on the straining face of the foredeck hand (if the yacht doesn't have an electric winch). There is undoubtedly a certain amount of hard physical labour involved in raising the anchor and chain, but many foredeck hands abandon their cool and become embroiled in a battle with the anchor, chain, wind and the full inertia of the boat. Whether or not the boat has a windlass, the skipper should use the engine to move the boat up to a position where the chain becomes vertical. Hand signals to keep the person at the helm steering straight to the anchor are useful here.

Normally, with a vertical pull the anchor will break out without incident, but if it starts to pull the foredeck hand overboard, he or she should take a few quick turns of the chain around the bollard and then call for the person at the helm to give a short burst ahead with the engine. If the yacht's nose dips violently and it spins around, the anchor is snagged, and direct confrontation is likely to be of no avail.

An anchor snagged in coral will not let go as long as there is pressure on it. Release the strain: let out plenty of slack. Ideally, if the yacht is in shallow water and there is a capable hand aboard, to avoid doing further damage to the coral, someone should dive down and free it manually. Otherwise, motor slowly to the right or left and upwind. If the anchor snags again, stop, retrieve the slack, then let it all out again and try going to the left. By slacking off and pulling in a different direction you may free it. If the chain has wrapped itself around a bommie, ascertain the

When the wind drops and tide becomes the governing force in the anchorage, adequate swinging distance between yachts is important for peace of mind.

direction in which it is wrapped and then circle slowly, keeping a little tension on the cable. If all this fails, there may be no choice but to abandon the anchor and cable, but buoy it so that it can be retrieved later.

Protecting reefs from anchor damage

Reef protection markers

In recent years a great deal of destruction of corals in the Whitsundays has occurred as a result of yacht anchors. Growing concern on the part of Marine Parks and some local citizens resulted in the formation of a volunteer organisation called OUCH (Organisation of Underwater Coral Heroes). OUCH volunteers conducted underwater surveys of sensitive areas throughout the islands, and armed with that information, Marine Parks officers from the Queensland Department of Environment (QDE) have installed a series of reef protection buoys in a number of anchorages. These are white, pyramid-shaped buoys, measuring about three-quarters of a metre on the base and sides, fixed to the bottom along the edge of the fringing reefs. Anchoring inshore of an imaginary straight line between the marker buoys is prohibited.

Since the first marker buoys were installed the incidence of damage to the fringing reefs has declined dramatically. The marker buoys are *not* moorings, and tying up to them is both unsafe and prohibited.

Public moorings

In a further effort to reduce anchor damage to living corals, QDE has embarked on a programme of installing public moorings in some bays; for example, Blue Pearl Bay (map C13), Luncheon and Manta Ray bays (map C14/15), Langford Island (map C12), Black Island (map C12), Sunlover's Bay (map C9). Public moorings are white, cylinder-shaped buoys identified by a coloured Marine Parks sticker that provides instructions for use and information on limits that apply to its use. Some moorings are suitable only for dinghies, some for yachts up to 10 metres, or yachts up to 18 metres, for example. Public moorings are designed to provide an easy way to secure a vessel to allow reef appreciation and are not intended for overnight use (a limit of 2 hours in any 8-hour period applies).

Commercial moorings

A number of private charter operators in the Whitsundays have installed moorings for their own use, which is usually during the daytime, from about 10.30 am till about 4.00 pm. Some operators do not object to yachts using these moorings at other times. If you do pick up a private commercial mooring, be prepared to relinquish it immediately at the owner's request. Do not leave the boat unattended on a private mooring.

Reef protection buoy

White triangular buoy (73 centimetres)

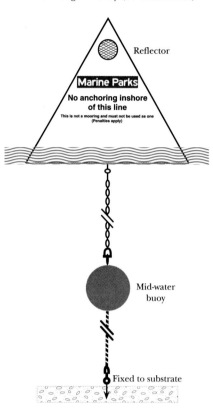

Reef protection buoys show anchoring limits (no anchoring inshore of an imaginary straight line between buoys). They have been installed in a number of sensitive anchorages to reduce anchor damage to corals. They are *not* moorings and may not be used as such.

A number of public moorings have been installed to facilitate reef appreciation activities. These have a coloured label (such as this one) which provides instructions for their use.

Planning the day's travel with likely sailing conditions in mind may provide a more pleasant trip. Wind against tide can produce lumpy seas in the Whitsunday Passage.

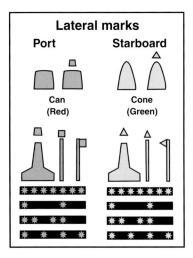

Lateral marks

Port — **Starboard**

Can (Red) — Cone (Green)

Port lateral marks are coloured red, have a basic can shape, the topmark is square, and if they have a light, it is red. Starboard lateral marks are green, the basic shape is conical, the topmark is triangular or cone-shaped, and if they have a light, it is green. Port marks are kept on the port side of the yacht, starboard marks on the starboard side, when proceeding into port.

There are a number of mnemonics to help keep this straight. One simple one is 'port to port to port', meaning that one should keep the port-coloured (red) mark on the port (left) side when going into port (PPP). Another is 'green gauche going' (keep the green (starboard) mark on one's left side (gauche is French for 'left') when going out of port) (GGG).

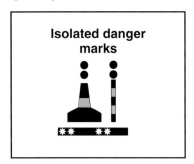

Isolated danger marks

The topmark of isolated danger marks is two black spheres, one on top of the other, clearly separated. At night they exhibit a white flashing light in a group of two flashes (two balls, two flashes).

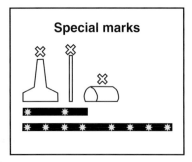

Special marks

Special marks have a yellow 'x' topmark; at night they exhibit a yellow light with any rhythm other than that used for the white lights on cardinal or isolated danger marks.

IALA Maritime Buoyage System 'A'

Queensland employs the IALA (International Association of Lighthouse Authorities) 'A' buoyage system – navigation buoys, beacons and marks designed to safely guide the mariner. The types of these beacons and marks most frequently encountered in the Whitsundays include lateral marks, cardinal marks, isolated danger marks, and special marks (see the marginal notes).

Lateral marks are usually positioned to show well-established channels and they indicate the constraints of the safe navigation route *into* a port. They are red or green floating buoys (anchored to the bottom) or beacons or marks fixed to the substrate. Ports in the Whitsunday area include the Port of Mackay to the south or the Port of Bowen to the north. Thus, marks south from Pioneer Point (map C2) are laid towards Mackay, and marks along the coast northwards from Pioneer Point are laid towards Bowen. In some instances marks are laid towards the obvious destination; for example, going into Nara Inlet (map C10), where the mark on the entrance shoal is a port mark identifying the left side of the navigation route into Nara Inlet.

Cardinal marks indicate the direction in which the safest course lies; for example, a north cardinal mark indicates that the 'best water' lies northwards from the mark, an east cardinal mark 'best water east', etc. Two examples of cardinal marks are those surrounding Low Rocks at the north-east entrance to Shute Harbour (map C3) and the south cardinal mark on the southern extremity of Langford Reef (map C12).

Isolated danger marks indicate a hazard to navigation of limited extent (i.e. with safe water around them). Don't pass too closely. A good example of this type of mark is on Pioneer Rocks (map C2).

Special marks indicate a special area (in major ports, things like spoil grounds, cables and pipelines, or perhaps a channel within a channel). In the Whitsundays these marks are employed, for example, on the northern and southern extremities of Black Island's reef (map C12), or on the south-east tip of the deceptive reef off the northern side of Refuge Bay, Nara Inlet (map C10).

'Red tide'

Visitors to the Whitsundays will sometimes see masses of 'red tide' – rust-coloured or yellow-green streaks of algae – floating in long slicks through the islands. Red tide is a misnomer in that, in other parts of the world, it is a term associated with a dinoflagellate algae that renders fish and some shellfishes temporarily poisonous. The Whitsunday 'red tide' is produced by the phytoplankton *Trichodesmium erythraeum*, a little hairy red bundle which periodically blooms (usually August–October) and blows in wind rows along the surface giving off a slightly rank smell. It is also called 'red sawdust', because that's what it looks like, or sometimes 'coral spawn'. *Trichodesmium* is a cyanophyte, a close relative of bacteria. Another type of slick is sometimes caused by coral spawn (late October to early December), and another by oil. The three types are sometimes confused. *Trichodesmium*, examined closely, always reveals bundles of tiny threads.

Going ashore

Mosquitoes, sandflies and various types of biting insects are abundant on some of the islands, including Whitsunday Island, home of the fabulous Whitehaven Beach which looks just too nice to have sandflies but which nevertheless does. Have plenty of insect repellent ready whenever you venture ashore.

The islands have the same wildlife as the mainland, including lizards, goannas, and snakes (some poisonous). Carry a torch with you at night. Resist the temptation to feed goannas by hand, or you may end up feeding one *your* hand.

Queensland has a stinging tree which Aboriginal people named the 'gympie' bush; it has heart-shaped green leaves covered with minute pale green hairs. If you brush the leaves with your bare skin you can get an intensely uncomfortable burning itch which is made worse by rubbing it and which does not respond particularly well to any treatment. The effects may last several days. Gympie bush is best avoided.

Making your way around the Whitsundays

Polaroid sunglasses are essential for the person at the helm and the lookout in coral waters. By cutting reflections on the surface they make it possible to distinguish reefs that are otherwise almost invisible. Reefs are difficult to see when the sun is low in the sky and on overcast days. They are impossible to see at night. It pays to move around when the sun is high and be in an anchorage not later than 1600 hours. While there are no real coral surprises in store among the islands, some of the island fringing reefs are extensive and deceptive.

Coral which is an immediate hazard to navigation has a brownish apearance in the water; shoaling coral and/or sand appears light green (beware); deep coral patches appear black or deep blue and are usually out of harm's way.

Reefs can provide hours of entertainment. Remember to leave the dinghy well out towards the edge if the tide is falling. Otherwise you may be stranded until the next tide (it is *very* difficult to carry a dinghy over a reef). Haslewood Island (map C31) and Neck Bay, Shaw Island (map S2) have very large expanses of drying reef, to mention a couple that catch the unwary.

Planning the day's travel

The first consideration of getting around in the Whitsundays is the tide – an assessment of what effect it will have in the prevailing winds and how this may affect the yacht. Wind against tide can create rough conditions, especially fresh winds against spring tides. The tide in the Whitsundays floods to the south and ebbs to the north. If the wind is fresh south-east and the tide is flooding, the Passage itself can be very lumpy, Solway Passage (map C26) can be hair-raising and Fitzalan Passage (map C22) can be breathtaking. You may well be advised to postpone a trip until the wind and tide are together.

The 'Index to anchorages and placenames' lists all the anchorages that have a name and also the most prominent placenames found on the maps. Their approximate geographic centre, in latitude and longitude, is given along with a map reference. At the beginning of each section (Northern, Central, Southern, Reef) is a map showing the area covered in that section, the area covered by individual sketch maps, and an index of maps and anchorages. Armed with these and the official Hydrographic Office charts, you should be able to locate, and get yourself into, any anchorage. It must be stressed that the offical charts are the final authority for navigators. The sketch maps, in some instances, may have small 'displacement errors' as they are based on uncorrected aerial photographs and other sources and have not been created with sophisticated map-making equipment nor by a professional cartographer. They are designed to assist with visual pilotage, giving additional detail, but they are not the ultimate authority, which is the offical charts of the area.

So, always have the chart with the largest scale available and use it as your primary navigation aid. The sketch maps will help you to get around with confidence, but they are not a substitute for the official charts. (The sketch maps indicate, in the upper right-hand corner of the page, the largest-scale chart that covers the particular area.)

There is a temptation to try to see too much of the Whitsundays in a short time, particularly for those with only a week on their hands. A leisurely look at four anchorages is about as much as you can really digest in one week; doing more will tend to make you feel rushed.

The most popular anchorages are Cid Harbour and Nara Inlet because they are all-weather anchorages and are close to Shute Harbour. The further south you go the more alone you will be. South-exposed anchorages, such as Waite Bay (White Bay) (map C31) and those along the south side

Cardinal marks

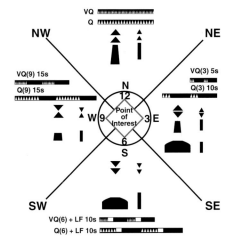

Cardinal marks have distinctive triangular or conical topmarks, which are relatively easy to remember (see below), and a code of coloured stripes, which are not so easy to remember.

North (cones/triangles pointing upwards, following the convention that north on a map is upwards)

South (cones/triangles pointing downwards following the convention that south on a map is downwards)

East (cones/triangles with apexes apart)

West (cones/triangles with apexes together)

The east and west marks are perhaps easier to confuse than the north and south. The following will help: 'E' comes before 'W'; apexes apart (aa) comes before apexes together (at).

At night, cardinal marks exhibit a white flashing light with easily identified patterns (3, 6, 9 and continuous flashing). These can be related to the positions of 3, 6, and 9 on a clock face, which also represent east, south and west on a compass rose.

Airlie Beach offers shelter for trailer sailers when the wind is blustery from the south-east.

of Whitsunday Island should not be used overnight during the trade winds season (May through September) because of the possibility of a strong southerly change in the middle of the night. Areas requiring particular caution are:

(1) the Stonehaven/Hayman area (map C12), particularly the passage between Hook and Hayman islands; the extensive and deceptive reef off the south side of Hayman; and the reef off the south side of Black Island;
(2) the shoal area to the south-east of the passage between Hook and Whitsunday islands (map C17), where there are isolated bommies;
(3) the entrances to Nara and Macona Inlets (map C10);
(4) the patch of reef just south-west of the entrance to Gulnare Inlet (map C20);
(5) French Shoal, off Whitehaven Beach (map C27);
(6) the area south-east of the southern tip of Haslewood Island, between Haslewood and Nicolson islands (map C31);
(7) Solway Passage, because of currents and sometimes rough conditions (map C26);
(8) Fitzalan Passage, because of currents and disturbed water (maps C21 and C22); and
(9) Long Island Sound, between Long Island and the mainland, because of strong currents and rough seas.

The prudent sailor always has the route out of the anchorage planned (a note of the compass course recorded) in the event of the unexpected; this is very worth doing if anchored in the south-exposed anchorages, such as those along the southern side of Whitsunday Island and Haslewood Island.

Trailer sailing in the Whitsundays

Are trailer sailers safe in the Whitsundays? This question is often asked, and the answer is a qualified 'yes'. A trailer sailer is safe in competent hands – if the skipper knows the limitations of the yacht, of the crew, and can handle the boat with these limitations. If no one else in the crew is capable of taking the helm and reefing the mainsail, then the skipper will sooner or later be in an awkward situation. Whitsunday weather can be blustery, seas can be short and steep, and currents can be strong. These test a trailer sailer just that much more than a fixed-keel yacht. Trailer sailers are overpowered more easily and demand more expertise from the crew when the going gets stiff.

With that in mind, the following tale is of a trailer sailer skipper who got caught out in some fresh Whitsunday weather.

> We had been camped in Hill Inlet (Whitsunday Island) because it had been blowing 30–40 knots for eight to ten days. It eased down to 30 knots, and we were out of food, so we sailed out of the inlet (through a surf!) and went to the bottom of Whitehaven. We anchored near the bombie for about two days. We ate oysters, and we got sick of oysters (and sick from oysters, too!) so we said 'Well, there's only one thing to do, and that's go'.
> We went through Solway Passage, and it was still blowing 30 knots. The waves were hitting Frith Rock and going 100 feet in the air. We had no chance of going between Frith Rock and Whitsunday Island; that was just a boiling cauldron. So we went round the eastern side of Frith Rock, and as we got near, it got too rough for us. So we decided to go back. But we couldn't go back, because there was a wall of water behind us. So we kept going. We had everything closed up and had a 'pocket handkerchief' sail on. We even had our life jackets on. The trailer sailer was like a dish – fairly flat – and it weathered the business very nicely. When we got opposite Craig Mountain, we were getting awkward, reflected waves from Craig Point. It's very rough a long way out from each of the headlands along the south of Whitsunday Island in heavy weather; reflected waves were coming back at an angle under the other ones, and they formed holes that were bigger than our boat was long. We went down one and we were heading straight for China!

The intrepid crew survived, apparently undaunted by the experience and continued exploring the area in their trailer sailer. Not all trailer sailer skippers are up to facing these sorts of conditions, but it all comes back to a matter of individual self-knowledge and competence. Many

Above:
Yacht racing in the Whitsundays reaches its peak each year during Hamilton Island Race Week, a series conducted by the Hamilton Island Yacht Club. It draws contestants from all over Australia who come for the brisk sailing and for the fun after the racing is over.

Left:
The high point of the day's cruising – enjoying a sunset after dropping anchor
in a peaceful anchorage.

people bring trailer sailers to the Whitsundays every year, and here are a few tips from some of those who have.

Before you set out

The trip can be long and punishing – three to four pretty solid days from Sydney or Melbourne – and it can place heavy demands on the trailer. Many trailers arrive wrecks, tyres shredded, frames cracked. Perhaps they were all right for metropolitan duty, but they were not up to the long haul over some bumpy patches on the way to Proserpine. So the first question is: 'Is the trailer up to it?' Tyres should be in good condition.

Travel as light as possible and stow all heavy gear, particularly the outboard motor, in the towing vehicle. Keep weight well forward in the boat. Check that all hull supports are correctly positioned so that the boat can't slide. Weigh the trailer fully laden before you leave to be sure that it is within limits for trailers without brakes and within the towing capacity of your vehicle. Some people recommend taking along a spare set of bearings, seals, split pins, wheel studs and nuts. A set of extra-large, extra-heavy rear flaps on the towing vehicle will protect the yacht's gelcoat from stones thrown up by the wheels.

On the way

Check the trailer frequently along the way.

Get a list of caravan parks from your local motoring organisation or the local office of the Queensland Tourist and Travel Corporation, and book ahead, especially if you're travelling during school holidays. Fresh fruit and vegetables get increasingly scarce as you get north of Nambour, so it may be wise to stock up before going too much further.

When you arrive

There are a number of private caravan parks on the Shute Harbour Road between Cannonvale and Shute Harbour. Launching ramps are located at Abell Point (just west of the marina – possibly the best in the area), Shingley Beach (just west of Abell Point – this is an older one and is not as good as the previous-mentioned), at Muddy Bay, east of the Esplanade, Airlie Beach, in front of the Whitsunday Sailing Club at Airlie Beach, and at Shute Harbour (next to the public jetty). Be sure to wear sand shoes when launching, as the ramps are in areas where giant toadfish have attacked the feet of fishermen wading in the water. Sheltered anchorage is available along the lee side of Abell Point and Airlie Beach. Shute Harbour ramp is sometimes particularly busy, especially at weekends, and it is sometimes not well protected.

Caravan parks offer supervised parking. There is a lock-up garage next to the service station at Shute Harbour. Boat trailer parking is available at Shute Harbour (along the road just before you reach the harbour, next to the sailing club at Airlie Beach, in the public parking area at Abell Point and next to the ramp at Shingley Beach.

Gear

Trailer sailers should carry a 15 or 20 pound CQR anchor, must have at least 10 metres of 6 millimetre or 8 millimetre chain (depending upon the yacht) and 40 metres of rope cable of a good-sized diameter (breaking strain has nothing to do with it; line should be sufficiently thick to be comfortable to pull on). If you've been trailer sailing on the Gippsland or Myall Lakes and are using clothesline for anchor cable, get rid of it before you go to the Whitsundays. CQR anchors are preferred to Danforths (see notes on anchoring earlier in this chapter). A small reef anchor is a useful addition.

Trailer sailers can get up to some of their usual anchoring tricks in the Whitsundays, close in and stern-to next to a sandy beach, but if you wish to explore an island where you must anchor offshore, your ground tackle and anchoring technique will need to be different. The importance of having anchor line of sufficient circumference to be easy on the hands cannot be stressed too much. A leadline is useful to determine the depth

in an anchorage, for calculating the amount of scope to put down (allowing always for high tide). A simple and effective leadline can be made using a good solid lead sinker, some venetian cord and a large fishing reel. Mark the line with a waterproof marker at regular intervals so that you can tell how much line is out.

Check that your reefing system is working efficiently, and have a No. 3 or storm jib aboard. Other useful items of equipment are: a boom tent (for protection from sun, dew and rain); containers for transporting water to the yacht; a portable transistor radio for receiving weather reports; and a 27 MHz radio for use in emergency.

It is necessary to carry certain items of safety equipment – the usual gear, including a proper liquid-damped compass, flares, oars, buckets with lanyards, bilge pump, waterproof torch, etc. (a complete list is contained in the *Queensland's Official Tide Tables & Boating Guide*, which itself is essential and which contains a wealth of other useful information about weather, fishing, navigation, buoyage, etc.). You will need a copy of chart AUS 252.

An outboard motor is an absolute necessity in the Whitsundays, and it should be in good working order. Take a spare 20-litre fuel can if you have enough space. Outboard motor fuel is available in reasonable proximity to the water at Abel Point Marina, the service station at Shute Harbour, at Mandalay Point jetty and at Hamilton Harbour.

A dinghy is also a necessity. The island fringing reefs are extensive and anchorage is sometimes a long way from shore; a small outboard motor for the dinghy may be a desirable 'luxury' as well.

On the water
With the usual caveat about the unreliability of flat statements about the weather, the best time in the Whitsundays for trailer sailers is from September onwards, when the winds are generally lighter.

Pay particular attention to the little wavy lines and curlicues on the chart, which indicate that disturbed water or eddies occur in some conditions. Remember that the tide floods south and ebbs north through the Passage and that it gets rough when fresh winds oppose spring tides. Plan your trip accordingly. Avoid Long Island Sound – the narrow strait between Long Island and the mainland – which can be dangerous for trailer sailers in all sorts of conditions – wind against tide, wind with tide, fresh winds. Be sure not to attempt Fitzalan Passage (maps C20 and C22) and Solway Passage (map C26) in fresh winds with contrary tides.

The most popular trailer sailer anchorages are Cid Harbour (map C19), which has a large all-tide sand beach and national parks campsites; water is available here for much of the year. Nara Inlet has a number of good little beaches, the best trailer sailer spot being anchorage No. 5 (map C10). Water is available here during much of the year from a waterfall at the head of the inlet. Hill Inlet (map C27) was made for trailer sailers (take plenty of insect repellent). Other sand beaches where you can moor stern-to and let the boat dry out are Cateran Bay (map C29), Windy Bay (map C31), Macona Inlet (map C10), Butterfly Bay (map C14/15) and a number of others (often where there are camping symbols shown on the maps). Camping is permitted at some of these sites provided you have a permit. Water is available in tanks or from streams at a number of anchorages (see 'Camping in the Whitsundays'). Not all resorts are able to provide water for itinerants.

Airlie Beach and Shute Harbour have public facilities where you can empty your toilet.

A final reminder of particular importance to trailer sailers, who use the land more than keel yachtsmen: take plenty of insect repellent with you when you go ashore. Sandflies and mosquitoes are prevalent at some locations, particularly Hill Inlet and Whitehaven Beach.

Bareboating is the ideal way to get the most out of the Whitsundays, giving virtually complete freedom to explore at your own pace with company of your own choice. Yachts available for charter vary from 7 metres to over 15 metres, from trailable yachts to catamarans to luxurious modern cruising vessels. Power craft are also available.

Bareboat chartering in the Whitsundays

Yacht charter began in the Whitsundays in the early 1970s when a Sydney couple, Yvonne and Bernie Katchor, sailed into Shute Harbour, fell in love with the Whitsundays and stayed. They used to take day-trippers around the islands in their auxiliary ketch *Nari*, and in those days *Nari* used to be the only way that visitors could savour a tantalising bit of these islands in a way that took full advantage of the remoteness and beauty of the setting.

It wasn't until about 1978 that the first drive-it-yourself yachts were licensed by the Queensland Department of Harbours and Marine, years after 'bareboat' was part of the international yachting vocabulary and only after a certain amount of official red tape had been unwound by two enterprising Sydneysiders, David Bradley and John Landau. They succeeded in overcoming a bureaucratic scepticism about the ability of unlicensed sailors to survive the rigours of the Queensland coast, and they were able to negotiate a compromise on the exacting survey regulations that were written for commercial passenger and fishing vessels. In 1978 they opened for business as Whitsunday Yachting World, a company that is no longer operating but which set a standard new to the charter industry in Australia for everyone else to follow. From that time on the industry really began to grow, and more and more sailors from the south were able to live out fantasies of tropical sailing that were previously only to be hankered after. The size of the bareboat fleet grew and charter companies have proliferated.

Bareboating is the ideal way to get the most out of the Whitsundays. It offers virtually complete freedom to go anywhere you want, at your own pace. Bareboating means you are the skipper, your friends the crew. In spite of the name, most bareboats these days are rather luxuriously appointed. Those over ten metres in length will usually be equipped with freezer and fridge, stereo cassette/radio, elaborate galley, hot and cold running water, shower, roller-furling headsail, electric anchor windlass, and so on. In order to become licensed the boats have to be solidly constructed, with safety features that most sailors wouldn't put on their own yachts. Charter yachts are available ranging in size from about seven metres up to about fifteen metres, with four berths up to ten berths. For comfort, as a rule of thumb subtract two from the number of berths available, and limit your crew to that number. Yachts under ten metres have a more restricted cruising area.

How to go about it

Bookings may be made either directly with the charter company or through travel agents. At the time of booking a deposit must be lodged, and the balance of the charter fee is payable 30–60 days before the charter commences. A security bond on the vessel and equipment must also be paid before heading off on the holiday; this acts as collateral against any damage or loss during the charter, and it represents the limit of the charterer's liability for the yacht (except in cases of wilful negligence). The bond is refunded immediately after (or within a few days of) completing the charter, less any deductibles (lost winch handles, etc.). Some companies offer insurance on a daily basis which further reduces any liability for damage sustained to the yacht or equipment.

Cancellations received more than 60 days before the charter attract only an administration fee; notice given in less than 60 days renders the charterer liable for the full fee unless an alternative charterer is found by the company (one frequently is). Cancellation insurance is available, although there are some limitations on what constitutes a legitimate excuse for cancelling.

How much experience is needed?

Charterers don't need any formal qualifications or licence. Someone in the crew should have a few clues about handling a boat. Anchoring is the most demanding task undertaken, and prospective charterers should be familiar with good anchoring technique (described earlier). Navigation is quite simple among the islands because land is always in sight, so one really only needs to be able to interpret a nautical chart.

Charterers are given a briefing and check-out aboard the yacht before being permitted to sail away. If the charter company is uncertain about your ability to handle the yacht, you may be required to take an experienced sailing guide along for a couple of days until you are ready to go it alone. Or, you may prefer to have a skipper for the duration. You will pay extra for the skipper.

A charter in the Whitsundays is not the ideal time and place for beginners to cut their baby teeth or to learn for the first time how to drop an anchor, but anyone with some experience and a crew capable of helping them should not be frightened off by tall tales. History has shown that it is often the most experienced sailors who come unstuck; perhaps less confident skippers are more vigilant.

How long to charter?

Charters are measured in 'nights' and begin at midday on day one. Most of the first afternoon is spent being briefed and checked out on the boat, and thus charterers need to anchor nearby on the first night because there won't be time to sail very far. All companies insist that charterers be anchored by 4.00 pm due to the difficulty of seeing coral when the sun is low. Charters end, depending upon the company, from 9.00 to 11.00 am on the last day, so one needs to anchor nearby on the last night. That leaves five nights of real freedom of choice of anchorages (on a one-week charter). Unless you are a roadrunner, it's much better to allow at least ten days to experience a number of different anchorages at leisure. Seven days just isn't enough; you may be just getting into the pleasant rhythm of life aboard a yacht in the Whitsundays when it's time to come home.

One imponderable as to how long is long enough is the compatibility of the crew. This wild card can make a few days seem like a lifetime, or time may fly. Living at very close quarters as one does aboard a yacht, hidden dimensions even in old mates may be uncovered. The charter boat log books tell all manner of tales, mostly of laughter, love and good times. There are a few tales of mutiny and abandonment, crew being put ashore on a deserted isle with a message sent to the charter base to have the water taxi go pick up the marooned member who will have to pay for the taxi – himself. It goes without saying that one should choose companions carefully.

In bareboating, you are the skipper, your friends the crew. The cost of a bareboat charter, divided amongst four or six members of the crew, is not a particularly expensive holiday. Friendships are forged and new dimensions are sometimes discovered in old mates.

What costs are involved?

Costs of a bareboat holiday include the hire of the vessel and food, and may also include fuel used while motoring, plus perhaps a few extras such as mooring fees when visiting an island resort.

Vessels range in size from about seven to fifteen metres in length, and the prices vary accordingly. Rates are higher during holiday seasons. Shared amongst a group, the costs of a bareboat holiday are not particularly high.

Provisioning the yacht with food can be done for you, and most companies offer several different standards, from survival rations to gourmet dining. This saves you the bother of planning meals and is a decided plus for whoever has the job of chief galley slave. The most frequently selected regime, for a seven-night charter, caters for seven breakfasts and lunches and five dinners, the assumption being that the other two dinners will be eaten at an island resort (this is referred to as 'partial provisioning'). You can opt to have your own list of food put aboard by the charter company, for which a handling fee (usually 15%) is charged. The same applies for liquor (the fee is usually 10%). If you're on a tight budget and don't mind the inconvenience, you can provision the yacht yourself.

All companies charge for fuel used by power vessels; some charge fuel used on sailboats, others don't. Mooring and marina fees vary from resort to resort, but having paid the fee, you usually have complete freedom to use all resort facilities; shared amongst all those on the yacht, it is a small expense.

The charter area

There are well over one hundred rocky islands, islets, rocks and shoals in the Cumberland Islands which are spread out over one degree of latitude (20° to 21° south). The charter area extends from George Point (map N9) to Hayman Island (map C13) to Goldsmith Island (map S9), although not many first-time charterers find time to get all the way to either the western or the the southern anchorages. Smaller yachts have a slightly more restricted area, and some restrictions apply when strong wind warnings are current. There are more than enough good anchorages within a twenty-mile radius of Shute Harbour to make it unnecessary to travel further. Seven of the islands in this area have resorts, and most will accommodate visiting sailors provided that certain procedures are followed (see 'Island resorts of the Whitsundays'). Many charterers at some time during their charter go ashore at a resort, providing that unique sensation in cruising of 'making port', to have a shower and a meal and enjoy the entertainment.

When is the best time to come?

For most people, the time of their holidays is the determinant, but if you have some flexibility, here are a few considerations. The weather is pleasant almost any time in the Whitsundays, with temperatures seldom above 30°C in summer nor below 20°C in winter. You can swim year-round. The trade winds are re-established after the summer monsoon in April–May, providing brisk sailing for the most part throughout the winter; the weather is generally more settled after June, and the winds get progressively lighter after mid-September. Charter rates are lower in non-holiday seasons, and from mid-October until Christmas is a 'shoulder season' with lower prices and balmy weather, making it possible to get into some south-exposed anchorages that cannot be used overnight during the trade winds season. Christmas holidays are a very busy time.

Crewed charter

A number of companies offer crewed charters; you charter the yacht and the company supplies a skipper and mate who do all the worrying and work for you. And, there are also a number of luxurious charter vessels ranging in size from about fourteen to twenty-one metres, with full-time crew, completely equipped with everything that might be wished for.

VISITING THE OUTER REEFS

The individual coral reefs of the Great Barrier system lie on Australia's eastern continental shelf, generally towards its outer margin. Along the northern Queensland coastline the shelf is narrower than it is in the south, and the reefs are closer to the mainland. In the Whitsunday region (south-central Queensland) the continental shelf is about seventy-five nautical miles wide (measured from the mainland out to the 200-metre depth contour in a north-easterly direction). The first reef to be reached from Shute Harbour is Bait Reef, about thirty nautical miles away. It is one of a group of reefs associated by name; their particular shapes and proximity to each other suggested, to early chart-makers, the angler's basic equipment – hook, line, sinker and bait. Immediately east is a large lagoonal platform reef, Hardy Reef, separated from the rest by a very long, deep channel through which tidal currents flow swiftly. These reefs are the focal point of Reef day-trip activity in this part of the Barrier Reef Marine Park.

Pontoons are moored in current-swept channel between Hardy and Line reefs, and it is protected on all sides from oceanic swells and from any chop whipped up by local winds. It is an ideal spot for coral-viewing along a dramatic reef wall. Visitors can also snorkel, scuba dive, or have a ride in a specially designed coral-viewing craft.

The lagoon at Hardy Reef also serves as the landing strip for amphibious aircraft. These bring sightseers out from the mainland and island resorts, and they sometimes pick up passengers from island anchorages.

Bait Reef, about eight nautical miles west of Hardy Reef, is a beautiful, pristine, kidney-shaped reef that is one of the favoured sites for scuba diving in this area, particularly its 'Stepping Stones', a series of large coral bombies on its western side. A number of vessels take divers to this reef, on day trips and overnight cruises.

How to get to the Reef

Motorised catamarans revolutionised travel to the Barrier Reef making it practicable to take large numbers of tourists out and back in a single day. Prior to the 'cats' the trip took six hours each way, in a rolling, mono-hulled vessel. The catamarans have reduced the travel time to about two and a half hours each way, and they have dramatically reduced the cost. Catamarans have a more comfortable motion than ordinary mono-hull vessels, making for a more comfortable ride when seas are choppy.

Motorised catamarans depart from Shute Harbour almost every day of the week. A smorgasbord lunch is included in the price. On the trip out and back, videos about the Barrier Reef are shown, and passengers are free to walk about the ship or to work on their sun tans on the sundeck, or to enjoy a drink at the bar.

Visitors to the outer reefs have a two-hour-plus journey via catamaran to a pontoon permanently moored in the channel between Hardy and Line reefs. Here they spend three hours snorkelling, scuba diving, looking at corals in specially designed craft, or just relaxing in the sun and enjoying a smorgasbord lunch.

Out at the Reef, visitors can go coral viewing in specially designed craft with glassed-in compartments below the level of the water. Glass-bottom boats are also used, and it's worth experiencing both types of craft, as each offers its own particular perspective. Glass-bottom boats give a bird's-eye view, and the semi-submerged craft allows lateral views along the edges and underneath ledges of the reef. Photography is easier from subs, particularly if using flash (tip: hold the camera right against the glass to avoid unwanted reflections).

Snorkelling is available from the pontoons – one of the most satisfying ways of experiencing a reef, right in the water with it. Snorkelling equipment is made available at no charge. Visitors who wish to go scuba diving can do so for an extra charge.

Another way of getting out to the Reef is with the area's air taxi service whose mainland operations are based at Whitsunday Airstrip and Hamilton Island. This is a most exciting means of travel, offering, as a bonus, magnificent aerial views of the islands and reefs (and, in late winter, frequent sightings of whales). Pick-ups can also be arranged for bareboat charterers from some locations, such as at resorts or at certain anchorages.

The flight to the Reef takes about twenty-five minutes, and visitors then spend two hours exploring Hardy Reef on foot (tide permitting), in glass-bottom boats, sub, or snorkelling.

A number of vessels do Reef trips for special interest groups, such as divers or those who are on an extended cruise throughout the islands.

What to take with you
Remember to take plenty of sunscreen, wear a broad-brimmed hat and be sure that you have stout footwear if you intend to go reef-walking. A light-weight cotton long-sleeved shirt is also a bonus on hot afternoons. Take along a windcheater for the trip out and back.

Special-interest boats, such as the *Whitsunday Diver*, take scuba enthusiasts to Bait Reef, where students and divers who are already qualified can enjoy a variety of excellent dive sites.

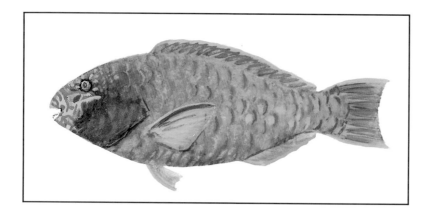

Above:
Fishes of the coral reef (top to bottom): blue tuskfish (*Choerodon albigena*),
coral trout (*Plectropomus leopardus*) and surf parrotfish (*Saurus rivulatus*).
Opposite:
Coral trout.

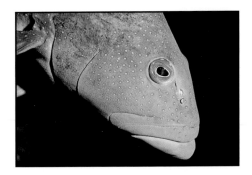

FISHING IN THE WHITSUNDAYS

Fishing in the Whitsundays can mean drifting along island reefs waiting to hook a coral trout or sweetlip; or it may mean trolling the deeper waters of the Molle Channel for big mackerel, queenfish and trevally or rod fishing from rocks along the mainland shore. The many estuaries and mangrove inlets of the Whitsunday coast are virtual fish nurseries.

Tips for coral fishing

If it's your first experience of coral fishing, there are a few tips that will be helpful. It's always desirable to fish as 'light' as possible, using minimum weight and hardware. Having said that, one must add that coral fishing requires a line of *at least* 25 kilograms breaking strain, not so much because of the monstrous fish waiting to pull you from the dinghy but because coral is hell on fishing gear. Take plenty of spares. Thin line will be chewed to pieces by coral in no time, and coral-dwelling fish tend to take the bait and run for cover under the nearest bombie. This line attached to a fleeting fish can be quickly severed and it can also cut your fingers (many fishermen tape their finger joints). Keep enough tension on the line to register bites and to avoid snagging. The weight of sinker can be adjusted to suit the current.

Fish over the edge of the reef one hour before or after high tide for best results (neap tides are better); early morning and evening are also better than when the sun is high. Night-time on a rising tide can be excellent.

Trolling along the edge of a reef may also produce dividends; the Nils Master lure is effective for coral trout (and may also yield cod or mangrove jack in estuaries).

Baits readily available in the Whitsundays are prawns, squid, a small fish known locally as 'herring', and garfish. If you have a throw net, small fresh fish from the shallows make excellent bait.

It is said that cutting the fish's throat immediately and bleeding it will improve the quality of eating.

Gear

Whether you use a rod or hand line is your own choice; rods may have advantages when fishing from rocks on the mainland, and hand lines may be easier to manage on a yacht. If you do use a hand line, be sure it has a large-diameter casting reel, which makes line management much easier than with a small hand reel. The basic recommended configurations of hooks and sinkers are shown on the following page.

Totally protected species
- Ceratodus or lungfish
- Helmet, trumpet and clam shells
- Female mud and sand crabs
- Whales, porpoises, dolphins, dugong and other marine mammals
- Turtles
- Egg-bearing female spanner or frog crabs
- Egg-bearing female Moreton Bay bugs and any other egg-bearing female sea bugs
- Egg-bearing slipper lobsters
- Corals
- Sea fans
- Estuary, greasy and potato cods greater than 1200 millimetres
- Giant groper greater than 1200 millimetres

Prohibited
- Fishing in a Marine National Park 'B' Zone
- Fishing within 100 metres of the Hook underwater observatory
- Spear fishing in Marine Park 'A' or 'B' zones
- Spear fishing anywhere with scuba gear
- Use of power head on spear/spear gun
- Spear fishing within 400 metres of:
  - ▲ the area between Brampton and Carlisle Islands;
  - ▲ the south and west sides of Lindeman Island;
  - ▲ Seaforth Island;
  - ▲ South Molle Island between Ker Point and The Causeway and in Bauer Bay;
  - ▲ Daydream Island;
  - ▲ the east, south-east and south sides of Hook Island from 800 metres north of the observatory around to the west side of Nara Inlet;
  - ▲ Hayman Island (south and west) from Groper Point to Blue Pearl Bay.

Fishing gear for the Whitsundays

For sand and mud

Line, running ball sinker (threaded but not attached), swivel, wire trace and hook. Good over sand and mud, where some movement helps to attract fish such as flathead. Bean-shaped sinkers are sometimes preferred when line must be kept in place.

For reef fishing

Recommended by pros for working reef areas. A line threaded through a ball sinker and attached to the hook runs freely and maximises sensitivity to bites, minimises snagging, and does not deter timid fish that might baulk at the sinker's dead weight.

For deep channels

The snapper rig is useful for deep channels where currents may be swift. Pass a loop through the eye of the hook and back over the shank (or use a three-way swivel). Attach a heavy sinker (perhaps as much as 225 grams).

For trolling

The 'floater' is for trolling and is simply a gang of hooks at the end of a long wire trace which in turn is attached to the line with a swivel. The hooks are embedded in a garfish (or other bait) and made to look as natural as possible. A single live fish may also be used, hooked through the back above the spine. Size, number of hooks and bait depend upon the quarry sought. Use shock cord or rubber tube as a shock absorber where the line is fixed to the boat.

Where to fish
Fishing is permitted in most areas of the Whitsundays, but there are some areas that are totally protected and others where some fishing restrictions apply. Fishing is not permitted in Marine National Park 'B' Zone (green area on the zoning map) or in a Special Management Area, e.g. the south-western section of Bait Reef. Also see the specific and miscellaneous prohibitions in the margins of these pages. Always wear footwear when fishing around the mainland harbours and estuaries, where kinky giant toadfish have been known to nibble toes (see 'Avoiding tropical hazards' for lurid details).

Where not to fish
In a Marine National Park 'B' Zone. Some examples:
- All along the northern side of Hook Island from Alcyonaria Point on the western side of Butterfly Bay to the Wood Pile (see map C14/15)
- Border Island, for 100 metres off the reef edge all around the island (see map C29)
- All along the eastern side of Haslewood Island and all around Lupton Island, for 100 metres off the reef edge (see map C31)

Restricted fishing areas
In a Marine National Park 'A' Zone (yellow areas on the zoning map) you may use only *one* hook on one *hand-held* line or rod (per person); no set lines are permitted. Trolling for pelagic fishes is allowed.

Size and bag limits
Some species of fishes are subject to size and bag limits. These are shown in the chart on pages 102–103. Fish are under general heavy pressure from commercial and recreational fishing all along the Australian coastline, but particularly in heavily used areas in Queensland. Catches in the Whitsundays have generally been in decline for the past ten years. Take only what you need for the next meal, and observe the size limits.

Avoiding anchor damage to coral
Use all care not to damage live coral when anchoring. Considerable coral damage has occurred in some locations, and further damage needs to be minimised. Avoid anchoring directly over coral (dark patches on the bottom) and try not to allow the anchor chain to drag through coral. Always try to anchor over sand or mud away from coral. In the dinghy, use a lightweight

reef anchor with heavy plastic tubing over the length of chain. When hauling in, motor towards the anchor until directly over it rather than dragging it towards the boat. Wherever possible, drift rather than anchor while fishing.

Spear fishing

Most of the Whitsunday area is closed to spear fishing. Spear fishing is totally prohibited in all Marine National Park 'A' and 'B' zones (yellow and green areas on the zoning map). Spear fishing with scuba gear is prohibited throughout Queensland. Other restrictions are outlined in the marginal note on the page opposite (see 'Prohibited').

Season and bag limits

There is no particular season for fishing in the Whitsundays with the following exclusions: barramundi may not be taken from midday 1 November to midday 1 February. Bag limits for all Queensland have been placed on certain species:

- Barramundi (5 taken or in possession at any one time)
- Mud crabs (10 taken or in possession at any one time)
- Molluscs (50 of any species (excluding oysters) taken or in possession at any one time)

The limits apply all year around, except during closed season when none of those species may be taken. You are not supposed to fillet or otherwise mutilate any fish so that the fish inspector can't see what you've been up to (cutting off the heads is all right).

Oysters

Oysters may be taken only for immediate consumption *on the spot* in most of the Whitsundays, except in the totally protected Marine National Park 'B' Zone where they may not be taken at all. Under Queensland fisheries legislation you *may not collect oysters in a container to eat later.*

Identifying your fish

The best way to identify your fish caught in the Whitsundays is to ask a local. Otherwise, have a look at a book called *Fishes of the Great Barrier Reef and Coral Sea* by J. Randall, G. Allen and R. Steene, or the *Guide to Fishes* by E.M. Grant.

One man's fish may be another's *poisson*, but coral trout has the reputation of being king of reef fishes (incidentally, these have a cyst, visible in the skin, which is off-putting but harmless). Fishes commonly caught are coral trout, coral cod, scarlet sea perch (nannygai), red emperor (juveniles are known as 'government bream' because of their broad arrow marking), parrotfish, blue tusk fish, and many types of emperor (sweetlip, spangled, squire and red throat).

Fish poisoning

There are a few fishes in Queensland which are known to cause tropical fish poisoning (ciguatera) and which should not be eaten: Chinaman fish, paddle tail, red bream, barracouta and moray eel. It's a good idea to check with locals to see that others have not temporarily been added to the list, as the toxin is sometimes a transitory phenomenon. Generally, larger fishes are more likely to be ciguatoxic; avoid eating any fish larger than four kilograms and don't eat repeated meals from the same fish. There are illustrations of the main ciguatoxic species and more details about ciguatera in 'Avoiding tropical hazards'. Puffer fishes are inherently poisonous and should never be eaten.

Game fishing

The Whitsundays are renowned for billfish and the area holds a number of world light tackle records. The outer islands from the Edward Group to 'The Paddock' north of Hayman is generally best for pelagic fishing, and excellent catches of mackerel and tuna may be had during the season when these fishes are running. The outer islands and near offshore reefs yield black marlin, sailfish, turum, barracouta, Spanish mackerel, cobia, yellowfin and bluefin tuna, kawa kawa and various species of shark. Game-fishing charters are available ex Hamilton Island, Abel Point Marina, Shute Harbour, and Hayman Island (for guests only).

Crab measurement and identification

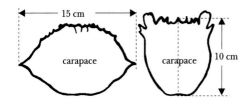

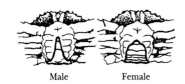

Male   Female

Crabs

Mud crabs are caught in drop nets called 'dillies' or in wire 'pots' baited with fish heads; they may also be raked out of their holes amongst mangroves with a hook on a pole. Only males should be taken (see identification diagram). Some anglers catch 'muddies' by filling a woman's stocking with bait and lowering this on a line. Pulled up quickly from time to time, crabs entangled in the mesh sometimes come too. Crabs should be handled with care. Their big nippers can sever a broom handle with ease!

To prepare crab: (1) remove the carapace and break the body in two; (2) clean out the lungs and organs; (3) break off the nippers; (4) place bodies, nippers and legs in a saucepan of cold sea water (or salted fresh water approximating sea water); (5) simmer (never boil) for 20 minutes. Some find the flesh of the sand crab, or blue manna, more delicate than mud crab, although these are not always easy to find in the Whitsundays.

Tagged fish and crabs

Tagging of fish is undertaken for fisheries research. If you catch fish or crabs with a tag attached, you can assist the advance of science by returning the tag to the Director, Fisheries Research Branch, GPO Box 46, Brisbane 4001 together with information about the date and place of capture, the length of fish or width of crab shell, the method of capture and your name and address. If you live near Brisbane, Cairns or Burnett Heads, ring the local Fisheries Research Laboratory; they will probably want to have a look at what you've caught.

Miscellaneous general prohibitions

- Jagging or foul-hooking fish
- Poisons or electrical devices to take fish
- Possession or carriage of prohibited apparatus in closed water unless the apparatus is dismantled, secured or stowed
- Collection of coral without lawful authority
- Selling fish without a licence or permit

Reef fish species to which size and bag limits apply

Fingermark
Lutjanus johnii
35 cm/10 fish

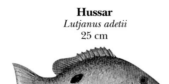

Hussar
Lutjanus adetii
25 cm

Large mouth nannygai
Lutjanus malabaricus
40 cm/10 fish

Mangrove jack
Lutjanus argentimaculatus
35 cm

Moses perch
Lutjanus russeli
25 cm

Red emperor
Lutjanus sebae
45 cm/10 fish

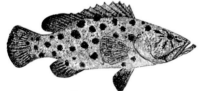

Small mouth nannygai
Lutjanus erythropterus
40 cm/10 fish

Stripey
Lutjanus carponotatus
25 cm

Estuary cod
Epinephelus tauvina (= coioides)
35–120 cm/10 fish

Potato cod
Epinephelus tukula
35–120 cm/1 fish

Queensland groper
Epinephelus lanceolatus
35–120 cm/1 fish

Pearl perch
Glaucosoma scapulare
30 cm/10 fish

Grass sweetlip
Lethrinus fletus (= laticaudis)
30 cm

Red throat emperor
Lethrinus miniatus
35 cm/10 fish

Spangled emperor
Lethrinus nebulosus
40 cm/10 fish

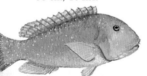

Coral trout
Plectropomus species
38 cm/10 fish

Black spot tusk fish
Choerodon schoenleinii
30 cm/10 fish

Purple tusk fish
Choerodon cephalotes
30 cm/10 fish

Venus tusk fish
Choerodon venustus
30 cm/10 fish

Maori wrasse
Chelinus undulatus
75 cm/1 fish

Silver jew
Nibea soldado
45 cm

Reef and pelagic fish species to which size and bag limits apply

Spotted (black) jew
Protonibea diacanthus
45 cm/10 fish

Teraglin jew
Atractoscion aequidens
45 cm/10 fish

Mulloway
Argyrosomus hololepidotus
45 cm/10 fish

Silver teraglin
Otolithes ruber
30 cm

Snapper
Pagrus auratus
30 cm/30 fish

Reef fish subject to size and bag limits

The 26 species of reef fishes shown and 10 pelagic species are among those under particularly heavy pressure from recreational and commercial fishing.

For the purpose of assessing a bag limit, two fillets equal one fish. No more than a total of 30 reef fishes may be taken in any combination. Recreational fishers are required to leave the skin on all fillets to provide a means of identification for bag-limit monitoring.

The figures shown beneath the scientific name of each species indicate (a) the minimum size that may be kept and (b) the bag limit.

Broad barred (grey) mackerel
Scomberomorus semifasciatus
50 cm/10 fish

School mackerel
Scomberomorus queenslandicus
50 cm/30 fish

Sharkey mackerel
Grammatorcynus bicarinatus
50 cm

Spanish mackerel
Scomberomorus commerson
75 cm/10 fish

Examples

45 cm/10 fish
The smallest size of this species that may be kept is 45 centimetres. The maximum number of this species that may be in one's possession at any one time is 10.

35–120 cm/1 fish
Where a range of size is given as above, fishes smaller than 35 centimetres or larger than 120 centimetres must be returned to the water.

Spotted mackerel
Scomberomorus munroi
50 cm/30 fish

Wahoo
Acanthocybium solandri
75 cm/10 fish

Black kingfish
Rachycentron canadus
75 cm/10 fish

Yellowtail kingfish
Seriola lalandi
50 cm

Rosy job fish
Pristipomoides species
30 cm/10 fish

Dolphin fish
Coryphaena hippurus
45 cm

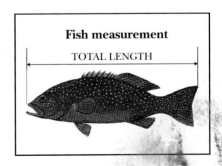

Fish measurement

TOTAL LENGTH

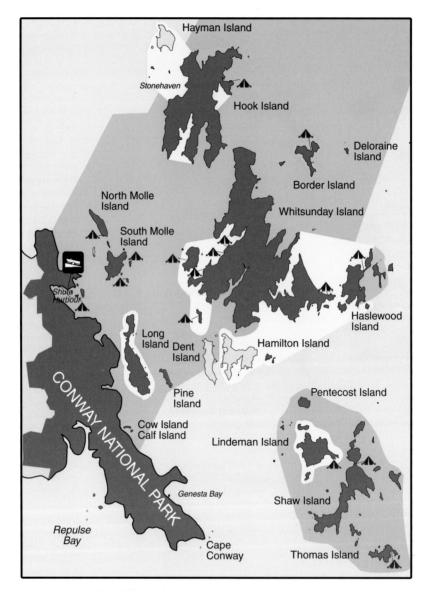

Camping in the Whitsundays

Campsites are available on a number of national park islands (shown in green) throughout the Whitsundays. The most popular and easily accessible sites are in the central area, from Hook Island to Thomas Island (red tents), although there are sites as far north as Gloucester Island (map N4) and as far south as Scawfell Island (map S16).

Camping permits must be obtained from the Queensland Department of Environment, which has complete details of all available sites.

CAMPING IN THE WHITSUNDAYS

Almost all of the Whitsunday Islands are national parks, and they provide a chance to indulge in what many believe to be the ultimate camping experience, sleeping out under the stars on a 'south sea isle'. A staging ground used by some campers before they set off for the islands is the mainland campsite at Conway Range National Park campsite, on Shute Harbour Road (about three kilometres from Shute Harbour). Some campers use one of the several backpackers establishments or caravan parks located along the highway from Cannonvale, immediately west of Airlie Beach, to Shute Harbour.

On the islands a number of national parks sites are available, and the choice may depend upon the size of your party and whether you prefer to go to one of the 'developed sites', which offer amenities such as pit or mulch toilets, defined tent sites, picnic tables and (sometimes) tank water, or whether you prefer bush camping – roughing it at a site without facilities, completely on your own. The park rangers provide a complete list of recommended sites which have been selected for their natural attributes, and one of these will probably suit you. You may also request a location of your choice. Commercial camping is also available – for example, on Hook Island next to the underwater observatory – and there are a few operators who take campers on safari to island sites.

Permits

Campers require a permit to camp in all Queensland national parks. Bookings are a must in the Whitsundays as these islands are popular year round. The Conway National Park site has limited space and is frequently busy. Booking information for all mainland and island sites is available from the Whitsunday Information Centre, Queensland Department of Environment (QDE), corner Mandalay Road and Shute Harbour Road (about one and a half kilometres towards Shute Harbour from the town of Airlie Beach) (PO Box 332), Airlie Beach, Qld 4802, telephone (079) 467 022, FAX (079) 467 023. For the southern islands, which are reached from Mackay, book through the Mackay District Office, Lands Office, corner Wood Street and River Street (PO Box 623), Mackay, Qld 4740, telephone (079) 518 788, FAX (079) 572 036. Give details of the number in your party, the dates you wish to camp, where you wish to camp, details of what you will camp in; for example, tent, tarpaulin, overturned cardboard box with breathing holes …

Campers with a permit must comply with a few conditions designed to preserve the park and to ensure an enjoyable time for all. Permits are granted for up to two weeks at any one site.

Important notes on Whitsunday camping

Campers arrange their own transport to the islands (see 'Getting to the islands' next page). They need to take their own water; 3 litres per person per day is a *survival* ration, which doesn't allow for showering, and the rangers recommend 5 litres per person per day. Campers need to take fuel for cooking (gas cookers are highly recommended).

* Flora includes everything from dead wood to leaves, and 'interfere', according to the legislation, includes 'destroy, get, damage, mark, move'. 'Taken' means 'to collect, pick, pluck, poison, disturb, cut, pull up, dig up, destroy, damage, remove, injure or attempt or permit any of these acts'. In relation to fauna, 'taken' means 'to hunt, shoot, kill, poison, net, snare, trap, catch, pursue, disturb, stupefy, disable, pluck, injure, destroy, damage or to attempt any of these'.
One can only imagine the wide-eyed excuses offered to park rangers over the years that inspired this list of prohibitions.

Fires are not permitted at:
Cockatoo Beach, North Molle
  Island (C9)
Dugong Beach, Whitsunday Island (C19)
Joe's Beach, Whitsunday Island (C19)
Sawmill Beach, Whitsunday Island (C19)
Stockyard Beach (Chalkie's Beach),
  Haslewood Island (C26)
Whitehaven Beach, Whitsunday
  Island (C26)

All flora and fauna in Queensland national parks are protected – no flora may be interfered with and no fauna taken*. The Whitsundays are also part of the Great Barrier Reef Marine Park and certain areas are offered additional special protection (see 'The Whitsundays and the Marine Park').

Rubbish

All rubbish must be brought back to the mainland – bottles, tins, bits of fishing line, garbage bags, even biodegradable rubbish, which should not be disposed of at the water's edge or buried. The approach should be 'ship it in, ship it out'. Don't bury, burn or sink rubbish.

Fires

While camping without a campfire may seem a bit like dry toast, the arguments against fires are persuasive. The islands are heavily used; the vegetation is fire-sensitive, and it has been damaged by campfires in some places. There is often a risk of wildfire, particularly in areas of acacia scrub, which is highly flammable. Fuel for fires is virtually non-existent on the islands and campers may be tempted to use island vegetation (dead or alive) which, for obvious reasons of conservation, is prohibited in national parks. Fires often cause unsightly contamination of foreshores and beaches which, among other things, spoils their natural beauty as well as the sense of wilderness.

Fires are totally banned on a number of beaches (see note at left). Any fires that are lit in the open elsewhere must be: (a) of driftwood only; (b) small cooking fires (0.5 metre diameter); (c) constructed either in fireplaces provided or on the beach below the level of high tide. All fire debris must be completely cleaned up afterwards. Campers must supply their own fuel for cooking; gas apparatus is recommended. *All vegetation (dead or alive) is protected in national parks and may not be used for firewood.* The rangers take a very dim view of violations, and there are stiff penalties. During the dry season there may be complete fire bans. Check before lighting a fire.

Getting to the islands

One of the most popular and least expensive ways of getting to the islands for those without their own boat is via one of the cruise yachts that take day-trippers out for scenic cruises. Arrangements for containers of water may be made at the same time. Information about cruise boats is available from any of the many travel and booking agencies in Airlie Beach, Cannonvale or Shute Harbour.

Not all island sites are accessible at low tide, and this needs to be discussed with your skipper as tide times may have some bearing on your choice of campsite. The Water Taxi at Shute Harbour jetty also takes campers and their water to the islands, and its schedule is more flexible than that of cruise boats, but for special trips it may cost a little more.

A few camping tips

One thing that might be overlooked is the importance of having good substantial footwear that you don't mind getting wet. Good footwear (not thongs) is essential for reef and beach walking to avoid coral and shell cuts and to protect against the possibility of stepping on a stonefish (see 'Avoiding tropical hazards').

Take a good first-aid kit. The islands have essentially the same wildlife as the mainland, including the occasional snake, so the normal camping cautions apply – don't romp barefooted through long grass, don't attempt to show off to friends by playing 'crack the whip' with the taipan you just found. Mosquitoes and other biters have, unfortunately, also discovered paradise in the Whitsundays, and the most beautiful, fine silica sand beach – Whitehaven – has its own particular breed of fine white sandflies; take plenty of insect repellent with you. The itchy aftermath of sandfly bites can persist for weeks, so prevention is very much preferable to cure.

Queensland has a stinging bush which the Aboriginal people called 'gympie'; it is also referred to by the somewhat dreamy name of 'moonlight', which bears little relation to the very real, uncomfortable sting that it is capable of inflicting. The plant has green heart-shaped leaves covered with very fine pale green hair. If you brush against these with your bare skin you will get a very unpleasant burning itch for which there isn't an immediate ready cure. It's not serious but can make you uncomfortable, perhaps for several days. Stinging trees tend to spring up in areas where bush has been disturbed. They are not everywhere, but keep an eye out for the heart-shaped leaves.

The above are the standard precautions and do not necessarily mean that, while camping in the Whitsundays, campers will be carried off by swarms of man-eating insects, attacked by vipers or savaged by noxious shrubs.

Campers should always take enough food and water for at least two more days than the planned stay in the event that bad weather delays pick-up. (Should you be forgotten entirely, the extra food will enable you to have two additional well-fed days during which to contemplate your fate. For those who are anxious about being 'isolated' on an island, a hand-held citizens band radio with marine distress frequency (27.88 MHz) may afford some peace of mind by permitting communication with the local coast guard.

Campers should read pages 'Tips for tropical holidays' for more discussion of how to keep out of trouble, as well as 'Avoiding tropical hazards', paying particular attention during the stinger season to information on jellyfish. Box jellyfish have not been a problem on the islands, but there have, in recent years, been instances of irukandji sting with its delayed and sometimes baffling symptoms.

Camping philosophy

Whitsunday camping offers a great opportunity to enjoy one of the very beautiful parts of the Queensland coast. The islands are unique in offering a whole range of different situations, with tropical birds and marine life, and water that is comfortable to swim in year round. The popularity of the islands is growing every year.

'Minimal impact camping' is a term which recognises the importance of remembering that, as campers, we do have an impact on nature no matter how considerate of nature we are. The Whitsundays are still, for the most part, as unspoilt as they were thousands of years ago when they were cut off from the mainland at the end of the last ice age. They are, however, under increasing pressure of use. If campers always leave the islands just as they find them, there is some chance that the Whitsundays will still be a special place when the next generation comes along.

THE WHITSUNDAYS AND THE BARRIER REEF MARINE PARK

The Great Barrier Reef Marine Park has been created to protect and preserve the largest and richest system of coral reefs in the world so that the Reef can be used and enjoyed by future generations. The Park includes continental islands such as the Whitsundays, with their beautiful fringing coral reefs and their fascinating marine life.

The Marine Park is similar to, yet different from, our usual idea of a national park. In national parks all flora and fauna are totally protected; hunting animals or picking flowers is prohibited. The Marine Park is more flexible and allows for all reasonable uses provided these are consistent with conservation of the Great Barrier Reef. Just what constitutes reasonable use is interpreted in Marine Park zones, which are discussed below. For practical purposes, the Park includes everything *below low water mark*.

Australia, in the 1920s, had the foresight to protect most of Queensland's islands by granting them national park status, and nearly all of the Whitsunday islands have been saved from serious incursion by man. As national parks, all flora and fauna *above high water mark* on these islands are totally protected – one reason for their great appeal to tourists.

Between high and low water the islands are protected by a complementary system of Queensland State Marine Parks; thus the whole continuum, from sea bed to island mountain top, is now provided for.

Zoning plans

The Great Barrier Reef Marine Park Authority (GBRMPA), which has the responsibility for planning in the Marine Park, has worked out a flexible system for preserving and conserving the Great Barrier Reef through zoning plans, which ensure a balance between short-term human needs and long-term conservation of the Great Barrier Reef. These zoning plans allow multiple use of the Reef and its resources but they separate conflicting uses, and they restrict or prohibit certain activities in specified areas. Levels of protection vary from almost no restrictions to areas where almost no human activities are permitted.

The majority of the Whitsunday islands fall in the Central Section of the Great Barrier Reef Marine Park. This section extends from Dunk Island in the north to just below Thomas Island in the south. It covers 77 000 square kilometres and comprises approximately one-fifth of the total area of the Marine Park.

Marine Park zones

The map on pages 110–111 shows the various zones that apply in the Whitsundays, colour coded for easy recognition. The Activities Guide summarises what may or may not be undertaken. The light blue and dark blue areas (General Use 'A' and General Use 'B') are virtually unrestricted as far as the average tourist is concerned. Two activities that are not permitted *anywhere* in the Park are spear fishing with scuba or hookah, and littering.

Marine National Park 'A' Zone

The zone most commonly employed, immediately around the frequently visited islands, is Marine National Park 'A' (yellow). These are areas of intense recreation and include the reefs and local waters associated with tourist resorts, camping areas and popular overnight anchorages. Marine National Park 'A' allows most people to do what they want, within reason, but restricts activities that are likely to conflict with the interests of tourists as a whole. In these zones, for example, one can still catch the evening

(continued on page 113)

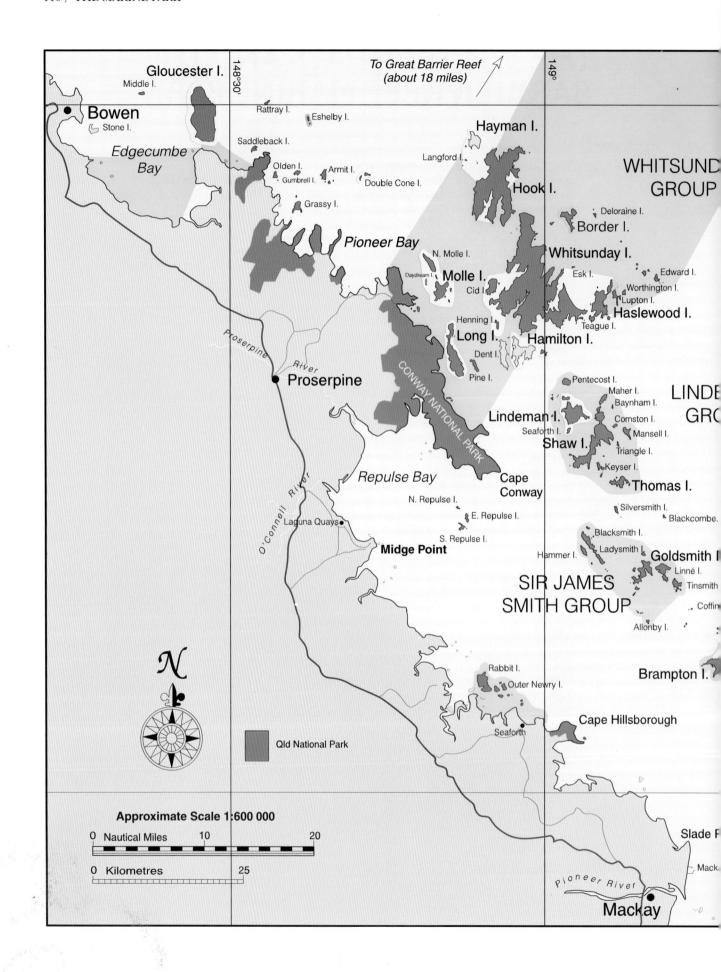

To Great Barrier Reef
(about 18 miles)

148°30'

149°

Gloucester I.

Middle I.

Bowen

Stone I.

*Edgecumbe
Bay*

Rattray I.

Eshelby I.

Saddleback I.

Olden I.

Gumbrell I.

Armit I.

Double Cone I.

Grassy I.

Pioneer Bay

Hayman I.

Langford I.

Hook I.

WHITSUND
GROUP

Deloraine I.

Border I.

N. Molle I.

Daydream I.

Molle I.

Cid I.

Whitsunday I.

Esk I.

Edward I.

Worthington I.

Lupton I.

Haslewood I.

Proserpine

River

Proserpine

CONWAY NATIONAL PARK

Henning I.

Long I.

Dent I.

Pine I.

Hamilton I.

Teague I.

Lindeman I.

Seaforth I.

Shaw I.

Pentecost I.

Maher I.

Baynham I.

Comston I.

Mansell I.

Triangle I.

Keyser I.

LINDE
GRO

Thomas I.

O'Connell River

Laguna Quays

Repulse Bay

N. Repulse I.

E. Repulse I.

S. Repulse I.

Midge Point

Cape
Conway

Silversmith I.

Blackcombe.

Blacksmith I.

Ladysmith I.

Hammer I.

Goldsmith I

Linné I.

Tinsmith

SIR JAMES
SMITH GROUP

Coffin

Allonby I.

Brampton I.

Rabbit I.

Outer Newry I.

Cape Hillsborough

Seaforth

Slade

Mack.

Pioneer River

Mackay

N

Qld National Park

Approximate Scale 1:600 000

| 0 | Nautical Miles | 10 | 20 |

| 0 | Kilometres | 25 |

		Bait netting and gathering	Trawling	Collecting (recreational – not coral)	Crabbing and oyster gathering	Diving, boating, photography	Line fishing (bottom fishing, trolling, etc.)	Spear fishing
	General Use 'A' Zone	Yes	Yes	Limited	Yes	Yes	Yes	Yes
	General Use 'B' Zone	Yes	No	Limited	Yes	Yes	Yes	Yes
	Marine National Park 'A' Zone	Yes	No	No	Limited	Yes	Limited	No
	Marine National Park 'B' Zone	No	No	No	No	Yes	No	No
	Preservation Zone	No	No	No	No	No	No	No

General Use 'A' Zone (light blue)
An area where you can do just about anything, within reason, consistent with conservation of the Reef. Spear fishing with scuba is prohibited throughout the Park, as are commercial drilling, mining and littering. The taking of estuary or greasy cod, or giant gropers over 1200 millimetres in length is also prohibited anywhere in the Park without a permit. Commercial trawling, shipping and limited collecting are allowed.

General Use 'B' Zone (darker blue)
Basically the same as General Use 'A' but with no trawling or commercial shipping.

Marine National Park 'A' Zone (yellow)
This zone is similar in concept to a national park on land, that is, natural resources protected; but it is different in that some fishing activity is permitted, e.g. trolling (for pelagic fishes, such as mackerel, line fishing (with one hand-held rod or line used with one hook or lure), and bait netting. This zone has been applied to protect significant areas from intensive extractive activities; for example, netting, collecting and spear fishing (without scuba) conflict with many tourist activities and have been excluded adjacent to resort and camping islands.

Marine National Park 'B' Zone (light green)
This is a 'look-but-don't-take' zone; fishing of any sort and collecting are prohibited. The purpose of this zone is to protect areas of special value so that people may appreciate and enjoy them in a relatively undisturbed state.

Preservation Zone (pink)
The objective of this zone is to preserve areas of outstanding value in a totally natural state, undisturbed by man except for purposes of scientific research which cannot be carried out elsewhere. Important breeding and nesting grounds may be given this status.

Above:
The Stepping Stones, a series of coral bommies on the western side of Bait Reef, are a favourite diving and snorkelling site about seventeen nautical miles north-east of Hook Island. This part of Bait Reef has been declared a Special Management Area, where fishing is prohibited, in order to preserve the quality of the site for underwater sightseers.

Right:
Snorkelling is one of the best ways to really enjoy a reef, from right in the water where the full colour and activity can be appreciated. Glass-bottom boats and other special craft for coral viewing are also available for those who prefer to keep dry while enjoying a reef.

(continued from page 109)

meal of fish (with a single line with a single hook), gather bait and gather oysters (for one's own immediate consumption); but spear fishing is not allowed (because it scares the fish away so that snorkellers and divers don't see them), and shell collecting is not permitted (even collection of dead ones) because if every tourist who visited the Whitsundays removed just one shell it would be a matter of only months before there were none at all for anyone to look at.

Marine National Park 'B' Zone

The green Marine National Park 'B' Zone is a 'look-but-don't-take' zone. This zone is employed in those areas where extractive activities would be in conflict with preserving especially good marine habitats where tourists can appreciate corals, fishes and other marine life in a relatively undisturbed state. Fishing and spear fishing are obviously inappropriate here.

Four areas among the islands and one at the outer Reef complex (Hardy Reef) have been designated Marine National Park 'B', areas requiring special care, which are:

Butterfly Bay and northern Hook Island (map C14/15). The area enclosed by a line between Alcyonaria Point has some of the best corals in the Whitsunday area and is very popular with divers and snorkellers. No fishing is permitted in this area. A number of bays in this area have reef protection buoys delineating areas of no anchorage. In some parts of this area considerable anchor damage has already been done and, to preserve the coral, the exceptional Manta Ray Bay has been designated a Special Management Area where anchoring is prohibited.

Border Island (map C29) has a beautiful fringing reef on the north side in Cateran Bay and along the eastern and western bays. This bay also has reef protection buoys to delineate anchoring limits.

Haslewood Island (map C31) has an extensive fringing reef that at low tide joins it to Lupton Island, and in Waite Bay (White Bay) and along the eastern side of Lupton Island the snorkelling is excellent. This reef can provide hours of fascinating fossicking. Haslewood Island, from the southern extremity right around the south and east sides and up to Pallion Point, is protected by Marine National Park 'B' status.

Cow Island and Calf Island are adjacent to the mainland south of Long Island and are zoned Marine National Park 'B' because they represent an important habitat with adjacent mangrove communities.

Hardy Reef (map R1) is a centre for Barrier Reef activities, with pontoons semi-permanently anchored, a 'landing strip' for amphibians, coral-viewing subs, and glass-bottom boats. This is where the big catamarans deposit their reef-trippers. As such it has been appropriately classified Marine National Park 'B'.

Special Management Areas

Bait Reef (map R1), an especially beautiful, pristine reef, is classified Marine National Park 'A'. Much used by divers and snorkellers, the part most frequented for these activities has been afforded special status to preserve the wildlife and the quality of the reef for sightseers. From the Stepping Stones, on its western side, down around the middle of the south side, is a Special Management Area, a 'look but don't take' zone; fishing and shell collecting are prohibited.

Manta Ray Bay (map C14/15), where there is some of the best underwater scenery to be found in the Whitsundays, has suffered anchor damage in recent years, and anchoring is now prohibited. There are several public moorings and some private commercial moorings in the bay.

Definitions of activities

Bait netting/gathering
Bait netting and bait gathering can be undertaken only in the General Use 'A', General Use 'B' and Marine National Park 'A' zones.
Recreational bait netting is the use of a cast net or a recreational bait net as defined by Queensland Fisheries Regulations.
Commercial bait netting is using a commercial bait net as defined by relevant Queensland Fisheries legislation when used by a licensed commercial fisherman.
Bait gathering is taking of yabbies, eugaries (pippies), bait worms or crabs, when taken by hand or hand-held implement.

Camping
Camping on Commonwealth islands and all Queensland National Park islands within the Marine Park requires a permit, which may be obtained from offices of the Queensland Department of Environment.

Spear fishing
Spear fishing may be undertaken in General Use 'A' and General Use 'B' zones except in certain designated areas . Throughout the Marine Park the following are prohibited:
● commercial spear fishing
● spear fishing with scuba or hookah
● use of a powerhead

Collecting
The taking, by any means, of any aquarium fish, invertebrates (includes shells), mammals and reptiles, whether dead or alive, may only be undertaken with a permit.

Limited collecting
In General Use 'A' and 'B' zones the taking of not more than five of any particular species, e.g. aquarium fish, shells and other invertebrates) in any 28-day period is allowed.

Commercial collecting
The taking of any species, including corals, commercially requires a permit.

Crabbing and oyster gathering
Crabbing may be undertaken by a licensed commercial fisherman or a recreational fisherman in the General Use 'A' and 'B' zones, using only certain apparatus (i.e. crab pots, dillies or inverted dillies). Crab hooks are no longer allowed.
Limited crabbing may be undertaken in Marine National Park 'A' Zone, using any combination of crab pots, dillies or inverted dillies that total not more than four devices. Note: limitations apply on the apparatus used, and restrictions apply on the numbers, size and sex of certain species taken, in accordance with the Queensland Fisheries Act.
Oyster gathering by hand may be undertaken in the General Use 'A' and General Use 'B' zones. However, while commercial operations may be carried out in these zones, subject to provisions of the Fisheries Act, the construction of racks or other structures in the Marine Park requires a permit.
Limited oyster gathering is gathering of oysters for immediate consumption and may be undertaken in Marine National Park 'A' Zone.

(continued next page)

The reef group including Hook, Line, Bait and Hardy reefs is the centre of outer reef activities for the Whitsundays. These are the reefs of the Barrier system nearest to the Whitsundays; they lie on the continental shelf about twenty-five nautical miles from the islands. Hardy Reef, with its magnificent lagoon, is the destination of amphibious aircraft, helicopters and high-speed catamarans which bring tourists out for a day on the Reef. Hardy is a Marine Park 'B' Zone, a 'look-but-don't-take' area. From the Stepping Stones, on the western side of Bait Reef, down to its southern extremity is a Special Management Area, where fishing is prohibited and there are restrictions on anchoring.

Definitions of activities
(continued from previous page)
Line fishing
Line fishing includes fishing by both recreational and licensed commercial fishermen. The term line fishing includes fishing with either a handline or rod and reel, bottom fishing, drift fishing or fishing with a floating bait. Tackle and equipment regulations are complementary to Queensland Fisheries Regulations: for example, no more than six hooks are to be used on one line.
Line fishing is allowed in the General Use 'A' and General Use 'B' zones and limited line fishing is allowed in the Marine National Park 'A' Zone. Limited line fishing allows fishing by a person using equipment comprised of either one hand-held rod or one handline attached to either one hook, one artificial fly, or one lure.
Trolling means fishing with a line, trailed behind a vessel that is underway, but does not include drift fishing or fishing without a floating bait. Trolling may be carried out in General Use 'A', General Use 'B', and Marine National Park 'A' zones.
Tourist/ educational programmes
The conduct and operation of any facility or programme for tourism (e.g. charter vessels, cruise boats, observatories, pontoons, etc.) or educational programmes may be undertaken in the Marine Park only with a permit.
Diving, boating and photography
These activities are considered to cause minimal disturbance to the Marine Park and are allowed in all zones with the exception of Scientific Research and Preservation Zones. Commercial operators have similar freedom of access within the conditions of permits granted by GBRMPA.

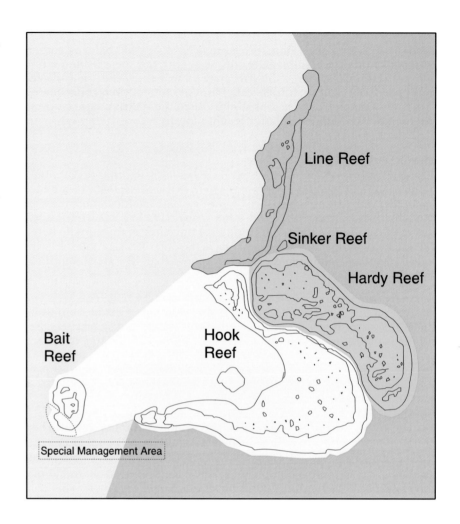

Preservation Zone
One Preservation Zone has been designated in the Whitsundays – the isolated Eshelby Island (map N8b). Eshelby is a Commonwealth lighthouse island and is also an important breeding area for several species of sea birds, particularly the bridled tern. It has a very good representative fringing reef community. Entry within 500 metres is prohibited, except in an emergency which threatens the safety of a vessel or its crew.

Above:

One of the Whitsunday's most expansive fringing reefs is that which extends between Waite Bay, on the south side of Haslewood Island, and Lupton Island. Waite Bay is a beautiful anchorage which offers good snorkelling and reef fossicking. Its exposure to the south makes it a poor, or at least risky, *overnight* anchorage until the trade winds have abated, in about October.

Left:

Border Island's Cateran Bay is another location at the northern end of the Whitsundays where coral development is very good. A lovely, remote anchorage, the saddle of the island offers beautiful views south-west across to Whitsunday Island and the magnificent Whitehaven Beach.

AVOIDING TROPICAL HAZARDS

These notes are provided for curiosity seekers as much as for any real hazards posed by tropical marine creatures. One has to marvel at the ingenious behaviour and weaponry that have evolved, and no matter how remote the danger posed by any of the animals discussed below, it's useful to be aware of them. Unlike man, the creatures described here almost always inflict their damage in self-defence only, or after extreme provocation.

Poisonous fishes

Of the many and varied fishes that may be found in the waters of the Whitsundays, there are a few which can be poisonous. Some are rendered so by their behaviour (such as Thomas the Terrible Toadfish), some can cause poisoning if eaten (such as Thomas the Terrible Toadfish, Chinaman fish, paddletail, etc.), and some cause poisoning if stepped on (such as the stonefish).

Toadfish

The toadfish belongs to the order of tetraodontiformes, a mouthful which describes these fishes' four (tetra) large, fused teeth (odontiformes). Toadfish lurk around shallow coastal estuaries and inlets; they lie waiting for passing crabs which they crunch up with their beak-like teeth. They are normally only about 13 centimetres long, but certain species grow as big as 96 centimetres, with teeth to match and capable of shearing through a number 4/0 hook.

Giant toadfish have from time to time conducted campaigns of terror in the Whitsundays. For example, during the Easter weekend of 1979, six-year-old Margaret Lewis had two toes bitten off at the first joint while wading barefoot in Shute Har-

Thomas the Terrible Toadfish had this portrait taken in 1979 after he unsuccessfully attempted to eat the sneaker-clad toes of a fisherman in Shute Harbour. This giant toadfish was 65 centimetres in length, but they can grow as large as 96 centimetres.

bour. Some time later that year a toadfish removed a walnut-sized chunk from the leg of a boy wading in Cid Harbour, and Richard Timperley was fishing

in water about thirty-five centimetres deep over gravel near the Shute Harbour ramp when a 65 centimetre toadfish came like a torpedo for his sneakered feet. Undeterred by jabs from a fishing rod, the toadfish pursued the rapidly retreating fisherman until it had almost beached itself. Timperley later made up a 'wanted' poster to warn local residents about a vile fish which he dubbed 'Thomas the Terrible Toadfish'.

In early March 1984 sixty-one-year-old Robert Crompton was prawning at Earlando (map N11) in waist-deep water when a giant toadfish tore away the top of the middle toe on his left foot. In spite of Robert's kicking, the fish circled back in a second attack and took yet a little more of the toe, which later had to be amputated completely. (As fate would have it, this was the first time Crompton had ever gone into the water barefoot.)

Toadfish are sometimes referred to in the area as 'toefish', and the lessons of the past should be heeded. Never wade in coastal inlets in bare feet.

Toadfish are members of the family of puffers which are capable of inflating themselves like basketballs, a practice which evidently intimidates would-be predators, or at least it makes the puffers jolly difficult to swallow. Puffers were known to be poisonous well before Christ. Hieroglyphics of 2700 BC mention the toxicity of Red Sea puffer fish, and there are biblical warnings against eating fish with no scales (puffer fish have no scales). The Greeks and Chinese knew of the danger, and it is surprising that neither Captain James Cook nor his cook were aware of it, for the great explorer was poisoned by a puffer in New Caledonia on his second voyage of discovery in 1774.

The Japanese play a form of culinary Russian roulette with puffer fish and, like so much of what they do in Japan, the game is taken to the extremes of art. Fugu, as it is called, is a prized delicacy which may be prepared only by licensed fugu chefs, who have gone to school and taken exams on the subject of its preparation. These chefs create *tours de forces* in their restaurants, laying out the thin slices of the fish in delicate floral patterns. Traces of tetrodotoxin (TTX) produce a pleasant tingling sensation which has been likened by enthusiasts to that produced by a white Burgundy of a good year. The sense of danger obviously heightens the experience, and it is said that to eat fugu liver, in which the concentration of toxin may be very great indeed, is the ultimate in fugu culture; even trained chefs are prohibited from serving it; but what can they do when a dejected haiku poet comes in and says:

I cannot see her tonight.,
I have to give her up,
So I will eat fugu.

TTX is one of the most toxic poisons known. James Bond, at the end of *From Russia with Love*, was left for dead on the floor after being kicked in the leg by a poison-tipped boot which, 'M' explains in the sequel, *Dr No*, was tainted with fugu poison, from the sex organs of the Japanese globe fish (the sex organs, roe, viscera and skin also have very high concentrations of toxin). Nine millionths of one gram (0.000009 gram) per

kilogram of TTX administered intravenously will kill 50% of mice injected with the poison.

Symptoms of puffer poisoning

The onset of symptoms is relatively rapid (10–45 minutes); the speed of onset and severity is relative

Puffer fishes can inflate themselves to relatively enormous proportions, making them difficult to swallow and, perhaps, formidable to predators.

to the amount of toxin ingested. Symptoms begin with a tingling sensation and numbness about the mouth and lips; sometimes there is nausea but seldom vomiting. Symptoms progress to numbness of the tongue and face, followed by slurred speech and progressive muscle paralysis, with ultimate respiratory paralysis and death, which evidently occurs in about 60% of cases. TTX is said to be used by voodoo specialists in Haiti to create their 'zombies' – the walking dead who survive being 'buried alive'. Conventional medicine reports that, in some serious cases where the patients have apparently been unconscious, they have recovered and reported being mentally alert right throughout the ordeal. (Don't say anything that you wouldn't say in front of the hapless patient or he may remember you for it later.)

First aid

If the victim is conscious, induce vomiting; stick fingers down the throat or administer an emetic (syrup of ipecac).

Prevention

Don't eat puffer fishes or, as the Bible says, any scaleless fishes.

Ciguatera (tropical fish poisoning)

The word ciguatera comes from a Spanish word, 'cigua', and was coined by a Cuban ichthyologist, F. Poey, in 1866. Cigua is the name for a small mollusc which causes digestive and nervous disorders when eaten. Ciguatera is usually acquired by eating predatory tropical reef fishes, or reef-feeding pelagic fishes, that have accumulated a toxin through eating smaller fishes which contain the toxin. Ciguatoxin is believed to originate from a dinoflagellate (plankton), *Gambierdiscus toxicus*, which is passed along the food web via small herbivorous fishes; the toxin is firmly tissue-bound, very little being excreted, and it thus can reach high concentrations in larger carnivorous fishes.

Gambierdiscus toxicus proliferates around coral reefs where the corals have been killed either by storms or by the intervention of man, or by silting after heavy rainfall.

Poisonous fishes

The toadfish (Spheroides hamiltoni) *is normally about 13 centimetres long. It patrols shallow mud flats looking for crabs. Like all puffer fishes, it is poisonous to eat.*

Red Bass
(Lutjanus bohar)

Thus, from time to time, many different species of fish may be affected by ciguatoxin, and the list of fishes that have been implicated at one time or another reads like a peerage, everything from coral trout to scallops having been named. The list is of little practical value as a guide to which fish to avoid if you want to eat any fish at all. It is a good idea to check with local fishermen as to which fish to avoid.

Certain species of fish in Queensland are known to be frequently toxic, and these should always be avoided: Chinaman fish *(Symphorus nematophorus)*, paddletail or red snapper *(Lutjanus gibbus)*, red bass *(Lutjanus bohar)*, and moray eel *(Gymnothorax sp.)*.

Because of the cumulative nature of the poison, it is possible that one may on one occasion ingest a dose which is not sufficient to produce symptoms, and then on a subsequent occasion develop a full-blown case after eating what would normally be a subclinical dose of toxin.

Several members of Cook's crew got ciguatera in the New Hebrides (now Vanuatu), and a pig on board which was fed some of the suspect fish died the next day, in spite of the fish having been cooked together with a silver spoon. Other folklore heard even today says that ciguatera may be avoided by boiling the fish together with a coin, and perhaps both of these fables have a common origin. There is no fact known to support either notion. Ciguatoxin is heat stable and is not destroyed by cooking. While the water soluble fraction may be reduced by repeatedly soaking fillets and discarding the water (incidentally, the broth of boiled ciguatoxic fish is very poisonous), this will not prevent poisoning by the insoluble fraction.

Symptoms of ciguatera – abdominal pain, nausea, vomiting and diarrhoea – develop between two and twelve hours after ingestion (usually in about five hours). There is a developing numbness or tingling about the mouth and in the extremities, and victims experience a characteristic inversion of hot and cold perception (ice cream and cold drinks burn the mouth and throat, a cold can of beer feels hot). Muscle aches and pains are common. Sometimes victims say their teeth feel like they're falling out of their sockets, and that they have a metallic taste in the mouth. Rash is common. Recovery usually occurs in forty-eight hours to one week. Tingling and disturbance of temperature perception may last much longer. A good dose of poison may produce subsequent allergic reactions, particularly to fish.

First aid
If the victim is conscious, induce vomiting; stick fingers down the throat or administer an emetic (syrup of ipecac). If a large amount of toxin has been ingested symptoms can be life-threatening, and medical attention should therefore always be sought.

Prevention
- Never eat Chinaman fish, red bass or red snapper, paddletail, moray eel. And always ask the locals which fish to avoid.
- Avoid eating any fish larger than four kilograms; bigger fish are likely to have larger accumulations of toxin.
- Don't eat repeated meals from the same fish.
- If there are more than the usual number of dead sea birds around, don't eat any fish for several weeks.

Envenomation
The kind of serious envenomations that visitors to the Queensland coast are at all likely to have to deal with are stonefish stings, box jellyfish stings, snake bite, stingray wounds, cone shell stings, blue-ringed octopus bites, anal sea snake bites. As unlikely as it is that any of them will occur, these are all discussed along with tips for avoiding trouble and measures to be taken when they happen.

Fortunately our scientists have developed specific antivenoms for some of the worst offenders, but prevention is better than treatment, which may be many hours away.

Venoms have a number of ways of working their mischief – by such means as destroying blood cells, by inactivating nerves which control vital muscles, by poisoning muscle tissues themselves. Some venoms do most damage at the site of injection; others, usually with more significant results, travel via the circulatory system to places where they can disrupt the functioning of the body. In the latter case it is important to prevent the systemic spread of venom by keeping the victim as still as possible; for example, walking should not be attempted in cases of snake bite on the leg. In other cases, venoms do local damage at the site of injection but do not produce serious systemic effects, and in these cases it is best not to restrict the movement of venom from the wound. The use of arterial tourniquets and the making of incisions is no longer recommended for envenomations. Experience has taught that both procedures very often do more harm than good. The use of Condy's crystals (potassium permanganate), it is felt, also does only harm.

Pressure-immobilisation
A procedure known as 'pressure-immobilisation' is now widely accepted in first aid for venomous bites and stings. It simply involves applying pressure generally to the bite and surrounding tissues which restricts the flow of venom through the circulatory system; immobilising the affected limb prevents systemic spread of the poison. Pressure-immobilisation is indicated in all cases of bites and stings *which are not immediately painful* (pain signifies that local tissue damage is taking place, and in these cases the procedure is sometimes not recommended). Pressure-immobilisation is recommended in all cases of snake bite, cone shell stings, blue-ringed octopus bite; it is not recommended for fish envenomations.

- Apply a broad crepe bandage (or any flexible material) over the site of the bite as soon as possible. Don't struggle with removal of pants or shirt if this requires a lot of movement of the affected limb. In cases of bites to the trunk, administration of pressure-immobilisation is more difficult but may be used if it doesn't impair breathing. In bites to the groin and neck, it is probably not feasible.
- Bandage over the wound and upwards (away from the toes or fingers) as tightly as you would bind a sprained ankle, extending the bandage as high as possible. If the victim complains of discomfort it probably means that the bandage is too tight and it should be readjusted.
- Bind a splint firmly to as much of the limb as possible (up to the elbow in the case of an arm).
- Reassure the victim. Seek medical assistance.
- Bandages should be left in place until the victim is in capable hands and emergency resuscitation measures have been prepared.

Stonefish
There are two principal species of stone fish in Queensland – the estuarine stonefish *(Synanceia trachynis)* and the reef stonefish *(S. verrucosa)*. The estuarine stonefish is much more common than the reef stonefish, but they are both equally ugly and equally poisonous.

Stonefish are usually about twenty centimetres long, are scaleless, and their skin is covered with 'warts' and a slime which is toxic to small marine animals and which evidently tastes bitter (the mind boggles at the desperate hunger of the man who established this fact, his bravery far exceeding that even of the man who ate the first oyster). Stonefish have spines along their back which become erect when the fish is disturbed; these thirteen spines (which will appeal to the superstitious) are fitted with venom sacs. Normally, stonefish lie in rubble, defying detection. They scoop out a little nesting place with their large pectoral fins and wait for an unsuspecting fish to come by, whereupon the prey is 'inhaled as if by a rock with a hideous upturned frog mouth'. Man describes stonefish as 'lethargic' because they make little attempt to move even when discovered. Discovery must be a rarity; having managed to find one, if you take your eyes off it for one second it will be gone when you look back (actually, it won't have moved, but such is the quality of their deception). Stonefish can remain exposed at low tide apparently without ill effect – to themselves.

The skin on the spines, when these are trodden on, presses down over the venom sacks causing venom to explode upwards along the sheath. The spines are capable of penetrating the sole of a sneaker, and the experience of a local general practitioner over the past eight years shows that about one-half of treated cases were wearing something on their feet. About three-quarters of stonefish wounds are to feet, one-quarter to hands.

Stonefish stings are agonisingly painful. No deaths have been reported in Australia (although some have been reported in the Indo-Pacific). There is laboratory evidence that the venom can produce loss of function in all types of muscle. The wound is usually accompanied by acute swelling, spreading up the limb from the wound, which may persist for many weeks.

First aid
- Control of pain is most important. Do not apply pressure-immobilisation. The venom is protein; soaking in hot water has been found useful in relieving pain (it should not be so hot as to scald).
- Antivenom is available and probably should be administered in all but mild cases.

Avoidance
- Always wear substantial footwear when reef fossicking or when walking on rubble around mainland beaches. Don't run in these areas.

Stingray
Stingrays are flattened sharks that lie on the sea bottom looking for shells to crunch up with their pavement of flat teeth. They flick sand onto their backs, and very often the first hint of their presence is when one 'explodes' from the sand immediately in front of or just between your feet! Rays are timid, and given the chance they will move away rather than

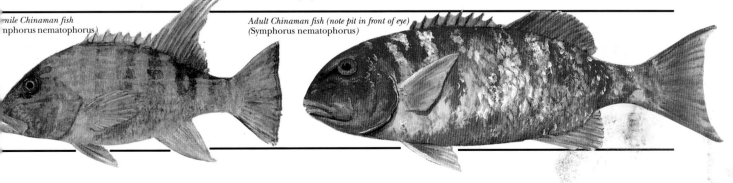

enile Chinaman fish
nphorus nematophorus)

Adult Chinaman fish (note pit in front of eye)
(Symphorus nematophorus)

do battle. For this reason it is always a good idea to shuffle one's feet or to carry a stick with which to 'test' the sand in front.

A foot planted on the back of a stingray makes it very difficult for the ray to fly away; its response is a forwards/downwards flick of the tail, the latter which is armed with venomous serrated spines. A similar response may be evoked by divers or snorkellers cruising close over the bottom, in which case the whole torso is offered as a target instead of just a foot or leg. Wounds to the trunk are possibly worse than those to the limbs.

As much damage, if not more, is done by the physical trauma caused by the barbed spines as is done by the stingray venom itself, which, like that of the stonefish, is protein. The wounds may be ugly, painful, and they are invariably contaminated with animal tissue and foreign matter which needs to be cleaned out. It is likely that proper treatment will be beyond the capability and the resources of the average holidaymaker, and medical attention for these wounds is a good idea. Considering the great number of rays that are about, it is surprising that there are so few wounds inflicted by them.

As is true with a number of venomous fishes, the sting apparatus can be dangerous long after the animal is dead, so treat dead rays with some respect.

First aid
● Pressure-immobilisation is not recommended.
● Wash the wound and clean it out thoroughly to remove venom and foreign tissue that may be in it.
● Hot water may be useful in controlling pain. Because of the nature of these wounds and possible loss of sensitivity in the affected limb, it is recommended that the unaffected foot or leg also be soaked in hot water of the same temperature to provide some gauge as to how much heat is 'too much'; overcooking the wounded limb may lead to serious complications.

Avoidance
● Shuffle your feet or prod the sand in front of you with a stick when walking in stingray country, i.e. shallow sand and mud flats.
● Don't cruise close along the bottom when diving or snorkelling.

Pterois volitans – butterfly cod, lionfish, zebrafish, fire cod
Butterfly cod are found around coral reefs. Curious creatures, they will sometimes approach divers in the water, pointing their dorsal spines in front of them as they get near. These spines have glands which produce venom akin to that of one species of stonefish. It produces a severely distressing sting, which usually subsides within a couple of hours (although it can last for several days). Local effects of the sting are usually the most significant (vomiting and fever are sometimes reported).

First aid
● Immerse the wound in hot (but not scalding) water. Do not use pressure-immobilisation.

Conus sp. – cone shells
Cone shells are numerous (some seventy species) in Australian waters, some seven species being potentially dangerous to man. They have beautifully patterned and coloured shells, although their beauty is not always obvious due to a thick green covering of slime.

Butterfly cod
(Pterois volitans)

Cones are carnivorous gastropods that inhabit shallow intertidal waters of coral reefs, where they remain buried or under a rock by day and come out at night to do their marauding. They eat worms, fish, other gastropods and octopuses, all of which they immobilise with a poisoned 'harpoon'. This barbed tooth, of up to a centimetre in length, is firmly held in the end of the proboscis and is jammed into their prey while venom is squeezed through the tooth cavity. Each barbed tooth is used only once, which is usually enough, although cones have a quiverful of them held in reserve. Cones can distend their proboscis to envelope an object about their own size. They have an acute sense of smell which they localise by sampling the water with their waving tube-like siphon.

The species that eat fish are potentially most dangerous to man, but since you cannot ask them what they eat it is best to assume that, whatever that cone is that you shouldn't have in your hand, it is potentially lethal. A myth has been perpetuated that cones can safely be held by the thick end; alas, they can reach *either* end from the cleft in their shell, so don't pick them up without barbecue tongs and don't slip them into your pocket.

The sting is sometimes very painful, and it may be followed by incoordination and muscular weakness, blurred vision, difficulty in swallowing, slurred speech; the ultimate symptom is respiratory paralysis. There have been some sixteen reported fatalities.

First aid
● Immediately apply pressure-immobilisation and be ready to give resuscitation. Keep the bandages in place until medical assistance and resuscitation equipment are available. Prolonged resuscitation may be required.

Avoidance
● Don't pick up cone shells in your bare hands.

Sea snakes
Virtually unknown in the Atlantic Ocean, there are some thirty-two species of sea snakes recorded in northern Australian waters. Lucky us! Sea snakes look like their land brethren but have flaps over their nostrils and a paddle-like tail which aids their swimming. Their nostrils, flattened tail and scaly appearance helps to differentiate them from eels. They can

absorb about one-fifth of their oxygen requirements directly from the water and are capable of extended (two-hour), deep (100 metre) dives. They shed their skin frequently, perhaps every two weeks, which solves their antifouling problems. Most are born alive at sea.

One hears some conflicting opinion about the danger of sea snakes, and caution is prudent. Their venom is very toxic, but they do not put out a great deal; pain is notably absent and this may be a distinguishing feature in the case of bites of unknown origin received at night. Clinical illness following bites is evidently uncommon.

Some say sea snakes are curious, some say they can be downright aggressive (at mating time), and both of these observations may be valid. Divers say that their 'curiosity' can be a damned nuisance. When they bite a flipper, they continue to hang on, probably behaviour required in the marine environment to avoid losing prey. Sea snakes are not a problem in the Whitsundays.

Where first-aid measures are not taken, symptoms of bites occur within half an hour and include visual disturbance, muscular weakness, pain, progressing in severe cases to paralysis and respiratory failure. Antivenom is available for treatment of bites.

First aid
● Pressure-immobilisation and resuscitation.

Hapalochlaena maculosa – blue-ringed octopus
The blue-ringed octopus is found all around Australia and is the only octopus with a potentially lethal bite. It is very small (only about twenty centimetres from the tip of one arm/leg to another) and has a characteristic dark brown to ochre coloured body with blue rings which 'glow' brightly when it is disturbed, making it 'irresistible' to people who happen upon it in shallow rock pools where it fossicks for crabs, its favourite food. The octopus has a small beak at the junction of its eight arms and, unlike many other octopuses, it manufactures a toxic saliva rather than ink. The toxin closely resembles tetrodotoxin, and its bite can produce flabby paralysis very much more rapidly than after puffer fish is consumed because the poison is injected rather than absorbed from the victim's gut. The bite may be almost imperceptible, many victims having been unaware that they were bitten except for a tiny drop of blood at the site. Bites have always occurred when the creature is being handled out of water, e.g. picked up and draped over an arm, hand or shoulder.

First aid
● Speed of action is important. Apply pressure-immobilisation immediately.
● Give resuscitation if necessary. Get the victim to medical help as soon as possible.

Avoidance
● These octopuses never bother any human unless picked up out of water. Tell children to leave them alone, irresistible though they may be with their glowing blue circles.

Box jellyfish
The box jellyfish *(Chironex fleckeri)* is a potential hazard to swimmers along the Queensland coast north from Rockhampton from November through May.

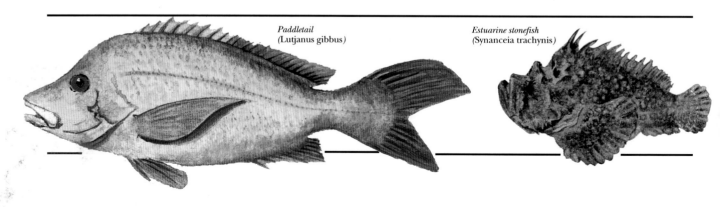

Paddletail
(Lutjanus gibbus)

Estuarine stonefish
(Synanceia trachynis)

The box jellyfish (Chironex fieckeri), almost invisible in the water, is the most poisonous jellyfish known with a potentially lethal sting. Swimmers on the central and northern Queensland mainland coast are advised to wear clothing when swimming in unprotected areas during the November–May period. These jellyfish are a mainland phenomenon and are rarely found among the islands.

The peak season along the Whitsunday mainland seems to be March–April.

Chironex belongs to a class of cuboid jellyfishes so-called because of their box-like shape. They are agile swimmers and are capable of maintaining a pace of three to four knots all day; they can swim at a rate of five knots in a sprint. They have four sensory organs that register posture and attitude, change of direction, change of light intensity, and one of their 'eyes' has a convex lens capable of forming crude images. When approached slowly at an oblique angle (not directly ahead or behind) they will move away, and they tend to avoid dark objects in the water. Stings have sometimes occurred when swimmers have rushed headlong into the water and dived on top of one, not giving it a chance to get away.

The extended threads of the nematocysts are 0.2 millimetres long – long enough to penetrate the skin of most adults (except that on the palms of the hands and undersides of the fingers, where the skin is thicker). They are not long enough to penetrate clothing. An encounter with the tentacles can produce a very high number of individual envenomations over a broad area. Only those nematocysts in contact with the skin discharge.

The venom is an extremely toxic protein that affects the skin, blood and the heart muscle. Stings by box jellyfish about fifteen centimetres diameter are extremely severe, with death a probability if the total length of weals is greater than six to seven metres. The stings produce a characteristic frosted crosshatching on the skin. Children are very susceptible because their skin is thin and because, relative to their body weight, they receive a high dose of venom.

Box jellyfish are creatures of the mainland coast rather than islands. The adults breed in coastal rivers and estuaries, and in summer they come out of the rivers and cruise along the coastal shores, patrolling for little prawns which they find in dense accumulations just outside the 'chop zone' where detritus is stirred up from the bottom by the waves. They tend to stay offshore from beaches in rough weather. They are seldom found far from the mainland. The classic weather to watch out for is glassy calm or light northerly winds.

Household vinegar is the most effective readily available commodity to inactivate the nematocysts, and this is the recommended first step before attempting to remove any adhering tentacles. Vinegar is recommended for all cuboid jellyfish stings (e.g. *Chironex*, *Tamoya* sp., irukandji, jimble) but not *all jellyfish* stings. Vinegar has no effect on the venom nor the damage it has caused, but it does prevent any unfired nematocysts from going off and causing a more serious envenomation.

'Stinger suits' are sold throughout Queensland and are worn by many locals during the stinger season, November–May.

First aid – *Chironex*
- Remove the victim from the water. Douse the area of the sting and any adhering tentacles with household vinegar for at least thirty seconds before attempting to remove them. Do not rub with sand.
- Be prepared to give resuscitation. Seek medical help.
- Pain is usually only temporarily relieved by topical applications.
- Antivenom is available; early administration will help reduce the incidence of scarring.

Avoidance
- Listen for jellyfish alerts and observe signs on beaches during the November–May season.
- During the season when swimming on mainland beaches (if not in a stinger-free enclosure) wear protective clothing or a 'stinger suit'.
- Don't rush headlong down the beach into the water.

Tamoya sp.
There may be several species of tamoya in Australian tropical waters, and their taxonomy (and the giving of specific scientific names) is currently being worked out. Like *Chironex*, it is a cuboid but is a slightly larger, flabbier species with only four flat tentacles (up to one metre long, perhaps green in colour), one emanating from each corner of the ten-to-fifteen-centimetres bell. The body is covered with pinkish papules which can also sting.

First aid – *tamoya*
- Douse with vinegar if any tentacles are present.
- Apply cold packs for ten minutes. Reapply cold packs if skin pain persists.
- Send for medical aid if symptoms persist.

Carukia barnesi – irukandji
Irukandji is a very small jellyfish (two to two-plus centimetres), with tiny red dots on the surface, found in north-central and northern Queensland coastal and sometimes oceanic waters. A cuboid, it has four solitary tentacles, white and hair-like when extended. It can produce a unique sting syndrome with delayed symptoms twenty to thirty minutes after the sting. Initially only mildly painful, the sting develops into a 'goose pimple effect' with mild redness around the site, perhaps five to seven centimetres wide. Twenty to thirty minutes later a symptom complex develops – limb pains, severe backache, abdominal and chest pains, perhaps accompanied by nausea, vomiting, restlessness. Because of this post-sting syndrome, victims should not go back into the water for at least two hours. If similar symptoms are experienced within an hour of swimming in the summertime, the possibility of irukandji sting should be considered.

First aid – irukandji
- Douse with vinegar followed by the application of vinegar-soaked pad and compression bandage. Send for medical aid immediately.
- Don't go back into the water for at least two hours. In case of severe abdominal pain or backache which occur within two hours of leaving the water, especially if a jellyfish sting has been noted, suspect irukandji before submitting to surgical removal of the appendix or exploratory abdominal surgery (this has happened!).

Carybdea rastoni – jimble
The jimble is another small (one to three centimetres) cuboid jellyfish, transparent, with four tentacles, one at each corner, measuring five to thirty centimetres depending upon whether or not they are retracted. Jimbles rise to the surface in the morning and evening, are active swimmers, and can deliver an immediately painful sting (characterised frequently by four weals, sometimes with a sharp bend producing a box-like shape on the skin) which may last for several hours.

First aid – jimble
- Douse adhering tentacles with household vinegar.
- Apply cold packs for ten minutes. Reapply cold packs if skin pain persists.
- Send for medical aid if symptoms persist.

Cyanea capillata, C. sp. – sea slubber, hairy stinger, sea nettle, hairy jelly, lion's mane
The sea blubber has been described as a repulsive big slimy jellyfish that resembles a mop hiding under a dinner plate (Barnes). It has a large, flattened bell (twenty-five to thirty centimetres across) and is found all around Australia. The sting is characterised by white weals which rapidly change to bright red zigzags with surrounding red flare. Sometimes nausea and abdominal pains develop after stings.

First aid – *Cyanea*
- Wash sting area with water.
- Apply cold packs for ten minutes; reapply if skin pain persists.
- Send for medical aid if symptoms persist.

Pelagia noctiluca – little mauve stinger
'Little mauve stinger' pronounced rapidly and indistinctly sounds like what a resident of Harlem would say after being stung by one. They are found all around Australia, have a rounded mushroom shape body (four to twelve centimetres in diameter) with wart-like nematocysts on their mauve to pink-coloured bodies. The brownish-yellow tentacles vary in length from ten to thirty centimetres. The sting can be painful, but is seldom serious, producing irregularly shaped weals that look like insect stings or hives.

First aid – *Pelagia*
- Wash sting area with water.
- Apply cold packs for ten minutes; reapply if skin pain persists.
- Send for medical aid if symptoms persist.

Physalia physalis – bluebottle, Portuguese man-of-war
Bluebottles occur right around Australia. This jellyfish with its inflated pale translucent blue bag for a sail is actually a colony of specialised animals, some of which are the sail trimmers and some the executioners (the latter being the mass of deep blue stingers, some quite long). The sting is painful and produces a characteristic line of separate oval weals, white in the centre with red edges.

First aid – *Physalia*
- Wash sting area with water.
- Apply cold packs for ten minutes; reapply if skin pain persists.
- Send for medical aid if symptoms persist.

Catostylus sp. – blubber jellyfish
The blubber jellyfish has been called a giant mushroom wearing frilly pants. It is milky-white to brown with a large bell (up to thirty centimetres). Easily seen and avoided, the sting is usually mild.

First aid – *Catostylus*
- Wash sting area with water.
- Apply cold packs for ten minutes; reapply if skin pain persists.
- Send for medical aid if symptoms persist.

Lytocarpus phillipinus – stinging hydroid
These beautiful white fern-like 'plants' pack a sting which belies their appearance. They have a penchant for finding the gaps in divers' wet suits, and any contact can produce an extremely uncomfortable sting with rash and, in more severe cases, gastro-intestinal symptoms.

First aid – stinging hydroid
- Apply cold packs for ten minutes. Reapply if skin pain persists.

Millepora sp. – fire coral, stinging coral
Millepora looks like greenish-brown staghorn coral with white–yellow tips. It has thousands of minute 'pores' (hence the name) through which it can poke its nematocysts. If it touches bare skin *millepora* can produce an uncomfortable burning itchy sting with swelling and, in severe cases, associated nausea and vomiting.

First aid – stinging coral
- Apply cold packs for ten minutes. Reapply if skin pain persists.

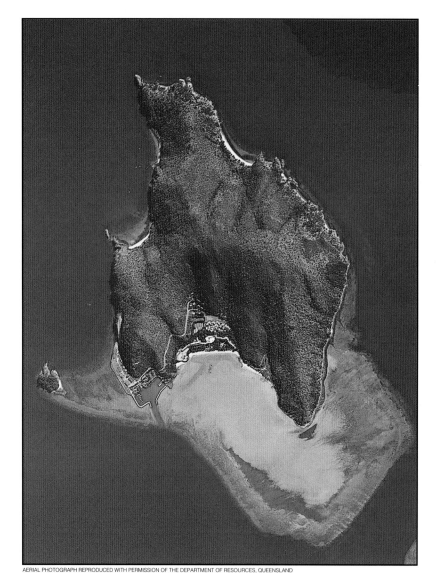

Hayman Island (see map C13), the most northerly island of the Whitsundays.

A BIRD'S-EYE VIEW
OF THE WHITSUNDAYS

The striking appearance of the Whitsundays has seldom failed to impress visitors to the islands. The first recorded thoughts about the area by European man were those of Lieutenant James Cook who, in June 1770, felt moved to name the group after that day on the religious calendar when he discovered them – Whit Sunday. Cook was taken both with the appearance of the islands, with their 'woods and lawns that looked green and pleasant' and with the abundance of anchorages they seemed to afford.

To the mariner or mainland traveller today the same lofty peaks rise abruptly from a turquoise sea, proud vestiges of a coastal mountain range that relinquished its hold on the Queensland coast when sea level rose at the end of the last ice age, some ten thousand years ago.

The Whitsundays are no less impressive when viewed from above. Bathed in the afternoon sun their voluptuous green hills glow against a background of deep blue, their margins iridescent green, their shorelines often dazzling white.

This chapter gives you an aerial tour of the islands. It begins at Hook Island, at the magnificent twin fjords, Macona and Nara inlets; thence it proceeds westabout around Hook Island, past Butterfly Bay, around and through the Hook Passage (between Hook and Whitsunday islands) and southwards along the west side of Whitsunday Island. It continues anti-clockwise right around this largest island of the group, thence east to Border Island. From Border it proceeds southwards to Haslewood, Lindeman, Shaw, Keyser, Thomas, Goldsmith, Linné and, finally, to the bottom of the Cumberland Island chain, finishing at Brampton Island.

The aerials cover some of the remotest and most peaceful retreats of these Barrier Reef Marine Park continental islands. Sailors, divers, campers and resort visitors alike will find that these pictures reveal secrets usually discovered only after many years of first-hand experience, painstakingly gained.

A few notes about the photographs

Most of the photographs were taken at mid-tide one clear sunny afternoon in December. The scale varies from about 1:28 000 to 1:31 000.

Each photograph has been numbered to correspond as nearly as possible with a sketch map in the section that follows this one; the number of the corresponding sketch map is given at the lower right-hand corner.

At the top of each photograph is the name of the island or islands pictured and the approximate geographic centre of the photograph, in latitude and longitude. Numbers of adjacent photographs are indicated, where appropriate, at the sides.

NARA INLET and MACONA INLET (C10)
HOOK ISLAND 10°09'S, 148°55'E

C11a

C11

C17

See map C10

Nara and Macona inlets are two fjord-like indentations on the southern side of Hook Island. They make magnificent anchorages for small ships, being deeply embayed and surrounded by lofty hills. In these hills have been found a number of shelters used by Aboriginal people in the distant past; some shelters have paintings on their walls and have yielded shell remnants dating back some eight thousand years. Park rangers have constructed a track to one such shelter deep in Nara Inlet, on the eastern side (see map C10 for the exact location).

FALSE NARA INLET (C11)
HOOK ISLAND 20°10'S, 148°55'E   **C12**

NARA/STONEHAVEN (C11a)
HOOK ISLAND 20°08'S, 148°54'E

See map C11

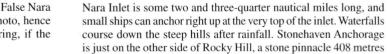

C10   *See maps C10 & C12*

The entrance to Nara Inlet is sometimes confused with False Nara Inlet, which is the indentation on the left side of the photo, hence its name. False Nara has some good coral for exploring, if the weather is suitably light, but it isn't a good anchorage.

Nara Inlet is some two and three-quarter nautical miles long, and small ships can anchor right up at the very top of the inlet. Waterfalls course down the steep hills after rainfall. Stonehaven Anchorage is just on the other side of Rocky Hill, a stone pinnacle 408 metres in height.

HOOK ISLAND NORTH-WEST (C12)
HOOK/LANGFORD/BIRD/BLACK/HAYMAN ISLANDS 20°05'S, 148°53'E   **C13**

C14/15

AERIAL PHOTOGRAPH REPRODUCED WITH PERMISSION OF THE DEPARTMENT OF RESOURCES, QUEENSLAND   **C11a**   *See map C12*

Hayman Island's fringing reef has a deceptive bulge, almost at its southern extremity, which has caught many yachts unawares. Black Island (centre), sometimes referred to as 'Bali Hai', has an extensive fringing reef. Langford Island (left) with its large kidney-shaped reef, is a popular day-visitor spot, affording good snorkelling. Bird Island sits at the western edge of the Langford Island reef and offers divers a good drift dive, if conditions are sufficiently calm.

HOOK ISLAND NORTH/EAST (C14/15)
HOOK ISLAND 20°05'S, 148°57'E

C12

C16

See map C14/15

The northern side of Hook Island affords some of the best diving in the Whitsundays in a series of bays, the largest of which is Butterfly Bay, a very popular anchorage. Reef development in many of these northern bays is excellent, fostered by the strong tidal currents that sweep around the island and flood southwards towards Mackay and Broad Sound. The water is frequently turbulent around Pinnacle Point (the north-eastern extremity of the island), and divers in the water along these shores must watch out for swift currents. All of the area, from the western side of Butterfly Bay to The Wood Pile (the northern extremity of the island) is a Marine National Park 'B' Zone, a 'look but don't take' zone (fishing and shell collecting are prohibited).

SABA BAY (C16)
HOOK ISLAND 20°07'S, 148°56'E   C14/15

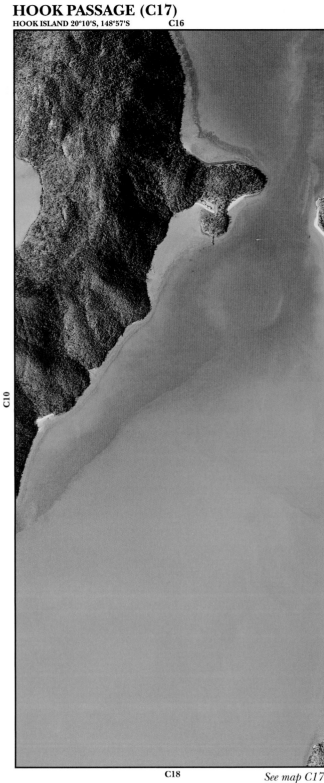

C17   *See map C16*

Saba Bay, on the eastern side of Hook Island, is exposed to the prevailing south-east winds and is thus frequently not habitable as an anchorage. When the wind is from the north, however, it offers a beautiful, isolated anchorage with some excellent coral reef.

HOOK PASSAGE (C17)
HOOK ISLAND 20°10'S, 148°57'S   C16

C18   *See map C17*

In the narrow passage between Hook and Whitsunday islands is an underwater observatory where visitors can watch marine life going about its business on the local fringing reef. The water is not always as clear as it might be here due to swift currents, but the observatory offers a unique opportunity to view fish at close quarters.

MAY'S BAY and DUGONG INLET (C18)

WHITSUNDAY ISLAND 20°13'S, 148°57'E

C17

See map C18

The north-western side of Whitsunday Island is surrounded by very shallow waters that harbour some isolated coral heads; navigators beware and keep well over towards Hook Island. At the bottom of the photo is Dugong Inlet, in Cid Harbour. The small bay on the left side of the peninsula at the bottom left is May's Bay, a peaceful anchorage. Peter Bay, with its labyrinth of coral reef, on the eastern side of Whitsunday Island, can be seen at the top right.

CID HARBOUR (C19)
WHITSUNDAY ISLAND 20°16'S, 148°57'E

C18

C20

See map C19

Cid Harbour is a favourite spot in the Whitsundays because it offers protection from virtually all winds, has beautiful sand beaches, campsites and a good anchorage. A sawmill was operated here in the late 19th century. Swift currents flow through the narrow passage between Cid Island and Loriard Point (bottom).

GULNARE INLET (C20)
WHITSUNDAY ISLAND 20°19'S, 148°56'E

C19

C24

C22

See map C20

Just south of Cid Harbour are Yvonne's Coves, which offer some good reef-fossicking. The deep indentation further to the south-east is Gulnare Inlet, a popular all-weather anchorage with quite shallow water near the entrance; it is safest to enter on a rising tide. Gulnare Inlet cuts deeply into Whitsunday Island and has extensive mangrove creeks that provide territory for exploration in a dinghy. Henning Island (middle-lower portion of the picture) has some good beaches.

GULNARE INLET and FITZALAN PASSAGE (C20a)
WHITSUNDAY ISLAND 20°18'S, 148°58'E
C20

See map C20

It is possible, at high tide, to go in a dinghy for many miles up Gulnare Inlet, following its tortuous course through mangrove creeks. Remains of an old timber-getter's tramway may be seen in one such creek; the tramway was built to move pines from the hills down to the shore, from where the logs were floated back to Cid Harbour for sawing.

Fitzalan Passage (bottom right) is a very narrow gut, with Fitzalan Island in the middle, between Whitsunday Island and Hamilton Island. Currents run swiftly in this passage, and the water may be rough and churning when the trade winds from the south-east vie with a southwards-flooding tide.

DENT and HAMILTON ISLANDS (C22)

DENT and HAMILTON ISLANDS 20°22'S, 148°57'E

C20 & C20a

AERIAL PHOTOGRAPH REPRODUCED WITH PERMISSION OF THE DEPARTMENT OF RESOURCES, QUEENSLAND

See map C22

The face of Hamilton Island (right) was transformed in the early to mid-1980s when the largest island resort in Australia was constructed there. What was a narrow channel blasted through the reef on the north-western side is now a completely dredged boat harbour with floating marina, one of the busiest yachting centres on the Queensland coast. The jet runway has changed the geography of the south-west corner of the island, reclaiming much of Crab Bay for an airport that is now the major trans-shipment point of the Whitsundays.

Dent Island (left) has one of the lighthouses that guide shipping through the Whitsunday Passage. At the upper right of the photo is Fitzalan Island, which sits in the narrow passage between Hamilton and Whitsunday islands, where the waters can become very disturbed when the wind and tidal currents are moving in opposite directions.

TURTLE BAY (C24)
WHITSUNDAY ISLAND 20°19'S, 148°59'E

Turtle Bay is a beautiful complex of small bays on the southern side of Whitsunday Island. *See map C24*

CHANCE BAY (C25)
WHITSUNDAY ISLAND 20°19'S, 149°03'E

Chance Bay on the south-eastern side of Whitsunday Island comprises two beautiful, isolated sandy bays which offer those cruising the Whitsundays a real chance for solitude. *See map C25*

SOLWAY PASSAGE and WHITEHAVEN BEACH (C26)

WHITSUNDAY ISLAND 20°18'S, 149°04'E

C27

C25

C31

See map C26

Solway Passage is a deep channel separating Whitsunday Island and Haslewood Island, and when the tide is flooding south against a fresh south-east trade wind, this passage may be quite 'spectacular', with overfalls, cresting waves and wild whirlpools. Those in yachts must use caution in such conditions. Whitehaven Beach, a magnificent 6-kilometre strip of pure white silica sand, stretches northwards along the east side of Whitsunday Island. This is a favourite destination in the Whitsundays for campers, day-trippers and sailors alike.

Teague Island, immediately south of Solway Passage, is separated from Haslewood Island by a very narrow channel which is passable but not recommended (prohibited for bareboats) if travelling to Waite Bay, Haslewood Island.

HILL INLET (C27)
WHITSUNDAY ISLAND 20°16'S, 149°02'E

C28

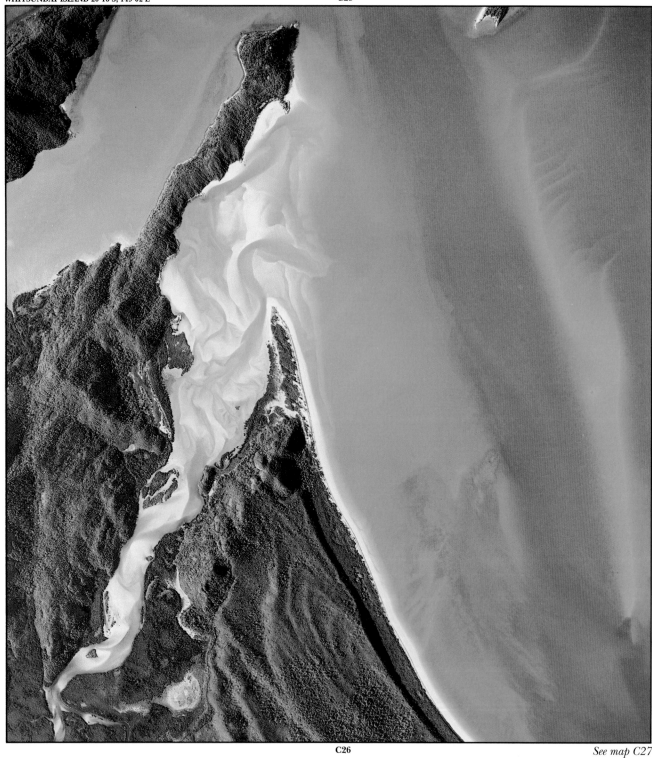

C26

See map C27

Hill Inlet, with its shifting sands and mangroves, is of major importance to the local ecology, being a major source of food for fish. It is an ideal spot for trailer sailers, which can penetrate deeply into the inlet at high tide. There may be sandflies and mosquitoes, so be prepared. Tongue Bay, immediately north, provides anchorage for keel yachts.

WHITSUNDAY NORTH-EAST (C28)

WHITSUNDAY ISLAND 20°14'S, 149°00'E

C18

C27   *See map C28*

Apostle Bay (bottom) and Peter Bay (top) provide anchorage in the vicinity of Whitehaven Beach, good alternatives to anchoring at Whitehaven itself, which is sometimes uncomfortably 'rolly'.

BORDER ISLAND (C29)
BORDER ISLAND and DUMBELL ISLET 20°10'S, 149°01'E

See map C29

Border Island is one of the outlying islands of the Whitsunday Group. Cateran Bay, on its north shore, offers a degree of solitude and very good fringing coral reef. The anchorage is surrounded by hills which produce sharp gusts when the wind is fresh, and the bay may be 'rolly' as swell is refracted around the north-eastern point of the island. The area for 100 metres all around Border Island is classified Marine National Park 'B', a 'look-but-don't-take' zone; fishing and shell collecting are prohibited.

WINDY BAY and WAITE BAY (C31)
HASLEWOOD ISLAND and LUPTON ISLAND 20°17'S, 149°06'E

C26

See map C31

Haslewood Island and Lupton Island are separated by a narrow passage which dries at low tide, exposing a massive fringing reef, which can provide endless hours of good reef-fossicking. When the tide comes in, an abundance of marine life can be seen swarming back onto the reef – turtles, fishes, and reef sharks. Waite Bay is on the south side, Windy Bay on the north, the latter so called because during the trade winds season it is not often quiescent. This area, including Waite Bay and right around the eastern side of Lupton Island to the northern tip of Haslewood Island, is classified Marine National Park 'B'. No fishing or shell collecting.

LINDEMAN ISLAND (S1)
LINDEMAN ISLAND and SEAFORTH ISLAND 20°27'S, 149°03'E

S2

See map S1

Lindeman Island, the home of one of the earliest resorts of the Whitsundays, now has a modern resort with a nine-hole golf links. Most of the island is a Queensland national park, and there are some excellent graded tracks, including one to the top of Mt Oldfield, from where magnificent views of the surrounding islands are available. Little Lindeman, immediately north, is connected to Lindeman by a drying fringing reef, and passage between the two islands is not possible for yachts.

SHAW ISLAND NORTH (S2)

LINDEMAN, SHAW, MAHER and BAYNHAM ISLANDS 20°27'S, 149°05'E

S1

S3

See map S2

As one moves south through the Whitsundays the tides become greater, and the narrow passage between Shaw Island (centre) and Lindeman Island is subject to very strong currents. Neck Bay is a beautiful anchorage, with an extensive fringing reef and sand beach lined with whispering casuarinas.

SHAW ISLAND SOUTH (S3)

SHAW, SEAFORTH and LINDEMAN ISLANDS 20°29'S, 149°03'E

S1

S3a

See map S3

Shown are the western side of Shaw Island (right), Brush Island (centre), Yellow Rock (above Brush Island), Seaforth Island (upper left) and the south-west corner of Lindeman Island (top). Yachts proceeding south along the west side of Shaw Island will find the deepest water by passing between Shaw Island and Yellow Rock or Brush Island.

SHAW ISLAND SOUTH and KEYSER ISLAND (S3a)
SHAW ISLAND, KEYSER ISLAND, and LONG ROCK 20°31'S, 149°04'E

See maps S3 and S4

The south side of Shaw Island offers peaceful anchorage in northerly winds.

SHAW ISLAND (S5)
SHAW and TRIANGLE ISLANDS 20°29'S, 149°06'E

See map S5

The south-eastern side of Shaw Island has several pleasant, isolated anchorages in the right weather conditions.

THOMAS ISLAND (S6)
KEYSER ISLAND, LONG ROCK and THOMAS ISLAND 20°32'S, 149°06'E   S5

S3a

See map S6

Thomas Island (bottom) is a beautiful small island towards the southern reaches of the Whitsundays, and it is thus less frequently visited by yachts sailing from Shute Harbour. It offers safe anchorage (although the northern anchorage can be 'swelly') and has some beautiful sand beaches. Keyser Island (top left) is rarely visited and makes a good daytime stopoff when winds are from the north.

GOLDSMITH ISLAND (S9)
GOLDSMITH ISLAND 20°40'S, 149°09'E

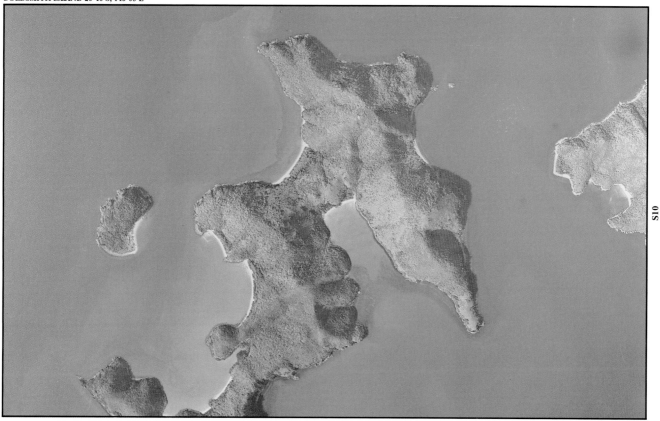

Goldsmith Island has a series of relatively remote anchorages, peaceful in the right conditions.

See map S9

LINNE ISLAND (S10)
LINNE, GOLDSMITH and TINSMITH ISLANDS 20°41'S, 149°10'E

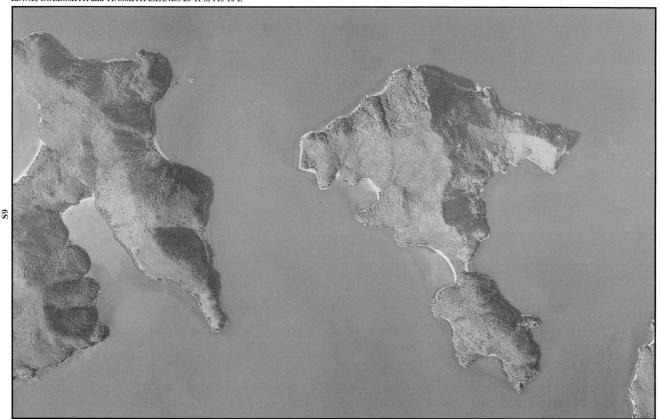

Linné Island (right) is infrequently visited and can be a pleasant lunch-time stopover.

See map S10

BRAMPTON ISLAND (S11)
BRAMPTON and CARLISLE ISLANDS 20°49'S, 149°15'E

See map S11

Brampton is one of the resort islands of the Cumberlands and is towards the southern end of the island chain. It is a national park and has some excellent graded walking tracks offering some of the most picturesque scenery in the Whitsundays. Carlisle Island (top right) can be reached at low tide by walking across the channel between the islands. It offers opportunities for campers seeking some escape.

ANCHORAGES IN THE WHITSUNDAYS

The following pages contain sketch maps and sailing directions covering the principal anchorages of the Whitsundays and some of the adjacent mainland from Bowen in the north to Mackay in the south. They will be immensely helpful to anyone making their way around the area, and they will provide an interesting, accurate souvenir record for others.

For convenience the maps are presented in four groups:

Group	Map	Location covered
Northern	N1–N15	Bowen to Airlie Beach
Central	C1–C33	Airlie Beach to Lindeman Island
Southern	S1–S19	Lindeman Island to Mackay
Reef	R1	Hook/Hardy/Line/Bait Reefs

Aerial photographs

Preceding the sketch maps is a section entitled 'A Bird's-eye view of the Whitsundays' which contains aerial photographs of many of the anchorages. These communicate a wealth of information at a single glance and are very helpful when used in conjunction with the maps. If there is an aerial photo of the area covered by a particular sketch map, this is noted (along with a page number and photo reference) at the lower right-hand corner of the map. The photographs are also referenced to the sketch maps.

A word of caution

The maps in this book have been prepared largely from vertical aerial photographs. Every attempt has been made to make them as accurate as possible using other maps and charts as cross-references. However, the user should be aware that the maps have not been created with sophisticated cartographic machinery, and some minor displacement errors may be present. The maps are not intended to be used for navigation but as a visual aid to pilotage in conjunction with the official Hydrographic Office charts of the area (chiefly AUS 252, 253, 254, 825).

We would like to think that in some instances the sketch maps may be more useful than official small-scale charts, but you are cautioned that you should *always have the largest-scale-available official Hydrographic chart at hand for navigation and reference.* The publisher and the author do not accept responsibility for errors or omissions or the consequences of these.

THE AREA COVERED

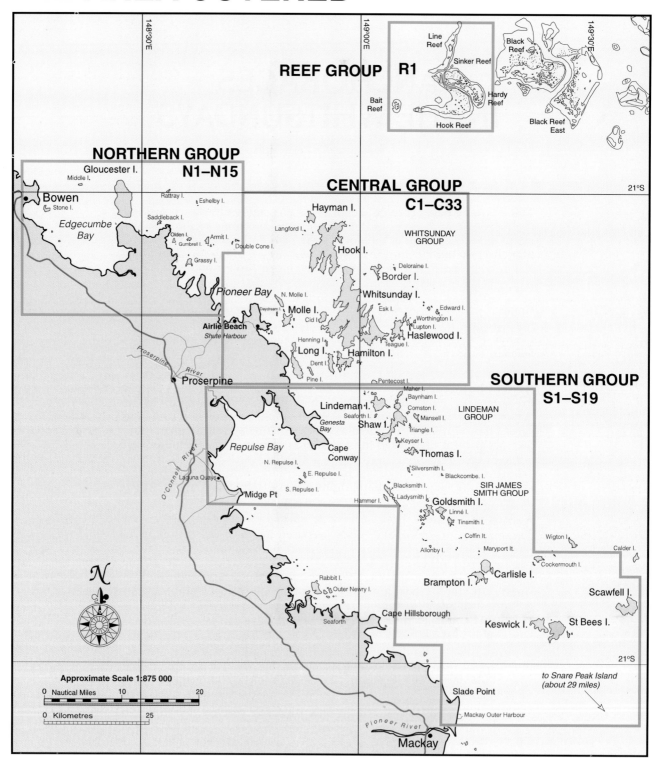

REEF GROUP **R1**

Line Reef
Sinker Reef
Bait Reef
Hardy Reef
Hook Reef
Black Reef
Black Reef East

NORTHERN GROUP
N1–N15

Gloucester I.
Middle I.
Bowen
Stone I.
Rattray I.
Eshelby I.
Edgecumbe Bay
Saddleback I.
Olden I.
Armit I.
Gumbrell I.
Double Cone I.
Grassy I.

CENTRAL GROUP
C1–C33

Hayman I.
Langford I.
WHITSUNDAY GROUP
Hook I.
Deloraine I.
Border I.
Whitsunday I.
Esk I.
Edward I.
Worthington I.
Lupton I.
Haslewood I.
Pioneer Bay
N. Molle I.
Daydream I.
Molle I.
Cid I.
Airlie Beach
Shute Harbour
Henning I.
Long I.
Hamilton I.
Dent I.
Pine I.
Teague I.
Pentecost I.
Proserpine

SOUTHERN GROUP
S1–S19

Maher I.
Baynham I.
Lindeman I.
Comston I.
Seaforth I.
Mansell I.
LINDEMAN GROUP
Genesta Bay
Shaw I.
Triangle I.
Keyser I.
Repulse Bay
Thomas I.
Cape Conway
N. Repulse I.
Silversmith I.
Blackcombe I.
E. Repulse I.
Blacksmith I.
Ladysmith I.
SIR JAMES SMITH GROUP
Laguna Quays
S. Repulse I.
Goldsmith I.
Midge Pt
Hammer I.
Linné I.
Tinsmith I.
Coffin It.
Wigton I.
Calder I.
Allonby I.
Maryport It.
Cockermouth I.
Rabbit I.
Carlisle I.
Outer Newry I.
Scawfell I.
Brampton I.
Seaforth
Cape Hillsborough
Keswick I.
St Bees I.

Approximate Scale 1:875 000

0 Nautical Miles 10 20

0 Kilometres 25

to Snare Peak Island (about 29 miles)

Slade Point
Mackay Outer Harbour
Pioneer River
Mackay

148°30'E
149°00'E
149°30'E
21°S
21°S

N

About the sketch maps

Map sequence

The area covered has been divided into north, central southern and reef sections, and the maps have a letter prefix 'N', 'C', 'S' and 'R' accordingly (there is only one map in the 'R' section). The maps are presented from north to south, as illustrated below, according to the way many yachts circulate among the (central) islands. A few maps added more recently, e.g. Laguna Quays, the Repulse Islands, have been added on at the end of the southern group to avoid upsetting the existing numbering system.

At the top, bottom and sides of most maps an adjoining map reference is given, e.g. 'joins map N15' (where maps are contiguous) or 'next map N15' (where maps are not contiguous). The sides of contiguous maps may not necessarily butt squarely against each other.

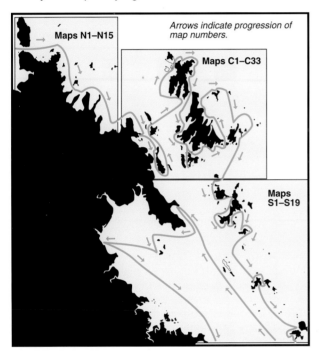

Maps N1–N15

Arrows indicate progression of map numbers.

Maps C1–C33

Maps S1–S19

Scale

The scale varies from approximately 1:20 000 to 1:32 000. It may be useful to note that on a 1:30 000 chart a 1 millimetre line represents a distance of 30 metres. Every attempt has been made to maintain the appropriate scale of charted objects, but this is not always practicable (as in the case of buoys, and the like).

Soundings, elevations, distances

Depths and elevations are in metres. Australia uses metric measures, and new Hydrographic Office charts are coming out in metric form; unfortunately, the present charts for the Whitsundays are imperial (fathoms and feet), which is a possible cause of confusion when using this book. Depths on the sketch maps are in metres and tenths of metres (e.g. 3_4 is 3.4 metres). Elevations of principal landmarks (in metres) are shown in parentheses. Distances over water continue to be measured in nautical miles (generally referred to as 'miles' in this book) in spite of our metric

system for most other measurements. This is simply because the foundation of our navigation system is the concept of angles and arcs subtended by them; one nautical mile is the distance on the earth's surface subtended by one minute of angle (latitude) at the earth's centre. One exception to use of nautical miles on the sketch maps is those cases where a rock, shoal or island is only a short distance away, for example 100 metres, in which cases a figure in metres is easier to comprehend than '0.054 mile' would be.

Anchorage symbols

Anchorages are noted by ⚓ ⚓ ⚓ ⚓

Numbers are used to differentiate anchorages where there are several in close proximity. In some cases anchor symbols are not numbered (where there is no ambiguity, or where maps overlap and the unnumbered anchorage is discussed on a different page). A small anchor denotes a temporary anchorage provided the weather is suitable; these are rarely suitable overnight anchorages. An anchor with a black circle and white numeral indicates an all-weather anchorage (offering protection in winds from any direction).

Wind diagrams

The wind directions and strengths (in knots) in which an anchorage is considered habitable (with some degree of comfort) are shown with arrows around an 8-point compass rose. An infilled blue arrow indicates that the anchorage offers protection in winds from that direction; the number next to the arrow indicates in how much wind it will be 'comfortable'. White arrows without numbers indicate that not a lot of protection is available, i.e. if it's blowing more than 10 knots from that direction, the anchorage may not be comfortable.

GPS positions in the Whitsundays

The advent of the Global Positioning System brought some headaches for chartmakers. The basic surveys for many Australian charts date back to the last century, and the datums of individual charts vary. Thus, charts for the Whitsundays carry a note as to corrections that need to be applied to positions read from a GPS receiver before they can be plotted on the chart. In some cases GPS positions cannot be accurately plotted. No reference to GPS positions is made in this book, among other reasons because the sketch maps in this book are *not* designed for navigation and should not be used for navigating.

Reef protection buoys

Reef protection buoys ▲ have been installed in a number of bays where coral damage has been a problem. They delineate no-anchor areas, i.e. anchoring inshore of an imaginary straight line between the buoys is prohibited.

Moorings

Park managers have embarked on a programme of installing public moorings to facilitate reef appreciation particularly in areas where no-anchoring buoys have been necessary. These moorings have coloured labels with instructions for their use (e.g. size of vessel, time limit). There are also a number of private commercial moorings in use by charter operators, who probably don't object to yachts

General legend

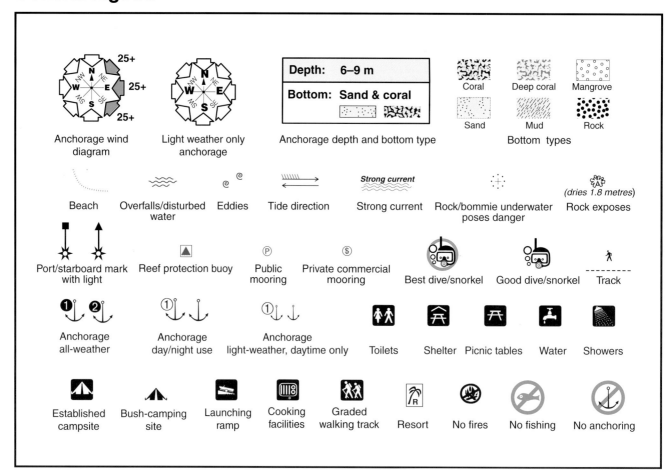

picking them up provided it is not at a time when they wish to use them themselves. If you are on a private mooring, never leave the yacht unattended while tied to one, and relinquish it immediately when asked to do so .

A note on names

Work by a local historian, Ray Blackwood, has shown that a number of placenames in use in the Whitsundays are incorrect; for example, Abel Point, White Bay (Haslewood Island), Arkhurst Island, and others). These found their way onto the charts and some local road signs by accident of fate. However, it is anticipated that, in the not-too-distant future, they will be officially corrected by the authorities concerned. With this in mind, an effort has been made to amend the maps in this book to show correct names. Thus, readers may wonder at such spellings as Abell Point, Akhurst Island, Waite Bay, and so on, which are actually the right names rather than those in common use. (The case of Abell Point is further complicated by the fact that the company that owns the marina (Abel Point Marina (Whitsundays) Pty Ltd) was incorporated in that style, and thus this name will undoubtedly remain confusing for some years to come.

Caution on use of maps

Although every effort has been made to make the maps and descriptions given in this book as accurate as possible, there may be errors, including some displacement errors in the maps (caused by using uncorrected aerial photographs). The maps cannot, therefore, be used for position fixing. The publisher and the author of this book have taken pains to insure that all information is accurate; however, no responsibility can be accepted for any inaccuracies in the maps or other information, nor can any responsibility be taken for the consequences of any inaccuracies.

THE NORTHERN GROUP

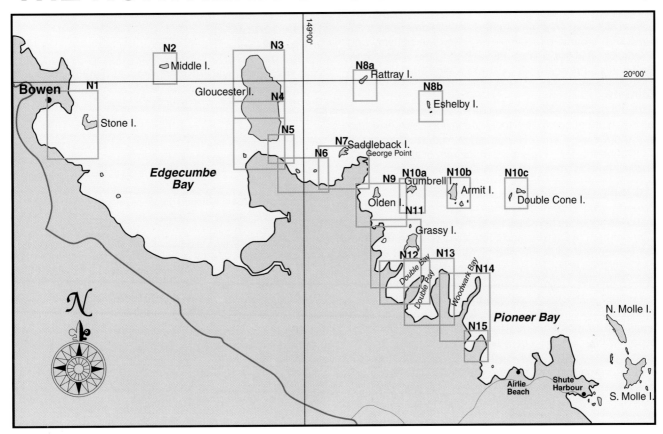

Map index

Anchorage index

Bowen

Bowen is a seaport town situated 1165 kilometres by rail north of Brisbane, exactly midway between Mackay and Townsville. It is the closest official port to the Whitsunday Group, a 40-nautical-mile sail from Airlie Beach.

Climate

Situated in the dry tropics, Bowen's average annual rainfall is just under one metre, most of it falling between January and March. Temperatures range from a mean maximum of about 28.5°C to a mean minimum of about 20.4°C. The average relative humidity is sixty-five per cent.

Industry

Bowen's major enterprise is small-crop farming – tomatoes, mangoes, rockmelons, capsicums, chillies and watermelons. Fifty per cent of Queensland's tomato crop is produced in the Bowen district; it has one of Australia's most efficient rural industries and is known as 'the salad bowl of the north'.

Bowen Shire is a significant cattle-producer, and the freezing works is the major secondary industry of the area. The Bowen Coke Works supplies Mt Isa Mines. There is a small salt evaporation industry and a growing fishing industry with a fleet of about twenty-five trawlers permanently based at Bowen Harbour. Large quantities of prawns, crabs and reef fish are processed and exported.

The port of Bowen has been made redundant by the huge coal export facility at Abbot Point, about twenty-four kilometres to the north.

History

Founded in 1861, Bowen was the first white settlement north of Rockhampton. It was to be the base for the complete exploration and settlement of northern Queensland. George Dalrymple, whose name is now on the point that juts out south-east from the harbour, made an epic trek overland from Rockhampton during a wet season to link up with sea parties that were sent to establish the settlement. Bowen was the first governor of Queensland; Port Denison was named after the then governor of New South Wales.

General

Bowen's 'front door' on the world is the harbour and a pleasant esplanade of shady Moreton Bay figs, she-oaks and coconut palms which overlook it. Behind is a backdrop of attractive coastal hills. Unspoilt beach areas line the northern side of Cape Edgecumbe, which is the promontory on which Bowen is situated.

Edgecumbe Bay yawns for some 19 kilometres to the south and east, and the lofty Gloucester Island can be seen on the distant eastern horizon. Along the mainland coast to Gloucester Passage, this whole expanse of bay is lined with beaches and creeks which are excellent fishing and picnic grounds. They are popular haunts for hundreds of small boats at weekends and during holidays.

Bowen has an atmosphere of an unhurried and unspoilt northern Queensland town.

Bowen services
(Area code 077)

Air Sea Rescue

Call sign VMR487, 8.00 am to 5.00 pm 2182 kHz, 2112 kHz, 2524 kHz, 27 MHz and VHF channels 16, 21. Tel. 861 061.

Chandlery

Bowen Boat Services (next to Air Sea Rescue). Tel. 862 612.

Fuel

Pioneer Seafoods pontoon.
Bowen Fisherman's Seafood Co. pontoon, by arrangement.

Mooring enquiries

Queensland Transport, Bowen Boat Harbour. Tel. 861 966.

Slipway

Bowen Slipway (Boat Harbour). Facilities include water sprayer and sandblasting. Tel. 861 760.

Water

Public pontoon adjacent to the yacht club and at Pioneer Seafoods pontoon; by arrangement at Bowen Fisherman's Seafood Co.

Yacht club

The North Queensland Cruising Yacht Club welcomes visiting yachtsmen. Tel. 863 490.

The launching ramp on the south-western arm of Bowen boat harbour, with public jetty and pile moorings in the background

The marina of the North Queensland Cruising Yacht Club.

BOWEN BOAT HARBOUR

Bowen Boat Harbour is another of Queensland's man-made harbours that require maintenance to keep them open, which is why itinerant vessels are asked to pay a fee for a berth. It is a very busy little harbour with only 15 berths for casual visitors and a long waiting list for permanents. Itinerants can usually obtain a berth, on an 'as available' basis (berths cannot be booked in advance).

The entrance to the harbour is marked by three pairs of port and starboard beacons on either side of a dredged channel with 1.6 metres depth (on a '0' tide).

The harbour has two arms, the main, south-western arm and a north-eastern arm.

The south-western arm has a variable depth, generally from about 2 to 3 metres. It has 120 moorings in the middle (8 available for casuals), most of which are the pile type. On the south-western side of this arm is a public pontoon jetty, where water may be obtained. A 30-minute time limit applies to hanging alongside the jetty, so there isn't time to go into town leaving a yacht tied up at the pontoon. On this side of the harbour there is also a launching ramp, a small marina belonging to the North Queensland Cruising Yacht Club, a parking lot and an amenities block.

On the north-eastern side of the main arm is a private jetty operated by Pioneer Seafoods (fuel is available here by arrangement; no fish sold to the public); a private pontoon operated by Bowen Fisherman's Seafood Company (diesel and water are available by arrangement; fish available to the public); an amenities block, a launching ramp, a slipway, a chandlery and the office of Queensland Transport, which manages the harbour and where arrangements can be made for berthing (VHF channel 16, telephone (077) 861 966, emergency only telephone 019 493 175).

The North Queensland Cruising Yacht Club is usually open after 4.00 pm. This friendly club welcomes visiting yachties, offering honorary membership for those staying only a short time. Those wishing to use the bar and shower facilities for longer periods should seek temporary membership.

The north-east arm has a depth of 3 to 4 metres and has 26 fore-and-aft moorings (8 are available for casual visitors).

BOWEN BOAT HARBOUR

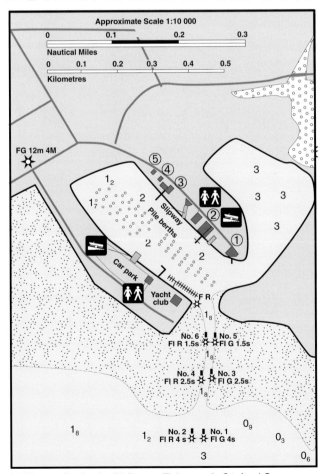

(1) Pioneer Seafoods; (2) Bowen Fisherman's Seafood Company
(3) Queensland Transport; (4) Air-Sea Rescue; (5) Chandlery.

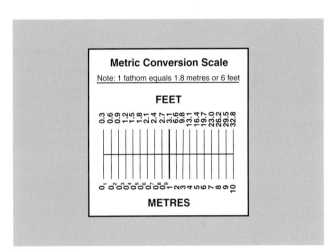

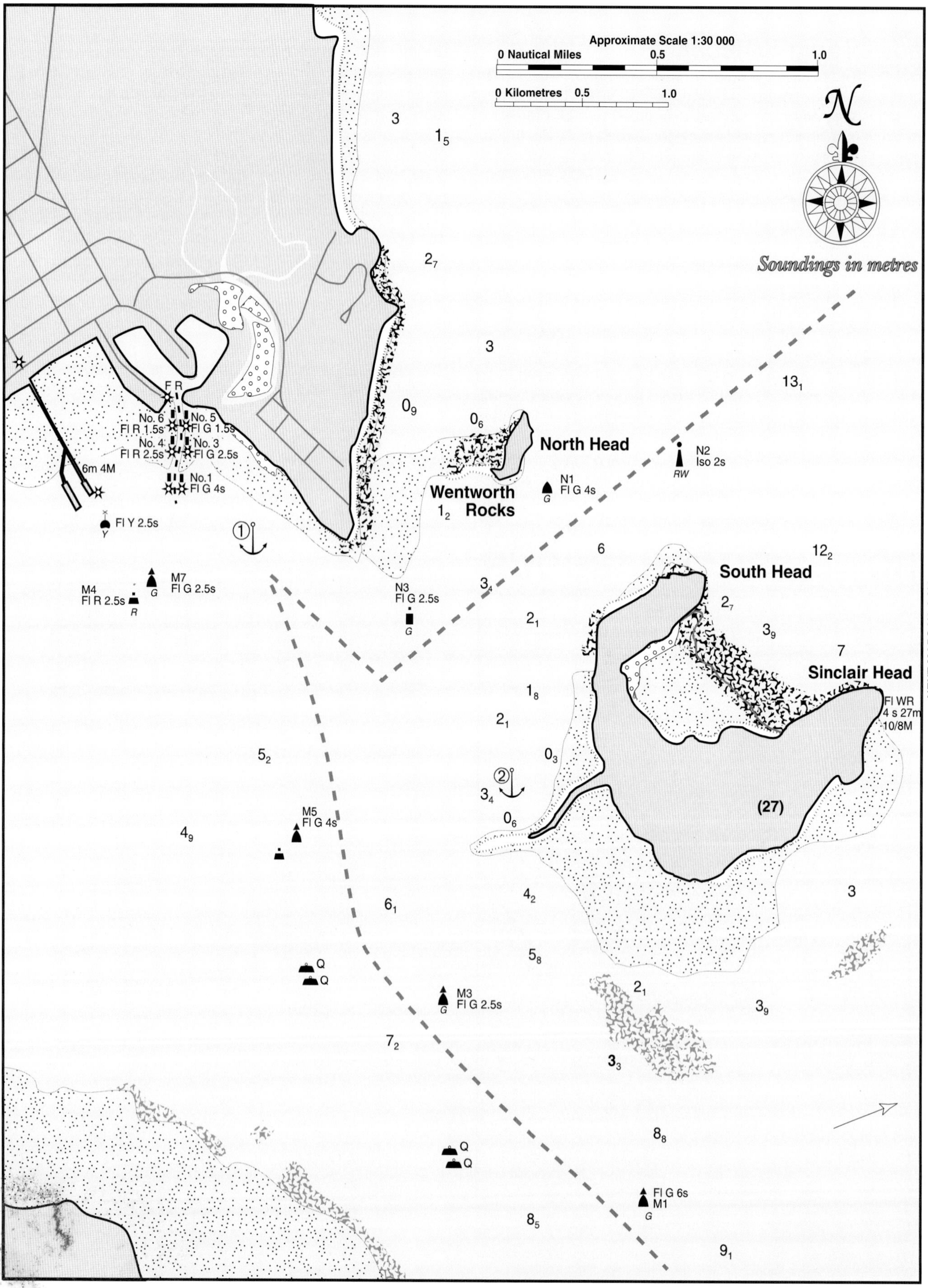

Approximate Scale 1:30 000

0 Nautical Miles 0.5 1.0

0 Kilometres 0.5 1.0

N

Soundings in metres

3

1₅

2₇

3

13₁

F R

No. 6   No. 5
Fl R 1.5s   Fl G 1.5s
No. 4   No. 3
Fl R 2.5s   Fl G 2.5s

0₉

0₆

North Head

N2
Iso 2s
RW

6m 4M

No.1
Fl G 4s

Wentworth Rocks

1₂

N1
Fl G 4s
G

Fl Y 2.5s
Y

①⚓

6

12₂

South Head

2₇

3₉

7

M4   M7
Fl R 2.5s   Fl G 2.5s
R   *G*

N3
Fl G 2.5s
G

3₄

2₁

Sinclair Head

Fl WR
4 s 27m
10/8M

1₈

2₁

5₂

0₃

②⚓
3₄

0₆

(27)

3

4₉

M5
Fl G 4s

4₂

6₁

5₈

2₁

3₉

Q
Q

M3
Fl G 2.5s
G

3₃

7₂

8₈

Q
Q

Fl G 6s
M1
G

8₅

9₁

NEXT MAPS N3 & N4

BOWEN BOAT HARBOUR (N1)

Depth:	2–3 m
Bottom:	Mud

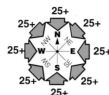

Most yachts will approach Bowen from Gloucester Passage, and the easiest approach is to simply lay a course to the north of Stone Island, a more interesting sail than coming in via the main shipping channel south of Stone Island.

The entrance to the harbour is marked by port and starboard beacons (three pairs) on either side of the dredged channel. Watch the state of the tide before attempting to enter; the channel has a depth of about 1.8 metres at low water.

Berthing is arranged with Queensland Transport, whose office is on the north-eastern side of the main arm (VHF channel 16, telephone (077) 861 966) during office hours 8.00 am–2.30 pm Monday–Thursday and 8.00 am–12.00 pm Friday. There is also a telephone number for use only in emergencies: 019 493 175.

The North Queensland Cruising Yacht Club has a small marina in front of the clubhouse. Enquire at the club regarding availability of berths.

DALRYMPLE POINT (N1)

Depth:	3–6 m
Bottom:	Mud & sand

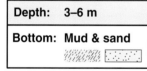 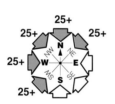

Approach as shown. This anchorage can be swelly.

STONE ISLAND (N1)

Depth:	3–6 m
Bottom:	Sand

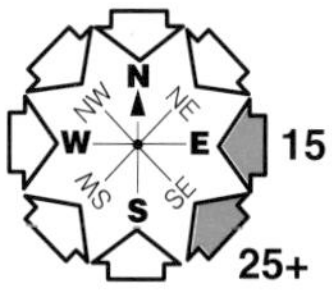

A very good anchorage. It can be swelly, especially as the wind moves more easterly.

MIDDLE ISLAND N2

NOT FOR NAVIGATION: SEE CHART AUS 825

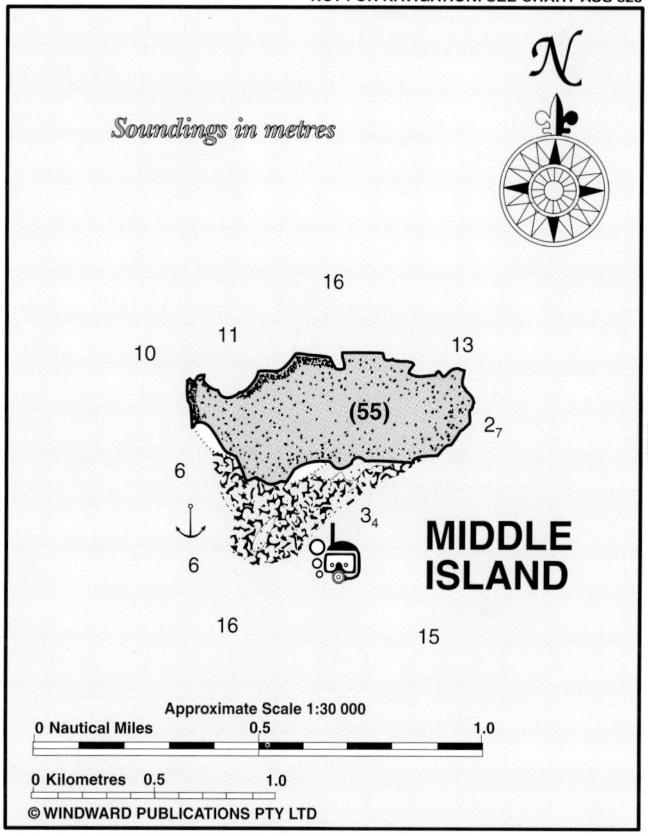

Soundings in metres

NEXT MAP N3

Approximate Scale 1:30 000

0 Nautical Miles   0.5   1.0

0 Kilometres   0.5   1.0

© WINDWARD PUBLICATIONS PTY LTD

MIDDLE ISLAND (N2)

Depth:	6–9 m
Bottom:	Sand & coral

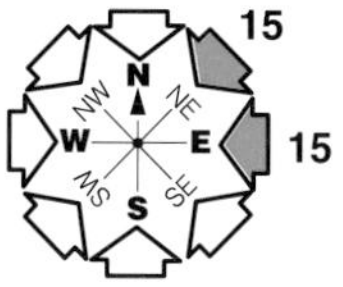

In calm conditions, Middle Island can offer pleasant daytime anchorage. Years ago it boasted some of the most spectacular coral in the district, but cyclone damage has somewhat diminished its lustre. It is still a good snorkelling and diving spot. The reef on the south-south-east side is best. Good fishing.

GLOUCESTER NORTH

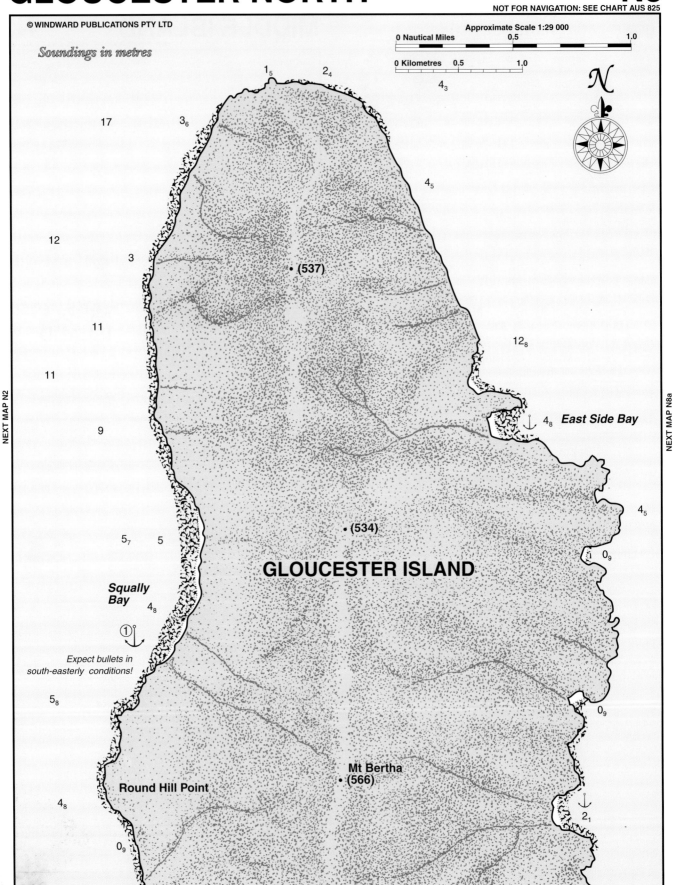

© WINDWARD PUBLICATIONS PTY LTD

Soundings in metres

Approximate Scale 1:29 000

0 Nautical Miles   0.5   1.0

0 Kilometres   0.5   1.0

N

1_5 2_4

3_6 17

4_3

4_5

12

3

• (537)

11

12_8

11

4_8 *East Side Bay*

9

4_5

5_7 5

• (534)

0_9

GLOUCESTER ISLAND

*Squally
Bay*

4_8

①

*Expect bullets in
south-easterly conditions!*

5_8

0_9

Mt Bertha
• (566)

Round Hill Point

4_8

2_1

0_9

NEXT MAP N2

NEXT MAP N8a

JOINS MAP N4

SQUALLY BAY (N3)

Depth:	3–6 m
Bottom:	Mud

Anchorage is good virtually anywhere along the west side of Gloucester Island; there are no real dangers, nor is there much tidal run. Bona Bay is the only good sand anchorage.

Squally Bay, popular with trawlers, lies in between the 566-metre-high Mt Bertha and another 534-metre hill to the north. These hills funnel and accelerate the wind very efficiently, hence the name of the bay, which it lives up to in fresh conditions. This anchorage may not be exactly quiescent; it does offer a long, lonely expanse, and solitude. The holding is good.

GLOUCESTER ISLAND (east side) (N3)

Depth:	2–6 m
Bottom:	Mud & sand

On the eastern side of Gloucester Island are two very nice bays for daytime anchorage in calm conditions. Both offer deserted, sandy beaches. East Side Bay has a lagoon which abounds with crabs and fish.

GLOUCESTER PASSAGE (N4)

Gloucester Passage marks the favoured route to Bowen from the Whitsundays and takes you in between a vast and lofty wind generator, Gloucester Island, and the mainland. The passage has ample water at all tides for vessels drawing up to 1.8 metres; deeper draught vessels should go through on the flood tide. The tidal stream flows easterly on the flood and westerly on the ebb. It may be as swift as 2-3 knots.

The passage is marked with a mixture of IALA lateral marks (laid towards Bowen) and IALA cardinal marks (best water east, west, and so forth). Gloucester Shoal is marked by an IALA east cardinal mark (best water east) at the east end and an IALA west cardinal mark at its west end. Don't attempt to go between the cardinal marks, and give them a healthy berth as this passage has strong currents and constantly shifting sands.

The final marker is a starboard lateral mark; give this a generous berth as there is some shoaling off to the south of it.

Entrance from the east

Entry from the east requires avoidance of a dangerous reef extending north-east from the mainland; keep well to the north. From Saddleback Island, for example, to clear the reef head directly for the south-east corner of Gloucester Island before entering the passage.

When approaching from the south – Jonah Bay or Dingo Beach – head far enough to the north-east to clear the protruding reef, and line up the north side of Saddleback Island with the south-east corner of Gloucester Island (to keep you north of the reef area) before entering.

Proceeding from the east, you will pass two port lateral marks. There is a shoal in the middle of the passage marked by east and west cardinal marks, and it is possible to pass either north or south of it. Shifting sands make it difficult to get unanimous agreement upon which is the best way to go. The general feeling of locals (including those at the North Queensland Cruising Yacht Club) is that the southern route is the easier and preferred route. After passing port beacon No. 4, turn south-west and travel parallel with the shore towards Monte's (Anchorage No. 2). Then hold the port marks on the reef areas (east and north of Shag Islet) to port and the west cardinal mark on Gloucester Shoal to starboard. Turn to the south-west around Shag Island. The final marker is a starboard lateral mark on the edge of the foul ground at the western end of the Passage.

The route north of the shoal is as shown on map N4, turning south-west after the west cardinal mark and proceeding between Passage Islet and the starboard beacon which marks the foul ground at the end of the passage.

Entrance from the west

Head directly for Passage Islet, leaving the 'green' marker to port and giving it a generous berth. Directions are then just the reverse of coming from the east.

Beware the shallow area westwards of the bay, although it can be crossed by shoal-draught vessels at the top of the tide.

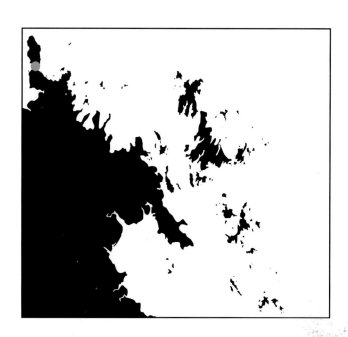

GLOUCESTER PASSAGE WEST

N4

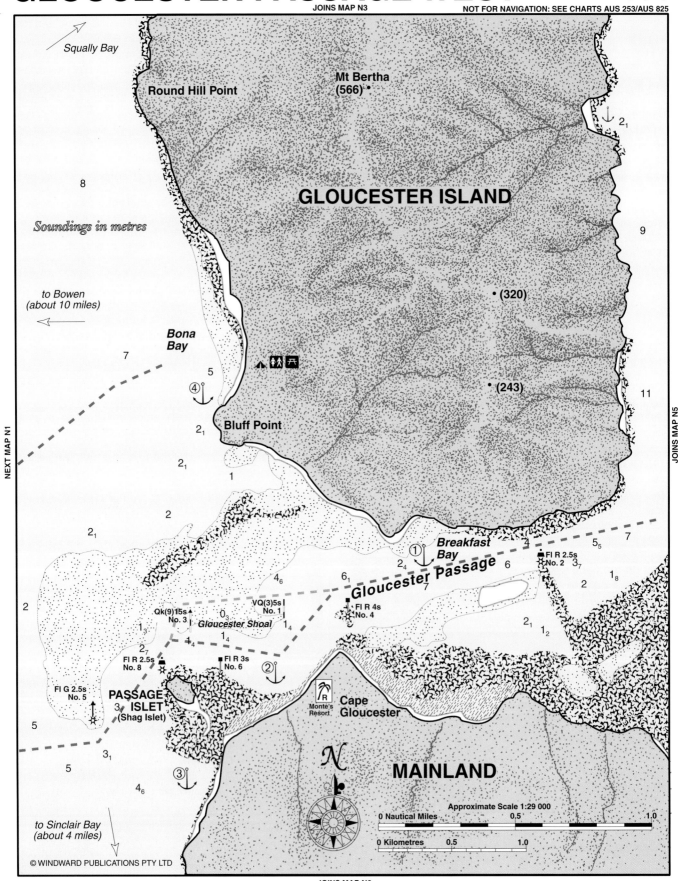

Squally Bay

Round Hill Point

Mt Bertha
(566) •

8

GLOUCESTER ISLAND

Soundings in metres

9

*to Bowen
(about 10 miles)*

• (320)

*Bona
Bay*

7

5

④ ⚓

• (243)

11

Bluff Point

2₁

1

2₁

2

*Breakfast
Bay*

2₁

① ⚓

4

5₅

7

Gloucester Passage

Fl R 2.5s
No. 2 3₇

2₄

6₁

6

1₈

4₆

7

2

Qk(9)15s
No. 3

VQ(3)5s
No. 1

Fl R 4s
No. 4

2₁ 1₂

2

0₃

1₄

Gloucester Shoal

1₄

1₃

4₄

Fl R 2.5s
No. 8

Fl R 3s
No. 6

② ⚓

2₇

Fl G 2.5s
No. 5

**PASSAGE
ISLET**
(Shag Islet)

3₁

⟨R⟩ 🌴
Monte's
Resort.

**Cape
Gloucester**

5

3₁

5

③ ⚓

4₆

𝒩

MAINLAND

*to Sinclair Bay
(about 4 miles)*

Approximate Scale 1:29 000

0 Nautical Miles   0.5   1.0

0 Kilometres   0.5   1.0

© WINDWARD PUBLICATIONS PTY LTD

BREAKFAST BAY (N4)

Depth:	3–5 m
Bottom:	Mud & sand

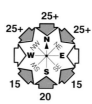

Anchor within 30 metres of the beach.

Breakfast Bay is a popular little bay with an extensive beach leading west to Bona Bay. It has several creeks with freshwater ponds in the wet.

Be sure to wear something on your feet when you go ashore; in the past the beach has had a significant component of silica in the form of broken 'stubbies' (that familiar species of stunted Queensland beer bottle, the contents of which are consumed at breakfast as well as all other times and which a species of stunted yahoo abandons on an otherwise beautiful beach).

MONTE'S RESORT (N4)

Depth:	3–5 m
Bottom:	Sand

Watch out for reef area to the west. This is good anchorage in most weathers except from the north-west and south-west.

Monte's Resort is a very pleasant, relaxed, low-key place where you can eat at the restaurant or buy a barbecue pack and cook for yourself on the facilities provided. You can sit under a shady palm or on the beachfront terrace with a drink, or enjoy a game of pool or tennis.

There is a public bar and restaurant. Limited supplies – groceries, ice, bait and tackle – may be purchased from the shop. Visitor's showers and laundry are also available at a small charge.

The resort itself caters for about 50 people in nine separate self-contained bungalows set in the gardens along the beachfront. Visitors by sea are welcome. It is a popular 19th hole for the North Queensland Cruising Yacht Club, of Bowen.

PASSAGE ISLET (SHAG ISLET) (N4)

Depth:	3–6 m
Bottom:	Sand

Do not attempt passage between Passage Islet, so-called 'Shag Islet' (there are a lot of shags), and the mainland. The anchorage is reached from the western side of the island. Anchor behind the island close to the beach. Watch for isolated bommies just off the beach. If necessary, anchorage may also be found anywhere for a mile or more south.

Shag Islet provides good alternative deeper anchorage

for visiting Monte's Resort. Go by dinghy, keeping close to shore, or take a pleasant walk around the foreshore.

Further anchorages and beaches may be found for several miles to the south, all of which offer good shelter in south-east to east winds up to 25 knots, but beware on-shore south-west winds that often blow during the night (i.e. anchor far enough out). Sinclair Bay also has a small settlement, coconut plantation and excellent beach, but anchor well off, as it is shallow.

BONA BAY (N4)

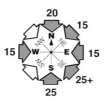

Depth:	3–6 m
Bottom:	Sand

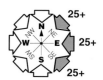

If coming from Gloucester Passage, give the foul ground at the west of the passage a sufficient berth. Although this may be crossed by shoal-draught craft at the top of the tide, it is not the recommended approach, especially without good local knowledge.

Anchorage at Bona Bay can be close to the beach, but leave enough swinging room in case the wind changes to the south-west at night.

During heavy south-east weather this is also a favourite shelter for trawlers.

Bona Bay is popular with Bowen weekenders and particularly at holiday time. It has a lovely beach.

There are death adders about; if you are moving around at night, always carry a torch so that you can see where you are going.

GLOUCESTER PASSAGE E. N5

JOINS MAP N4   NOT FOR NAVIGATION: SEE CHARTS AUS 253/AUS 825

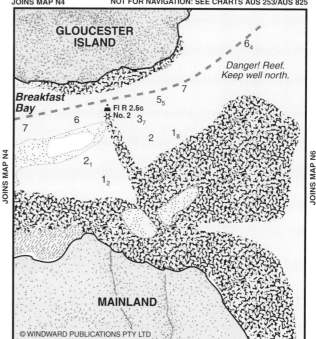

JOINS MAP N6

DINGO BEACH

N6

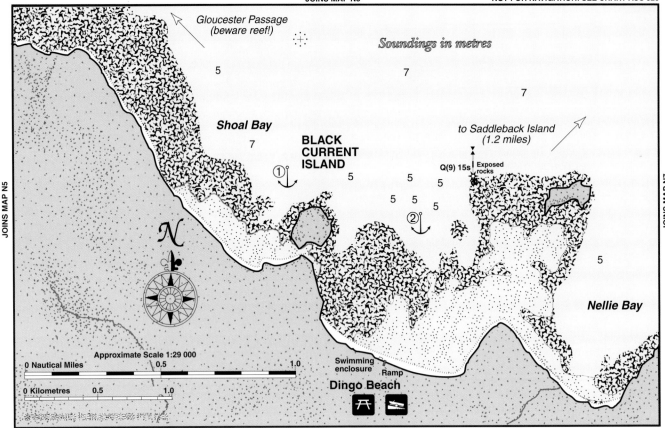

Gloucester Passage (beware reef!)

Soundings in metres

5

7

7

Shoal Bay

7

BLACK CURRENT ISLAND

to Saddleback Island (1.2 miles)

① 5

5

Q(9) 15s | Exposed rocks

5 5 5

② 5 5 5

5

Nellie Bay

N

Approximate Scale 1:29 000

0 Nautical Miles 0.5 1.0

0 Kilometres 0.5 1.0

Swimming enclosure

Ramp

Dingo Beach

DINGO BEACH and NELLIE BAY (N6)

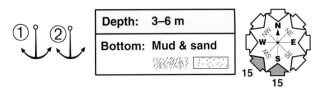

Depth:	3–6 m
Bottom:	Mud & sand

The waters off Dingo Beach are shoal, and there are extensive reef areas, particularly north-east of Nellie Bay. It is not suitable for keel boats. Use care, particularly if your draught is more than 0.7 metres.

This area is probably best known for its fishing. Much of the reef exposes at low tide. Dingo Beach is accessible by road, and it is a very busy spot during holiday periods.

Dingo Beach was so named because of (guess?) the preponderance of dingoes that used to frequent the area.

SADDLEBACK ISLAND (N7)

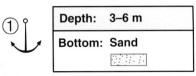

Depth:	3–6 m
Bottom:	Sand

When approaching from George Point, keep well off the point, where there are frequently overfalls. From Gloucester Passage head straight for the northern side of Saddleback to avoid reefs and shoals south-east of the Passage.

Saddleback is not a brilliant anchorage, although the holding is fine. On the southern tip of the island are the remains of a hut which once contained a toilet and emergency supplies, but it was burned down in 1979.

Anchorage is also possible on the south-east to east side of the island in north to north-west winds.

Saddleback has been reported to have a considerable number of death adders on it (which could possibly mean that it's someone's favourite fishing spot, or that there's buried treasure there … or just that there are a large number of death adders).

GEORGE BAY (N7)

Depth:	3–6 m
Bottom:	Sand & coral

The whole area from George Point to Gloucester Passage is subject to quite a large, long swell. Anchorage is possible along much of the whole expanse as far as Dingo Beach, in suitable weather. The deeper bays are less subject to swell; all may be gusty in fresh conditions.

As with many mainland areas, the water around these anchorages is often murky and unsuitable for snorkelling. However, in weather ranging from light to medium, they

GEORGE POINT

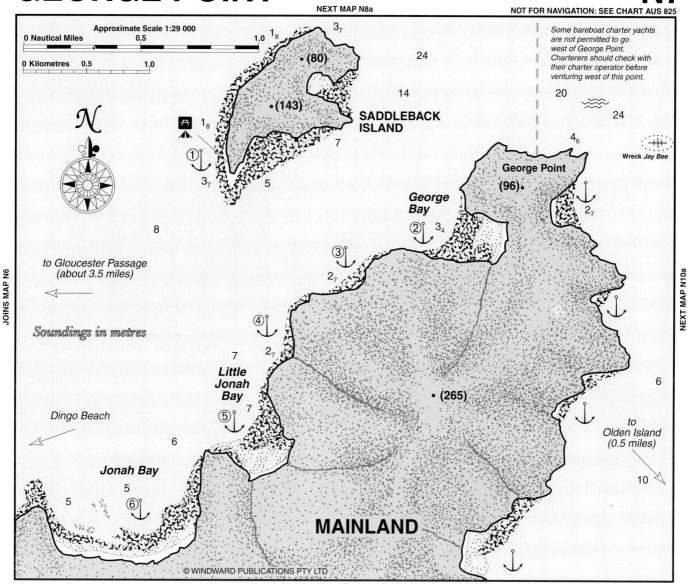

Some bareboat charter yachts are not permitted to go west of George Point. Charterers should check with their charter operator before venturing west of this point.

SADDLEBACK ISLAND

George Point

George Bay

Wreck *Jay Bee*

Little Jonah Bay

Dingo Beach

Jonah Bay

MAINLAND

to Gloucester Passage (about 3.5 miles)

Soundings in metres

to Olden Island (0.5 miles)

Approximate Scale 1:29 000

JOINS MAP N6

NEXT MAP N10a

JOINS MAP N9

---

offer good beach barbecue areas and may constitute 'new territory'. George Bay can be subject to occasional bullets in fresh south-easterly conditions; it starts to get swelly after winds reach 20 knots from the south-east.

SOUTH-WEST OF GEORGE BAY (N7)

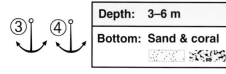

Depth:	3–6 m
Bottom:	Sand & coral

These anchorages are not as protected as George Bay to the north or Little Jonah and Jonah Bay to the south, but in moderate conditions they are quite habitable. They are prone to swelliness.

LITTLE JONAH BAY (N7)

Depth:	3–6 m
Bottom:	Mud & sand

Excellent holding.

JONAH BAY (N7)

Depth:	3–6 m
Bottom:	Mud & sand

Excellent holding.

RATTRAY ISLAND   N8a

NOT FOR NAVIGATION: SEE CHART AUS 825

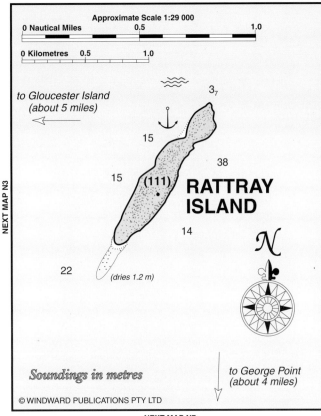

ESHELBY ISLAND   N8b

NOT FOR NAVIGATION: SEE CHART AUS 825

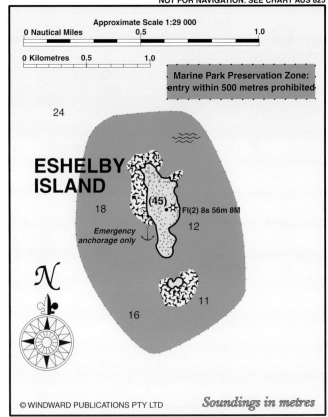

RATTRAY ISLAND (N8a)

Depth:	6–9 m
Bottom:	Sand & coral

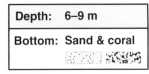

Rattray Island was named after Alexander Rattray, RN, ships surgeon aboard the survey ship *Salamander*, which conducted surveys of the Whitsundays in the 1860s.

ESHELBY ISLAND (N8b)

Depth:	3–9 m
Bottom:	Sand & coral

Eshelby Island is in a Marine Park Preservation Zone, which means that entry is prohibited within 500 metres except in cases of dire emergency. The anchor shown in map N8a is therefore of academic interest. The special status of Eshelby is because this island is a significant nesting area for bridled terns, one of the few such areas left in Australia, and these threatened species need to be protected without disturbance by man, which upsets their nesting.

Albert Eshelby was a sub-lieutenant on the survey ship *Salamander*.

MAINLAND ANCHORAGES (N9)

Depth:	3–4 m
Bottom:	Sand & coral

Opposite Olden Island on the eastern side of George Point there are a number of beautiful, deserted mainland beaches which offer good shelter in south-west to north-west winds. Anchor about 100 metres off the beaches to avoid scattered coral heads.

OLDEN ISLAND

JOINS MAP N7 NOT FOR NAVIGATION: SEE CHART AUS 825

to George Point (about 1.6 miles)
Excellent beach
Excellent beach
Excellent beach
OLDEN
ISLAND
(85)
GUMBRELL
ISLAND
MAINLAND
Approximate Scale 1:29 000
0 Nautical Miles 0.5 1.0
0 Kilometres 0.5 1.0
Soundings in metres
N
to Earlando Resort
(about 1.5 miles)
to Grassy Island (1.5 miles)
and Double Bay (3 miles)
11 9 0₉ 14 9 16 9 8 20 9 10 11 12 7 3₇
JOINS MAP N7
JOINS MAP 10a
© WINDWARD PUBLICATIONS PTY LTD.

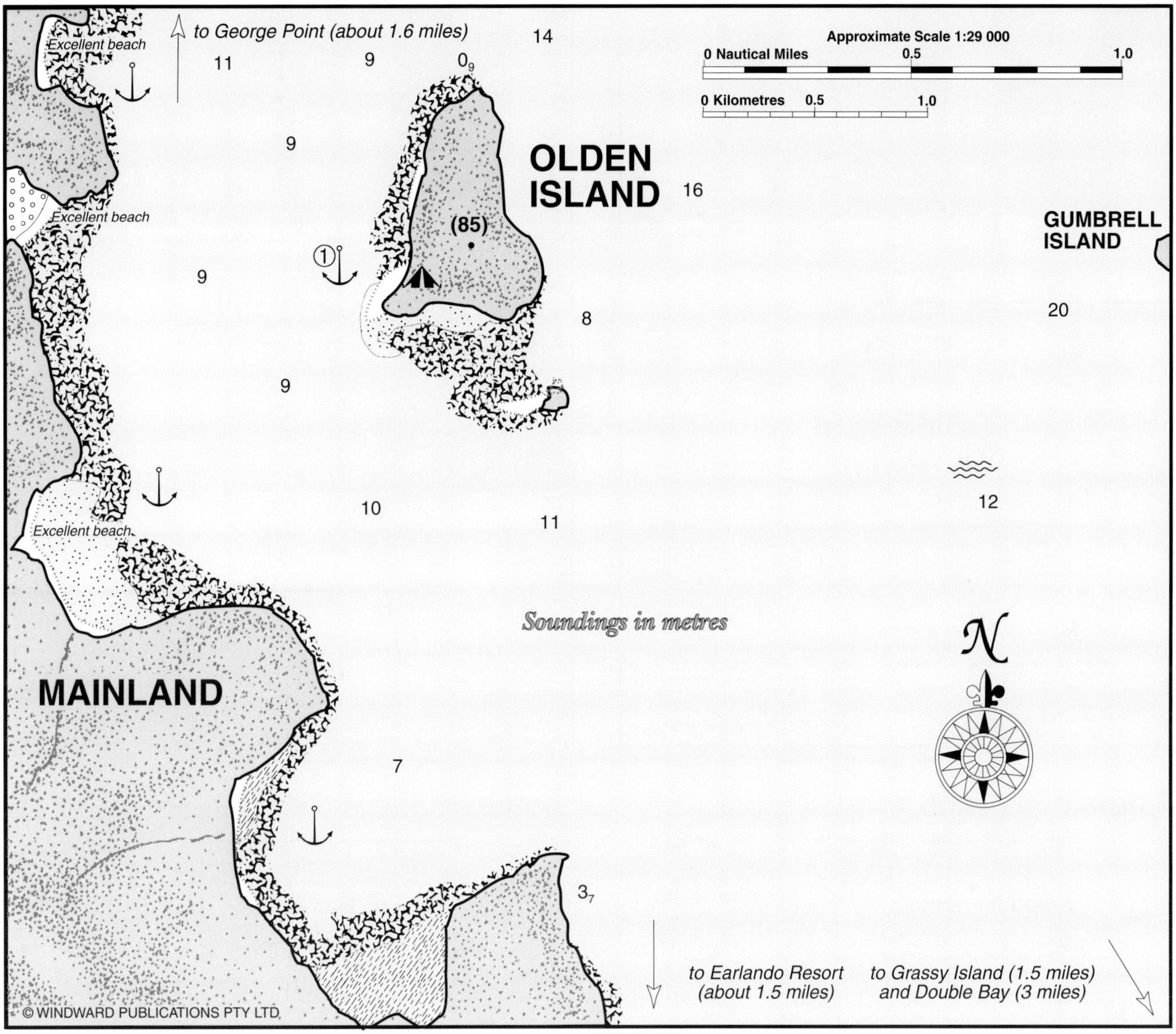

JOINS MAP N11

OLDEN ISLAND (N9)

①

Depth:	3–4 m
Bottom:	Sand & coral

N
NE
E
SE
S
SW
W
NW
25
25
25

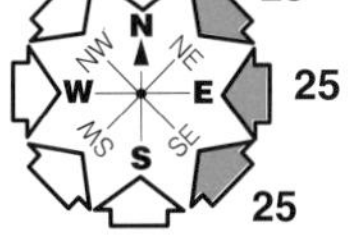

Watch out for shallow area south of the beach if approaching from that direction. Anchor at the south-west end of the beach (perhaps a little further north if staying overnight).

The anchorage can be swelly in 25-knot winds but the holding is very good. Olden has a pleasant sand beach. It is a deserted, peaceful anchorage, ideal for a lunch stop and used by some overnight.

GUMBRELL ISLAND (N10a)

①

Depth:	3–5 m
Bottom:	Sand

N
NE
E
SE
S
SW
W
NW
15

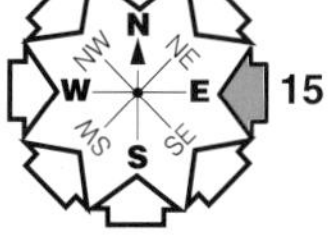

A pleasant daytime stopping-off spot. A lonely, deserted island with some nice beaches.

GUMBRELL I. N10a
NEXT MAP N8b NOT FOR NAVIGATION: SEE CHART AUS 825

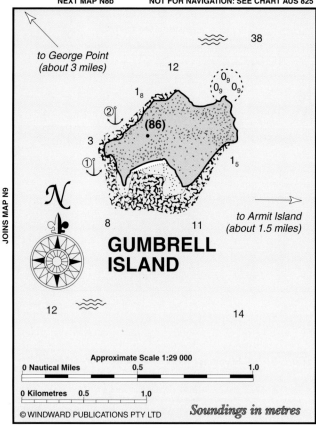

to George Point
(about 3 miles)

38

12

1_8

②

(86)

3

①

1_5

N

8   11

GUMBRELL
ISLAND

0_9
0_9 0_9

to Armit Island
(about 1.5 miles)

12   14

Approximate Scale 1:29 000

0 Nautical Miles   0.5   1.0

0 Kilometres   0.5   1.0

© WINDWARD PUBLICATIONS PTY LTD

Soundings in metres

JOINS MAP N9

NEXT MAP N11

NEXT MAP N10b
NEXT MAP N10a

ARMIT ISLAND N10b
NEXT MAP N8b NOT FOR NAVIGATION: SEE CHART AUS 825

15   2_1 2_1 2_1 13

9

13

Soundings in metres

3_4 162   ARMIT
ISLAND   22

3_4

①   11

4

17   58 2_1

17   LITTLE ARMIT I.

© WINDWARD PUBLICATIONS PTY LTD

to Airlie Beach
(about 8 miles)

19

N

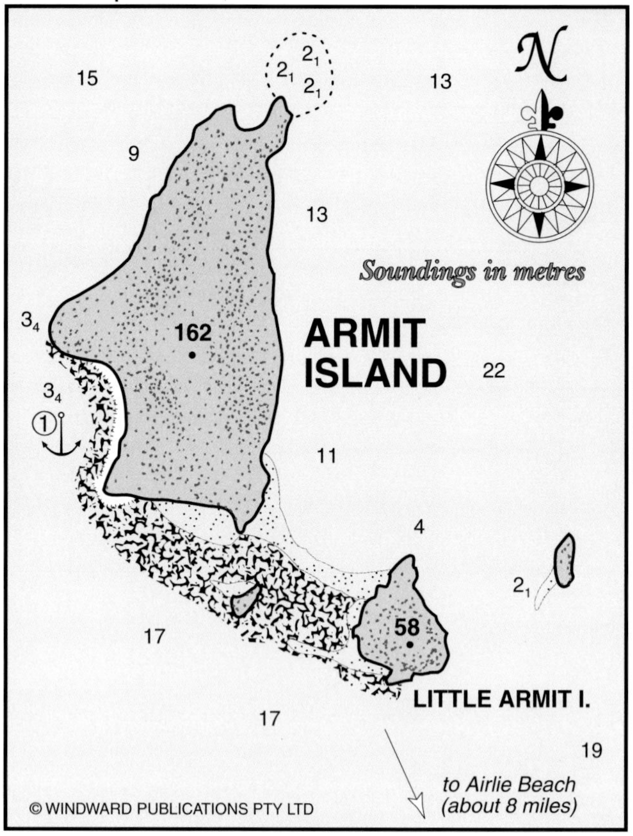

NEXT MAP N10c

GUMBRELL ISLAND (N10a)

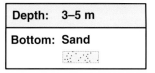

Depth:	3–5 m
Bottom:	Sand

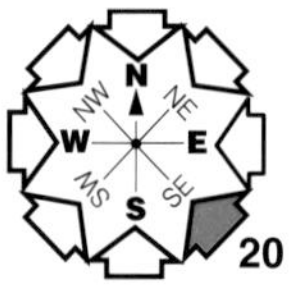

20

This anchorage gives better protection in south-east conditions.

ARMIT ISLAND (N10b)

Depth:	6–8 m
Bottom:	Sand

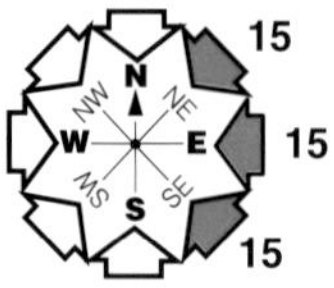

15
15
15

Avoid the reef areas which join Armit and the small islets to the south-east.

Anchor close in as the bottom slopes steeply off. Good holding, although the anchorage is not particularly comfortable in fresh conditions.

Armit was named for Sub-lieutenant Robert E. Armit, RN, of the survey ship *Salamander*.

DOUBLE CONE ISLAND (N10c)

Depth:	4–6 m
Bottom:	Mud & sand

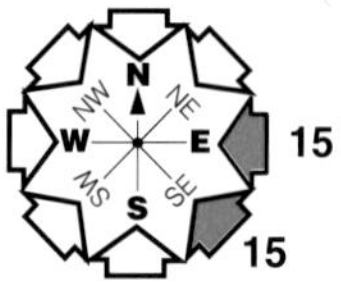

15
15

Approaching from the south, keep well off the south-west tip where the reef runs off for several hundred metres.

Double Cone Island is seen for miles from the south-east, sitting up prominently on the horizon. It is an interesting daytime stopoff spot (in suitably light weather) that offers excellent beach fossicking and good fishing. Some time ago a trawler was wrecked on the south-western end of the eastern 'cone', and some remains may still be visible on the beach.

An ironic aspect of its name is that it is indeed an island of double cones – in addition to its two conic hills, there are reportedly significant numbers of the poisonous cone shell, *Conus geographus*, in residence (these, needless to say, are best left to their poisonous selves).

Double Cone Island is an important nesting site for the Torresian imperial pigeon (*Ducula spilorrhoa*) of which there are about 2500 pairs. Other bird species nesting there are the beach thick-knee (*Burhinus mangirostris*), the white-bellied sea eagle (*Haliaeetus leucogaster*) and the osprey (*Pandion haliaetus*). The island is closed seasonally (from October through March) to allow these species to nest in peace. Keep well away during this period.

DOUBLE CONE I. N10c
NOT FOR NAVIGATION: SEE CHART AUS 252

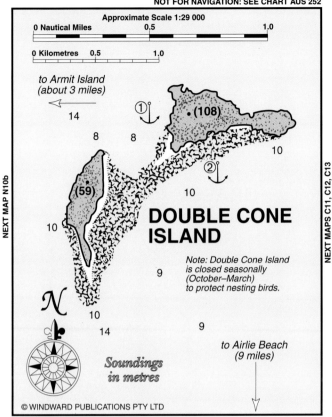

to Armit Island
(about 3 miles)

**DOUBLE CONE
ISLAND**

Note: Double Cone Island
is closed seasonally
(October–March)
to protect nesting birds.

to Airlie Beach
(9 miles)

*Soundings
in metres*

© WINDWARD PUBLICATIONS PTY LTD

NEXT MAP N10b

NEXT MAPS C11, C12, C13

NEXT MAP C1

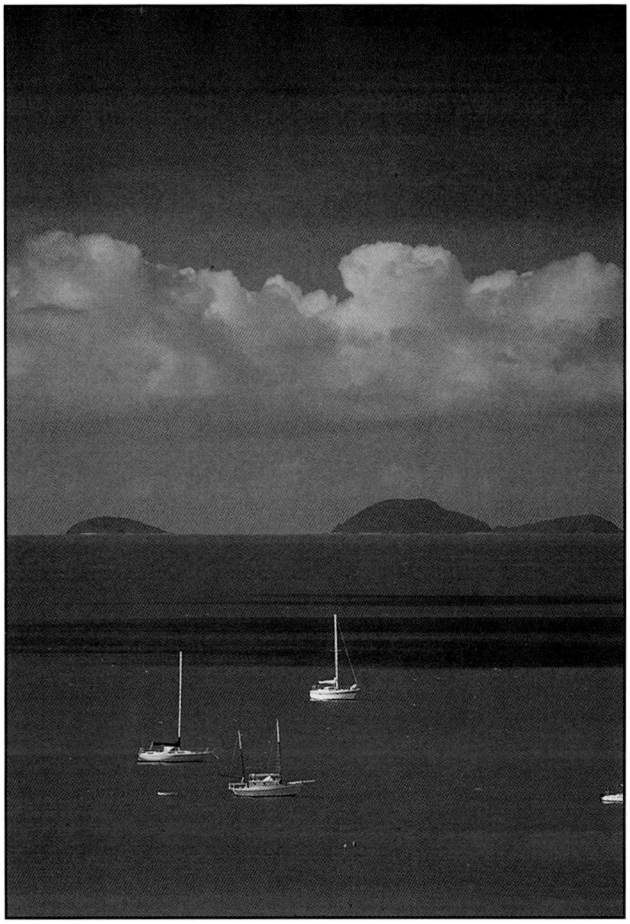

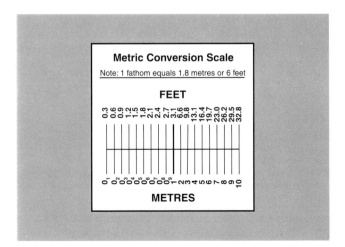

The 'three cones' of Double Cone Island as seen from Airlie Beach.

DOUBLE CONE ISLAND (N10c)

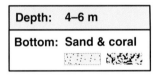

Depth:	4–6 m
Bottom:	Sand & coral

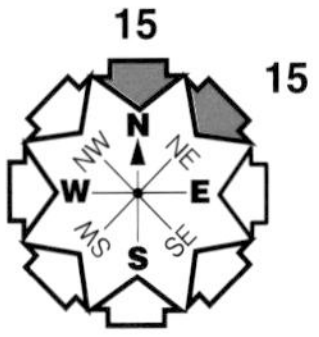

This is the preferred anchorage in northerly conditions.

Metric Conversion Scale

Note: 1 fathom equals 1.8 metres or 6 feet

FEET

0.3 0.6 0.9 1.2 1.5 1.8 2.1 2.4 2.7 3.1 6.6 9.8 13.1 16.4 19.7 23.0 26.2 29.5 32.8

0.1 0.2 0.3 0.4 0.5 0.6 0.7 0.8 0.9 1 2 3 4 5 6 7 8 9 10

METRES

GRASSY ISLAND

N11

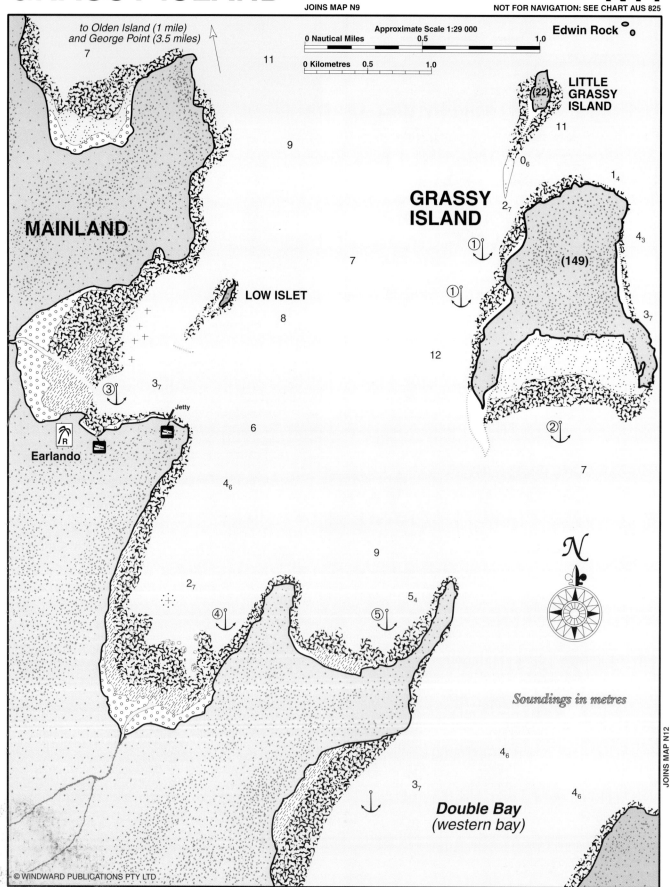

to Olden Island (1 mile)
and George Point (3.5 miles)

7

11

9

Approximate Scale 1:29 000

Edwin Rock

LITTLE GRASSY ISLAND

(22)

11

0₆

1_4

GRASSY ISLAND

2_7

(149)

4_3

MAINLAND

7

LOW ISLET

8

①

①

3_7

12

3_7

③

3_7

Jetty

R

Earlando

6

②

4_6

7

5_4

9

2_7

④

⑤

Soundings in metres

4_6

3_7

Double Bay
(western bay)

4_6

4_6

GRASSY ISLAND (N11)

Depth:	6–9 m
Bottom:	Sand

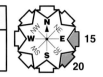

Coming from the south, watch out for the sand spit which extends for some distance off the south-western tip of the island.

Coming from the north, keep west of Edwin Rock and pass outside of Little Grassy Island (immediately north of Grassy Island).

This anchorage has good holding and is suitable for over-night stops; it may be swelly as the wind easts. The tidal flow past this side of Grassy Island tends to keep you point-ing either straight north or south, which is useful because of the depth and it also makes any swell less annoying. Beware of occasional bommies where the southern of these two anchors is shown.

GRASSY ISLAND (N11)

Depth:	3–5 m
Bottom:	Mud & sand

The south side of Grassy Island offers protection from northerly winds. Pleasant walking and fossicking.

EARLANDO RESORT (N11)

Depth:	3–5 m
Bottom:	Mud

Stay south of Low Islet and the reef which extends south-west from it. Earlando Resort welcomes visitors by sea.

MAINLAND (N11)

Depth:	3–5 m
Bottom:	Mud

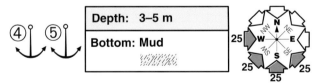

These anchorages are not frequently occupied and offer privacy and solitude. Good fishing, crabs.

DOUBLE BAY (western bay) (N12)

Depth:	3–5 m
Bottom:	Mud & sand

The western embayment of Double Bay offers several good anchorages, quiet and secure even in fresh south-east winds. As with many of these northern mainland bays, there is a rich food supply for fish and the fishing can be good.

Anchorage No. 1 may be swelly, especially as the wind gets into the east. Double Bay (eastern bay) is less swelly. Anchorage No. 2 may be marginally less swelly than No. 1 and offers slightly better protection from the south-west.

DOUBLE BAY (western bay) (N12)

Depth:	3–5 m
Bottom:	Mud

Anchorage No. 3 offers some protection from the north-west and west; it is also tenable in moderate south-east to east winds, but it may be swelly.

DOUBLE BAY (western)

N12

NOT FOR NAVIGATION: SEE CHART AUS 825

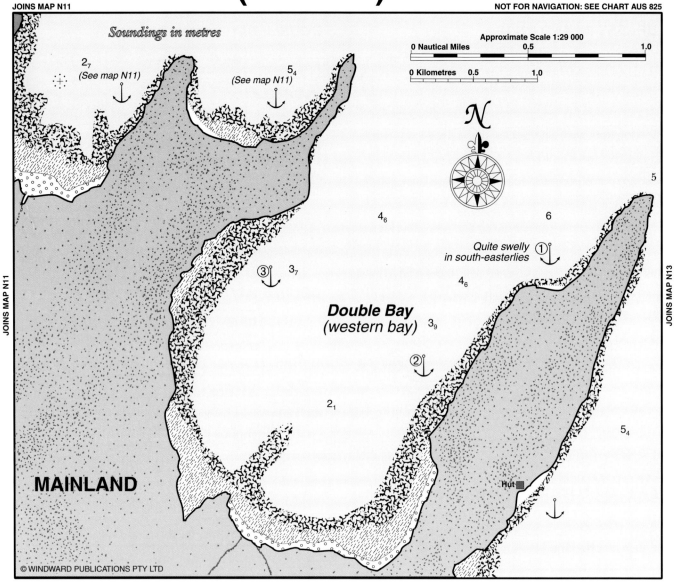

Soundings in metres

2₇ (See map N11)

5₄ (See map N11)

Approximate Scale 1:29 000

0 Nautical Miles   0.5   1.0

0 Kilometres   0.5   1.0

N

5

4₆   6

Quite swelly in south-easterlies (1)

 3₇

4₆

Double Bay *(western bay)* 3₉

(2)

2₁

5₄

MAINLAND

Hut

© WINDWARD PUBLICATIONS PTY LTD

JOINS MAP N11

JOINS MAP N13

DOUBLE BAY (eastern bay) (N13)

Depth:	3–5 m
Bottom:	Mud

Watch out for scattered bommies. Double Bay offers several good anchorages, quiet and secure even in fresh south-east winds. As with many of these northern mainland bays, there is a rich food supply for fish provided by the mangrove community, and the fishing can be good. The eastern bay has extensive areas of mangroves, which make interesting exploring at high tide. A delightful anchorage offering peace and solitude.

DOUBLE BAY (eastern bay) (N13)

Depth:	3–5 m
Bottom:	Mud & sand

Watch out for the reef area which extends some distance north-west of Datum Rock. Anchor off the pleasant little expanse of sand.

DOUBLE BAY (eastern bay) (N13)

Depth:	3–5 m
Bottom:	Mud

15

There are probably better choices for overnight

(continued on page 169)

DOUBLE BAY (eastern)
JOINS MAP N11

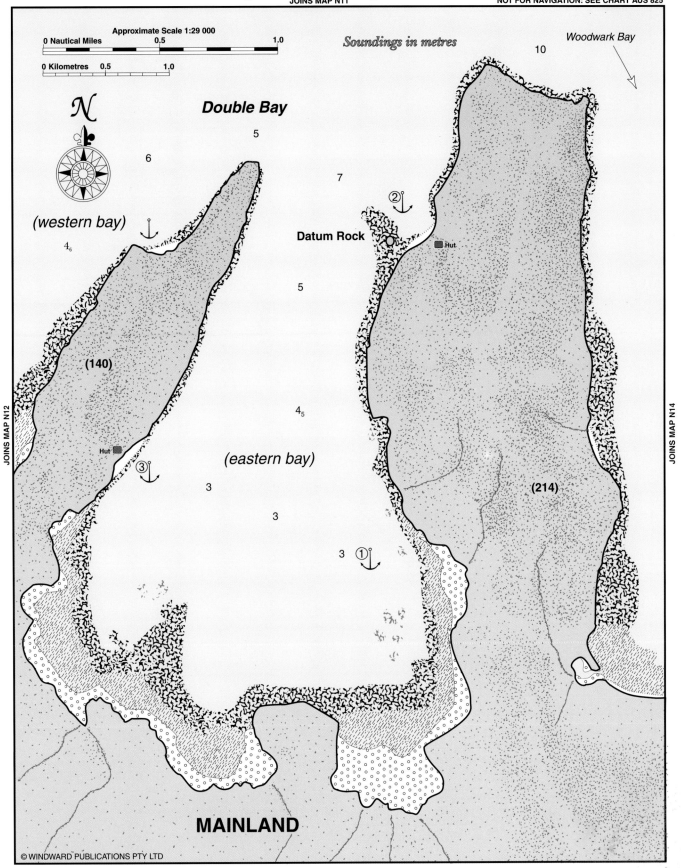

Double Bay

Soundings in metres

Woodwark Bay

10

5

6

7

② ⚓

(western bay) ⚓

Datum Rock

Hut

4₆

5

5

(140)

4₅

Hut

③ ⚓

(eastern bay)

3

3

3 ① ⚓

(214)

JOINS MAP N12

JOINS MAP N14

MAINLAND

© WINDWARD PUBLICATIONS PTY LTD

WOODWARK BAY

NEXT MAP N10b

NOT FOR NAVIGATION: SEE CHART AUS 825

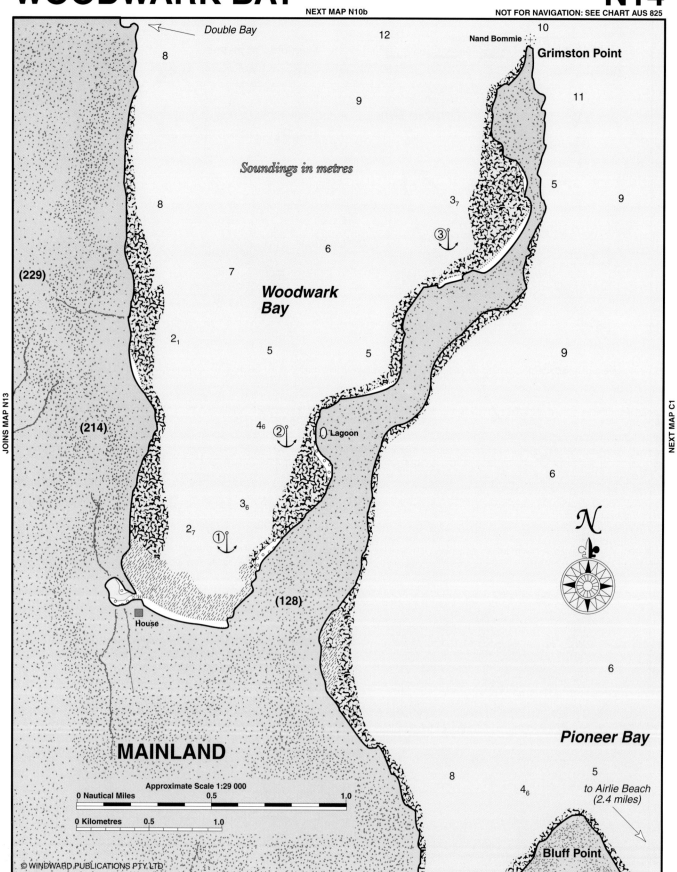

Double Bay

12

Nand Bommie

10

Grimston Point

8

9

11

Soundings in metres

5

③ ⚓

3₇

9

8

6

(229)

7

Woodwark Bay

5

5

9

2₁

4₆ ② ⚓

Lagoon

9

3₆

6

2₇ ① ⚓

(128)

House

MAINLAND

Pioneer Bay

8

5

4₆

to Airlie Beach (2.4 miles)

Bluff Point

Approximate Scale 1:29 000

| 0 Nautical Miles | 0.5 | 1.0 |

| 0 Kilometres | 0.5 | 1.0 |

© WINDWARD PUBLICATIONS PTY. LTD

JOINS MAP N13

NEXT MAP C1

JOINS MAP N15

(214)

BLUFF POINT   N15

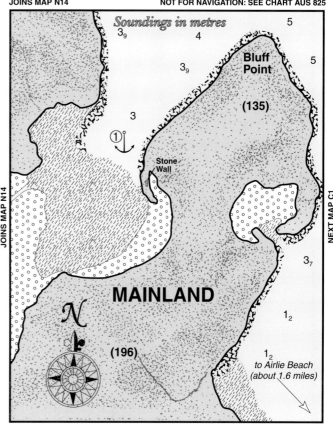

(continued from page 166)

anchorages than this one, but there is a little beach and hut on the shore which makes a pleasant picnic spot for lunch.

WOODWARK BAY (N14)

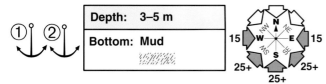

Depth:	3–5 m
Bottom:	Mud

15 W · E 15
25+ · 25+
25+

Woodwark Bay is a large lonely bay that offers a vast area for exploring, good fishing, and mangroves. At the very head is a hole which is suitable as a cyclone anchorage. This anchorage has a very nice beach.

Grimston Point, the headland at the eastern side of Wood-wark Bay, has strong currents flowing around it, like many headlands in this area. A vessel called *Nand* struck a bommie when rounding it not many years ago. Give it a good berth.

WOODWARK BAY (N14)

Depth:	3–5 m
Bottom:	Sand

15
15 W · E 25
15

This anchorage can be swelly. It has a lovely little sand beach with a spot in the corner for barbecues.

BLUFF POINT (N15)

Depth:	3–5 m
Bottom:	Mud

15
W · E 15
S 25
25

This anchorage may be swelly as the wind easts. It is another mangrove-filled mainland bay which can offer good fishing. A rarely visited anchorage, and perhaps not as good as Woodwark Bay or Double Bay, it is closer to Abell Point and is sometimes used as a first-night anchorage by bareboat charterers. Anchor just off the rocks north of the first mangrove trees (in a depth of about 3 metres at low tide).

THE CENTRAL GROUP

C1–C33

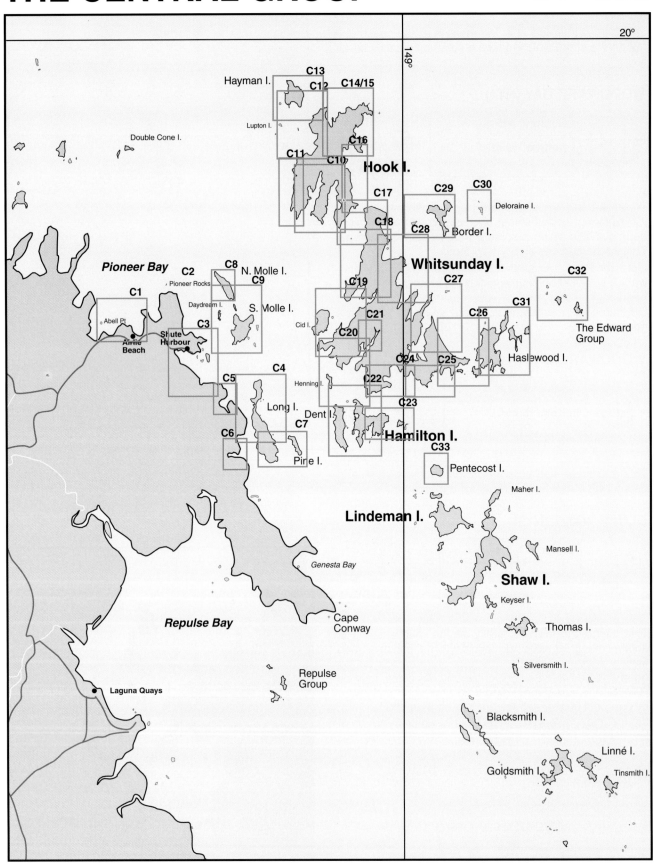

20°

149°

Hayman I.

C13

C12

C14/15

Double Cone I.

Lupton I.

C16

C11

C10

Hook I.

C29

C30

Deloraine I.

C17

Border I.

C18

C28

Pioneer Bay

C2

C8

N. Molle I.

Whitsunday I.

C27

C32

Pioneer Rocks

C9

C31

The Edward Group

C1

Daydream I.

S. Molle I.

C19

C26

Abell Pt

C3

Cid I.

C21

Haslewood I.

Airlie Beach

Shute Harbour

C20

C5

C4

Henning I.

C24

C25

Long I.

C22

C6

C7

C23

Dent I.

Hamilton I.

Pine I.

C33

Pentecost I.

Maher I.

Lindeman I.

Mansell I.

Genesta Bay

Shaw I.

Keyser I.

Cape Conway

Thomas I.

Repulse Bay

Silversmith I.

Laguna Quays

Repulse Group

Blacksmith I.

Linné I.

Goldsmith I.

Tinsmith I.

Map index

Anchorage index

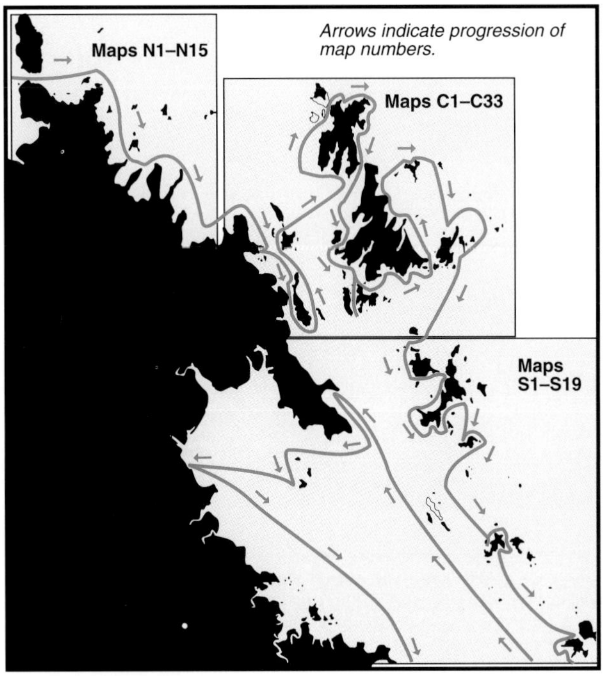

Maps N1–N15

Arrows indicate progression of map numbers.

Maps C1–C33

Maps S1–S19

AIRLIE BEACH

Airlie Beach and Cannonvale to its west are the principal coastal mainland centres for the Whitsundays, providing manpower, services and supplies for the island resorts and for the bareboat charter industry. These villages comprise a tourist destination in their own right, with resorts, motels, holiday flats, backpackers' resorts and hostels, camping and caravan parks, a variety of shops and services, and restaurants. Night-time entertainment is available at several establishments.

Airlie Beach looks northwards over Airlie Bay and Pioneer Bay onto a spectacular seascape, a brilliant blue expanse of still water, diamonds twinkling at mid-morning on a rippled surface. These waters are shielded from the prevailing south-east winds by the Conway Range. Airlie Beach has thus become a protected refuge for itinerant vessels in need of rest and provisions, particularly in the trade winds season. It must be added that, when the winds pipe in from the north, it's not a very good anchorage at all.

The town of Airlie Beach is small, and all shops and services are within easy walking distance along the main street, Shute Harbour Road. The Esplanade, a loop which runs from the main road around along the waterfront by the beach, is where you will find the pub.

Muddy Bay, on the eastern side of Airlie Point, is shallow and dries extensively; it is the principal careening* spot in the area. Two public launching ramps are on the Muddy Bay side of Airlie Point, the one most preferred being found further out towards the end of the point. Parking for trailers is available in the immediate area.

On the Airlie Bay side is the Whitsunday Sailing Club, which welcomes visiting yachts and their crews; it has a bar, restaurant, and its own launching ramp.

ABELL POINT**

Abel Point Marina

Abell Point is the site of the marina owned and operated by Abel Point Marina (Whitsundays) Pty Ltd. It is the first mainland marina in the area. Completed in 1989, it provides an 'all-weather anchorage' on the northern Whitsundays mainland, surrounded as it is on three sides by a massive breakwater that has been constructed to withstand extreme conditions. The marina has over two hundred berths, some of which are available for casual hire. Fuel (diesel, unleaded, outboard, LPG) and water are available. All berths have power. Several bareboat charter companies have offices above or on the marina. The marina office is open from 0800 to 1800 hours Monday to Friday and from 0800 to 1700 hours Saturday and Sunday.

The marina office can be contacted on VHF 16/68 and 27 Mhz channel 88.

Hawkes Boatyard

Hawkes Boatyard has been operating on the same site next to the marina for many years. It has recently come under new management and additional services have been made available, including workshops, shipwright, sailmaker, marine electronics, marine electrics, brokerage and chandlery. Tools, trestles, welding plant and airless

spray antifouling equipment is available for hire. The new slipway will haul boats up to 80 tonnes and the installation of a travel lift is imminent (if not already done).

Airlie area services (Area code 079)
Air Sea Rescue
The Volunteer Marine Rescue Whitsunday VMR442
Altmann Avenue, Cannonvale. Tel. 467 207.
Weekends 7.00 am to 5.15 pm. Volunteers are on a listening watch roster throughout the day all week at their private premises. 2524 kHz, 27.88 and 27.91 MHz, VHF channels 16, 22, 80, 81.
Fuel
Abel Point Marina, Abell Point. VHF 16/68. Tel. 466 695.
Yacht club
Whitsunday Sailing Club, Airlie Point, Airlie Beach.
Visiting yachts and their crews welcome. Licensed bar, meals.
Tel. 466 138.

---

*Careening is the practice of making a vessel lay over on its side so that the bottom can be maintained. This is usually accomplished by running the vessel aground at high tide and allowing it to lay over as the tide recedes.

**Abell Point is named after the Abell family, who were early settlers in the area. Some time ago signs were erected by the local council carrying the name spelled with only one 'l', and since that time the incorrect spelling has become widely used. The council has recognised the error, which will be corrected in due course. It is, however, likely that the marina will continue to be called 'Abel Point Marina' because that's the name on its certificate of incorporation.

ABEL POINT MARINA

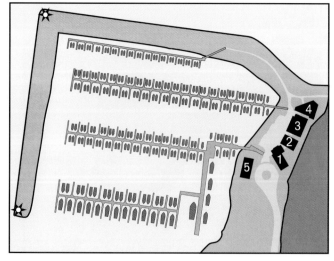

Building 1: kiosk, booking office, charter office, sailmaker, marine refrigeration, marine and electrical services. Building 2: chandlery and charter company. Building 3: dive shop, bottle shop, charter office and dive school. Building 4: restaurant. Building 5: marina administration (ground floor), laundry (ground floor) and charter offices (first floor).

AIRLIE BEACH

C1

NOT FOR NAVIGATION: SEE CHART AUS 252

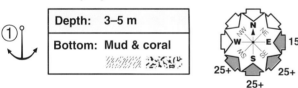
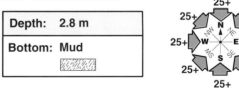

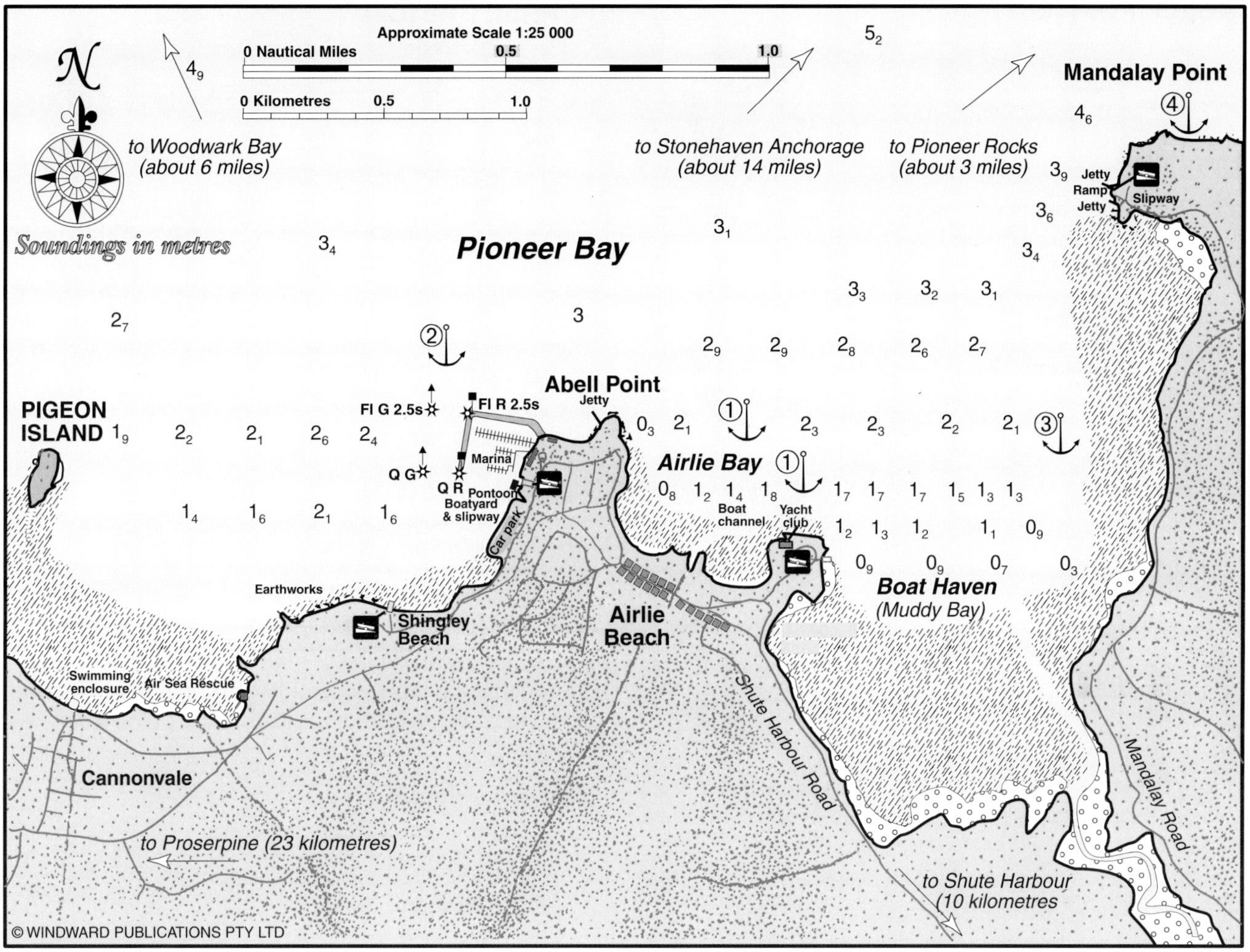

Approximate Scale 1:25 000

0 Nautical Miles — 0.5 — 1.0

0 Kilometres — 0.5 — 1.0

to Woodwark Bay (about 6 miles)

to Stonehaven Anchorage (about 14 miles) *to Pioneer Rocks (about 3 miles)*

Mandalay Point

Soundings in metres

Pioneer Bay

Jetty / Ramp / Jetty / Slipway

PIGEON ISLAND

Abell Point

FI G 2.5s   FI R 2.5s   Jetty

Marina

Q G

Q R   Pontoon / Boatyard & slipway

Car park

Airlie Bay

Boat channel   Yacht club

Boat Haven (Muddy Bay)

Earthworks

Shingley Beach

Airlie Beach

Swimming enclosure   Air Sea Rescue

Shute Harbour Road

Cannonvale

Mandalay Road

to Proserpine (23 kilometres)

to Shute Harbour (10 kilometres)

© WINDWARD PUBLICATIONS PTY LTD

NEXT MAP N15

JOINS MAP C2

AIRLIE BAY (C1)

Depth:	3–5 m
Bottom:	Mud & coral

This anchorage provides good protection from southerly winds but is very exposed to north. The anchorage may be swelly as the wind easts.

The coral/rock/sand/mud off Airlie Beach dries extensively. A dinghy channel through the reef allows access to the back of the supermarket and shops; negotiate this with care at low tide as silting has occurred in some places, and the bar dries at spring low tides. The Whitsunday Sailing Club has a dinghy harbour behind a breakwater which can make dinghy access easier in northerlies and at low tide. The club facilities are available at nominal charge. Muddy Bay dries extensively; careening piles are located at the north-west corner. Two launching ramps provide access to Muddy Bay; the most popular is the north-eastern one. Another launching ramp into Airlie Bay, a firm sand beach, is located just to the right of the Whitsunday Sailing Club.

There are two other launching ramps in the Airlie area, one immediately adjacent to the marina at Abell Point (probably the best in the area) and one at Shingley Beach, a little west of the marina.

ABEL POINT MARINA

Depth:	2.8 m
Bottom:	Mud

The marina has been dredged to 2.8 m (low water) throughout. Marina berths may be available for hire at overnight, weekly or monthly rates. The marina operates VHF channel 16/68. Fuel (outboard, diesel, unleaded, LPG) and water are available.

ABELL POINT (C1)

Depth:	2–4 m
Bottom:	Sand

Watch shoaling depth and make allowance for low water.

MUDDY BAY (C1)

Depth:	2–5 m
Bottom:	Mud

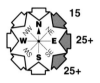

In easterly winds when Airlie Bay becomes uncomfortable, anchorage may be found in Muddy Bay. There is good holding in mud and sea grass.

MANDALAY POINT (C1)

Depth:	4–5 m
Bottom:	Sand & mud

This anchorage is exposed on its flanks; however it does provide comfortable anchorage in south to south-east winds up to about 20 knots and offers a couple of pleasant deserted beaches. Anchorage is also possible around the corner to the west.

Mandalay Point has a jetty and slipway capable of handling quite large vessels (up to 150 tonnes) The jetty is an 80-metre rock abutment with a 30-metre timber wharf and landing at the end, where the depth is 4 metres (LWS). Water and fuel (diesel, outboard, LPG refills) are available.

All services are provided.

FUNNEL BAY (C2)

Funnel Bay offers one of the 'cyclone anchorages' of the Whitsundays. Although there is '0 water' (at low tide) over the bar in front of the creek, just inside the entrance is a depth of 2.4 metres in a large pool. There are lots of mangroves.

If you are unfortunate enough to experience the thrill of a cyclone in Funnel Bay, tie to the mangroves along the bank (don't anchor 'mid-stream'; there will be heaps of water and piles of logs and debris racing down the valley). Keep your lines high, and tie so that your bow faces the onslaught. (See also 'Riding out a cyclone' in 'Boating in the Whitsundays'.)

Approaching Funnel Bay from the south and east, Almora Islet may be mistaken for Pioneer Rocks, with unfortunate results, as there is no passage between Almora Islet and the mainland. Pioneer Rocks is beaconed and lighted.

FUNNEL BAY (C2)

Depth:	3–6 m
Bottom:	Mud

Funnel Bay (and this anchorage) is at the northern end of a valley with high hills on both sides, hence its name. The area from the mouth of the bay seawards can be very squally, so be prepared for bullets in south-east conditions when sailing across to Airlie Beach or when approaching the Bay itself.

Like so many of these northern mainland anchorages, the fishing can be very good.

FUNNEL BAY (C2)

Depth:	6–9 m
Bottom:	Mud & sand

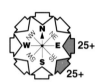

This anchorage has good holding and is suitable for overnight stops, although being close to the point, it can be a bit rolly.

PIONEER POINT (C2)

Depth:	5–8 m
Bottom:	Sand

Anchorage may be had just off Pioneer Point in suitably light conditions.

---

*'T' stands for 'true' bearing (as opposed to magnetic bearing). The difference between a true bearing and a magnetic bearing is the amount of local magnetic 'variation' caused by the compass needle pointing at the north magnetic pole rather than at the top of the globe (the north pole). The figure for magnetic variation is given on hydrographic charts, usually on the compass rose. In the Whitsundays, magnetic variation is about 9°, a figure which must be added to magnetic bearings to obtain true bearings (and subtracted from true bearings to obtain magnetic bearings).

FUNNEL BAY

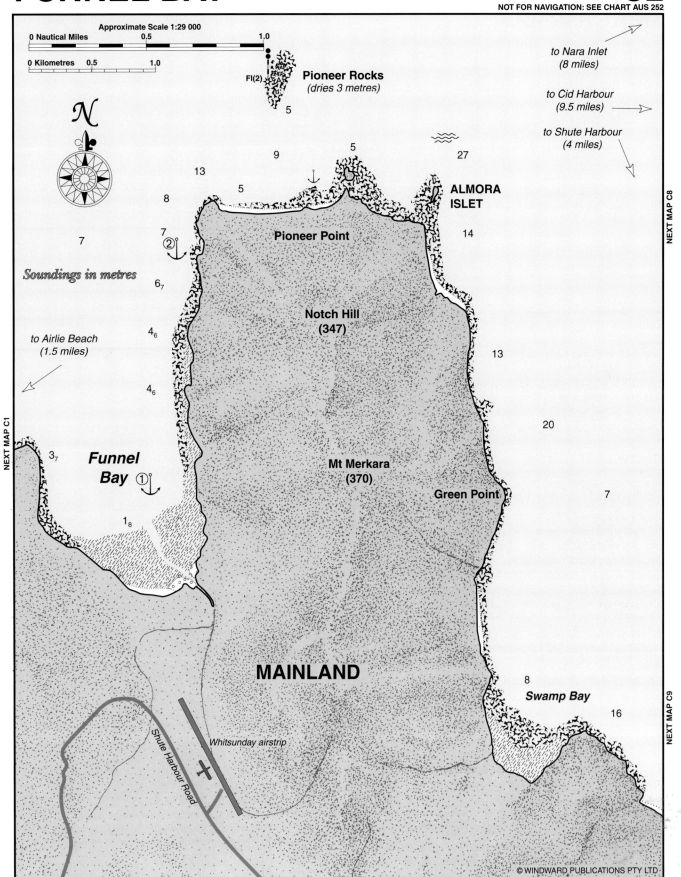

Approximate Scale 1:29 000

0 Nautical Miles 0.5 1.0

0 Kilometres 0.5 1.0

Fl(2) **Pioneer Rocks**
(dries 3 metres)

5

9 5 27

13

5

8 **ALMORA ISLET**

7 **Pioneer Point** 14

2

6 7

Soundings in metres

Notch Hill (347)

4 6 13

to Airlie Beach
(1.5 miles)

4 6

20

3 7 **Funnel Bay** ①

Mt Merkara (370)

Green Point 7

1 8

to Nara Inlet
(8 miles)

to Cid Harbour
(9.5 miles)

to Shute Harbour
(4 miles)

MAINLAND

8 *Swamp Bay*

16

Whitsunday airstrip

Shute Harbour Road

NEXT MAP C1

NEXT MAP C8

NEXT MAP C9

SHUTE HARBOUR

Shute Harbour is the focal point of communications between the mainland and the Whitsunday islands. Protected in all weathers, it is surrounded by the lofty hills of Conway Range. It is the best mainland natural harbour for some miles along this stretch of the south-central coast of Queensland.

Here the dreams of enchanted holidays among 'South Pacific islands' begin. At 0800 hours each day the island cruise boats assemble, their hulls gleaming in the morning sun, their skippers and crews spruced up in white. Shapely, suntanned girls stroll up and down the jetties, clutching clipboards, enticing clients to enjoy a day on one of the famous old yachts of Australian ocean racing – *Gretel, Apollo, Ragamuffin* – to enjoy a tropical lunch at Langford Island or Whitehaven Beach, some diving or snorkelling, sailboarding, and then an exhilarating sail up the Whitsunday Passage to finish off a perfect day.

Shute Harbour has two council jetties. Standing in the parking lot and looking to sea, the one on the right is the older, Lloyd Roberts Jetty, an enclosed rectangle with dinghies tied up in the middle, their bow lines secured to the jetty and their stern lines run through pulleys, with a weight tied to the end, so that as the tide rises and falls some 3.6 metres each twelve hours the lines always have the correct amount of tension. East of the Lloyd Roberts Jetty is a newer jetty, with the jetty supervisor's office and council ticket office at its landward end.

There are plans for some significant improvements at Shute Harbour which are taking shape as this edition goes to press.

Transport to and from Shute Harbour

Bus service

A regular bus service serves Shute Harbour, Airlie Beach and Proserpine, the latter being the location of the nearest mainland jet airport. There are buses to and from Airlie Beach all day (starting at 0615 hours and finishing about 1815 hours with a late run at about 2300 hours), and there are a number of daily services to Proserpine. It takes about one and a half hours to get to the Proserpine airport. Airlie Beach has a taxi service. Also, it is usually quite easy to hitch-hike between Shute Harbour and Airlie Beach.

Water taxi

The office of the water taxi (469 499) is on the upper level of the waterfront buildings. This taxi does several runs each day to Hamilton Island, where it meets the Ansett flights, and there are five services each day to Daydream Island and Long Island. The taxi will go anywhere you like in the islands, but the fare is much less if your destination is along the regular run. It also takes campers and their equipment to the islands and will make arrangements for transporting their water.

Air services

Whitsunday airstrip, a few kilometres down the road from Shute Harbour, is the base for several companies operating helicopters, amphibians and fixed-wing aircraft. These provide a wide range of services: helicopters and sea

planes can pick up passengers anywhere throughout the islands; fixed wing aircraft operate air taxi services to airports in the area.

Parking

Two-hour parking spaces may be found in the vicinity of the Lloyd Roberts Jetty, and there is also a 24-hour parking lot with space for 200 cars. Tickets for parking are purchased from an attendant from about 0800 to 0900 hours daily and at other times at Jilly's at the Jetty, the council booking office or the jetty supervisor's office. Up on the hill overlooking the harbour is free parking. Access is via Whitsunday Drive, which turns off to the left from Shute Harbour Road just beyond the service station. Steps lead down to the main car park. A 500-car lock-up garage (operated by private enterprise) is next to the service station. This is a better place to leave a car overnight or for a longer term.

Launching ramp

Shute Harbour has a concrete ramp for launching trailer yachts. Parking for trailers is available in designated space between the service station and the harbourside parking area.

Shute Bay, a shallow, muddy estuary which dries extensively at low tide, is territory favoured by the toadfish, a (usually) small species, with parrot-beak teeth, that patrols the shallows, picking off molluscs and crabs. Many years back there were a number of bizarre attacks by a giant toadfish in the Shute Harbour area, the victims being unsuspecting children and local fishermen, and the odd toe was lost. Never wade in muddy coastal areas without shoes on your feet. (For more lurid details about terrible toadfish, see 'Avoiding tropical hazards'.)

Shops and services

The kiosk on the Lloyd Roberts Jetty (Jilly's at the Jetty) sells souvenirs, T-shirts, postcards, film, books, sunscreen creams, maps, cruise tickets, and the like. Immediately adjacent is a café/sandwich/take-away shop where you can also get a hearty breakfast before departing for the islands.

SHUTE HARBOUR (C3)

| Depth: | 1.5–3 m |
| Bottom: | Mud |

Shute Harbour may be entered from two directions, the preferred one being from the north-east, passing on either side of Low Rock. Low Rock is actually a pile of rocks and coral north-east of Shute Island. As a result of several bareboat charterers having unintentionally careened their yachts there, it is marked on all four sides by cardinal marks. Give it a decent berth, and watch the tidal run, which can be particularly strong coming around The Beak. There are leading lights on the jetties (white by day, blue at night) to guide into the harbour. The channel into the harbour is thereafter deep and well buoyed.

(continued on page 178)

SHUTE HARBOUR

C3

NOT FOR NAVIGATION: SEE CHARTS AUS 253/AUS 252

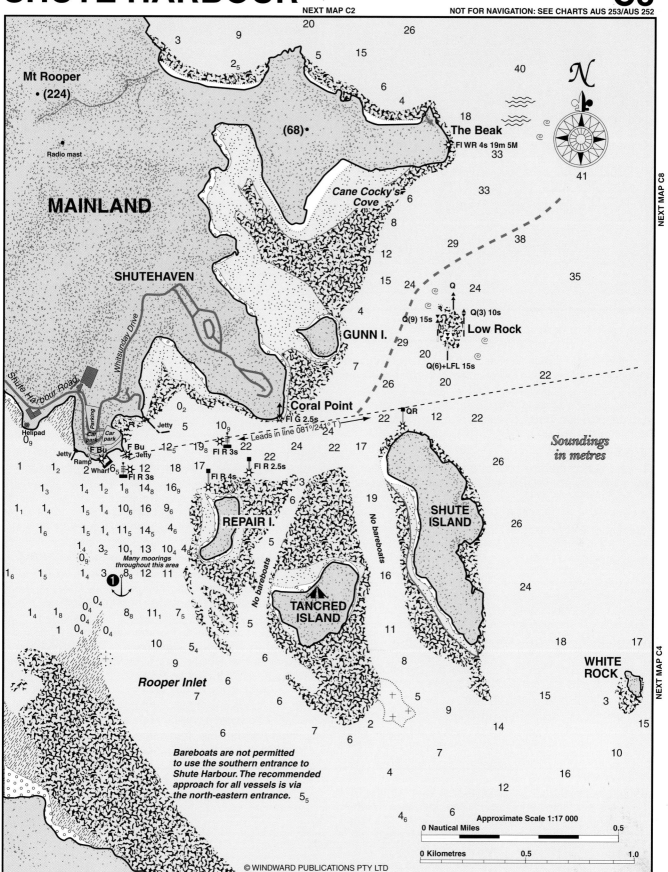

Mt Rooper
• (224)

Radio mast

MAINLAND

(68)•

Cane Cocky's Cove

The Beak
FI WR 4s 19m 5M

SHUTEHAVEN

Whitsunday Drive

GUNN I.

Low Rock
Q(9) 15s
Q(3) 10s
Q(6)+LFL 15s

Shute Harbour Road

Coral Point
☆ FI G 2.5s
Leads in line 081°/241° T

QR

Soundings in metres

Hellpad

Jetty

Parking
Car park
Car park

F Bu
F Bu
Jetty

Jetty
Ramp
Wharf
FI R 3s

FI R 3s

FI R 4s
FI R 2.5s

SHUTE ISLAND

REPAIR I.

Many moorings throughout this area

⚓①

No bareboats
No bareboats

TANCRED ISLAND

WHITE ROCK

Rooper Inlet

Bareboats are not permitted to use the southern entrance to Shute Harbour. The recommended approach for all vessels is via the north-eastern entrance.

Approximate Scale 1:17 000

0 Nautical Miles   0.5

0 Kilometres   0.5   1.0

© WINDWARD PUBLICATIONS PTY LTD

NEXT MAP C8

NEXT MAP C4

SHUTE HARBOUR
Approximate Scale 1:14 000

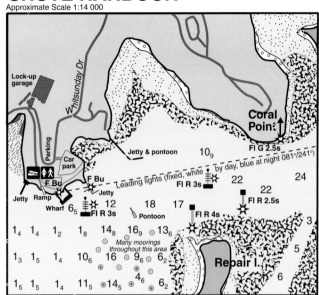

(continued from page 176)

Don't go too close to any of the beacons from Low Rock on in, as reefs sometimes extend a small distance beyond.

Entry to Shute Harbour is possible from the south, through Rooper Inlet, although it is prohibited by the bareboat charter companies. It should not be attempted at night because of the absence of navigation aids and the large number of moorings to the south and west of Repair Island which all but block the channel.

Tidal anomaly

Except during the first hour of the flood in the vicinity of the main jetty, the tidal stream always flows from south to north through Shute Harbour.

Anchorage is available where shown, depending upon the draught of your vessel and the height of the tide. Further west of the anchor symbol the bottom shoals rapidly.

The jetties

There are two public jetties, both designed for large vessels. The one on the left (looking from seawards) is the older Lloyd Roberts Jetty, with no ladders and with widely spaced piles; the new jetty on the right has ramps of a sort on the starboard arms, but it, too, is designed for large vessels. Between 0800 and 0930 hours, and again between 1600 and 1730 hours, yachts are not permitted to use either jetty (except in emergency) because these are chock-a-block with cruise vessels.

If you arrive during the day, call Shute Harbour Control on VHF channel 16. There is no charge for pulling up at the jetties; there is a small fee if water is required. Fuel is available at the Lloyd Roberts Jetty (by arrangement with the water taxi office).

Other places where fuel is available in the northern Whitsundays are Hamilton Island, Mandalay Point, Hayman Island and the marina at Abell Point. Water is not so readily available on the islands: from time to time when rainfall is low, water is of major concern to the resorts, and supplies have to be brought by barge from the mainland. It can be a precious and not inexpensive commodity, hence their reluctance to part with it.

HAPPY BAY (C4)

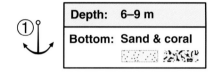

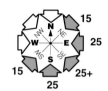

Depth:	6–9 m
Bottom:	Sand & coral

Historically, Happy Bay has been a popular first-night anchorage for bareboat charterers, who often haven't time to get to another overnight anchorage after their briefing in Shute Harbour but who want to get on their way rather than spending the first night at Shute. It is the site of the Club Crocodile Long Island Resort, which has changed names as many times in recent years as the cat has hats. If you wish to overnight at Happy Bay and visit the resort, radio ahead on VHF channel 16 to advise your arrival time and to book a mooring with the water sports manager. Payment of the mooring fee entitles you to the use of the resort, including showers. Moorings are infinitely preferable to anchoring in this bay because they are in the best location, out of the tide, and they will spare you the worry of avoiding isolated bommies which are difficult to see in the turbulent, often cloudy, waters. The jetty is for resort use only. If you wish to pick up or discharge passengers, before approaching the jetty, call the water sports manager for permission to pull alongside, which may be granted for a brief period only.

The reef at the southern end of the anchorage is deceptive; it extends *beyond* a line between Base Point at the north of the bay and Humpy Point at the south. If you do anchor on the south-west side, keep a healthy distance away from the reef to avoid several isolated bommies.

The stream which flows through 'The Narrows', between Spit Point and Fire Point, may reach 4-5 knots in spring tides. Approaching Happy Bay from the south, take special note of the prevailing wind and tide conditions. In fresh south-easterlies and a flooding tide, stong eddies and overfalls occur at the southern end of Long Island sound, and patches of similar conditions will be present within the Sound itself. Inside the Sound these disturbances can generally be avoided by steering for adjacent quieter waters, but conditions at the southern entrance may be unavoidable. Whether travelling north or south, it may be preferable to bypass the Sound and travel outside Long and Pine islands, avoiding the passage between the two which will also be disturbed.

LONG ISLAND NORTH

C4

NOT FOR NAVIGATION: SEE CHARTS AUS 253/AUS 252

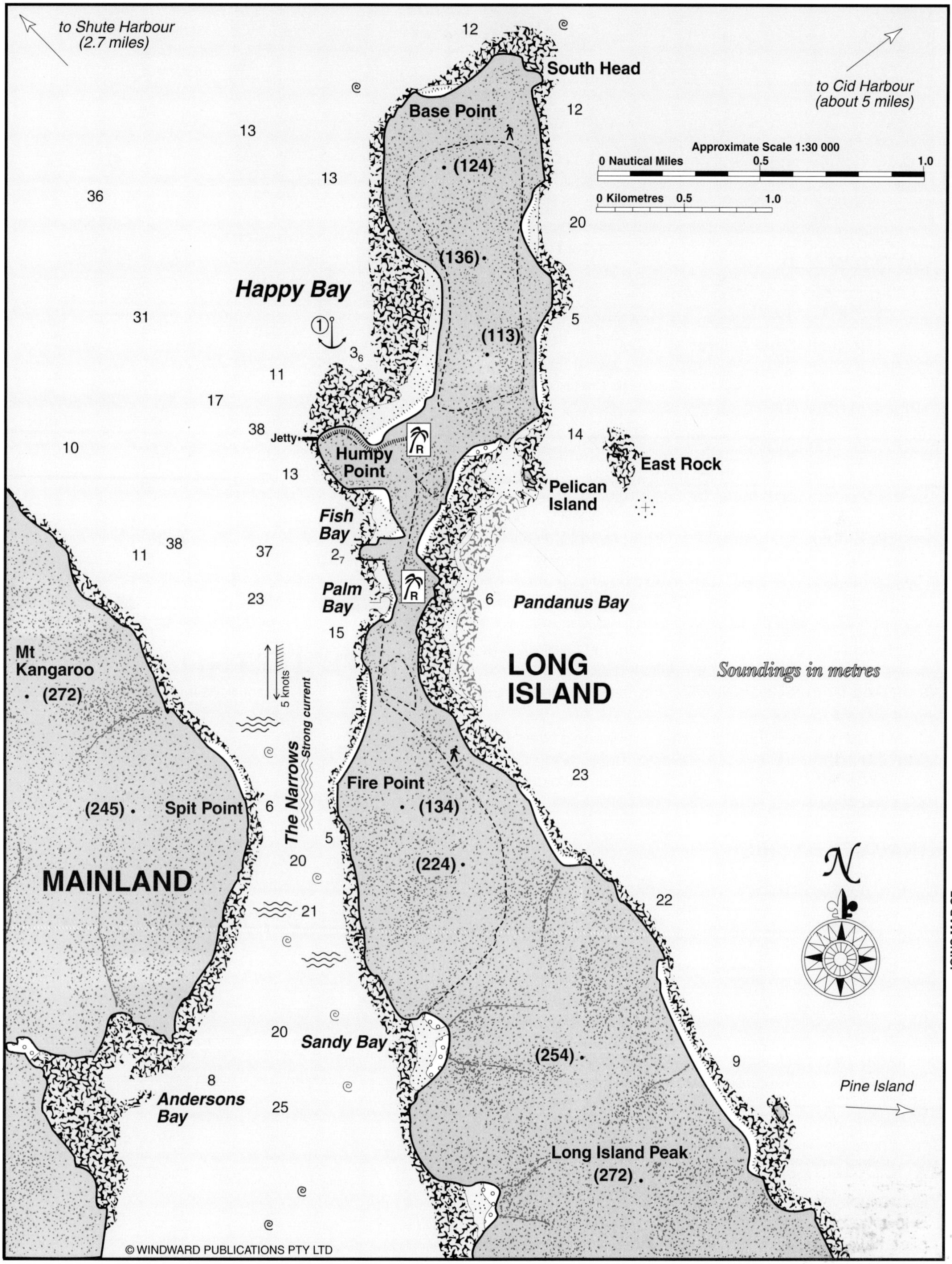

to Shute Harbour
(2.7 miles)

to Cid Harbour
(about 5 miles)

12

South Head

Base Point

13

13

Approximate Scale 1:30 000

| 0 Nautical Miles | | 0.5 | | 1.0 |

| 0 Kilometres | 0.5 | | 1.0 |

12

(124)

20

36

(136)

Happy Bay

5

31

①

3₆

(113)

11

17

38   Jetty

14

East Rock

10

Humpy
Point

13

Pelican
Island

*Fish
Bay*

R

11   38

37

Pandanus Bay

2₇

*Palm
Bay*

R

23

6

15

**LONG
ISLAND**

Soundings in metres

Mt
Kangaroo
(272)

5 knots   Strong current

The Narrows

Fire Point

23

(245)   Spit Point   6

(134)

5

MAINLAND

20

(224)

22

21

N

20

Sandy Bay

(254)

9

8

Pine Island

*Andersons
Bay*   25

Long Island Peak
(272)

NEXT MAP C5

NEXT MAP C20

JOINS MAP C7

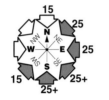

Palm Bay, Long Island

PALM BAY (C4)

Depth:	2.5 m
Bottom:	Sand & coral

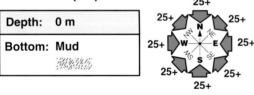

Palm Bay has a dredged channel and lagoon, offering another good overnight anchorage near Shute Harbour. There's room in the lagoon for eight vessels with draught up to 2.5 metres, and there are two moorings outside the lagoon as well. Radio ahead on VHF channel 16 for a booking (this is a popular spot with first- and last-night charterers, so it's essential to check to see if space is available).

Do not under any circumstances enter the harbour without a guide. There is a bar at the entrance. At a '0' tide at Shute Harbour there is only 1.5 metres in the channel; therefore, the tide must be a minimum 0.7 metres at Shute Harbour before boats are allowed in. The entrance is marked by port and starboard markers and there are lighted leads on the shore.

Once in the harbour, yachts pick up a mooring and tie to a stern line ashore. There is an overnight fee, and visitors are welcome to use the facilities of this informal hideaway, including showers, a small shop, and barbecues.

TRAMMEL BAY (C5)

Depth:	0 m
Bottom:	Mud

Trammel Bay is a shallow mangrove creek which is accessible at neap high tides to yachts with draught of up to 2.1 metres. In the past, stakes have been put in by private individuals to mark the channel(s), and there are private moorings. Care is obviously required in picking a suitable spot so as not to block access to moorings. (See 'Riding out a cyclone' in 'Boating in the Whitsundays'.)

WOODCUTTER BAY (C6)

Woodcutter Bay is another 'anchorage' that is only sought in an emergency (cyclone). It offers a number of spots among the mangroves where a yacht can be tied to weather a tropical storm.

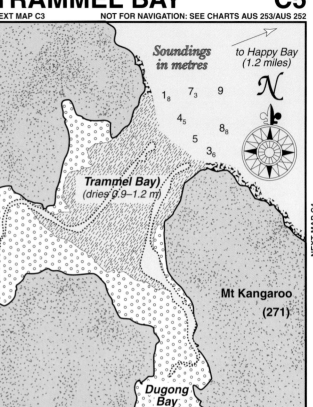

TRAMMEL BAY   C5
NEXT MAP C3   NOT FOR NAVIGATION: SEE CHARTS AUS 253/AUS 252

Soundings in metres

to Happy Bay (1.2 miles)

Trammel Bay) (dries 0.9–1.2 m)

Mt Kangaroo (271)

Dugong Bay

© WINDWARD PUBLICATIONS PTY LTD

NEXT MAP C4

NEXT MAPS C4 & C6

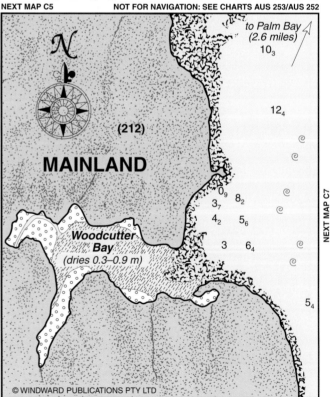

WOODCUTTER BAY   C6
NEXT MAP C5   NOT FOR NAVIGATION: SEE CHARTS AUS 253/AUS 252

to Palm Bay (2.6 miles)

(212)

MAINLAND

Woodcutter Bay (dries 0.3–0.9 m)

NEXT MAP C7

© WINDWARD PUBLICATIONS PTY LTD

LONG ISLAND SOUTH / PINE ISLAND C7

JOINS MAP C4 NOT FOR NAVIGATION: SEE CHARTS AUS 253/AUS 252

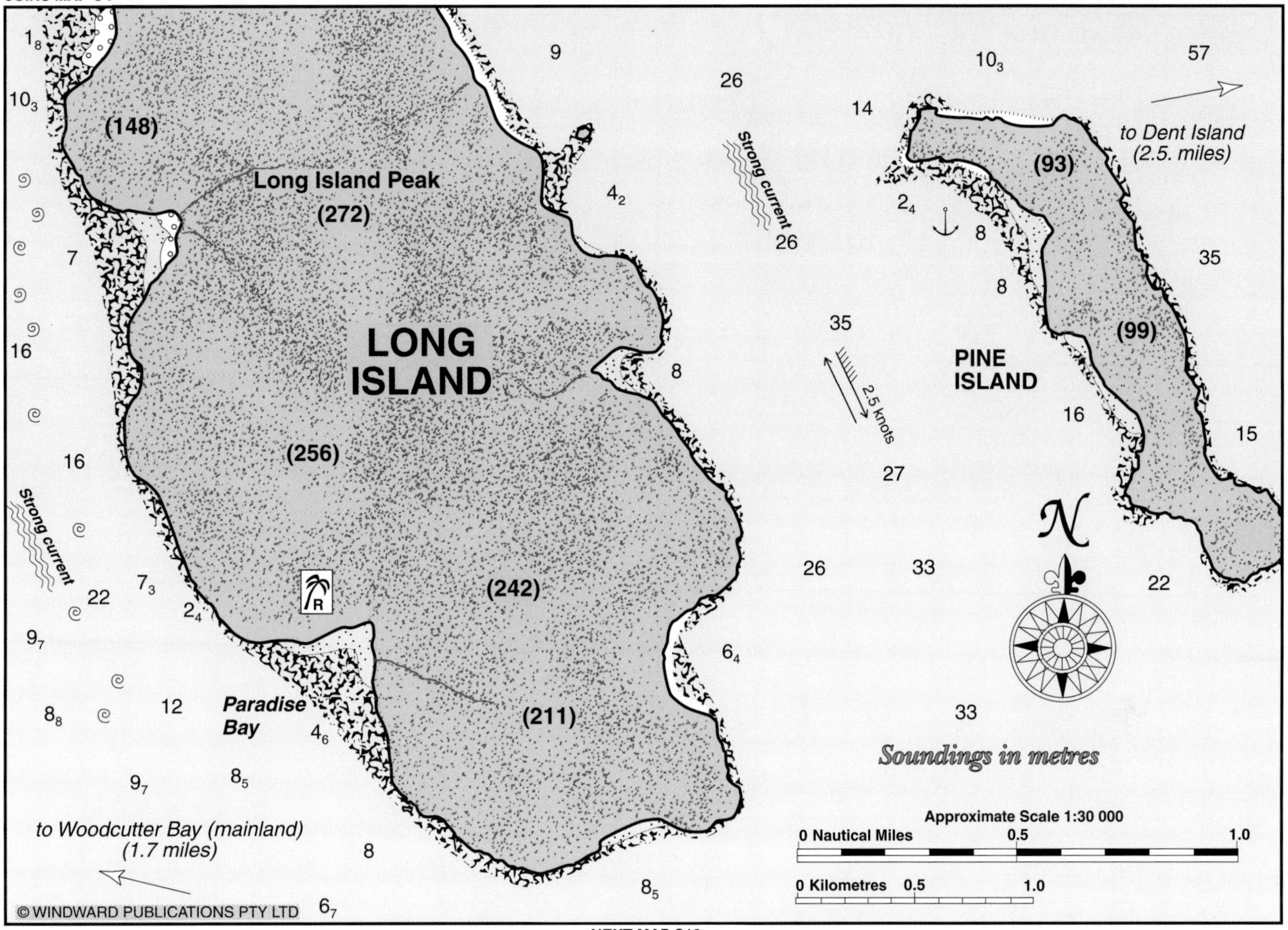

NEXT MAP C6
NEXT MAP C22
Long Island Peak
(272)
(148)
LONG ISLAND
(256)
(242)
(211)
Paradise Bay
Strong current
Strong current
2.5 knots
PINE ISLAND
(93)
(99)
to Dent Island (2.5. miles)
to Woodcutter Bay (mainland) (1.7 miles)
Soundings in metres
Approximate Scale 1:30 000
0 Nautical Miles 0.5 1.0
0 Kilometres 0.5 1.0
© WINDWARD PUBLICATIONS PTY LTD

NEXT MAP S19

PINE ISLAND (C7)

Depth:	**3–8 m**
Bottom:	**Sand & coral**

N
NE
E
SE
S
SW
W
NW

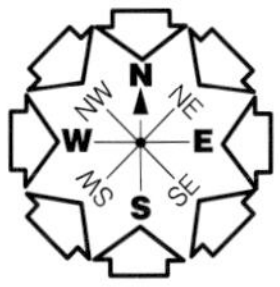

This anchorage offers limited protection and is adjacent to a channel with swift currents. It is suitable for a temporary anchorage in light conditions. There used to be a wreck on the reef at the north-western end of the anchorage.

HANNAH POINT (C8)

Depth:	**8–12 m**
Bottom:	**Coral**

N
NE
E
SE
S
SW
W
NW

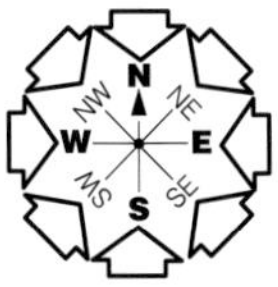

This anchorage on the north-west side of North Molle Island is a light-weather daytime stop and is a difficult anchorage because it drops off suddenly and is subject to tidal currents. You really need light wind and a neap tide to get the best of it.

There is a very nice sand beach; at its south end is a big rock and some interesting bommies for snorkelling. Hannah Point also offers some interesting diving, but watch out for current, particularly as you approach the Point. Should you feel yourself getting into current, back out straight away and don't let yourself stream on around the point.

Visibility for snorkelling and diving will not be especially good except in neap tides and when the wind is fairly light.

UNSAFE PASSAGE (C9)

Unsafe Passage was named by a surveyor who had the navigation of ships in mind; it is perfectly safe provided you exercise due caution. Watch the run of the tide carefully and stay on track using the leads on the north-east end of Daydream Island (they line up at 240°30'T). Hold them in line one above the other until you are through and for a safe distance beyond. The leads show fixed white lights by day (blue at night).

Do not mistake Unsafe Passage for The Causeway, which at high tide appears to separate Mid Molle Island from South Molle Island. As its name suggests, The Causeway actually *connects* the two islands.

If proceeding to Shute Harbour, watch out for the reef that extends for some considerable distance south from Daydream Island. Especially if the tide is ebbing, keep a close watch on your track to avoid being carried northwards by the tidal stream onto the reef.

NORTH MOLLE I. C8

NOT FOR NAVIGATION: SEE CHARTS AUS 253/AUS 252

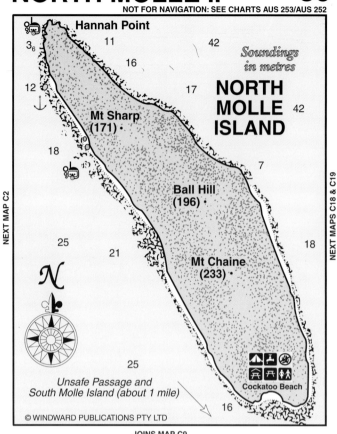

NEXT MAP C2

NEXT MAPS C18 & C19

Hannah Point

3₆ 11

16

42

*Soundings
in metres*

12

17

**NORTH
MOLLE
ISLAND** 42

18

Mt Sharp
(171) •

**Ball Hill
(196)** •

7

25

21

18

N

Mt Chaine
(233) •

25

*Unsafe Passage and
South Molle Island (about 1 mile)*

16

Cockatoo Beach

© WINDWARD PUBLICATIONS PTY LTD

JOINS MAP C9

SUNLOVERS BAY

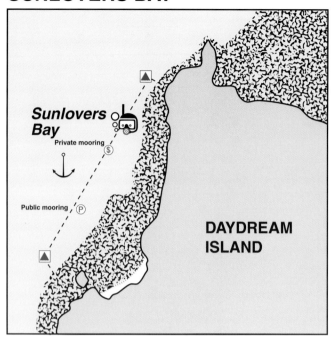

*Sunlovers
Bay*

Private mooring S

Public mooring P

**DAYDREAM
ISLAND**

DAYDREAM ISLAND (C9)

Depth:	5–10 m
Bottom:	Coral & mud

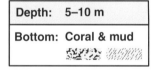

Daydream Island is not a good anchorage for yachts, and some bareboat companies discourage their charterers from anchoring here. The island is immediately adjacent to the Molle Channel and is subject to swift currents.

There is a resort at the northern end and a day-visitor facility on the southern end. If visiting the day-visitor area, anchor on the west side, north of the jetty, and leave some-one aboard to watch the anchor (when the tide changes direction, the anchor may become dislodged). If visiting the resort, radio ahead on VHF channel 16 to make arrangements to tie up at one of the two pile berths withinthe small harbour on the eastern side.

The anchorage shown at the north-western side is off Sunlovers Beach, a beautiful sand beach with obvious appeal for resort guests as well as visitors by sea. Reef protection buoys have been installed to protect what was some rather nice coral, and the snorkelling is still pretty good if the water hasn't been stirred up by fresh winds or spring tides. There is one public mooring for yachts up to 9.5 metres in length; there is also a private commercial mooring, which you will be asked to relinquish if you are tied there when the owner arrives. If anchoring, keep offshore of an imaginary straight line between the reef protection buoys.

BAUER BAY (C9)

Depth:	5–10 m
Bottom:	Coral & mud

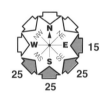

15

25 25

25

From Deedes Point southwards right around to the western side of the island, South Molle is surrounded by tidal rips and overfalls, some of which extend some distance offshore and which can give the appearance of reefs.

Bauer Bay is not one of the most quiescent anchorages among the islands. In fresh southerly conditions it is subject to bullets that funnel around the lofty Spion Kop, The Horn and Lamond Hill. It also tends to be swelly. As the wind easts the anchorage becomes quite rolly, and you may rock uncomfortably at night. It is a safe anchorage, however. The principal reason for using it is to do one of the walks on the island, or to visit the resort, or to take cover if you're suddenly caught out in bad weather. If visiting the resort, contact them on VHF channel 16 and announce your arrival before going ashore. Take the dinghy to the jetty, not to the beach.

The island is a national park and has some beautiful graded walking tracks with spectacular views of the Whitsunday Passage and Molle Channel.

THE MOLLE GROUP

NOT FOR NAVIGATION: SEE CHART AUS 253

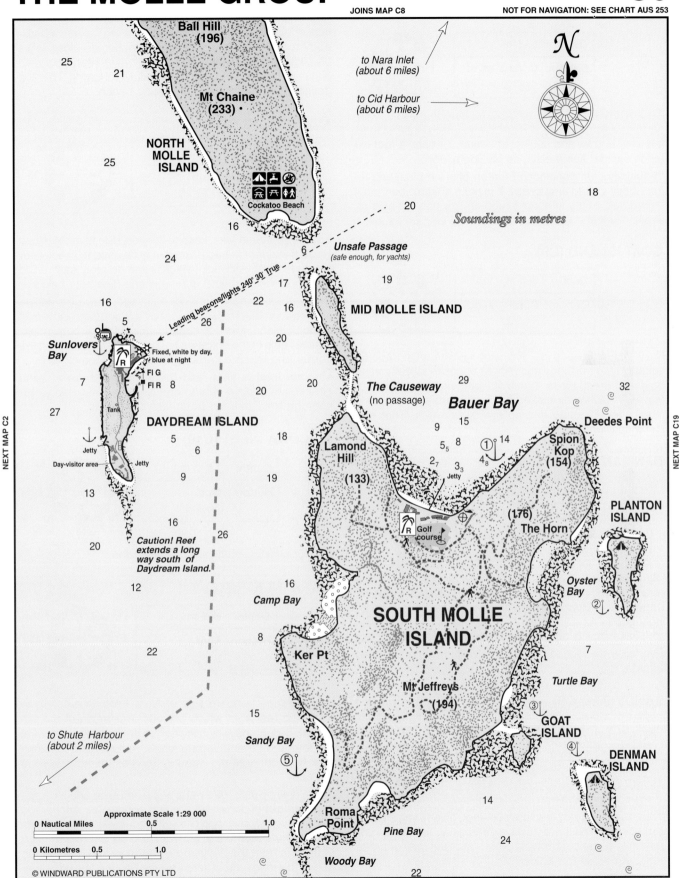

Ball Hill
(196)

25   21

Mt Chaine
(233) •

**NORTH
MOLLE
ISLAND**

25

25

16

to Nara Inlet
(about 6 miles)

to Cid Harbour
(about 6 miles)

18

Soundings in metres

20

Cockatoo Beach

6   *Unsafe Passage*
(safe enough, for yachts)

24

17   19

MID MOLLE ISLAND

22   16

Leading beacons/lights 240° 30′ True

16

26

20

*Sunlovers
Bay*

Fixed, white by day,
blue at night

FI G
FI R   8

The Causeway
(no passage)

29   32

Bauer Bay

20   20

9   15

Deedes Point

7

18

Lamond
Hill

5₅   8

Spion
Kop
(154)

Tank

27

DAYDREAM ISLAND

5

6

20   20

2₇

3₃

①   14

4₈

Jetty

(133)

Jetty

Day-visitor area   Jetty

9

19

(176)

The Horn

**PLANTON
ISLAND**

13

16

*Oyster
Bay*

②

20   *Caution! Reef
extends a long
way south of
Daydream Island.*

26

**SOUTH MOLLE
ISLAND**

7

12

16   *Camp Bay*

Turtle Bay

22   8

Ker Pt

③

**GOAT
ISLAND**

Mt Jeffreys
(194)

④   **DENMAN
ISLAND**

15

*to Shute Harbour
(about 2 miles)*

Sandy Bay

⑤

14

*Roma
Point*

24

Approximate Scale 1:29 000

0 Nautical Miles   0.5   1.0

Pine Bay

0 Kilometres   0.5   1.0

© WINDWARD PUBLICATIONS PTY LTD

Woody Bay   22

NEXT MAP C2

NEXT MAP C19

PLANTON ISLAND (C9)

Depth:	5–8 m
Bottom:	Coral & sand

It is not advisable (or permissible for bareboats) to use the narrow passage between Planton and South Molle islands. It is very narrow and subject to strong currents; a reef extends east for some distance off South Molle.

In suitably light conditions Planton offers a pleasant, infrequently visited anchorage. It is not a suitable overnight anchorage, and you should keep an eye on your anchor, especially if the tide is due to turn while you are ashore.

GOAT ISLAND (C9)

Depth:	5–8 m
Bottom:	Coral & sand

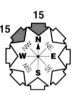

North of Goat Island is a pleasant daytime anchorage (in suitably light northerly conditions) opposite a pretty sand beach on South Molle. Watch out for the edge of the fringing reef. Anchor as close as you prudently can to minimise effects of tide flowing swiftly between Goat and Denman islands.

DENMAN ISLAND (C9)

Depth:	6–9 m
Bottom:	Coral & sand

Denman Island is a pleasant daytime stopoff spot that is rarely visited. Watch out for strong currents between Denman and Goat islands. This anchorage offers surprisingly good protection from the south-east, but the sweet spot is small; it is not a good overnight anchorage.

Overfalls may occur as much as 0.5 miles east of Denman Island.

SANDY BAY (C9)

Depth:	9–14 m
Bottom:	Sand & mud

If approaching from the south or west, give Roma Point a good berth as reef and rocks extend south for some considerable distance from this point. Overfalls may at times be seen west of this point.

The anchorage is well protected with good holding, but tidal effects make it less than ideal. During the ebb a back-eddy runs south from Ker Point. Anchor as close in as practicable to minimise tide effects while keeping a safe distance from the fringing reef to allow for swing. This is a delightful, isolated expanse of sand beach.

MACONA INLET (C10)

Depth:	4.5–6 m
Bottom:	Mud

Entering Macona Inlet, keep to the port side to avoid Proud Rock. If in doubt, a back transit may be used to check your progress; hold Hill Rock (which is immediately east of Cid Island) to the east (left) of Pine Island (see note below).

If you are coming from Hook Passage, stay outside the light beacon that marks the reef off the southern extremity of Hook Island, and don't head straight for the buoy marking the reefs in the entrance to Macona or you may cut the corner (the reef area around Proud Rock) too closely.

Macona Inlet is vast, and there are numbers of sand beaches to explore. Anchorage No. 1 is preferable to anchorage No. 2 in fresh south-east conditions.

MACONA INLET (C10)

Depth:	1.8–3 m
Bottom:	Mud

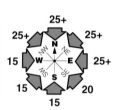

Anchor allowing sufficient swinging room.

NARA INLET (C10)

Depth:	6–9 m
Bottom:	Mud

Keep to the starboard side of Nara Inlet on entering to avoid the reef area which extends over much of the entrance. Bareboats may not attempt the narrow channel at the left, and no one is particularly well advised to. Once past this reef area the water is good all the way down to the end.

There may be disturbed water at the entrance and for some distance out in contrary wind/tide conditions. Anchorage No. 3 may get some chop or swell in south-south-east winds of 25+ knots as there is a clear (virtually unbroken) fetch straight in from the Whitsunday Passage and down to the end of this long narrow fjord. Refuge Bay may be smoother

NARA & MACONA INLETS

NEXT MAPS C13 & C14/15

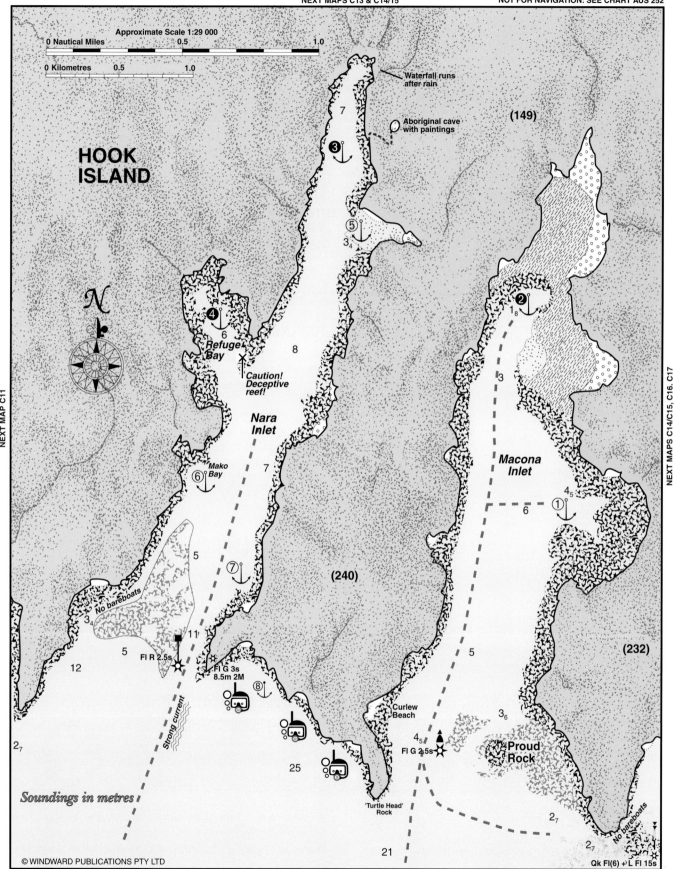

Approximate Scale 1:29 000

0 Nautical Miles   0.5   1.0

0 Kilometres   0.5   1.0

Waterfall runs
after rain

Aboriginal cave
with paintings

(149)

**HOOK
ISLAND**

7

❸

⑤
3₄

N

❹

6

*Refuge
Bay*

8

Caution!
Deceptive
reef!

*Nara
Inlet*

②
1₈

3

*Macona
Inlet*

4₅

⑥ *Mako
Bay*

7

①

6

⑦

5

(240)

5

No bareboats

3₄

5

11

FI R 2.5s

5

12

FI G 3s
8.5m 2M

⑧

Curlew
Beach

5

3₆

2₇

25

4₅
FI G 2.5s

*Proud
Rock*

(232)

Soundings in metres

'Turtle Head'
Rock

2₇

21

2₇

Qk FI(6) + L FI 15s

NEXT MAP C19

See photo C10, page 122

NEXT MAP C11

NEXT MAPS C14/C15, C16, C17

NARA INLET C10a

NEXT MAPS C13 & C14/15   NOT FOR NAVIGATION: SEE CHART AUS 252

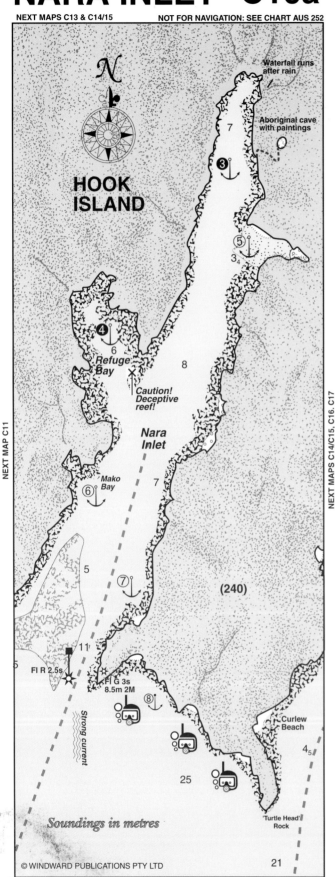

NEXT MAP C11

NEXT MAPS C14/C15, C16. C17

NEXT MAP C19   See photo C10, page 122

(as will Anchorage No. 5 for smaller yachts and trailer sailers).

It is possible to anchor quite close to the end of the inlet. The holding is excellent. Just before the end (on the starboard side) a waterfall runs after rain.

Marine Parks rangers have constructed a track up to an Aboriginal cave site (with paintings); it is reached from a small beach about 600 metres in from Anchorage No. 5. Anyone in reasonable health and with good footwear shouldn't find the climb too daunting. Be sure to shut the gate (to keep out the local art-loving goats), and stay on the boardwalk which is there to reduce dust, too much of which will eventually obliterate the paintings.

The names painted on some of the rocks on either side of the inlet have been put there by troglodytes. Their graffiti spoils for everyone the natural beauty of this magnificent inlet, and the practice is abhorrent. Visitors who observe such vandals should insure that the Marine Parks rangers find out who is responsible (see page 105 for their phone number at the Whitsunday Information Centre).

REFUGE BAY (C10)

Be very careful to avoid the deceptive reef extending from the point on the northern side. This is now easier to avoid, as a special mark has been placed on the end of it, but in the past it has been the undoing of more than one or so yachts.

Refuge Bay is less susceptible to swell than is anchorage No. 3 in heavy south to south-east winds; it may be blustery in winds of 25 knots and more.

This bay used to be known as Shark Bay, possibly because both Nara and Macona Inlets are reputed to be spawning grounds for hammerheads. On the other hand, some local skippers say they've never seen a shark here. Sharks have never yet been a problem in the Whitsundays. Enjoy a swim, but don't establish the presence or absence of sharks by thrashing around in the water making wounded fish sounds.

NARA INLET (C10)

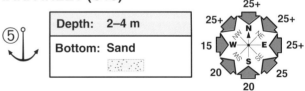

Smaller yachts and trailer sailers will be able to make use of this delightful cove with its lovely sand beach. It provides protection from chop and swell in fresh southerly conditions. Trailer sailers can anchor right over the sand beach; larger yachts should split the difference between the fringing coral reefs. There is very limited swimming room. It is shallow, and if your boat is threatening to swing the wrong way, a stern anchor may solve the problem.

MAKO BAY (C10)

Depth:	3–5 m
Bottom:	Sand

Mako Bay has a pleasant beach for swimming or a barbecue in northerly weather (when it is well protected). Anchor outside the reef, over sand.

NARA INLET (C10)

Depth:	7–11 m
Bottom:	Mud

There are more protected anchorages than this in Nara Inlet, but this one is tenable in suitably light conditions if you wish to remain close to the entrance. There is good snorkelling in the area between Nara and Macona. Or, you may just want to fish from the dinghy around the reef at the entrance to the inlet.

NARA INLET (C10)

Depth:	7–11 m
Bottom:	Mud & coral

In suitably light weather the fringing reef on the point of land that separates Nara and Macona inlets offers good snorkelling and exploring. Ideally, the conditions should be light easterlies and neap tides, at or near the bottom of the tide.

CAVES COVE (C11)

This shallow cove just south of Stonehaven has private commercial moorings in it. It is not the best of anchorages but may provide refuge, in a pinch, hanging off one of the moorings. When the owner comes along be prepared to relinquish your spot immediately.

FALSE NARA (C10)

Depth:	11–15 m
Bottom:	Mud & coral

False Nara gets its name because it masquerades as Nara Inlet. You won't get far if you try to go in here.
This is not an easy anchorage because it is fairly deep. At neap tides, and when the wind is quiet, it can provide a good dive or snorkel.

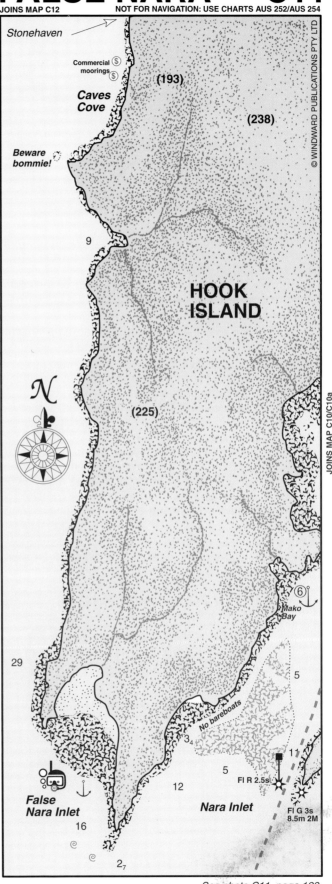

FALSE NARA C11

JOINS MAP C12   NOT FOR NAVIGATION: USE CHARTS AUS 252/AUS 254

© WINDWARD PUBLICATIONS PTY LTD

Stonehaven

Commercial moorings

Caves Cove

Beware bommie!

(193)

(238)

9

HOOK ISLAND

(225)

JOINS MAP C10/C10a

Mako Bay

29

No bareboats

5

3 4

5

12

16

Nara Inlet

Fl R 2.5s

Fl G 3s 8.5m 2M

False Nara Inlet

2 7

See photo C11, page 123

STONEHAVEN ANCHORAGE (C12)

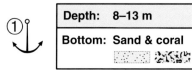

Approaching from the northern sectors there are a number of potential hazards, and caution is needed.

If approaching from Butterfly Bay, beware the extensive reef off Hayman Island; at high tide, when this reef is covered, you may be deceived; stay closer to Hook Island (about two-thirds of the total distance between Groper Point and Stanley Point).

If approaching from Hayman keep a lookout for the beacon which marks the considerable bulge on Hayman's reef south-south-west of Groper Point. Keep well south until you are past this and can see the next beacon on the southern tip of the reef and the yellow mark on the northern tip of Black Island's reef.

Sealark Patch (south-east of Black Island) is a shallow patch of shifting sand which is not a hazard to navigation.

Stonehaven is a majestic anchorage surrounded by some lofty hills; it is very blustery in fresh south-east conditions, and there may be 'bullets' in the anchorage – sharp gusts of much greater force than the average wind. Moreover, the anchorage is relatively deep. Because of these two factors, if there are other yachts in the anchorage put down plenty of anchor line, and take special care to allow enough swinging room. A yacht anchored where the maximum depth at high tide is 12 metres may have as much as 60 metres of scope out, and its maximum swinging circle may be almost 60 metres. Anchor at least five boat lengths away.

The bottom is sand and coral, with isolated bommies, and your anchor chain will make a dreadful noise scraping over the bottom. Rig a rope snubber. (See page 83 for more discussion of snubbers and swinging room.)

STONEHAVEN ANCHORAGE (C12)

Watch out for scattered bommies off the fringing reef.

There is a good sand beach here which offers good fossicking. A patch of coral (marked by the snorkeller/diver symbol) may provide some interesting exploring if the wind hasn't been too strong and the tides not too great.

STONEHAVEN ANCHORAGE (C12)

This anchorage possibly offers slightly more protection in gusty south to south-east weather, but it is not as 'cozy'.

LANGFORD ISLAND (C12)

If approaching from the west, keep well outside Bird Island. Reef protection buoys have been installed along Langford's eastern reef; anchor outside (offshore) of an imaginary straight line between these buoys. There are also some public moorings which will make life easier than anchoring, as this is not an easy anchorage (scattered coral heads on the bottom can snag your anchor). Langford offers a good dive all along the north-east side, but particularly where the 'best dive' symbol is. A nice island.

LANGFORD ISLAND (C12)

Watch out for scattered bommies lying along the reef margin. Anchorage No. 4 (above) is preferable, and the snorkelling is better there, too.

BIRD ISLAND (C12)

Watch out for strong currents that sweep by this side of Bird Island.

This anchorage is possibly of greatest interest to divers, and this side of Bird Island offers an excellent drift dive with dropoffs. Either be prepared for drift diving (i.e. have someone in the dinghy to pick you up), or go only at slack water on a neap tide. The current is reported to always run south along this side of the island.

HOOK ISLAND NORTH-WEST   C12

JOINS MAP C12

NOT FOR NAVIGATION: SEE CHARTS AUS 254/AUS 252

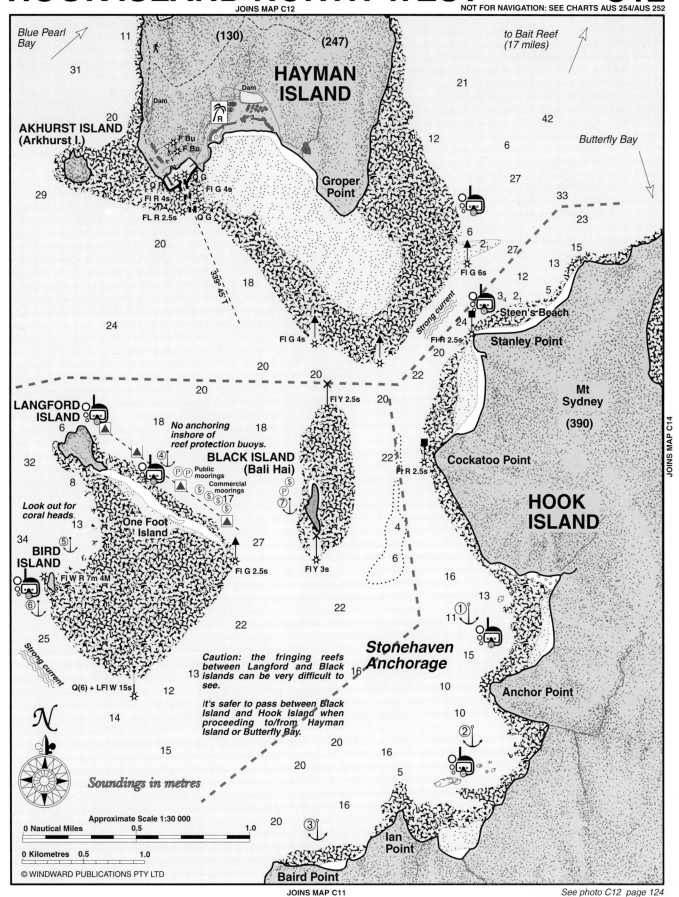

Blue Pearl Bay

11

(130)   (247)

HAYMAN ISLAND

Dam

31

to Bait Reef (17 miles)

21

42

AKHURST ISLAND (Arkhurst I.)

20

Dam

R

F Bu
F Bu

N

Q G

Fl G 4s

Groper Point

12

6

Butterfly Bay

27

33

23

29

Fl R 4s

FL R 2.5s Q G

6

2
1

27

15

13

Fl G 6s

20

3₄ 2₁

12

5

18

Steen's Beach

24

339° 45' T

24

Fl R 2.5s

Stanley Point

Fl G 4s

20

22

Mt Sydney

(390)

20

20

Fl Y 2.5s

20

LANGFORD ISLAND

6

18

No anchoring inshore of reef protection buoys.

18

20

22

Cockatoo Point

32

④

P P Public moorings

BLACK ISLAND (Bali Hai)

Fl R 2.5s

HOOK ISLAND

8

$ $ Commercial moorings

$ 17

$

P

⑦

4

Look out for coral heads.

13

One Foot Island

6

BIRD ISLAND

34 ⑤

f

27

16

Fl W R 7m 4M

Fl G 2.5s

Fl Y 3s

11 ①

⑥

13

25

Strong current

Stonehaven Anchorage

15

Anchor Point

Q(6) + LFl W 15s

12

Caution: the fringing reefs between Langford and Black islands can be very difficult to see.

13

16

10

14

It's safer to pass between Black Island and Hook Island when proceeding to/from Hayman Island or Butterfly Bay.

10

②

15

20

16

5

Soundings in metres

20

16

20

Approximate Scale 1:30 000

0 Nautical Miles   0.5   1.0

0 Kilometres 0.5   1.0

20

③

Ian Point

© WINDWARD PUBLICATIONS PTY LTD

Baird Point

See photo C12 page 124

JOINS MAP C14

HAYMAN ISLAND

C13

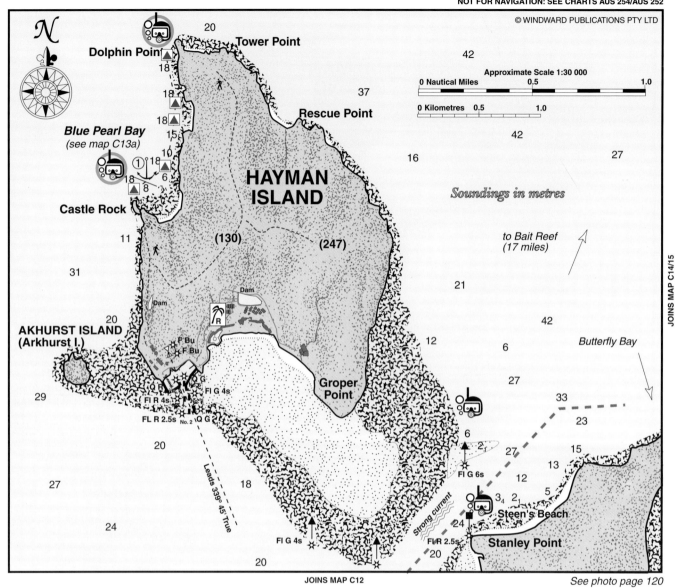

© WINDWARD PUBLICATIONS PTY LTD

Soundings in metres

BLACK ISLAND (C12)

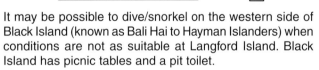

Depth:	5–11 m
Bottom:	Sand & coral

It may be possible to dive/snorkel on the western side of Black Island (known as Bali Hai to Hayman Islanders) when conditions are not as suitable at Langford Island. Black Island has picnic tables and a pit toilet.

See photo page 120

HAYMAN ISLAND (C13)

Hayman Island has one of Australia's most talked about resorts with a man-made boat harbour on the southern side where, in days gone by, there was a rather poor anchorage. Before entering the harbour, yachts must obtain permission from the Hayman marina office (on VHF channel 16 or HF 2436 kHz).

The harbour entrance is marked by six beacons (Nos 1 to 6) lighted at night. On the hill behind and in line with the entrance are two triangular leads (fixed blue lights at night) that line up 339°45'T.

The floating marina berths have power and water. The marina office is on the breakwater at the top of the marina. The island's functional facilities (e.g. power generation plant, desalination plant, sewage treatment plant) are located in the area beyond the marina office.

The waterway south from Hayman across to Hook Island is strewn with navigation hazards and is haunted by the spirits of defrocked mariners. A number of lights and beacons have been installed on the worst trouble spots; use extreme care in this area.

You will notice that Akhurst Island is 'Arkhurst' on the charts, a stuff-up in the Admiralty hydrographic office. John Akhurst was a crew member on HMS *Salamander*, which surveyed the Whitsundays in the 1860s. On the Admiralty chart of 1866 this island is shown as Akhurst. Somehow, from 1916 onwards, the charts show 'Arkhurst' Island. It was undoubtedly named Akhurst by *Salamander*'s captain, Commander Nares (*source:* local historian, Ray Blackwood).

BLUE PEARL BAY (C13)

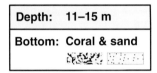

Do not attempt to go between Akhurst Island and Hayman Island when sailing around to Blue Pearl Bay.

Blue Pearl is a lovely expanse of bay with beautiful beaches. The excellent fringing reef has sustained anchor damage due to the popularity of the bay and the fact that the bottom slopes off somewhat steeply and yachts have tended to anchor too close to the reef. To prevent further assault and to preserve some excellent coral, reef protection buoys have been installed. Do not anchor inshore of an imaginary straight line between the marker buoys.

Outside the no-anchoring buoys you will be in 11–15 metres of water, so be sure to put out plenty of scope, and leave sufficient swinging room between yachts. This is not the most quiescent of overnight anchorages, there often being plenty of action due to swell refracting around the points and reverberating off the sheer rock faces of Hayman Island.

There are two public moorings (suitable for use by dinghies only) inside the no-anchoring limit in the southern end of the bay. A two-hour limit applies to the use of public moorings (to give more people a chance to use them). There may also be a commercial mooring or two.

The bay offers some excellent diving and snorkelling. The best snorkelling is in the southern bay. The best dive sites are off Castle Rock and Dolphin Point. There are a number of large bommies between Castle Rock and the middle of the bay. Be mindful of the state of the tide; the currents off Castle Rock can be very swift. Dolphin Point offers one of the best dives in the islands.

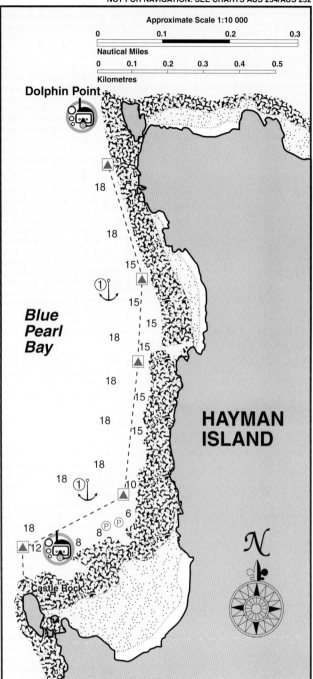

BLUE PEARL BAY   C13a
NOT FOR NAVIGATION: SEE CHARTS AUS 254/AUS 252

NORTHERN HOOK ISLAND

The north coast of Hook Island has beautiful fringing coral reefs that offer good diving and snorkelling. These have attracted lots of attention during the past ten years, and a considerable amount of anchor damage has been sustained by the reefs. To prevent further degeneration, the Organisation of Underwater Coral Heroes (OUCH) has conducted underwater surveys of much of this area, and park rangers have installed reef protection buoys in a number of bays.

All of the area along the north coast of Hook Island, between Alcyonaria Point (the western entrance of Butterfly

Bay) and the Woodpile (a distinctive rock formation at the western end of Pinnacle Bay) has been declared a Marine National Park 'B' Zone (a look-but-don't-touch zone – fishing and shell collecting (even dead shells) are prohibited). In addition, Manta Ray Bay has been declared a Special Management Area, where anchoring is totally prohibited.

The installation of reef protection marker buoys is continuing. Where these are not installed (and, indeed, at all times, skippers need to take special care to minimise damage to coral when dropping anchor. Anchor over sand (light-coloured bottom) and try to keep the anchor and chain away from coral (dark patches). This will not only help preserve the coral but will save any headaches should the anchor or chain become fouled by coral.

Approaches to Butterfly Bay

If coming from the west, i.e. the Hayman Island and Stonehaven areas, observe caution in negotiating the passage between Hook Island and Hayman Island. The reef extends a very long way off Hayman Island, and you should be considerably closer to Hook Island than to Hayman Island when negotiating this passage. If the tide is high, one can be deceived.

If approaching from the east side of Hook Island, be prepared for strong currents and overfalls around Pinnacle Point.

Butterfly Bay is tucked in behind the precipitous north-east face of Mt Sydney and is, like Stonehaven Anchorage, subject to bullets in fresh south to south-east conditions; these whistle down and strike anchored yachts

BUTTERFLY BAY (eastern wing)

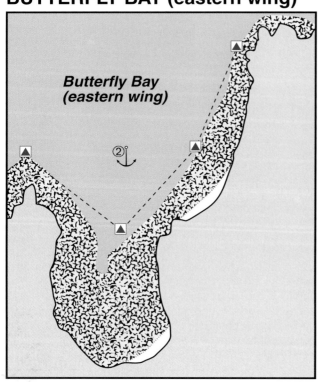

Butterfly Bay (eastern wing)

like a punch. You may experience sharp gusts off Alcyonaria Point when you approach, so it's a good idea to have the motor going and to get sails down before the yacht is where manoeuvring is restricted.

A shallow patch with 2.1 metres water at '0' tide is in the entrance to Butterfly Bay; this is not usually a problem for yachts, but if yours draws 2.1 metres or more, keep an eye out if the tide is low.

Set your anchor well. Some parts of the anchorage have restricted room; make sure you have allowed enough room to swing, to avoid both fringing reefs and other yachts already anchored.

Your anchor chain dragging across the bottom may keep you awake; rig a rope snubber (see 'Anchor noise', page 83). There are a number of living coral heads on the bottom, and Butterfly Bay has a reputation for snagging anchors. Anchor in a sandy spot and keep the chain away from dark patches, which are coral.

In light north-east conditions, you may find yourself rolling uncomfortably at night. If the anchorage around you is not crowded, rigging a stern anchor will make for a more restful night, and it may help to prevent your bow anchor from wrapping itself around a bommie. Buoying the stern anchor (a buoy tied to the crown on a line long enough to just reach the surface) may make it easier to retrieve.

As funds become available, public moorings are being installed to help prevent anchor damage and to assist reef appreciation.

Butterfly Bay is shaped somewhat like a butterfly with one underdeveloped wing. Coincidentally, colonies of butterflies may be found at times in the moist shade of trees along the creek beds. There are several very good dive/snorkel spots, particularly along the bay side of Alcyonaria Point, the latter named by local divers because of the abundance of that coral form there. (See 'Diving and snorkelling in the Whitsundays' for more information on diving in this bay.)

BUTTERFLY BAY (C14/15)

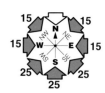

Depth:	6–9 m
Bottom:	Mud & coral

Anchorage No.1 offers the best protection, particularly from swell in north-east weather, and it is the most snug, but watch out for isolated bombies. Pick your way up along the left side of the reef, which is steep-to, and have a lookout posted at all times. There are bommies in the centre.

Allow enough swinging room. It is possible to go right up to the end; swinging room there is limited to about two boat lengths, and positioning the yacht is critical.

Butterfly Bay is high on the list of bays to have moorings installed when funds are available.

HOOK ISLAND NORTH & EAST C14/15

NOT FOR NAVIGATION: SEE CHART AUS 252

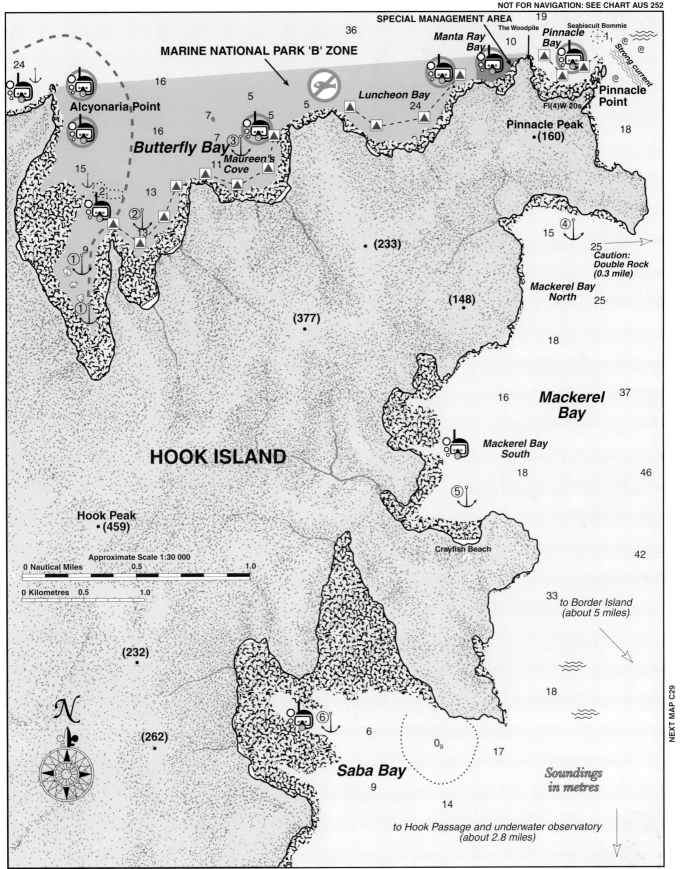

SPECIAL MANAGEMENT AREA

MARINE NATIONAL PARK 'B' ZONE

36

19

Manta Ray Bay

The Woodpile

10

Pinnacle Bay

Seabiscuit Bommie

1

Strong current

24

Alcyonaria Point

16

5

5

Luncheon Bay

24

Pinnacle Point

Fl(4)W 20s

7 6

5

16

5

Butterfly Bay

3

Maureen's Cove

7

11

15

2

13

2

13

9

1

1

Pinnacle Peak
• (160)

18

• (233)

15

4

25

Caution:
Double Rock
(0.3 mile)

• (148)

*Mackerel Bay
North*

25

18

• (377)

16

*Mackerel
Bay*

37

HOOK ISLAND

*Mackerel Bay
South*

18

46

5

Hook Peak
• (459)

Crayfish Beach

42

Approximate Scale 1:30 000

0 Nautical Miles   0.5   1.0

0 Kilometres   0.5   1.0

33 *to Border Island
(about 5 miles)*

• (232)

18

N

• (262)

6

6

0 9

17

*Soundings
in metres*

Saba Bay

9

14

*to Hook Passage and underwater observatory
(about 2.8 miles)*

JOINS MAP C13

JOINS MAP C16

See photo C14/15 page 125

NEXT MAP C29

BUTTERFLY BAY (C14/15)

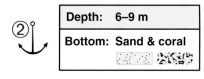

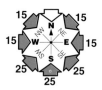

Anchorage No. 2 is less restricted and may be less crowded for those who prefer a bit of relative loneliness. However, it is subject to quite strong 'bullets'. Reef protection markers have been installed; do not anchor inshore of an imaginary straight line between the buoys. The reef and sand beach here (in the top of the 'underdeveloped wing') offer fascinating exploring. Watch out for stingrays when you walk on the sand flats (shuffle your feet). The point which separates this anchorage from No. 1 has nice flat elevated rocks for sunbaking.

MAUREEN'S COVE (C14/15)

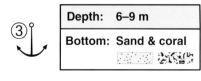

Maureen's Cove has some good snorkel/dive spots. Reef protection buoys have been installed here; do not anchor inshore of an imaginary straight line between the buoys. This anchorage has a pleasant sand beach.

MAUREEN'S COVE

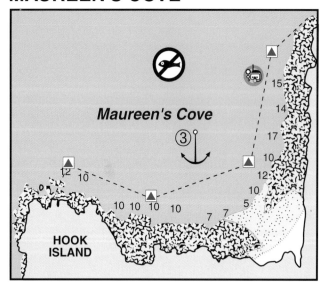

LUNCHEON BAY (C14/15)

Luncheon Bay has some good dive sites, and reef protection markers have been installed to prevent anchor damage. Don't anchor inshore of an imaginary straight line between these buoys. It is not a good anchorage, being subject to swift currents and being relatively deep. A number of moorings for yachts up to 18 metres in length

LUNCHEON BAY

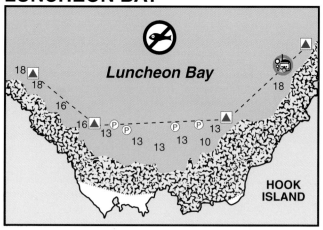

have been installed to facilitate reef appreciation. A very pleasant spot to stop for lunch.

MANTA RAY BAY (C14/15)

Approaching Manta Ray Bay from the east, watch out for Seabiscuit Bommie which lies immediately north-north-west of the Pinnacles and which is a potential hazard at spring low tides. Give the point a good berth. The north-eastern tip of Hook Island may be subject to strong currents, overfalls and very choppy seas in fresh south-east winds with a flooding tide.

Manta Ray Bay offers some of the best underwater scenery in the Whitsundays and is a favourite spot for diving and snorkelling. The bay has been declared a Special Management Area to help preserve the live coral, which has been reduced considerably over the past decade by anchor damage. Anchoring in the bay is totally prohibited. There are four public moorings, two for dinghy-sized craft and two for vessels up to 9.5 metres (and there may be more in the future as funds for moorings become available). A time limit of two hours applies to use of public moorings. There are also private commercial moorings here. If you pick one up, don't leave the vessel unattended

MANTA RAY BAY

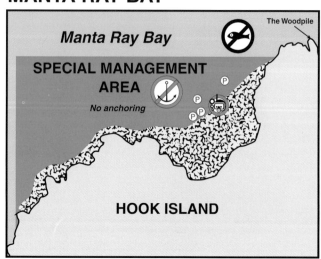

on the mooring, and be prepared to relinquish it when the owner comes along. Like many of the bays along this side of Hook Island, Manta Ray is a poor overnight anchorage.

PINNACLE BAY (C14/15)

The Pinnacles are some rather striking rocks on the north-eastern corner of Hook Island. The bay formed between them and 'The Woodpile' (a volcanic dyke on the most northern tip of the island that looks like a stack of logs) offers some excellent diving. Reef protection buoys have been installed in this bay; do not anchor inshore of an imaginary straight line between the buoys (see map below).

PINNACLE BAY

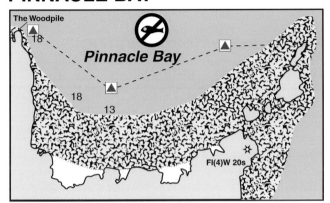

MACKEREL BAY (C14/15)

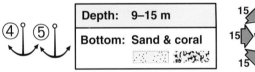

Depth:	**9–15 m**
Bottom:	**Sand & coral**

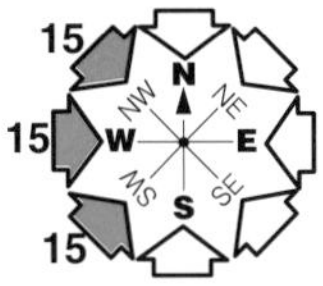

Mackerel Bay offers two infrequently explored anchorages in the right winds; both anchorages are exposed in sou'-easterlies, even No. 5, which suffers from refracted swells. The reef offers some interesting exploring with the dinghy or in the water with snorkelling gear. Good fishing.

SABA BAY (C16)

Depth:	**5–10 m**
Bottom:	**Sand & coral**

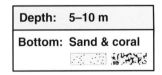

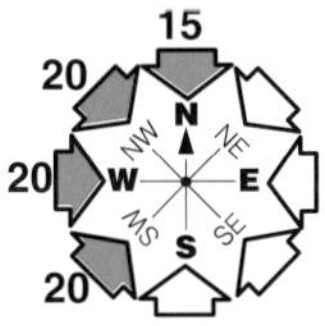

Exercise caution in negotiating the reef.

Saba Bay is not frequently visited because it is exposed to the south and east and therefore it is only habitable in winds from the north (and only safe as an overnight anchorage after the trade winds season is over (late October until about March). It has some excellent fringing reef and can provide some interesting snorkelling and diving. It is high on the list of bays to have reef protection markers installed; if none are evident, be careful not to drop your anchor over coral.

HOOK SOUTH-EAST   C16

JOINS MAP C14/15   NOT FOR NAVIGATION: SEE CHART AUS 252

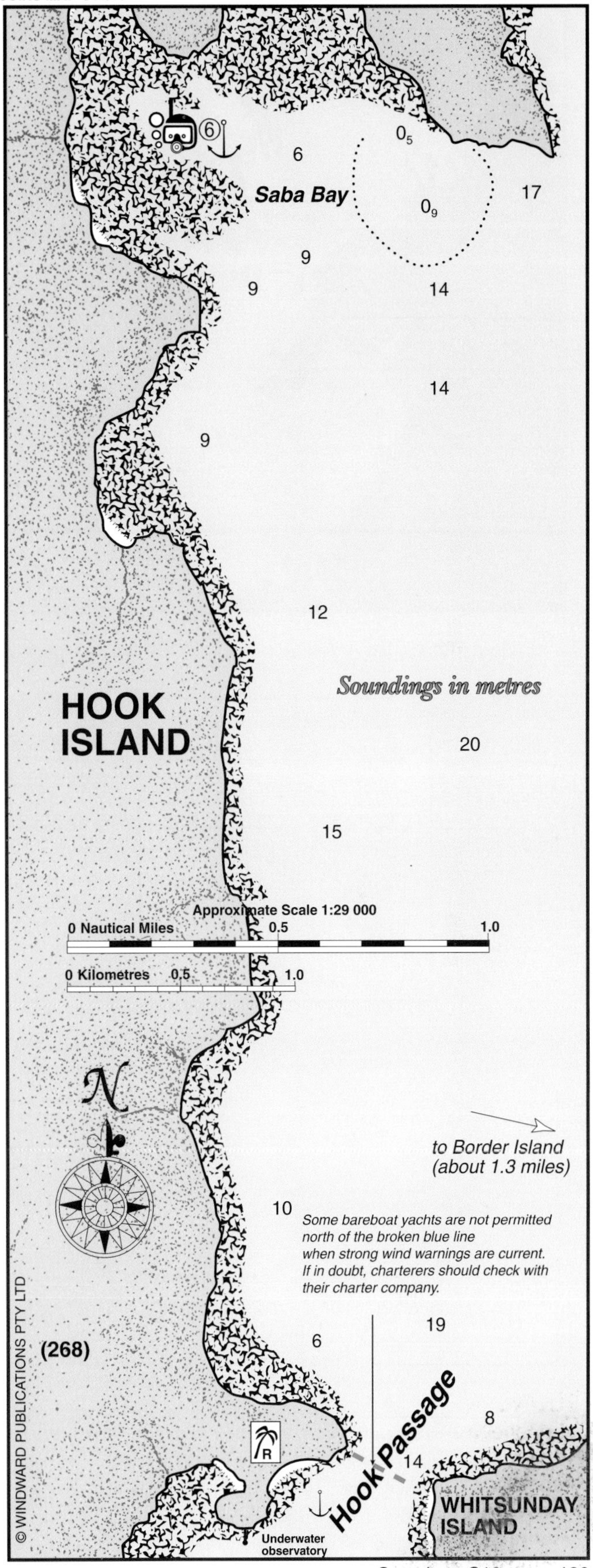

Saba Bay

HOOK ISLAND

Soundings in metres

Approximate Scale 1:29 000

0 Nautical Miles   0.5   1.0

0 Kilometres   0.5   1.0

to Border Island (about 1.3 miles)

Some bareboat yachts are not permitted north of the broken blue line when strong wind warnings are current. If in doubt, charterers should check with their charter company.

(268)

Hook Passage

WHITSUNDAY ISLAND

Underwater observatory

© WINDWARD PUBLICATIONS PTY LTD

JOINS MAP C10

JOINS MAP C29

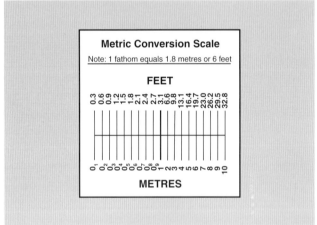

Metric Conversion Scale

Note: 1 fathom equals 1.8 metres or 6 feet

FEET

0.3 0.6 0.9 1.2 1.5 1.8 2.1 2.4 2.7 3.1 6.6 9.8 13.1 16.4 19.7 23.0 26.2 29.5 32.8

0.1 0.2 0.3 0.4 0.5 0.6 0.7 0.8 0.9 1 2 3 4 5 6 7 8 9 10

METRES

HOOK PASSAGE (C17)

Hook Passage offers a relatively narrow obstruction to the tidal stream and is therefore subject to strong currents and eddies. The high land on either side guarantees fickle winds which veer 180°. Be prepared.

When heading north through the passage in flood tides and when the wind is fresh from the south-east, be prepared for overfalls on the other side.

If you are proceeding south from from the passage, note that there is large shallow area with some dangerous bommies on the north-western side of Whitsunday Island. So, when heading south, keep to starboard (west of centre) between Hook and Whitsunday islands (steer about 200°M) until well south-west of the beacon marking the reef off Hook Island's south-eastern corner.

HOOK OBSERVATORY/RESORT (C17)

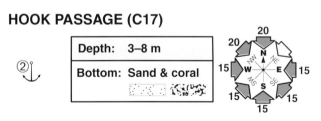

Depth:	10–12 m
Bottom:	Mud & coral

The Hook underwater observatory is located on the western side at the top of Hook Passage. This is not a good place to anchor, there being all manner of hazards on the bottom of the anchorage, and many an anchor that has been lost there is just waiting to snag the next one. The resort has eight moorings which are available for a small fee for day and/or overnight use (contact the resort office on VHF channel 16). Temporary anchorage is also available off the sand beach north of the observatory. The resort itself consists of 12 cabins with bunks, a shared amenities block, restaurant/coffee shop, kiosk, barbecue facilities and a small bar. The observatory operates a coral-viewing 'sub'; scuba diving and snorkelling are available at local reefs. (See also 'Island resorts of the Whitsundays'.)

The observatory is a sunken metal tube that allows you to descend and view, from underwater, coral and fish which inhabit the local reefs. Unfortunately the visibility is not always all that good in this restricted passage, particularly with winds from the northern sector which cause fine sediments to rise, or at times of spring tides with strong south-east winds. The observatory does provide an opportunity to view fish at very close quarters.

HOOK PASSAGE (C17)

Depth:	3–8 m
Bottom:	Sand & coral

This is a pleasant daytime stopoff with a lovely little beach.

HOOK PASSAGE

C17

19

6

29

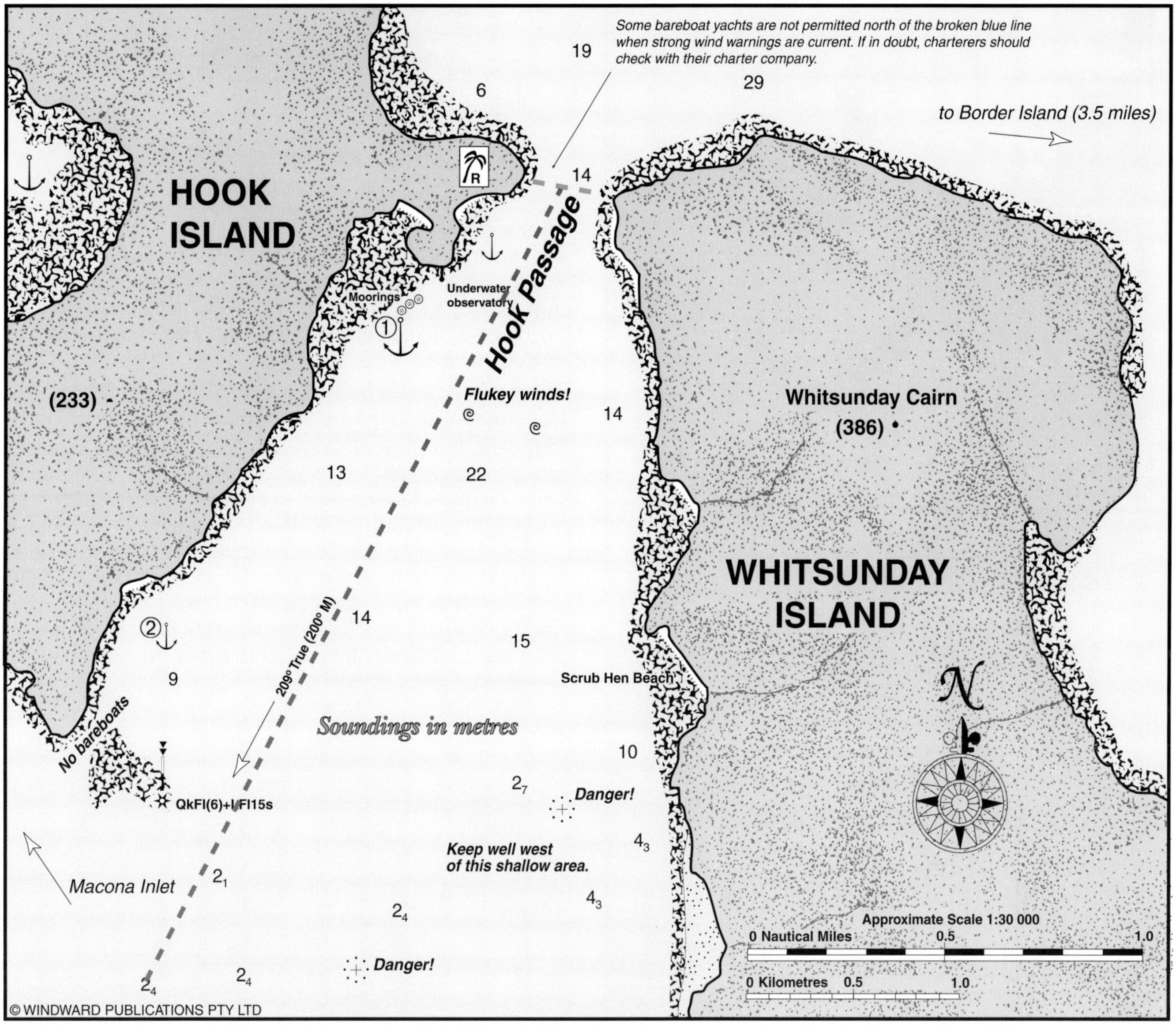

Some bareboat yachts are not permitted north of the broken blue line when strong wind warnings are current. If in doubt, charterers should check with their charter company.

to Border Island (3.5 miles)

14

HOOK ISLAND

14

Moorings

Underwater observatory

Hook Passage

Flukey winds!

14

WHITSUNDAY ISLAND

Whitsunday Cairn

(386)

(233)

13

22

209° True (200° M)

14

2_1

15

2_4

2_4

9

Scrub Hen Beach

Soundings in metres

10

2_7

Danger!

4_3

QkFl(6)+LFl15s

Keep well west of this shallow area.

4_3

Macona Inlet

Danger!

No bareboats

JOINS MAP C10

NEXT MAP C29

N

Approximate Scale 1:30 000

0 Nautical Miles   0.5   1.0

0 Kilometres   0.5   1.0

© WINDWARD PUBLICATIONS PTY LTD

See photo C17, page 126

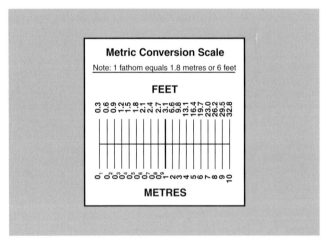

Metric Conversion Scale

Note: 1 fathom equals 1.8 metres or 6 feet

MAY'S BAY (C18)

Depth:	3–6 m
Bottom:	Mud

If coming from Hook Passage, watch out for two bommies off the north-western shore of Whitsunday Island which are hazards to navigation at low tide. Proceeding southwards, stay to the right of centre in the passage and don't turn for May's Bay until you are about half a nautical mile beyond the beacon marking the reef on the south-east tip of Hook Island.

The anchorage can be swelly as the wind easts. The water is deeper towards the western end of the beach.

May's Bay has a lovely sandy beach, called Bernie's Beach after Bernie Katchor, with whom it was a favourite spot when he started operations in the early '70s with the first crewed charter boat in the area, *Nari.* 'May' was the wife of Lindsay Heiser; she and her husband were early partners in the Hook underwater observatory, and before their accommodation was finished at the observatory site, they stayed on their boat. When the weather blew too strongly from the south-east, they used to move over and stay in this lovely sheltered anchorage.

WHITSUNDAY ISLAND NORTH-WEST   C18

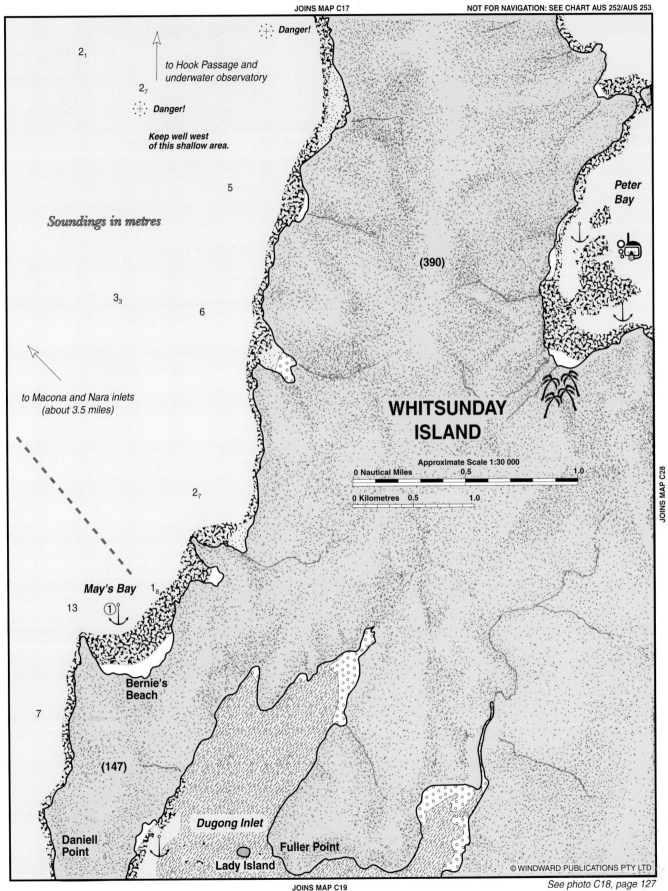

2_1

Danger!

to Hook Passage and
underwater observatory

2_7

Danger!

Keep well west
of this shallow area.

5

Soundings in metres

Peter
Bay

3_3

6

(390)

to Macona and Nara inlets
(about 3.5 miles)

WHITSUNDAY
ISLAND

2_7

Approximate Scale 1:30 000

| 0 Nautical Miles | 0.5 | 1.0 |

| 0 Kilometres | 0.5 | 1.0 |

May's Bay 1_8

13   ①

Bernie's
Beach

7

(147)

Dugong Inlet

Daniell
Point

Fuller Point

Lady Island

JOINS MAP C28

See photo C18, page 127

SAWMILL BAY (C19)

Depth:	3–6 m
Bottom:	Mud & sand

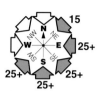

Watch out for strong currents and gusts of wind when entering from the south between Cid Island and Loriard Point. Give Reef Point a good berth.

Cid Harbour is a very large harbour and one of the all-weather anchorages of the Whitsundays. It is popular with yachts, trailer sailers and campers alike. There are several sand beaches. Campsites are located at Sawmill Beach and Dugong Beach; both of these have toilets, and you may be able to find tank water at Dugong Beach. Both of these beaches are popular with trailer sailers.

A 1-kilometre track follows the 200-metre contour from Sawmill Beach to Dugong Beach. About halfway along are arrows pointing to a very rough bush track which leads up to Whitsunday Peak – a steep climb and not a clearly marked track. Only those in good condition wearing solid footwear, and with bush sense, should attempt it. Needless to say the views will reward the effort.

Ross Islet, also called Orchid Rock, is sometimes a nesting place for sea eagles. It is best to stay away in nesting season (August to September). If disturbed, these raptors can, in fright, damage their eggs. As the island's other name suggests, it is one of many rocky places in the Whitsundays where wild orchids (Dendrobium discolor) grow. (Orchids are protected in Queensland.)

SAWMILL BEACH (C19)

Depth:	5–8 m
Bottom:	Sand & coral

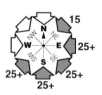

Approach cautiously and be aware of the state of the tide as the beach slope is fairly gradual.

This is the best of Cid's beaches and it also has an established campsite with tables. All rubbish created ashore must be taken away with you. Sawmill Beach is a great spot for a picnic.

DUGONG INLET (C19)

Depth:	1.5–3 m
Bottom:	Mud

Approach is from Cid Harbour. Stay about 150 metres off the port shore and keep a lookout.

This is a shallow anchorage but one in which the bottom is very soft mud, so not much damage can be done if you do find yourself settling in at low tide. If the wind changes you should be able to make your way across to one of the south-east anchorages without difficulty.

HOMESTEAD BAY (C19)

Depth:	2–4 m
Bottom:	Sand & coral

Homestead Bay is a small, pretty bay and makes a good picnic spot. There are excellent views of the Passage from Cid Island.

NARI'S BEACH, JOE'S BEACH (C19)

Depth:	4–6 m
Bottom:	Mud & sand

Nari's and Joe's are nice sand beaches that are good for a lunchtime stopoff. Because anchorage is either in, or very near, the narrow channel between Cid and Whitsunday Islands, these locations are subject to tidal influences and are not really satisfactory overnight anchorages. You should also keep an eye on your anchor. There are scrubfowl (Megapodius reinwardt) mounds behind some of these beaches. Don't climb on the mounds (both for the fowl's and your own sake – there are sometimes mites and snakes in them).

A channel in the coral by Joe's Beach can be an interesting place to puddle around, but the visibility may not always be particularly good in this current-prone channel. Never attempt to swim across Hunt Channel to Cid Island; the currents are very swift, and occasionally very large motorised catamarans and other cruisers come through the channel apace and may not see you in the water.

CID HARBOUR

C19

Soundings in metres

(138)

Fuller
Point

Lady
Islet

13   Daniell
Point

③

Jones
Point

Dugong Inlet

12

Dugong
Beach

Sawmill
Beach

Cid Harbour

Sawmill Bay ②

Hill Rock

12

Bolton Hill
(204)

Magnificent
stand of
paperbarks

④

Homestead Bay

Babieca
Summit
(204)

Ross Islet
(Orchid Rock)

Hughes Point ①

CID ISLAND

(167)

Whitsunday Peak
(437)

Bench
Point

Nari's
Beach

Hunt Channel

**WHITSUNDAY
ISLAND**

Gilling Point

Fl 6s 12m 3M

Joe's Beach

Strong current

Loriard Point

N

Gulnare
Inlet

Reef Point   *Yvonne's Coves*

Approximate Scale 1:29 000

0 Nautical Miles   0.5   1.0

0 Kilometres   0.5   1.0

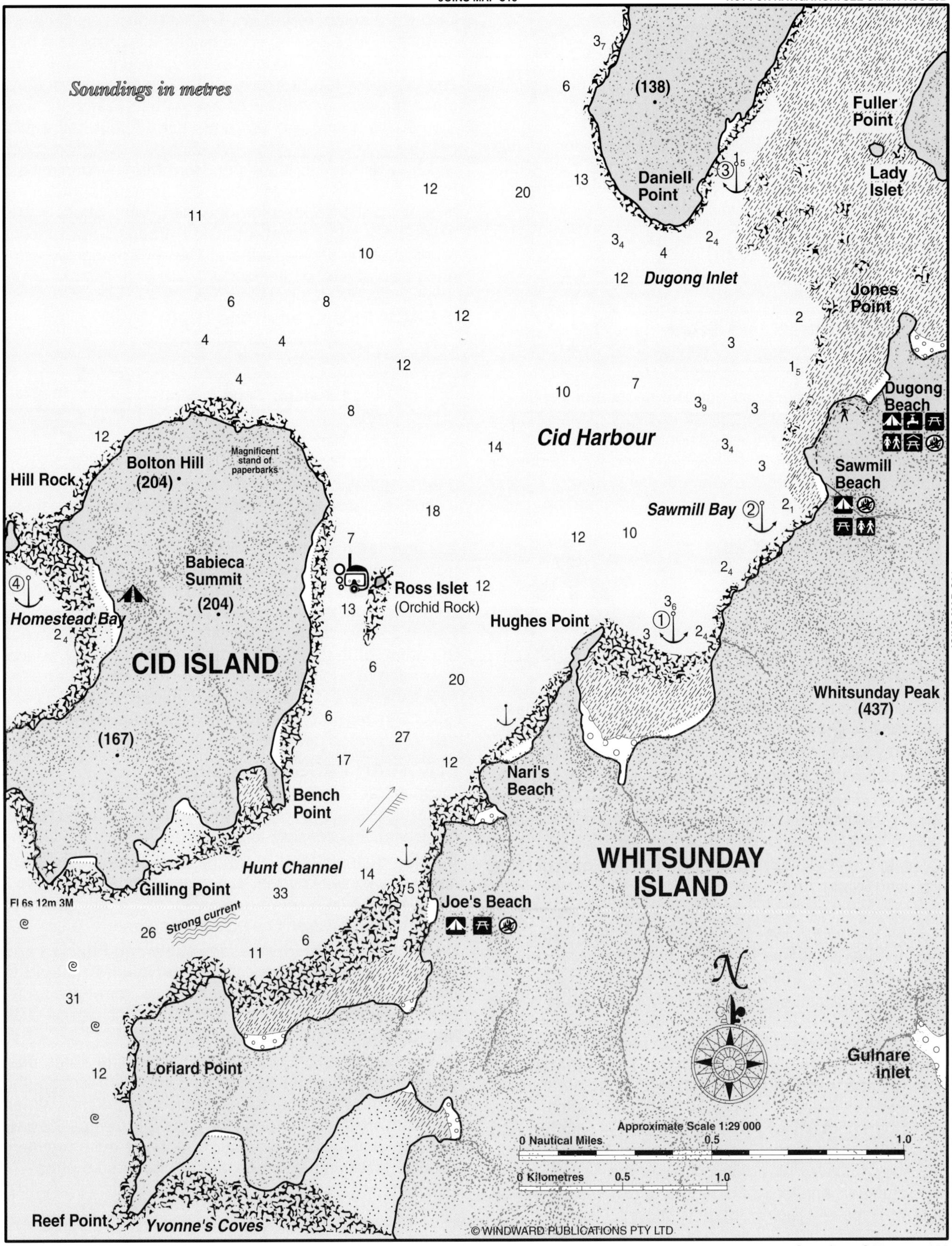

© WINDWARD PUBLICATIONS PTY LTD

See photo C19, page 128

YVONNE'S COVES (C20)

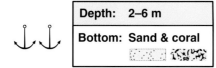

Depth:	2–6 m
Bottom:	Sand & coral

Yvonne's Coves offer fascinating reef fossicking in suitably light weather. Anchor off the edge of the reef, allowing enough swinging room. There is much interesting reef life, including armies of soldier crabs.

HENNING ISLAND (C20)

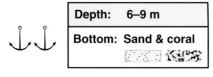

Depth:	6–9 m
Bottom:	Sand & coral

Henning Island offers two daytime anchorages, one off the north-east side, where there is a very pleasant sand beach, and one off a little sand beach in the middle of the western side. At times of neap tides and light southerly winds, the visibility may be good enough to enjoy the coral on the reef that extends west from the northern tip.

GULNARE INLET (C20)

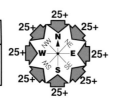

Depth:	2–5 m
Bottom:	Mud

Gulnare Inlet is a very protected anchorage, but it has a few shallow spots on the way in, so be aware of the state of the tide; it's probably best to enter on a rising tide.

Approaching from Fitzalan Passage, beware of the submerged reef area shown. Don't turn into the inlet until you are on the back bearing that aligns Dent and Pine islands (see below).

Coming from Dent or Hamilton islands, stay east of Plum Pudding Island.

Approaching from the north, keep well south until picking up the Dent Island/Pine Island bearing (see below). Don't mistake the rocks that lie off the northern entrance with the submerged patch of reef just to their east.

A back bearing, using Dent and Pine islands as leads, is a useful guide to the entrance: the south-east tip of Pine Island is held in line with the extremity of the rocks on the north-west tip of Dent Island. The outer rock on Dent Island submerges at high tide, so make a small allowance for this if the tide is high. This back bearing, which is approximately 202°M, avoids the patch of reef just inside the entrance on the port side. There is a shallow spot abeam of this patch. Once past the reef stay about mid-channel. Anchor at the mouth of an embayment on the port side where anchorage is shown.

Gulnare is a relatively shallow anchorage; there is room for quite a number of boats. The inlet offers endless opportunities for exploring in the dinghy. It is possible at high tide to go for miles up the estuary through mangroves, and the upper reaches have something of the 'great grey-green greasy Limpopo River' about them. Watch the tide, though; it's a long way up (and back). About half a mile from the anchorage, on the right, there is a mangrove creek which turns back to the south. Here Martin Cunningham built a tramway to move timber cut from the surrounding hills along the flat and into the inlet, from where it was towed back to the sawmill at Cid Harbour. There are still remains of the tracks. Gulnare, like most mangrove estuaries, can offer good fishing.

BEACH 25 and environs (C20)

Depth:	2–4 m
Bottom:	Sand & coral

Just north of Fitzalan Passage are a couple of anchorages that may be useful in the event of being blown out of a south-exposed anchorage at night, such as one of those along the south side of Whitsunday Island. Anchorage No. 2 is preferable in fresh conditions and it is more removed from the tidal stream which courses through Fitzalan Passage at a rate of knots. Both anchorages have nearby pleasant sand beaches. Watch out for scattered bommies. Beach 25 (incorrectly called Beach 23 by some locals) is the name of the beach east of Anchorage No. 2, which, according to a local historian, Ray Blackwood, was used by a fisherman, Harold Hurst, during the 1950s and early '60s to dry his nets. The '25' was the licence number of his fish trap located near the rocky point south of the beach.

FITZALAN PASSAGE (C20)

Fitzalan Passage is actually two passages, on either side of Fitzalan Island, between Whitsunday Island and Hamilton Island. It is possible to use either.

Fitzalan restricts the flow of the tidal stream, and there can be 4+ knots of current during spring tides, and up to 3 knots in neap tides. Always use your motor, and watch to be sure that you aren't being set off course.

If using the southern passage (between Fitzalan and Hamilton islands), keep closer to Hamilton Island to avoid a reef which extends south-west from Fitzalan Island towards Hamilton, the position of which can be quite deceptive.

In wind-against-tide conditions, particularly south-east winds against a south-east-moving flood tide stream, the passage may become quite turbulent and lumpy. When travelling south-east through the passage towards the east you may encounter a dramatic change to quite turbulent conditions within a distance of a few hundred metres.

GULNARE INLET

JOINS MAPS C19 & C21

C20

NOT FOR NAVIGATION: SEE CHART AUS 252

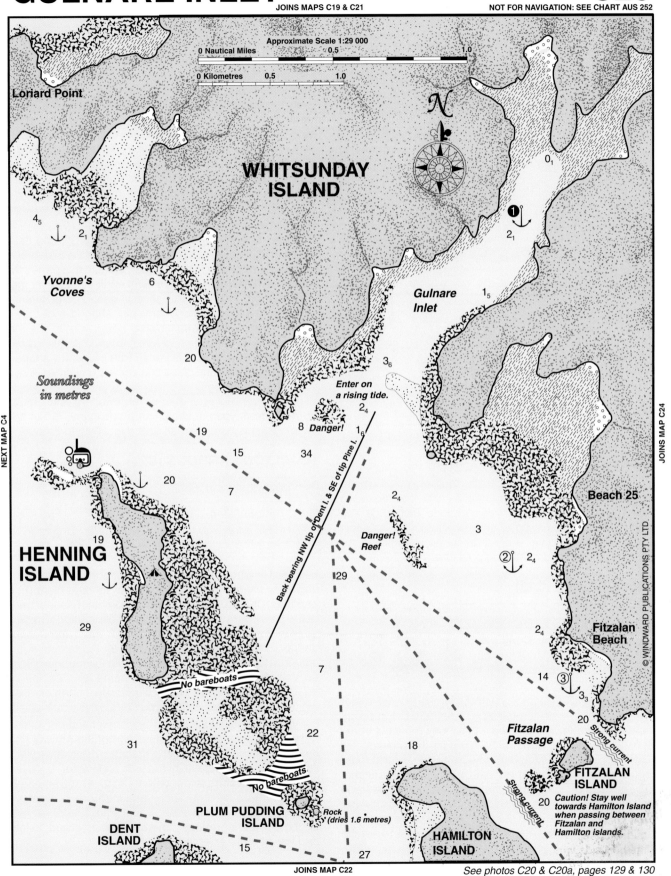

Approximate Scale 1:29 000

0 Nautical Miles   0.5   1.0

0 Kilometres   0.5   1.0

Loriard Point

WHITSUNDAY ISLAND

N

0_1

4_5 2_1

①

2_1

Yvonne's Coves

6

Gulnare Inlet

1_5

20

3_6

Soundings in metres

Enter on a rising tide.

2_4

8   Danger!

1_6

19

15

34

NEXT MAP C4

20

7

2_4

19

HENNING ISLAND

Back bearing NW tip of Dent I. & SE of tip Pine I.

Danger! Reef

3

② 2_4

Beach 25

29

129

2_4

Fitzalan Beach

7

14   ③

3_3

No bareboats

22

18

20

31

Fitzalan Passage

FITZALAN ISLAND

No bareboats

Strong current

20

DENT ISLAND

PLUM PUDDING ISLAND

Rock (dries 1.6 metres)

15

27

HAMILTON ISLAND

Caution! Stay well towards Hamilton Island when passing between Fitzalan and Hamilton islands.

© WINDWARD PUBLICATIONS PTY LTD.

JOINS MAP C22

JOINS MAP C24

See photos C20 & C20a, pages 129 & 130

UPPER GULNARE C21

NEXT MAP C18   NOT FOR NAVIGATION: SEE CHART AUS 252

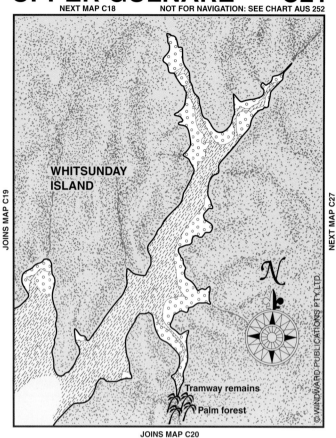

JOINS MAP C19

JOINS MAP C20

NEXT MAP C27

WHITSUNDAY ISLAND

Tramway remains

Palm forest

©WINDWARD PUBLICATIONS PTY. LTD.

UPPER GULNARE INLET (C21)

Just beyond the creek that courses south-west to the palm forest is another broader mangrove creek that has been used by some local skippers as a cyclone anchorage. You will obviously need to enter on a high tide. (The smallest high tide you are ever likely to strike here would be 1.9 metres at normal atmospheric pressure.)

DENT ISLAND (C22)

Depth:	0 m
Bottom:	Coral

Approaching Dent Island, watch out for the extensive reef areas south of Henning Island. Do not attempt passage north of Plum Pudding Island as you may run afoul of extensive reef there. Don't be tempted by the presence of other boats that may apparently be moored in this 'passage'; always pass south and east of Plum Pudding Island. The lee side of Dent Island (the north side during the trade winds season) is not a particularly easy anchorage because of the dropoff and currents. Anchorage is possible, but you'll want to have a windlass, and be sure to set the anchor securely. If you are visiting Coral Art on the northern tip of the island, it's definitely easier to pick up the

western one of two moorings, which is there for the use of visiting private yachts. The other mooring is for commercial vessels.

If anchoring, drop the anchor off the reef at the western end of the beach. If you're a bareboat charterer, your company may insist that you anchor right on top of the reef in order not to repeat history (bareboats drifting away unattended when the anchor became dislodged by contrary wind and tide). If you anchor on the reef you must do so on a rising tide to avoid getting trapped and, according to a local formula, there will be sufficient water for a vessel of 1.8-metre draught only if the next high tide is more than 2.6 metres at Shute Harbour (4.4 metres Mackay); you should get there one and a half hours before high tide and leave within an hour of the high.

Coral Art is a shell jewellery shop run by Bill and Leen Wallace, who have lived on the island since the mid-1950s. Bill, who is originally from Oregon, came to this part of the world during World War II as a flight engineer. Leen comes from Victoria. The Coral Art shop is based on a Samoan falé, with a unique aerodynamically shaped roof that is just about perfect for withstanding heavy winds. The roof battens are all hand shaped and lashed, the ceiling lined with tapa cloth. The floor is paved with irregularly shaped, thick pieces of antique glass that came to Australia in sailing ships for the original buildings of Sydney University. Bill and Leen make all manner of jewellery and articles from different types of shell. There are many Pacific artifacts on display and a small library in which to browse.

HAMILTON HARBOUR (C22)

Depth:	1.6–2.4 m
Bottom:	Mud

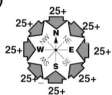

Hamilton Harbour is marked by four port and starboard beacons; the two outside ones show lights at night (Fl R and Fl G), the two inside do not. The lighthouse (port side of the breakwater as you enter) is for decoration. The harbour is dredged to 2.4 metres at low water throughout, deeper in the channel that runs just off the marina to the jetties in front of the Mariners Inn. Radio the harbourmaster on VHF 16/68 and make arrangements for a berth; call again on arrival and you will be directed to a berth or mooring. The overnight fee entitles you to 'the keys to the island'.

Hamilton with its jet airport is a yachting centre in its own right. Keep well away from either end of the runway (fifty times the length of your mast is the official doctrine). Hamilton has a full-service shipyard with fuel, water, supplies, shipwright, travel lift, refrigeration. electrical and engineering services available. There are many restaurants, a bakery, a fish-and-chip shop, Trader Pete's store, several boutiques, a supermarket, chemist, pub, showers, toilets, and lots of amusements.

HAMILTON ISLAND

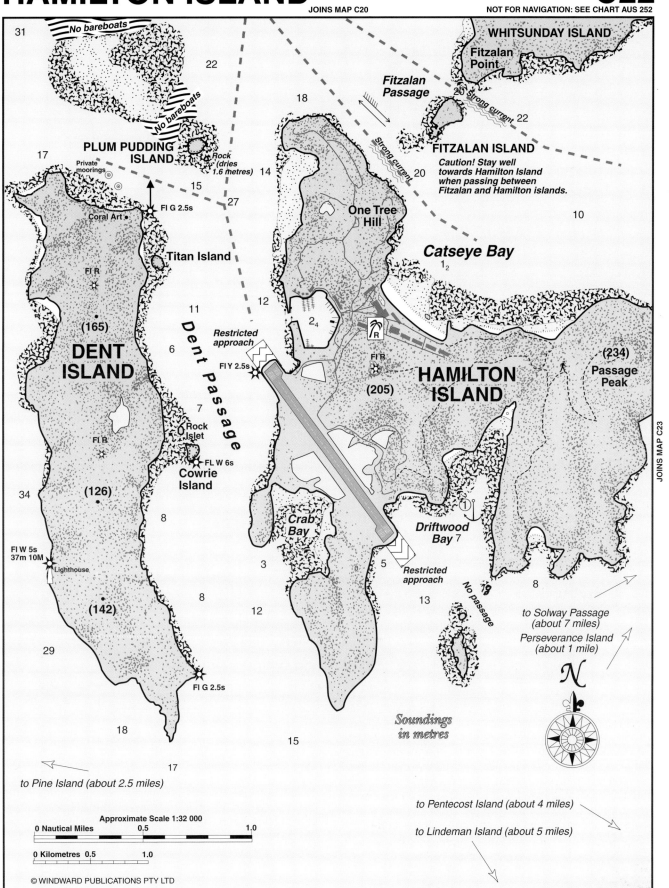

31

No bareboats

22

No bareboats

WHITSUNDAY ISLAND

Fitzalan Point

Fitzalan Passage

20 *Strong current* 22

18

PLUM PUDDING ISLAND

17

Private moorings

Coral Art •

Rock (dries 1.6 metres)

14

Strong current

20

FITZALAN ISLAND

Caution! Stay well towards Hamilton Island when passing between Fitzalan and Hamilton islands.

15

27

Fl G 2.5s

Fl R

Titan Island

One Tree Hill

Catseye Bay

1_2

10

11

12

DENT ISLAND

(165)

6

Dent Passage

Restricted approach

Fl Y 2.5s

2_4

Fl R

(205)

HAMILTON ISLAND

(234)

Passage Peak

7

Fl R

Rock Islet

Fl W 6s

Cowrie Island

(126)

Fl R

8

8

Crab Bay

3

5

Restricted approach

Driftwood Bay 7

①

Fl W 5s 37m 10M

Lighthouse

(142)

12

6

13

No passage

8

34

29

18

17

15

N

to Solway Passage (about 7 miles)

Perseverance Island (about 1 mile)

Fl G 2.5s

Soundings in metres

to Pine Island (about 2.5 miles)

Approximate Scale 1:32 000

0 Nautical Miles   0.5   1.0

0 Kilometres 0.5   1.0

to Pentecost Island (about 4 miles)

to Lindeman Island (about 5 miles)

© WINDWARD PUBLICATIONS PTY LTD

NEXT MAP C33   *See photo C22, page 131*

JOINS MAP C23

HAMILTON ISLAND EAST

NEXT MAP C4

NOT FOR NAVIGATION: SEE CHART AUS 252

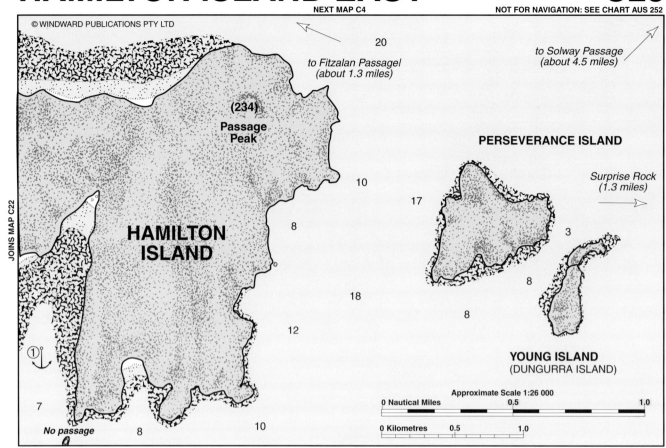

© WINDWARD PUBLICATIONS PTY LTD

to Solway Passage
(about 4.5 miles)

20

to Fitzalan Passagel
(about 1.3 miles)

(234)
Passage
Peak

PERSEVERANCE ISLAND

Surprise Rock
(1.3 miles)

10

17

HAMILTON ISLAND

8

3

18

8

12

8

JOINS MAP C22

①

7

No passage   8   10

YOUNG ISLAND
(DUNGURRA ISLAND)

Approximate Scale 1:26 000

0 Nautical Miles   0.5   1.0

0 Kilometres   0.5   1.0

NEXT MAP C33

DRIFTWOOD BAY (C22)

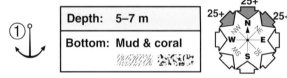

Depth:	5–7 m
Bottom:	Mud & coral

The enlargement of Hamilton's airport and the increase in air traffic has rendered this anchorage less desirable than it used to be. Post a lookout when going into the anchorage. There are some walking tracks around the bay.

TURTLE BAY (C24)

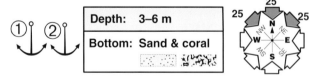

Depth:	3–6 m
Bottom:	Sand & coral

Turtle Bay comprises a beautiful series of bays just east of Fitzalan Passage. There are a number of good lunchtime spots in suitable weather during the April to August/ September trade winds season. At this time it is advisable *not* to stay overnight to avoid being caught on a lee shore by a sudden, middle-of-the-night burst of southerly air (which happens not infrequently during these months).

Anchorage No.1 offers the most protection. The water is shallower on the west side of the anchorage.

There is some good snorkelling on the reef just north of the Anchorage No. 2 symbol. Visibility will be best in neap tides and if the wind has been in the northern sectors for a day.

TORRES HERALD BAY (C24)

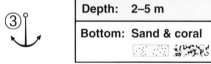

Depth:	2–5 m
Bottom:	Sand & coral

This used to be a favourite lunchtime spot of the charter vessel *Torres Herald*.

CRAYFISH BAY (C24)

Depth:	5–9 m
Bottom:	Sand & coral

Watch out for bommies. Leave adequate swinging room.

Note: Surprise Rock is not always visible. It dries some 2.1 metres and lies on a line between the pinnacle of Pentecost Island and Craig Point, approximately midway between the two. If you are on that line, watch out to avoid an unpleasant surprise.

TURTLE BAY

C24

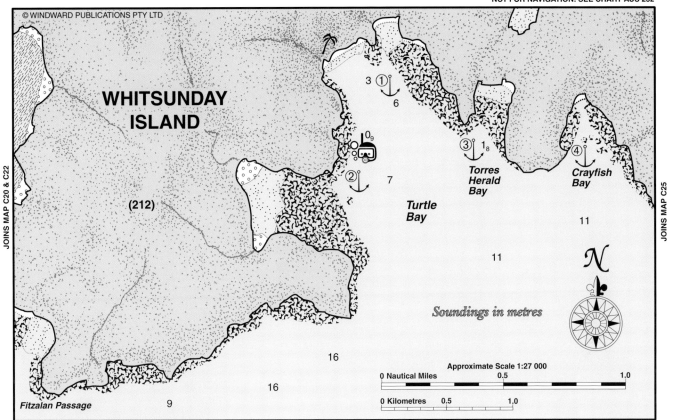

Soundings in metres

Approximate Scale 1:27 000

NEXT MAP C23

See photo C24, page 132

CHANCE BAY

C25

NEXT MAP C26

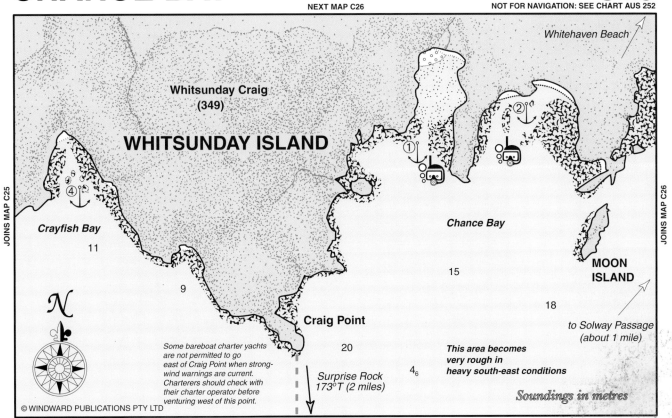

Some bareboat charter yachts are not permitted to go east of Craig Point when strong-wind warnings are current. Charterers should check with their charter operator before venturing west of this point.

This area becomes very rough in heavy south-east conditions

Soundings in metres

© WINDWARD PUBLICATIONS PTY LTD

NEXT MAP C33

See photo C25, page 132

WHITEHAVEN BAY

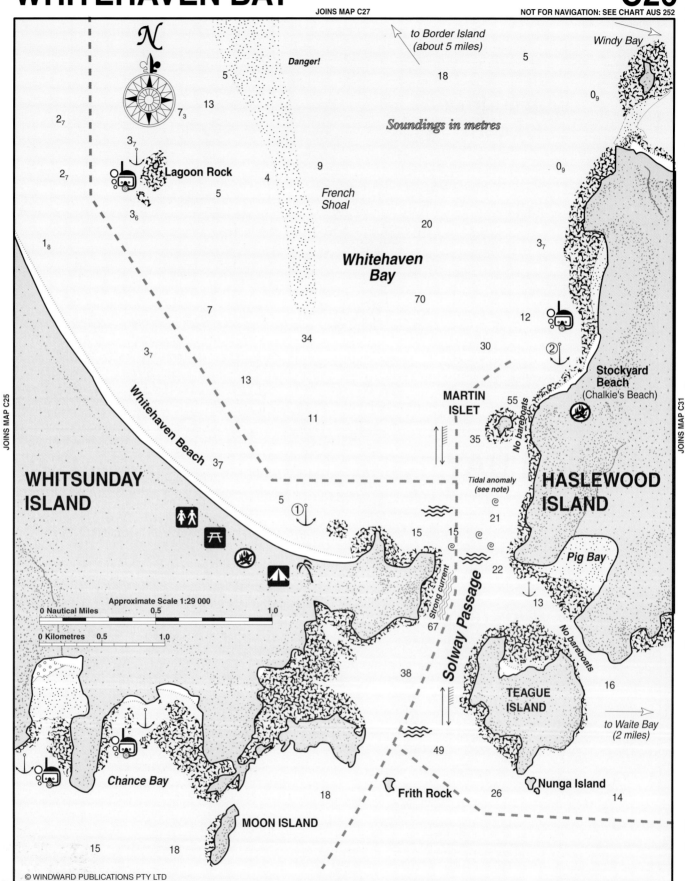

to Border Island
(about 5 miles)

Windy Bay

Danger!

Soundings in metres

French
Shoal

**Whitehaven
Bay**

Lagoon Rock

Whitehaven Beach

**WHITSUNDAY
ISLAND**

Approximate Scale 1:29 000

0 Nautical Miles   0.5   1.0

0 Kilometres   0.5   1.0

**MARTIN
ISLET**

Tidal anomaly
(see note)

Stockyard
Beach
(Chalkie's Beach)

No bareboats

**HASLEWOOD
ISLAND**

Pig Bay

Solway Passage

strong current

No bareboats

**TEAGUE
ISLAND**

to Waite Bay
(2 miles)

Chance Bay

Frith Rock

Nunga Island

MOON ISLAND

NEXT MAP C33

See photo C26, page 133

JOINS MAP C25

JOINS MAP C31

CHANCE BAY (C25)

Depth:	5–10 m
Bottom:	Sand

Keep a lookout posted, especially picking your way into anchorage No. 2.

Chance Bay is a 'double' bay with two beautiful sand beaches. There is good snorkelling around the reef areas and around the little islet to the west of anchorage No.1. Anchorage No. 2 may provide some protection in moderate south-east to east winds. As with other south-exposed anchorages along these islands, this one is risky for overnight use during the trade winds season (April to August/September) when strong southerlies may come roaring in during the night.

SOLWAY PASSAGE (C26)

Solway Passage is another of the Whitsundays' restricted passages through which spring tides race at about 5 knots. When a fresh south-east trade wind is bucking a south-flooding tide, Solway Passage can become 'spectacular' with curling waves, whirlpools that spin a yacht around 90° and overfalls. Some argue that it is not really dangerous; without debating the point, the average skipper in the average-sized yacht may, in these conditions, get a bit of a fright. Solway Passage should be avoided in strong wind-against-tide conditions, particularly by smaller craft, including trailer sailers. If possible it should be negotiated when the tide is slack or when wind and tide are together, i.e. in southerly winds when the tide is ebbing and in northerly winds when the tide is flooding.

Frith Rock is in the middle at the southern end of the passage and is always exposed, with good water on either side.

The passage between Teague Island and Haslewood Island is extremely narrow with an underwater reef extending out from Haslewood Island; it is also subject to tidal currents. Bareboats are not permitted to use this passage, and only the adventurous would use it in preference to going around Teague Island.

Note: A tidal anomaly has been reported near Haslewood Island south of Martin Islet; during ebb tide, which normally flows north, the stream runs south from Martin Islet for some half mile before recurving to join the north-moving main stream.

WHITEHAVEN BEACH (C26)

Depth:	5–10 m
Bottom:	Sand

If coming from Solway Passage, watch out for the reef area, which is always covered, at the south-east end of

Whitehaven Beach. Proceed north until you are well clear of the passage before turning to port and heading for the beach.

Approaching from the north, pass slightly to the west of Esk Island, avoiding the northern shallows of French Shoal (see map C27); then turn more south to avoid shifting sands at the mouth of Hill Inlet and head just west of Lagoon Rock. Follow your way down, closing gradually with the beach.

Alternatively, you can come straight down, leaving Esk Island and French Shoal to starboard until you are almost abeam of Martin Islet, then turn towards the anchorage. The former track avoids guesswork as to the exact whereabouts of French Shoal and the coral patches at the southern end of Whitehaven.

Note: The anchor is shown slightly *west of north* of the lone palm tree on the beach. If you're directly opposite the palm tree you may find yourself too close to the reef patch. Keep the palm tree to your south-east.

If you never anchor in less than 5.5 metres or in more than 9 metres of water, you will never have to worry whether the tide is coming or going.

Whitehaven can be very rolly and, therefore, an uncomfortable anchorage at night. Put a stern anchor in the dinghy and drop it on the beach at high tide level; then pull your stern around to keep your bow towards the swell. A buoy on the line may help to let others know not to pass between you and the beach.

Whitehaven is an incredible expanse of pure white sand, the legacy of a geologic era when the sea level was lower. It is a magnificent beach, and one that is understandably popular with all and sundry, from itinerant yachts to motorised catamarans complete with rock bands. It is also popular with sandflies and mosquitoes; take plenty of insect repellent with you. The 6-kilometre stretch of beach is big enough for all. Fires are completely prohibited at Whitehaven because of the highly flammable acacia scrub, which is vital to the stability of the foreshore dunes.

STOCKYARD BEACH (CHALKIE'S) (C26)

Depth:	8–12 m
Bottom:	Sand

Stay outside Martin Islet if coming from the south; approach from the southern end of the anchorage closing gradually to pick up the fringing reef. Anchor just off the gap in the reef; further south is deep water.

This anchorage has a magnificent beach. If Whitehaven is overcrowded, this is a good alternative. In neap tides and light southerly winds, snorkelling at the northern end of the beach is good. As with Whitehaven, fires are prohibited on this beach.

PIG BAY (C26)

Depth:	9–12 m
Bottom:	Sand & coral

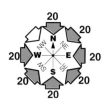

Temporary anchorage is possible opposite this pretty bay just north of Teague Island. Needless to say, watch the run of the tide.

HILL INLET (entrance) (C27)

Depth:	2.5–5 m
Bottom:	Sand

Hill Inlet is a large estuary, with mangroves and shifting sands. It is not really accessible to keel boats (although at high tide you could pick your way up one of the shifting channels for some little distance). It offers trailer sailers magnificent exploring and many spots for allowing the yacht to dry out at low tide. Because it is tidebound, go in near the top of the tide and be prepared to wait for the next tide to get out, if you're not staying overnight.

The anchorage shown is a light-weather temporary stop-off and may provide an opportunity to explore the inlet in the dinghy, or to go ashore and loll around on the northern end of the magnificent Whitehaven Beach, away from the crowd that may be madding away at the southern end.

Hill Inlet is very important to the local ecology, being a major source of food for hungry and growing young fishes. Humanoid visitors are also an important source of food for mosquitoes and sandflies. Take insect repellent with you.

TONGUE BAY (C27)

Depth:	2.5–4 m
Bottom:	Mud

Tongue Bay is quite a large anchorage that offers a secure haven for keel boaters who want to explore Hill Inlet or who have fled the crowds or the swell at Whitehaven. You can walk over Tongue Point to Hill Inlet or, if the weather is favourably light, go around the point in the dinghy.

LAGOON ROCK (C27)

Depth:	2–5 m
Bottom:	Sand

Lagoon Rock, in suitably light south-east to east weather and at neap tides, may provide some interesting exploring from the water. Anchor on the lee side as shown.

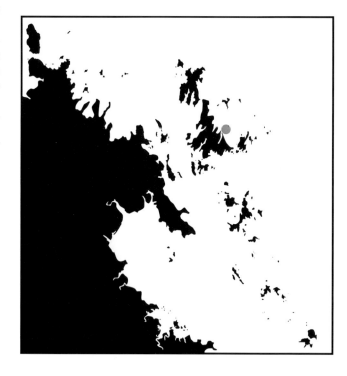

HILL INLET

C27

© WINDWARD PUBLICATIONS PTY LTD

Apostle Bay

Rock (dries 0.6 metre) and bommies

11

Tongue Point

ESK ISLAND

1_8

20

4_7

Soundings in metres

2_7

4_6

2_7

12

2_7

12

①

Tongue Bay

14

Hill Inlet

3_7

Shifting sand (dries)

0_5

3_7

16

1_2

3_7

9

5

Danger! Dries in places

2_7

7

12

3_7

2_7

Lagoon Rock

5

9

3_7

9

1_8

French Shoal

7

WHITSUNDAY ISLAND

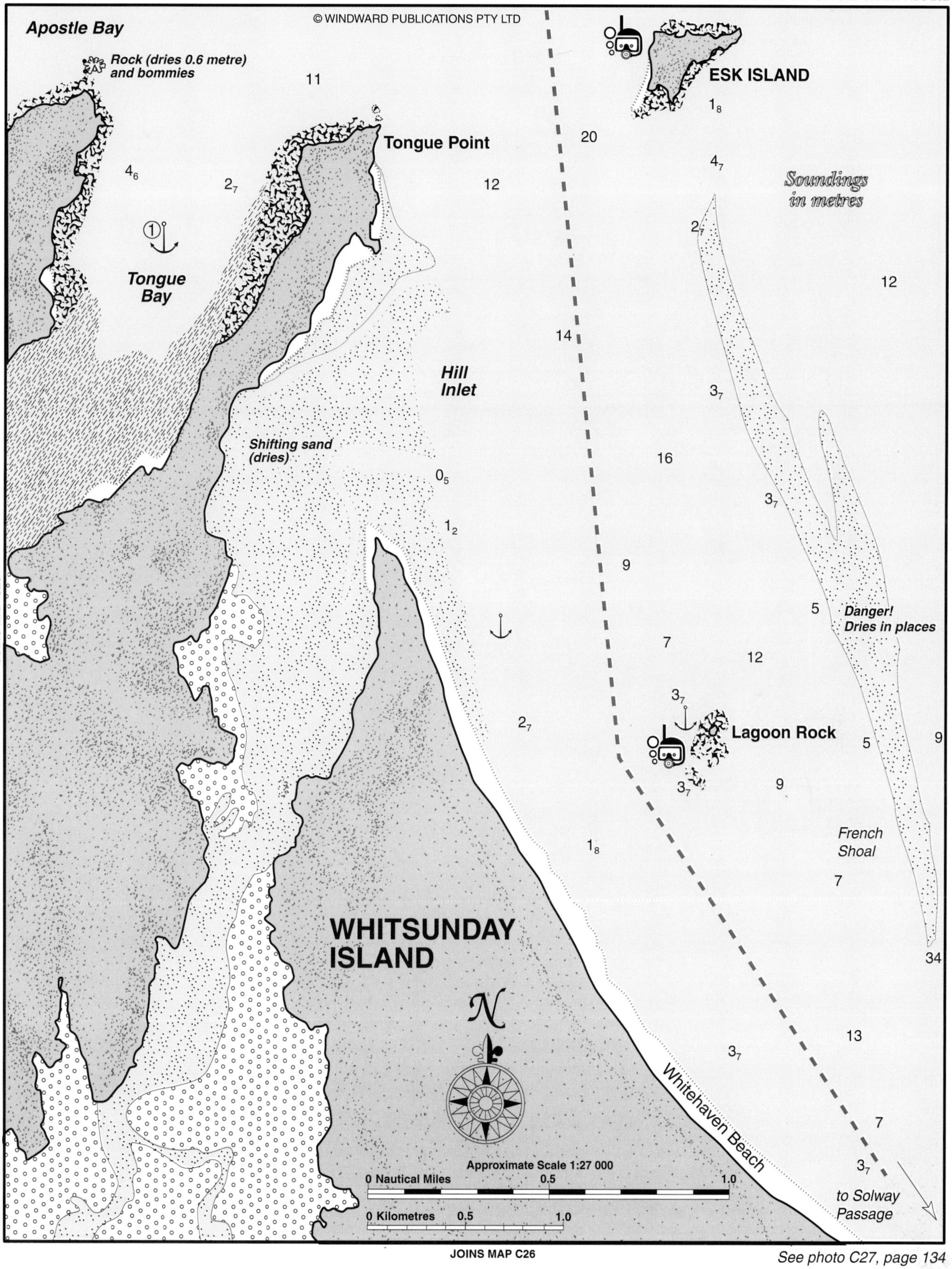

$\mathcal{N}$

3_7

13

7

3_7

to Solway Passage

3_7

34

Approximate Scale 1:27 000

| 0 Nautical Miles | 0.5 | 1.0 |

| 0 Kilometres | 0.5 | 1.0 |

Whitehaven Beach

See photo C27, page 134

JOINS MAP C28

JOINS MAP C26

WHITSUNDAY NORTH-EAST C28

NEXT MAPS C17 & C29

NOT FOR NAVIGATION: SEE CHART AUS 252

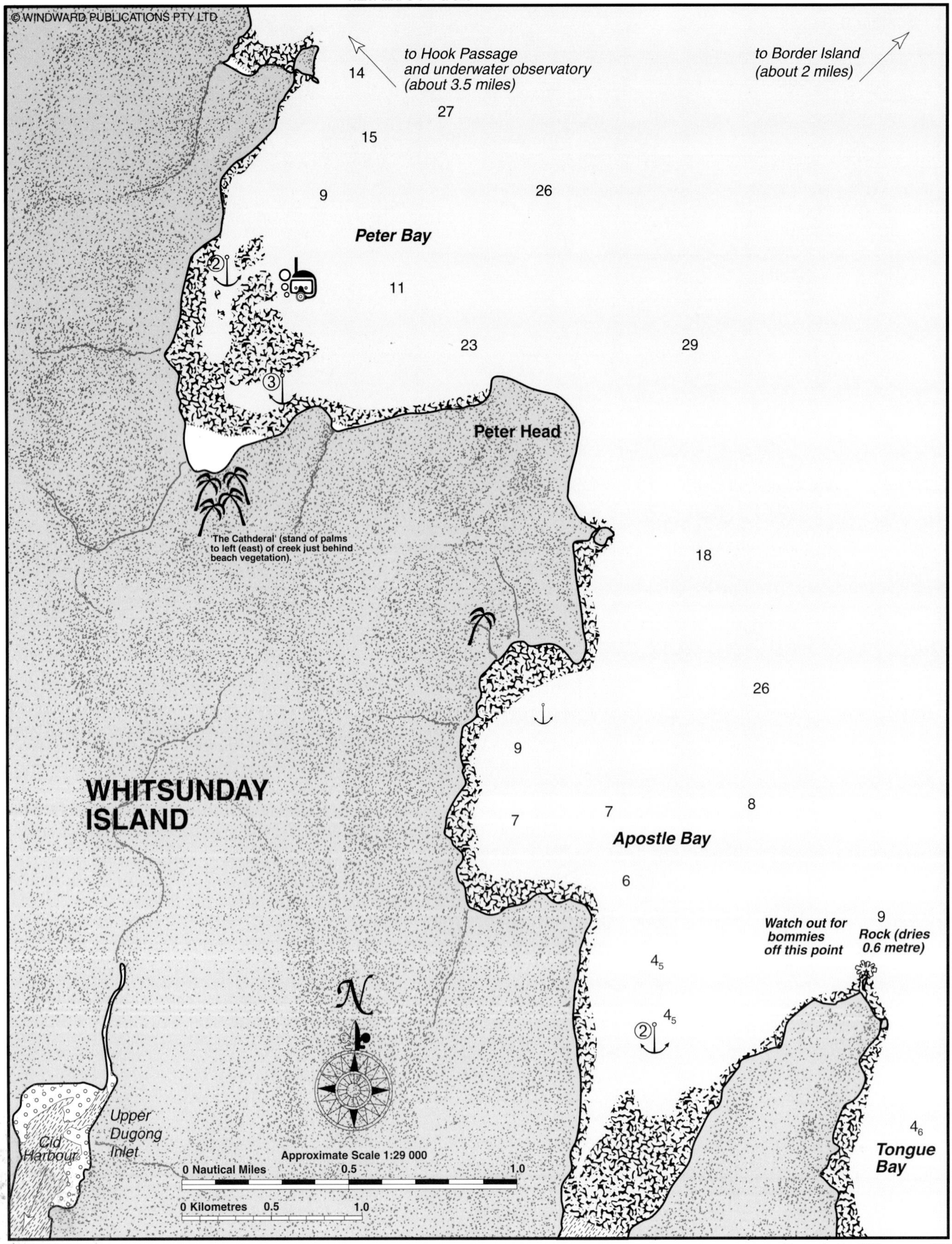

© WINDWARD PUBLICATIONS PTY LTD
to Hook Passage and underwater observatory (about 3.5 miles)
to Border Island (about 2 miles)
14
27
15
9
26
Peter Bay
11
23
29
Peter Head
'The Cathderal' (stand of palms to left (east) of creek just behind beach vegetation).
18
JOINS MAP C18
26
9
WHITSUNDAY ISLAND
7
7
8
Apostle Bay
6
Watch out for bommies off this point
9
Rock (dries 0.6 metre)
4₅
4₅
JOINS MAP C27
4₆
Tongue Bay
Upper Dugong Inlet
Cid Harbour
Approximate Scale 1:29 000
0 Nautical Miles 0.5 1.0
0 Kilometres 0.5 1.0

JOINS MAP C27

See photo C28, page 135

APOSTLE BAY (C28)

Depth:	3–5 m
Bottom:	Mud & coral

Apostle Bay is another quite large anchorage which may not be crowded. It may be a bit swelly as the wind easts. Be on the lookout for scattered bommies as you pick your way into the anchorage.

PETER BAY (C28)

Depth:	5–9 m
Bottom:	Sand & coral

Peter Bay is swelly in south-east conditions and, from some distance off, it normally looks foreboding. There are a couple of places to tuck in snugly, using great care to avoid the fringing reef, in suitably light conditions. It offers good fishing and snorkelling or diving. Behind the beach vegetation on the eastern side of the creek outlet is a fine stand of palm trees that has been likened to walking through a cathedral – imaginative, but the palms are lovely.

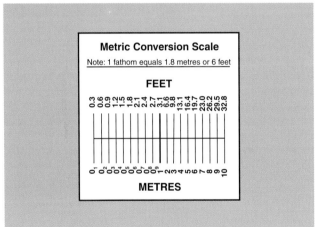

Metric Conversion Scale

Note: 1 fathom equals 1.8 metres or 6 feet

FEET

0.3 0.6 0.9 1.2 1.5 1.8 2.1 2.4 2.7 3.1 6.6 9.8 13.1 16.4 19.7 23.0 26.2 29.5 32.8

0 0.2 0.3 0.4 0.5 0.6 0.7 0.8 0.9 1 2 3 4 5 6 7 8 9 10

METRES

BORDER ISLAND

C29

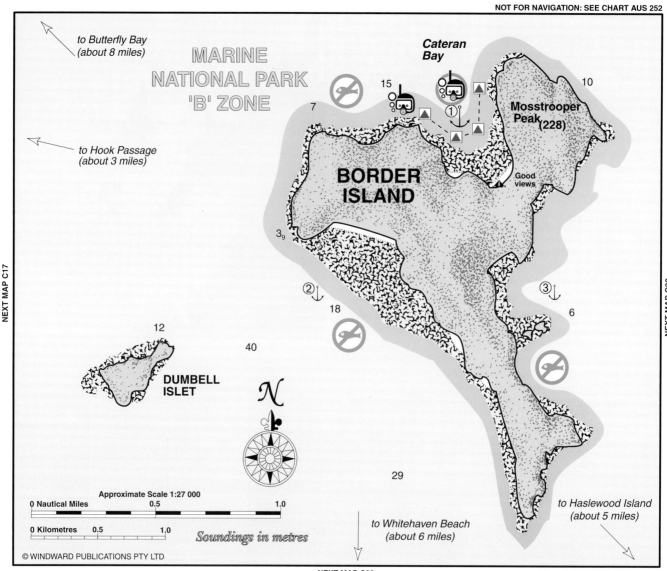

NEXT MAP C17

NEXT MAP C30

NEXT MAP C28

See photo C29, page 136

CATERAN BAY (C29)

 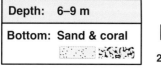

Depth:	6–9 m
Bottom:	Sand & coral

Border Island is one of the 'outlying' islands that will reward your efforts for going there. Reef protection marker buoys have been installed to prevent further damage to the island's excellent fringing reef. Do not anchor inshore of an imaginary straight line between the reef protection buoys.

Cateran Bay is subject to bullets when the wind is over 20 knots. It is swelly when the wind easts. If the wind is light, you will also roll around on your anchor as the tide changes. A stern anchor, if the anchorage is not crowded, may help. Your anchor chain will make a dreadful noise scraping over the bottom, so rig a rope 'snubber'. There are occasional bommies on the bottom. Try to drop the anchor over sand (light-coloured bottom – avoid dark patches).

If all that hasn't put you off, you will find it one of the most delightful anchorages in the islands. The bay has very good coral. The snorkelling/diving is best in neap tides and southerly winds (northerly winds cause the rising of fine sediments that are deposited on the 'lee side' of the islands, and visibility is poor). In spring tides some colourful coral exposes at the bottom of the reef, just off the sand beach. The beaches are accessible in the dinghy at high tide. There is good walking, with views from the saddle above the beach.

If you go ashore at low tide, be careful where you tread to avoid killing live corals (and to avoid stepping on a stonefish).

All around Border Island, for 100 metres beyond the low tide level, is Marine National Park 'B' Zone; fishing and shell collecting (even dead shells) are prohibited.

CATERAN BAY

NOT FOR NAVIGATION: SEE CHART AUS 252

DELORAINE ISLET   C30

NOT FOR NAVIGATION: SEE CHART AUS 252

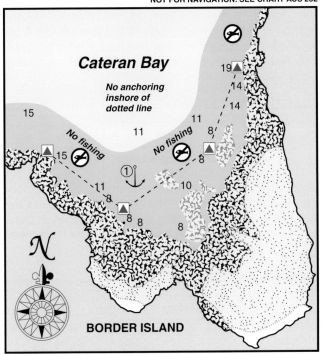

BORDER ISLAND (C29)

Depth:	5–9 m
Bottom:	Sand & coral

This is a daytime stopoff in light easterly or north-easterly weather. Watch the flow of the current, and keep an eye on your anchor.

BORDER ISLAND (C29)

Depth:	6–9 m
Bottom:	Sand & coral

Another pleasant lunchtime anchorage in north-westerly winds.

DELORAINE ISLET (C30)

Depth:	4–10 m
Bottom:	Sand & coral

Deloraine Islet stands aloof, east of Border Island; it shimmers in the sunlight, its dazzling beach punctuating vibrant blue water around it, lonely and beckoning. It is a difficult place to anchor, and should be attempted only in ideal conditions – light easterlies/north-easterlies.

Anchorage No. 1 is a magnificent but steep coral dropoff, and an anchor dropped on this face may be difficult to retrieve, quite apart from the damage the cable will do to the coral. A better plan, if tide, weather and draught permit, is to ease in over the reef flat and hang off a short anchor in one of the sandy patches that can be found there. Best to leave someone aboard if you make a shore visit, as the tide races through here.

DELORAINE ISLET (C30)

Depth:	2–5 m
Bottom:	Sand & coral

Anchorage No. 2 obviously requires very light conditions and excellent visibility. This anchorage is suitable only for small, shallow-draught boats (dinghies and runabouts). Watch the current.

Good beach fossicking and fishing. .

CAUTION
Approach to Waite Bay (White Bay)

This is another of those Whitsunday placenames in the process of correction. The original survey chart of this area shows Waite Bay, and as has happend in some other cases, this later somehow became 'White'. Waite is undoubtedly correct.

The area between Haslewood Island and Nicolson Island is hazardous. One vessel, *Pegasus*, was sunk there in 1982, and several have done themselves serious damage while heading through the passage between Nicolson and Haslewood. The culprit is an elusive bommie that has variously been reported over the years as being anywhere between the southern tip of Haslewood Island and Nicolson Island. It has moved around the chart like an ephemeral spirit, but investigations by harbourmasters and experienced local mariners have failed to find it. There *is* a bommie (which is marked on map C31 as 'Pegasus Rock') which is deceptive and which is probably the one that has done the defrocking and which has been reported elsewhere to spare red faces. It becomes a problem at spring low tide. **Keep well over to the Nicolson Island side if you use the passage between Nicolson and Haslewood islands.** If proceeding to Waite Bay from the south of Whitsunday Island or from Solway Passage, after coming around Teague Island don't head straight for the passage or you will probably run right onto Pegasus Rock. Keep well to starboard and favour the western side of Nicolson Island (or go right outside (east) of Nicolson Island).

If proceeding from Waite Bay to Solway Passage or to the south of Whitsunday Island en route to Fitzalan Passage, the same applies; favour the western side of Nicolson Island and keep well south of Teague before turning west.

WAITE BAY (C31)

 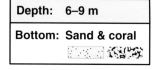

Anchorage No. 1 will provide better protection in north to north-east winds, which funnel through the opening between Lupton and Haslewood Islands.

There is a beautiful sand beach on Lupton Island, and the island offers easy walking with excellent views back over Waite Bay.

Haslewood Island has a massive reef which dries extensively, providing potentially endless hours of reef fossicking and, in suitable weather, snorkelling at the edge. As the tide comes up over the reef the sea life returns to feed, including turtles, small sharks, etc.

If the tide is falling when you land, remember to leave your dinghy close to the edge of the reef, or you may find yourself stranded until the tide comes back in.

Be careful where you tread, avoiding stepping on live coral (step *between* clumps or in places that appear like concrete, which will help to preserve the coral as well as yourself).

Keep an eye on the tide; it comes quickly once it gets over the edge of the reef, and you may find yourself in deeper water and further from the dinghy than you might like to be.

All of the area around this bay and Lupton Island is a Marine National Park 'B' Zone; fishing and shell collecting (even dead shells) are prohibited.

WAITE BAY (C31)

 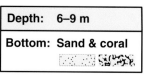

Go slow and keep a lookout for scattered bommies in and around the area marked (and even in the approach channel marked), especially at times of spring low tides, when they may constitute a hazard.

WINDY BAY (C31)

Approach cautiously, as you cannot get very deep into the bay. Windy Bay is lovely but not particularly quiescent at the best of times. It tends to be very rolly, and it can be gusty in fresh south-east conditions. It does offer an opportunity to explore the fascinating Haslewood/Lupton Reef in southerly weather.

LUPTON ISLAND (east side) (C31)

On the east side of Lupton Island, in ideal conditions, and preferably at times of neap tides, you can find temporary anchorage which will allow you to explore this isolated spot. Be careful where you drop anchor to avoid damaging coral. The area south of Lupton Island is marked by eddies and disturbed water.

LUPTON ISLAND (north side) (C31)

Be careful if using the passage between Worthington Island and Lupton Island, particularly at times of contrary wind and tide, when it may best be avoided. Watch out for the reef which runs for some considerable distance north-east
(continued on page 218)

HASLEWOOD ISLAND

C31

11

Pallion Point

7

27

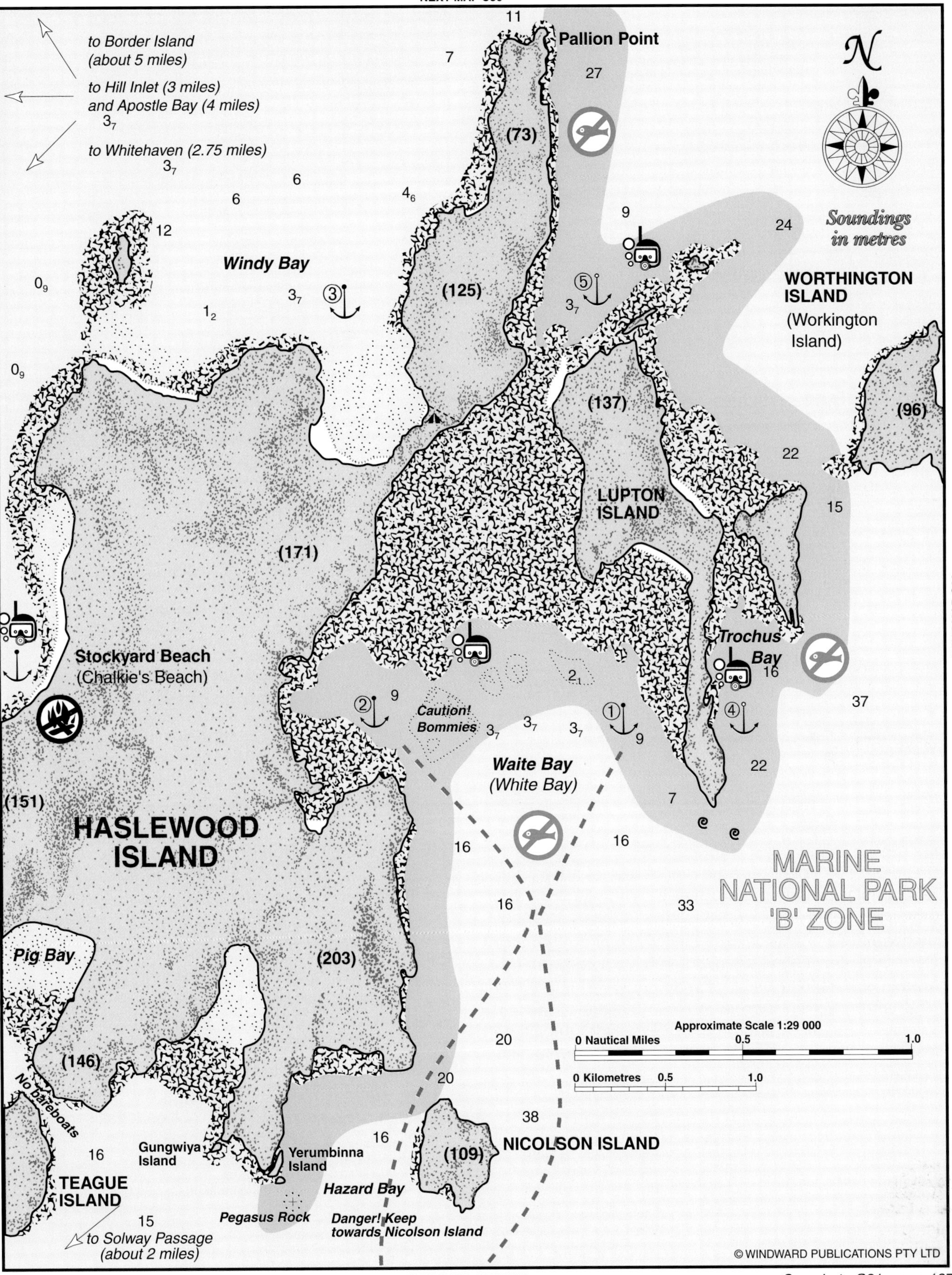

to Border Island
(about 5 miles)

to Hill Inlet (3 miles)
and Apostle Bay (4 miles)
3_7

to Whitehaven (2.75 miles)
3_7

6

4_6

(73)

9

24

6

6

$\mathcal{N}$

Soundings in metres

WORTHINGTON
ISLAND

(Workington Island)

12

Windy Bay

(125)

⑤

3_7

0_9

1_2

3_7 ③

(137)

(96)

0_9

**LUPTON
ISLAND**

22

15

(171)

Stockyard Beach
(Chalkie's Beach)

(151)

**HASLEWOOD
ISLAND**

*Trochus
Bay*

16

④

37

② 9

*Caution!
Bommies*

3_7

3_7 3_7

2_1

① 9

22

7

16

16

**MARINE
NATIONAL PARK
'B' ZONE**

Waite Bay
(White Bay)

16

(203)

33

20

Pig Bay

Approximate Scale 1:29 000

0 Nautical Miles   0.5   1.0

0 Kilometres   0.5   1.0

(146)

20

No bareboats

38

16

Gungwiya
Island

Yerumbinna
Island

16

(109)

NICOLSON ISLAND

**TEAGUE
ISLAND**

15

Hazard Bay

Pegasus Rock

**Danger! Keep
towards Nicolson Island**

to Solway Passage
(about 2 miles)

See photo C31, page 137

JOINS MAP C26

NEXT MAP C32

EDWARD GROUP

C32

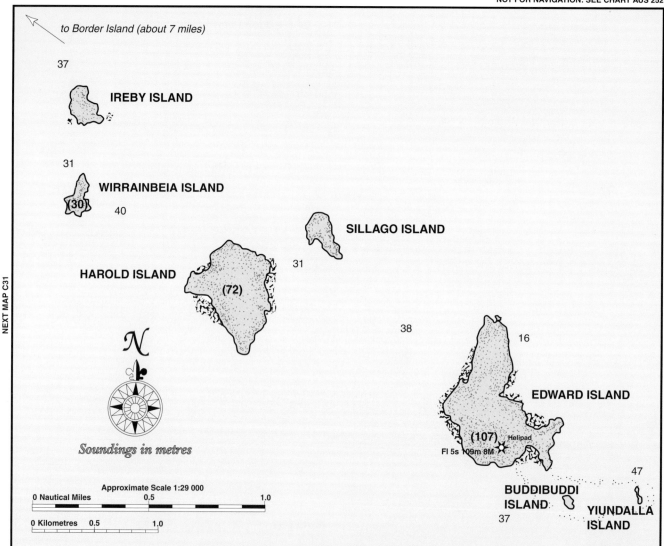

to Border Island (about 7 miles)

37

IREBY ISLAND

31

WIRRAINBEIA ISLAND

(30)   40

SILLAGO ISLAND

HAROLD ISLAND   (72)   31

38   16

EDWARD ISLAND

N

(107)   Helipad
Fl 5s 109m 8M

Soundings in metres

47

**BUDDIBUDDI
ISLAND**
37   **YIUNDALLA
ISLAND**

Approximate Scale 1:29 000
0 Nautical Miles   0,5   1,0
0 Kilometres   0.5   1.0

NEXT MAP C31

(continued from page 216)

of Lupton. For safety don't go south-west of a line from Pallion Point to the northern end of Worthington Island unless you can see your way clearly into the anchorage.

Anchorage No. 5 is a daytime stopover, not a night-time anchorage. Good snorkelling, but watch the current.

Worthington Island (Workington on the chart) is another case where somewhere along the line the name got changed through an error in the British hydrographic office. The original charts show 'Worthington' (*source:* Ray Blackwood).

THE EDWARD GROUP (C32)

The Edward Group lies east-north-east of Haslewood Island. These islands are not of interest as anchorages, but since the advent of the Hamilton Island Race Week they have seen more yachts, being a mark of one of the courses. Note the shaded line around Buddibuddi Island and Yiundalla Island, which indicates that passage between these islands is not advisable (although it may be possible at high tide, on a wing and a prayer, as one very keen yacht proved some years ago).

These islands are outside the bareboat charter limits.

Edward Island is the easternmost of the northern Whitsundays, a cliffy island with steep gullies. It has some good coral in very clear water (for the intrepid diver).

PENTECOST ISLAND (C33)

Depth:	4–8 m
Bottom:	Sand & coral

If approaching from Haslewood or from the east side of Hamilton Island, watch out for Surprise Rock, which lies on a line between the peak of Pentecost Island and Craig Point on Whitsunday Island.

A 4.9-metre rock which resembles a surfaced submarine lies one mile west-south-west of the island.

As you get further south in the Whitsundays, the tidal range increases considerably. At Lindeman Island, which is the next island south from Pentecost, the tides are almost half again as big as they are at Shute Harbour. Irregular tidal eddies may be experienced throughout this area and, in fact, from Long Island to Lindeman Island.

Temporary anchorage is possible on the south side of Pentecost opposite a small sand beach, a nice lunch spot.

Pentecost was so named by Lieutenant James Cook on his voyage of discovery which brought him through the Whitsunday Passage on Whit Sunday, 1770. It was the only island he named. Pentecost comes from the Greek word 'fifty', the association being with the religious festival celebrated on the fiftieth day after Easter, that is, Whit Sunday. Geologically, the island is a dyke of porphyry. Viewed from the west, some see, in the northern protruberance of the island, the likeness of a Red Indian head.

PENTECOST I.   C33
NEXT MAP C23   NOT FOR NAVIGATION: SEE CHART AUS 252

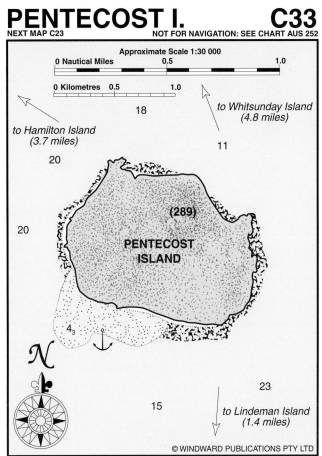

NEXT MAP S1

THE SOUTHERN GROUP S1–S19

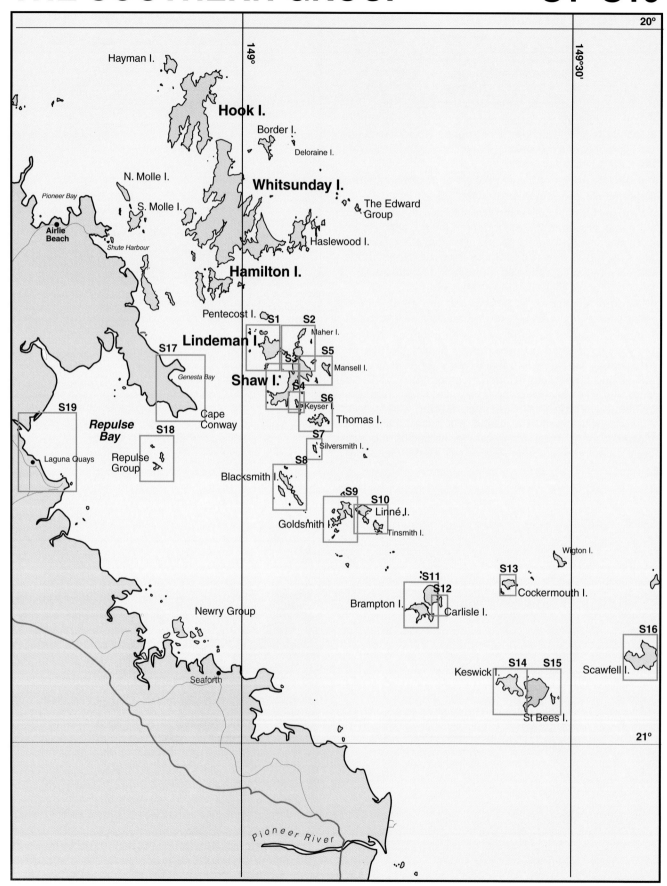

20°

149°

149°30'

Hayman I.

Hook I.

Border I.

Deloraine I.

N. Molle I.

Whitsunday I.

Pioneer Bay

The Edward Group

S. Molle I.

Airlie Beach

Haslewood I.

Shute Harbour

Hamilton I.

Pentecost I.

S1

S2

Maher I.

Lindeman I.

S17

S3

S5

Genesta Bay

Mansell I.

Shaw I.

S4

Cape Conway

S6

Keyser I.

Thomas I.

S19

S7

Repulse Bay

Silversmith I.

S18

S8

Laguna Quays

Repulse Group

Blacksmith I.

S9

S10

Linné I.

Goldsmith I.

Tinsmith I.

Wigton I.

S13

Newry Group

S11

S12

Brampton I.

Carlisle I.

Cockermouth I.

S16

Seaforth

S14

S15

Scawfell I.

Keswick I.

St Bees I.

21°

Pioneer River

Map index

Anchorage index

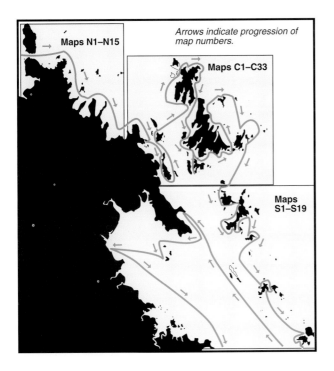

Arrows indicate progression of map numbers.

Maps N1–N15

Maps C1–C33

Maps S1–S19

LINDEMAN ISLAND (S1)

Depth:	6–10 m
Bottom:	Mud & coral

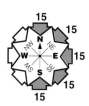

Tidal currents may reach 2 knots in the passage between Seaforth and Lindeman Islands. Anchor outside the reef as shown and tuck in close to get out of the stream. Don't go into the dredged channel.

Lindeman Island has a Club Med resort. Most of the island is national park, and the jetty is public. There are some marvellous graded walking tracks through vine forests and valleys where butterflies sometimes swarm. The bird life is abundant. Excellent views are available from the high ground, such as from the summit of Mount Oldfield, where there is a panorama – northwards to Hamilton and Whitsunday islands, westwards to the Conway Peninsula and mainland, and southwards over Shaw Island.

SEAFORTH ISLAND (S1)

Depth:	2–6 m
Bottom:	Mud & sand

It is possible to tuck in on the northern side of Seaforth Island and get shelter from south-east winds.

The island is sometimes referred to as 'Royal Seaforth', the result of a royal visit in 1954 by Queen Elizabeth and the Duke of Edinburgh, who spent an hour or so enjoying a bit of sand between their toes. Seaforth was declared a national park in 1962. In times past there have been fruit bats living there (a small colony of these lives next door on Lindeman Island (beside the resort).

BOAT PORT (S1)

Depth:	2–5 m
Bottom:	Sand & coral

There are frequently eddies around Thumb Point, and because, at high tide, the reef between Lindeman Island and Little Lindeman Island becomes covered, this anchorage is sometimes inclined to be rolly.

The water is frequently murky and visibility is limited. Use caution.

There are several nice beaches.

LITTLE LINDEMAN ISLAND (S1)

Depth:	2–5 m
Bottom:	Sand & coral

At high tide don't be tempted to go between Little Lindeman and Lindeman islands.

The water is frequently murky and visibility is limited. Use caution.

This anchorage may be rolly.

GAP BEACH (S1)

Depth:	2–5 m
Bottom:	Mud & sand

Gap Beach lies between two high pieces of land; it can be gusty when the wind gets above 20 knots, and it tends to be swelly. It offers beautiful views northwards towards Pentecost and the main islands of the Whitsunday Group.

LINDEMAN ISLAND

S1

NOT FOR NAVIGATION: SEE CHARTS AUS 253/AUS 252

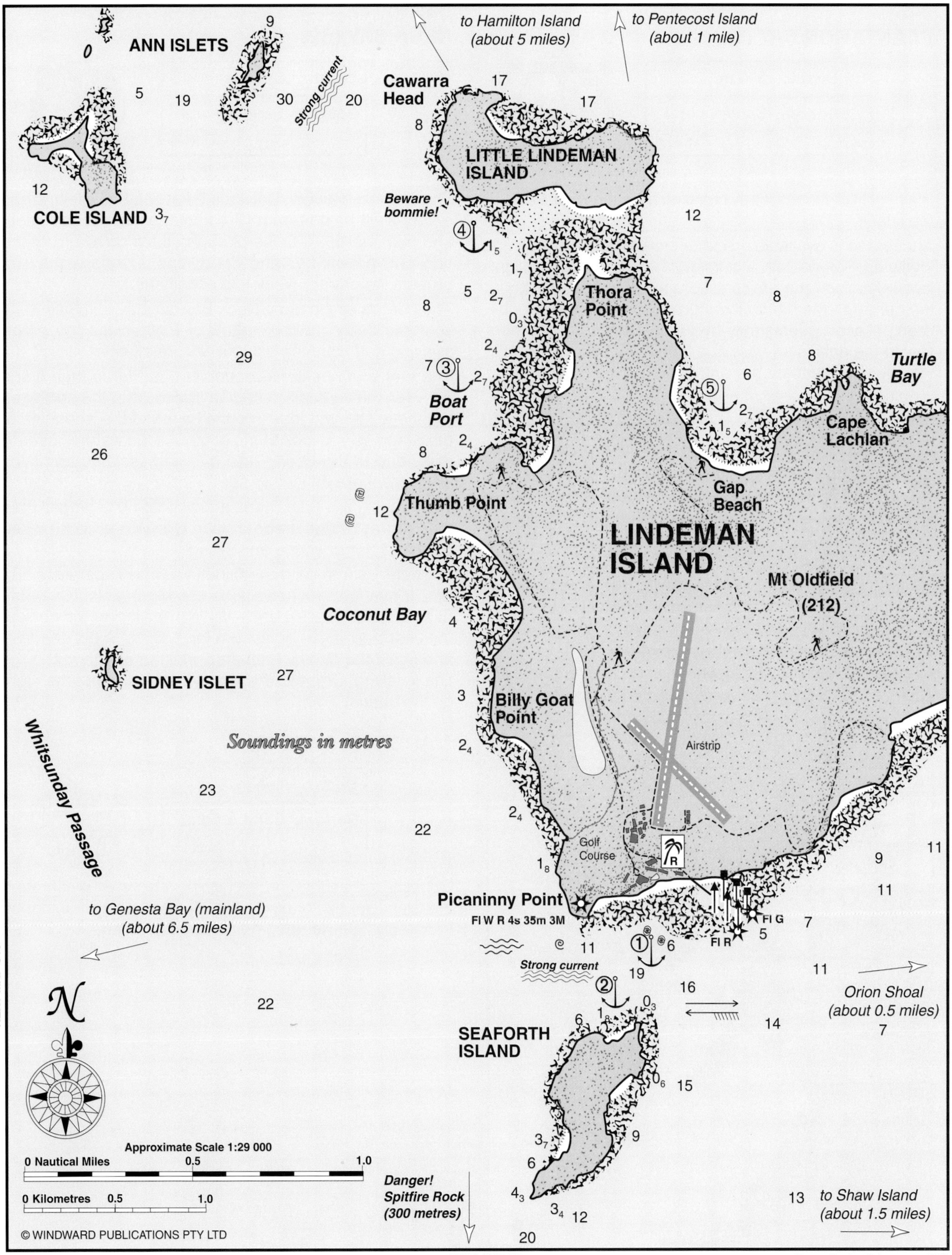

ANN ISLETS

9

0

5   19   30   20

Strong current

12

COLE ISLAND   3₇

to Hamilton Island
(about 5 miles)

to Pentecost Island
(about 1 mile)

Cawarra
Head   17

17

8

LITTLE LINDEMAN
ISLAND

12

Beware
bommie!   ④
5

1₇

7

8   5   2₇

0₃

2₄

7   ③
2₇

Boat
Port

2₄

8

Thora
Point

8

Turtle
Bay

8

6

⑤

2₇

1₅

Cape
Lachlan

29

26

12

Thumb Point

Gap
Beach

LINDEMAN
ISLAND

Mt Oldfield
(212)

27

Coconut Bay   4

SIDNEY ISLET   27

3

Billy Goat
Point

2₄

Soundings in metres

23

2₄

22

1₈

NEXT MAP S2

9   11

11

Whitsunday Passage

to Genesta Bay (mainland)
(about 6.5 miles)

Golf
Course

R

Fl G
Fl R   7   11

5

Picaninny Point
Fl W R 4s 35m 3M

①   6

NEXT MAP S19

Strong current

19

11

②

16

1₈   0₃

14

11

Orion Shoal
(about 0.5 miles)

7

22

N

SEAFORTH
ISLAND

6

0₆

15

3₇

6

9

Approximate Scale 1:29 000

0 Nautical Miles   0.5   1.0

0 Kilometres   0.5   1.0

4₃

3₄   12

13   to Shaw Island
(about 1.5 miles)

© WINDWARD PUBLICATIONS PTY LTD

Danger!
Spitfire Rock
(300 metres)

20

See photo S1, page138

PLANTATION BAY (S2)

Depth:	3–6 m
Bottom:	Sand & coral

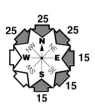

Stay north of Orion Shoal if coming from the resort side of the island.

Anchorage is available on either side of the reef. This is a lovely anchorage with a delightful beach, affording excellent swimming if the tide conditions are right. Inland at about the centre of the beach the old 'adventure camp' for children of resort guests may be found. Princess Alexandra Bay to the east is an easy ride in the dinghy in favourable weather – a pleasant bay and beach.

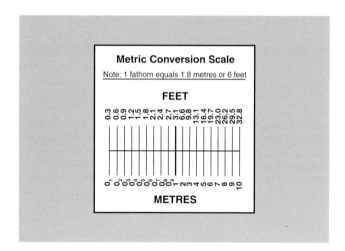

Metric Conversion Scale

Note: 1 fathom equals 1.8 metres or 6 feet

FEET

METRES

NECK BAY (S2)

Depth:	6–11 m
Bottom:	Sand & coral

The channel between Dalwood Point and Shaw Island has a very swift tidal stream (3-4 knots), which floods south and ebbs north. At times of spring tides be aware of the tide and prevailing wind conditions. Overfalls may be present in contrary wind–tide conditions.

The tide races close by Neck Bay, so stay as close in as you practically can to keep out of it; otherwise you will be swaying and spinning on your anchor all night.

The reef is very extensive; don't go further in than a line between the vertically fluted/faulted rocks at the north end (on the left as you look into the bay) and the 'shoulder' of the island as you look to the south. As the water is usually milky due to the strong tidal currents, isolated bommies off the reef are difficult to see.

Remember, the tides here are almost 50% bigger than they are at Shute Harbour; take this into account when calculating your scope and swing.

In blustery south-east conditions you may experience bullets. It may get a bit swelly as the wind easts. Neck Bay has a beautiful sand beach. You can walk over the neck to the east side. If you go ashore for a picnic, watch the tide, and leave the dinghy anchored well out on the reef if the tide is falling. Otherwise you may have to spend the night on the beach.

MAHER ISLAND (S2)

Depth:	5–8 m
Bottom:	Sand & coral

Opposite this anchorage is a nice beach and a 'hole through the island' for exploring. This is a pleasant daytime stopoff in suitably light weather, not a night anchorage.

SHAW ISLAND NORTH

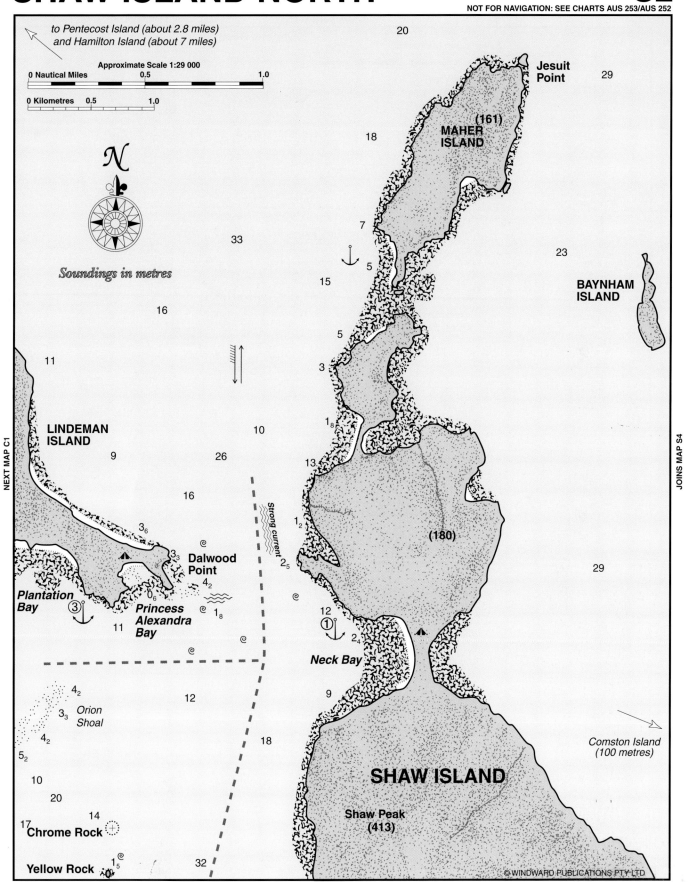

to Pentecost Island (about 2.8 miles)
and Hamilton Island (about 7 miles)

Approximate Scale 1:29 000

0 Nautical Miles   0.5   1.0

0 Kilometres   0.5   1.0

N

Soundings in metres

20

Jesuit
Point

29

(161)
**MAHER
ISLAND**

18

7

23

**BAYNHAM
ISLAND**

15

33

16

5

3

5

1_8

NEXT MAP C1

JOINS MAP S4

11

**LINDEMAN
ISLAND**

10

13

26

9

16

1_2

(180)

29

3_6

3_3

**Dalwood
Point**

4_2

Strong current

2_5

**Plantation
Bay**

③

0_6

**Princess
Alexandra
Bay**

1_8

11

12

①

2_4

Neck Bay

9

4_2

3_3

*Orion
Shoal*

12

18

4_2

*Comston Island
(100 metres)*

5_2

10

SHAW ISLAND

20

14

17

Chrome Rock

**Shaw Peak
(413)**

Yellow Rock

1_5

32

© WINDWARD PUBLICATIONS PTY LTD

JOINS MAPS S3 & S4

See photo S2, page 139

SHAW ISLAND SOUTH

S3

JOINS MAPS S1 & S2

NOT FOR NAVIGATION: SEE CHARTS AUS 253/252

⊕ **Chrome Rock**

Approximate Scale 1:29 000

0 Nautical Miles · · · 0.5 · · · 1.0

0 Kilometres · 0.5 · 1.0

3_6

SEAFORTH ISLAND

⊜

17

①⚓

8

⊛ **Yellow Rock**

Beware! Spitfire Rock

4

20

20

1_8

Caution! Mars Shoal

①⚓

9

🧭 N

3_3

26

BRUSH ISLAND

7

1_5 2_7

6

Soundings in metres

7

8

1_5

④⚓

5

10

14

Venus Shoal

10

29

26

NEXT MAP S17

⊜ **Burning Point**

②⚓

2_1

1_8

1_5

16

13

4_9

14

Volskow Island

4_6

⛺

SHAW ISLAND

Mt Arthur (253)

Danger! Rocks

18

23

10

1_8

✠ 10
VQ(9) 10s

Platypus Rock
(dries 2.1 metres)

25

KEYSER ISLAND

4_5 ③⚓

③⚓

7

Billbob Bay

5

to Cape Conway and Repulse Bay (about 6 miles)

3_9

10

to Thomas Island (about 2 miles)

Some bareboat yachts are not permitted east of the broken blue line when strong wind warnings are current. If in doubt, charterers should check with their charter company.

9

⚓

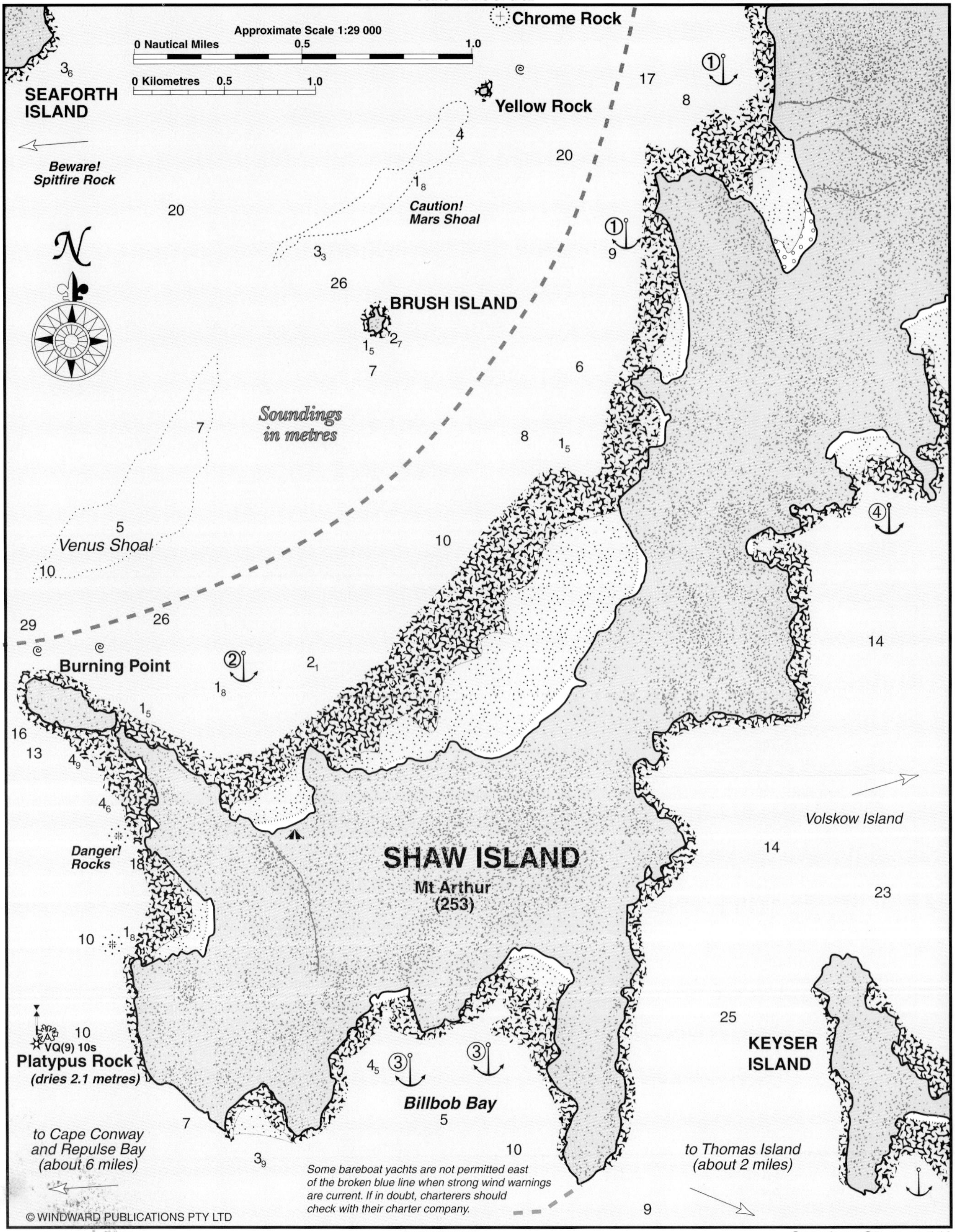

NEXT MAP S8

See photo S3, page 140

SHAW ISLAND SOUTH (S3)

Depth:	8–10 m
Bottom:	Sand & coral

This anchorage is not as snug as Neck Bay immediately to the north.

BURNING POINT (S3)

Depth:	5–8 m
Bottom:	Mud & sand

Note that the bottom is shoal for quite some distance off this little bay. Approach with care. This is indeed a lovely anchorage.

SHAW ISLAND SOUTH (S3)

Depth:	4–6 m
Bottom:	Sand

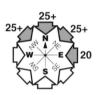

The tide sweeps around Burning Point at a rate of knots; in fresh winds from the south there may be overfalls and eddies.

Approaching Anchorage No. 3 from Burning Point, watch out for Platypus Rock, which is now marked as a result of one or two wrecks that have occurred there.

Look out for bommies off the reef, particularly on the eastern side.

There are beautiful little beaches – a nice, lonely anchorage.

As with all southerly exposed anchorages in the Whitsundays, you are potentially on a lee shore. These are not recommended for overnight during the trade winds season, from April to August/September.

SHAW ISLAND SOUTH (S3)

Depth:	5–9 m
Bottom:	Sand

Watch the reef on the north-east side, and leave enough room to swing. There is another small beach in the opposite cove.

Note: Some bareboats are not permitted south and east of a line between Cape Conway and the southern extremity of Shaw Island when strong wind warnings are current. If in doubt, check with your charter company.

KEYSER ISLAND S4

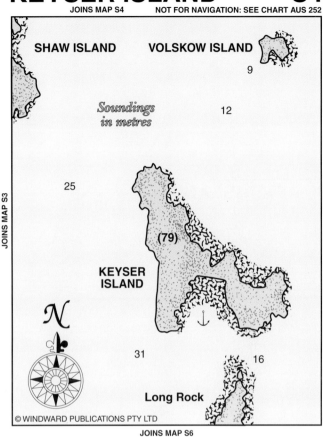

KEYSER ISLAND (S5)

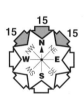

Depth:	6–9 m
Bottom:	Sand

In moderate winds from the northern quarter this can be a delightful, isolated anchorage. The shape of the island bears only a faint resemblance to that shown on the chart (AUS 252).

SHAW ISLAND EAST

S5

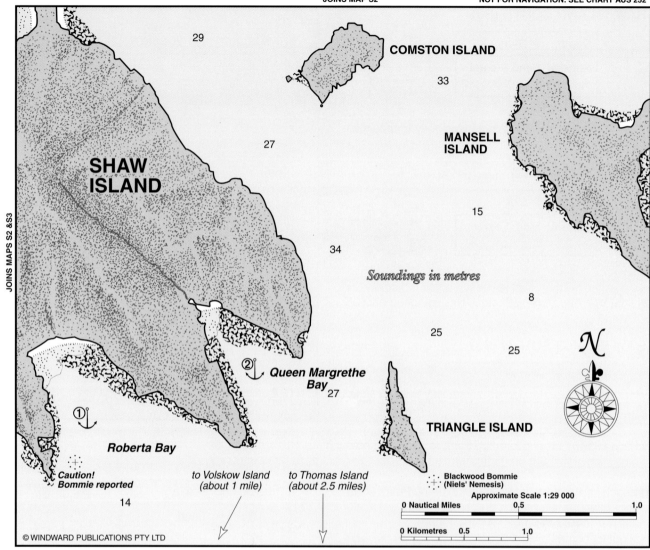

29

COMSTON ISLAND

33

27

MANSELL ISLAND

SHAW ISLAND

15

34

Soundings in metres

8

25

25

25

① ⚓

② ⚓ *Queen Margrethe Bay* 27

TRIANGLE ISLAND

⬦ **N**

Roberta Bay

⊹ **Caution!**
Bommie reported

to Volskow Island (about 1 mile)

to Thomas Island (about 2.5 miles)

⊹ **Blackwood Bommie**
⊹ **(Niels' Nemesis)**

14

Approximate Scale 1:29 000

0 Nautical Miles   0.5   1.0

0 Kilometres   0.5   1.0

© WINDWARD PUBLICATIONS PTY LTD

JOINS MAPS S2 &S3

NEXT MAPS S4 & S5

See photo S5, page 141

ROBERTA BAY (S5)

Depth:	6–10 m
Bottom:	Sand

Watch out for a bommie reported (but as yet unconfirmed) to lie some 250 metres off the point in anchorage No. 1 as shown, and give this side a wide berth just in case it's there. (Several intrepid mariners have scoured this bay looking for it as a result of earlier reports, without success. It may have been the bommie later confirmed south-east of Triangle Island.)

QUEEN MARGRETHE BAY (S5)

Depth:	6–10 m
Bottom:	Sand

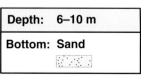

Queen Margrethe Bay will be less comfortable than Roberta Bay as the wind hauls more north-east.

Both Roberta Bay and Queen Margrethe Bay have nice beaches. These are not recommended as overnight anchorages during the trade winds season (April to August/September).

THOMAS ISLAND (S6)

Depth:	3–5 m
Bottom:	Sand

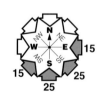

You can enter the anchorage on either side of the small island; watch out for the fringing reef which makes off for some distance from its south-west side.

This anchorage can be quite 'swelly' (i.e. uncomfortable), particularly in fresh south-east winds with a flooding tide.

THOMAS ISLAND

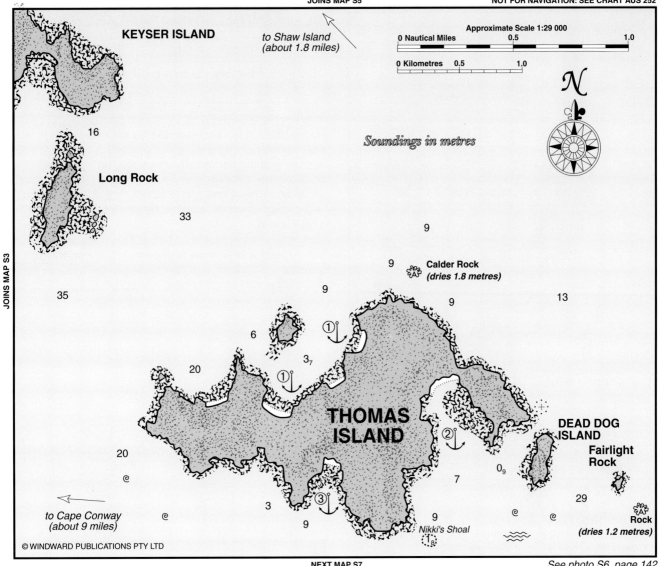

KEYSER ISLAND

to Shaw Island
(about 1.8 miles)

Approximate Scale 1:29 000

0 Nautical Miles 0.5 1.0

0 Kilometres 0.5 1.0

Soundings in metres

16

Long Rock

33

9

9 Calder Rock
(dries 1.8 metres)

9

35 9 9 13

JOINS MAP S3

6 ①

3₇

20 ①

**THOMAS
ISLAND**

② **DEAD DOG
ISLAND**

**Fairlight
Rock**

20 7 0₉ 29

to Cape Conway
(about 9 miles) 3 ③ Rock
(dries 1.2 metres)

9 9

Nikki's Shoal ①

© WINDWARD PUBLICATIONS PTY LTD

NEXT MAP S7 *See photo S6, page 142*

There are several sand beaches throughout the anchorage.

Thomas Island, being somewhat remote from the centre of the Whitsundays, is likely to afford more solitude than some of the central island anchorages.

THOMAS ISLAND (S6)

Depth:	3–5 m
Bottom:	Sand

There can be overfalls south of Dead Dog Island; watch the run of the tide if you are coming between Dead Dog Island and Fairlight Rock.

This is a lovely anchorage with a beautiful sand beach that is readily accessible at all tides through the break in the reef. It has a truly 'South Pacific' atmosphere. During the trade winds season it is not suitable for overnight use as southerlies sometimes spring up in the night.

THOMAS ISLAND (S6)

Depth:	6–9 m
Bottom:	Sand

This anchorage also has a nice sand beach, although access to it is not as easy as Anchorage No. 2 because there is no break in the reef.

SILVERSMITH ISLAND S7
NEXT MAP S6   NOT FOR NAVIGATION: SEE CHART AUS 252

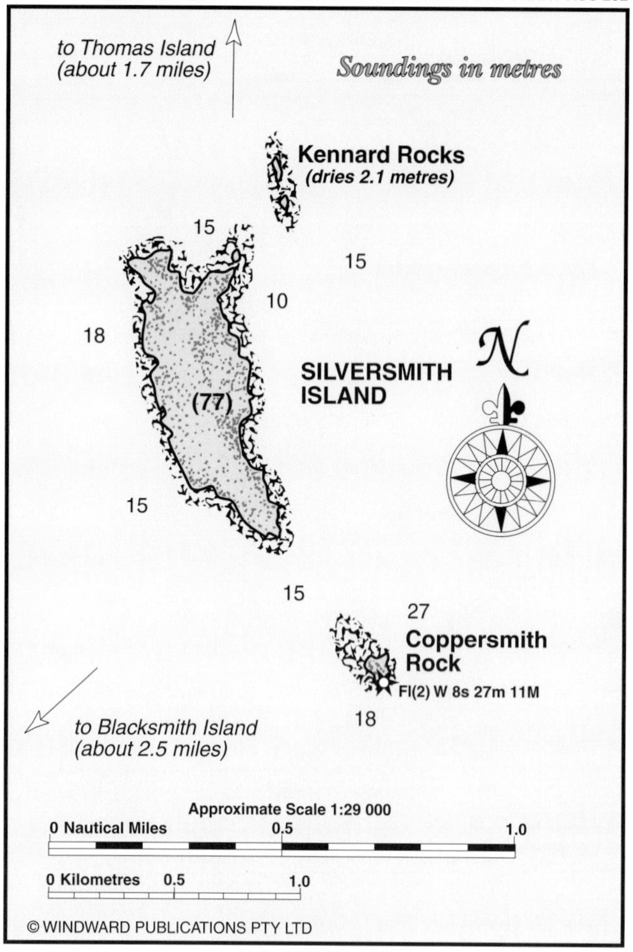

to Thomas Island
(about 1.7 miles)

Soundings in metres

Kennard Rocks
(dries 2.1 metres)

15

15

10

18

(77)

**SILVERSMITH
ISLAND**

15

15

27

**Coppersmith
Rock**
Fl(2) W 8s 27m 11M

18

to Blacksmith Island
(about 2.5 miles)

Approximate Scale 1:29 000

0 Nautical Miles   0.5   1.0

0 Kilometres   0.5   1.0

© WINDWARD PUBLICATIONS PTY LTD

NEXT MAPS S8 & S9

SILVERSMITH ISLAND (S7)
Silversmith Island doesn't offer any anchorage. There may be overfalls to the north of Kennard Rocks.

BLACKSMITH/LADYSMITH ISLAND (S8)

Depth:	6–9 m
Bottom:	Sand & coral

The Anchor Islands no doubt afforded the surveyor(s) who named them a few pleasurable minutes of name twizzling, but they do not afford the sailor very much more. They are remote and not particularly welcoming. In light conditions temporary anchorage may be had next to the sand beach at the south-west end of Blacksmith. The tide may be swift in the deep channel between Hammer Island and Blacksmith Island.

Ladysmith has prominent white cliffs on its north-eastern side. There is a shallow (4.3-metre) patch north-west of Bellows Islet which you can expect to be lively in fresh conditions with contrary wind and tide.

ANCHOR ISLANDS

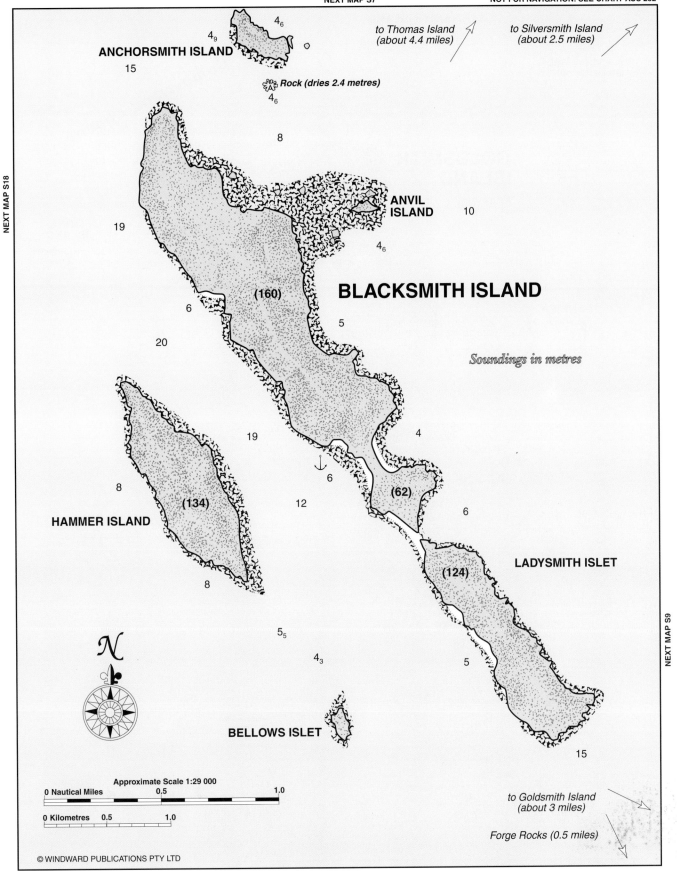

ANCHORSMITH ISLAND

4₉

4₆

15

to Thomas Island
(about 4.4 miles)

to Silversmith Island
(about 2.5 miles)

Rock (dries 2.4 metres)

4₆

8

ANVIL
ISLAND

10

19

4₆

BLACKSMITH ISLAND

(160)

6

5

20

Soundings in metres

NEXT MAP S18

19

4

(62)

6

8

(134)

12

6

HAMMER ISLAND

(124)

8

LADYSMITH ISLET

5₅

4₃

5

NEXT MAP S9

N

BELLOWS ISLET

15

Approximate Scale 1:29 000

0 Nautical Miles   0.5   1.0

0 Kilometres   0.5   1.0

to Goldsmith Island
(about 3 miles)

Forge Rocks (0.5 miles)

© WINDWARD PUBLICATIONS PTY LTD

GOLDSMITH ISLAND

NEXT MAP S7

S9

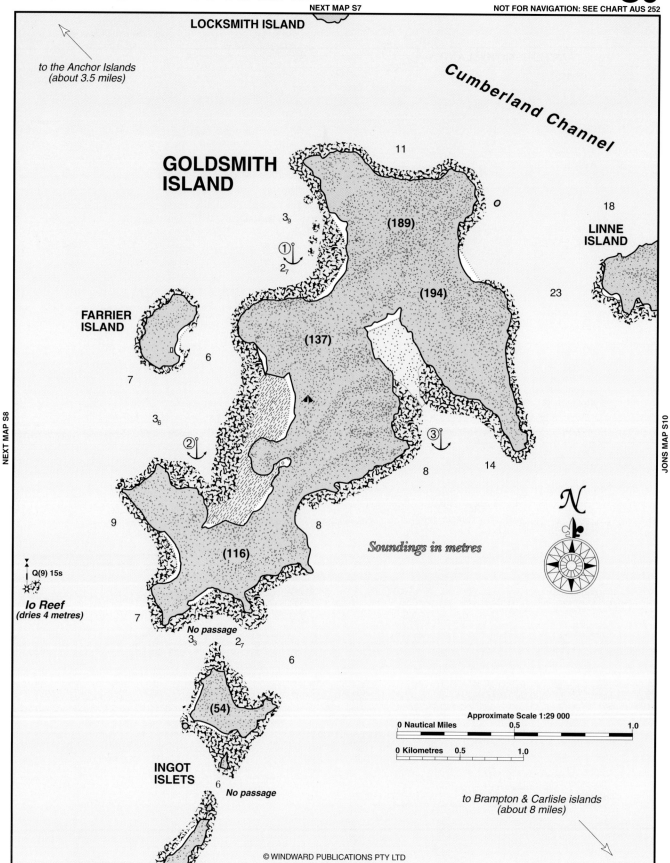

LOCKSMITH ISLAND

*to the Anchor Islands
(about 3.5 miles)*

Cumberland Channel

**GOLDSMITH
ISLAND**

11

(189)

18

**LINNE
ISLAND**

3₉

①

2₇

(194)

23

**FARRIER
ISLAND**

6

(137)

7

3₆

②

③

9

8

14

8

8

Soundings in metres

NEXT MAP S8

JONS MAP S10

Q(9) 15s

Io Reef
(dries 4 metres)

(116)

7

No passage

3₃   2₇

6

(54)

**INGOT
ISLETS**

6   *No passage*

Approximate Scale 1:29 000

| 0 Nautical Miles | 0.5 | 1.0 |

| 0 Kilometres | 0.5 | 1.0 |

*to Brampton & Carlisle islands
(about 8 miles)*

See photos S9 & S10, page 143

GOLDSMITH ISLAND (S9)

Depth:	2.5–4 m
Bottom:	Sand & coral

Approaching Goldsmith from the north, you may encounter overfalls between Locksmith Island and the northern end of the island, particularly in fresh wind-against-tide conditions.

From the south, the *Pilot* says not to attempt passage between Goldsmith and the Ingot Islets nor between the Ingot Islets themselves. About one mile south of the Ingots is Specie Shoal, which has only 4 metres of water in one spot. This whole area will be quite alive in fresh southeast conditions, particularly if the tide is making. Watch out for Io Reef west of the southern end of the island. Watch out for several isolated bommies just north of anchorage No. 1.

Goldsmith is a long way south of Shute Harbour and therefore enjoys solitude. The beaches are beautiful.

GOLDSMITH ISLAND (S9)

Depth:	6–9 m
Bottom:	Mud & coral

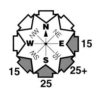

You can pass on either side of Farrier Island. There are sometimes strong currents between Farrier Island and Goldsmith Island, and this anchorage can be 'rolly' and subject to swell. Tidal effects may also cause the boat to ride up over the anchor.

There have, in the past, been moorings here, and room to anchor inside the moorings is limited.

GOLDSMITH ISLAND (S9)

Depth:	5–9 m
Bottom:	Sand & coral

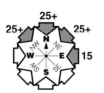

The reef extends a long way out from the sand beach; approach with care.

This lonely southern anchorage is not frequently visited both because of its distance from Shute Harbour (for bareboats) and because it is exposed to the south, which makes it not a good overnight anchorage from April to August/September when southerlies can arrive in the middle of the night. It is a magnificent anchorage, alive with reef life that seldom sees man. Sand extends out from the beach for some distance, making this a good spot for practising windsurfing. Small black tip sharks can be seen foraging in reef pools as the tide recedes.

The anchorage looks south to the lofty peaks of Carlisle and Brampton islands. Top spot in the right weather.

LINNE ISLAND (S10)

Depth:	6–9 m
Bottom:	Sand & coral

Linné Island is infrequently visited. The anchorage gives some protection in south-east conditions but is not an ideal overnight anchorage.

Linné was the second of the Cumberland Islands to have a European man set foot on it, according to recorded history – Lieutenant John Murray, in 1802 (the first was Calder Island). Murray and his crew on the *Lady Nelson* were assisting Matthew Flinders in his coastal explorations, and they made several landings on the beaches on the western side of the island, noting evidence of visits by Aboriginal people and retrieving a wrecked canoe (*source:* local historian, Ray Blackwood).

LINNE ISLAND

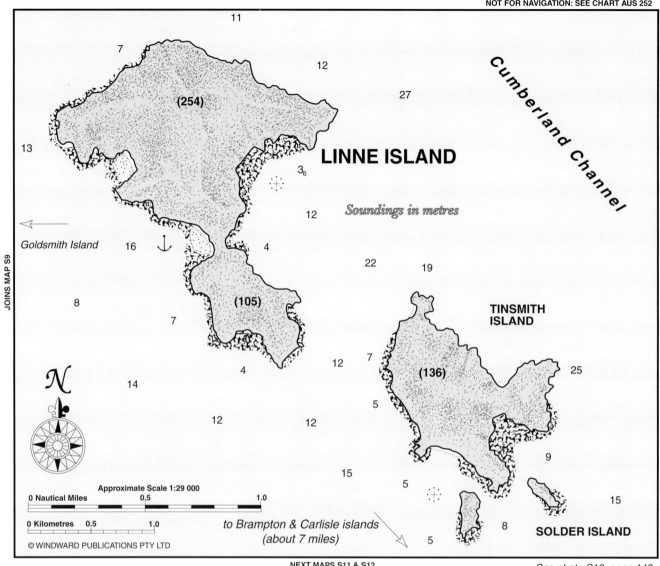

Cumberland Channel

11

7

12

27

(254)

13

LINNE ISLAND

3₆

Soundings in metres

12

4

Goldsmith Island   16   ⚓

22   19

TINSMITH ISLAND

8

(105)

7   12   7

(136)   25

4

5

14

12   12

15

5   9

12

15

5   5   15

to Brampton & Carlisle islands
(about 7 miles)   5   8   **SOLDER ISLAND**

JOINS MAP S9

Approximate Scale 1:29 000

0 Nautical Miles   0.5   1.0

0 Kilometres   0.5   1.0

© WINDWARD PUBLICATIONS PTY LTD

NEXT MAPS S11 & S12   *See photo S10, page 143*

BRAMPTON ISLAND (S11)

Depth:	3–5 m
Bottom:	Sand

Stay a healthy distance off southern and western points as in adverse wind/tide conditions there will be overfalls.

Brampton is one of the stopover anchorages for cruising yachts making their way to the Whitsundays. It is also a popular destination for the Mackay Cruising Yacht Club. There is a resort on the island, where visitors by sea are welcome as long as they register at reception on arrival, are dressed in a tidy manner (after 7.00 pm 'good Queensland casual' is required) and behave with proper consideration for the resident guests. Showers are available.

Water, fuel and food are not available unless it is an emergency.

BRAMPTON ISLAND (S11)

Depth:	6–9 m
Bottom:	Sand & coral

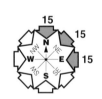

Approach with care and anchor off the extensive reef.

BRAMPTON ISLAND (S11)

Depth:	6–9 m
Bottom:	Sand

This anchorage offers good protection in north-east to north winds.

BRAMPTON & CARLISLE ISLANDS S11

NOT FOR NAVIGATION: SEE CHART AUS 252

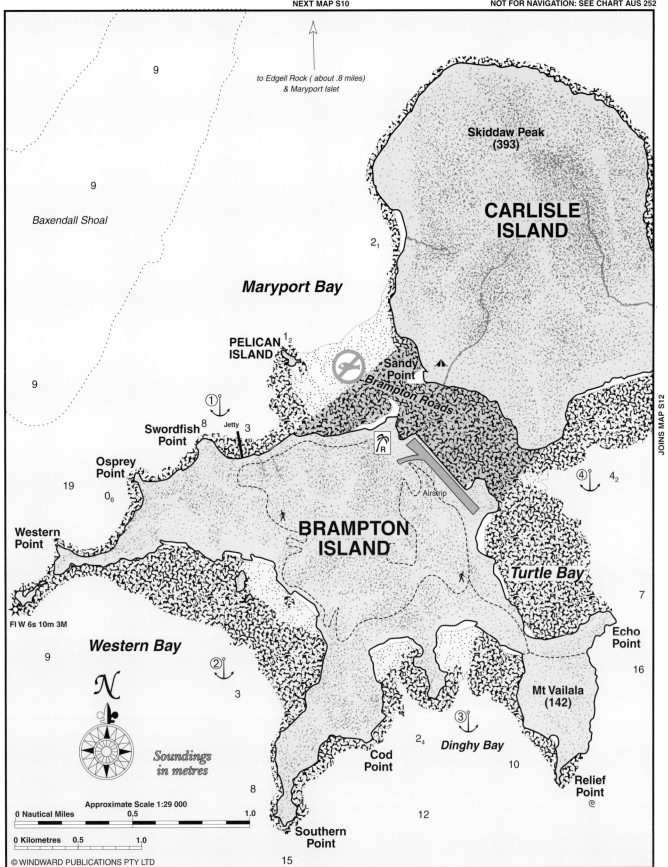

9

to Edgell Rock (about .8 miles)
& Maryport Islet

Skiddaw Peak
(393)

9

**CARLISLE
ISLAND**

Baxendall Shoal

2_1

Maryport Bay

9

PELICAN
ISLAND 1_2

Sandy
Point

Brampton Roads

① ⚓

Swordfish 8
Point   Jetty 3

Osprey
Point

19

0_6

④ 4_2
⚓

Airstrip

**BRAMPTON
ISLAND**

Western
Point

Turtle Bay

7

Fl W 6s 10m 3M

Echo
Point

Western Bay

16

9

② ⚓

Mt Vailala
(142)

3

③ ⚓

2_4 *Dinghy Bay*

Cod
Point

10

8

Relief
Point

*Soundings
in metres*

Southern
Point

12

Approximate Scale 1:29 000

0 Nautical Miles   0.5   1.0

0 Kilometres   0.5   1.0

15

JOINS MAP S12

See photo S11, page 144

CARLISLE EAST   S12

NOT FOR NAVIGATION: SEE CHART AUS 252

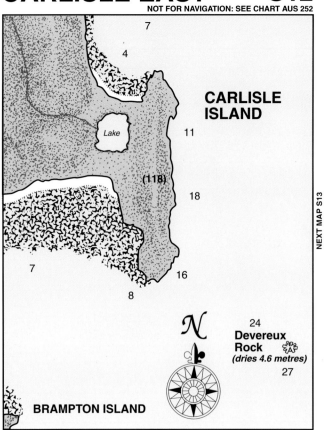

COCKERMOUTH I.   S13

NOT FOR NAVIGATION: SEE CHART AUS 824

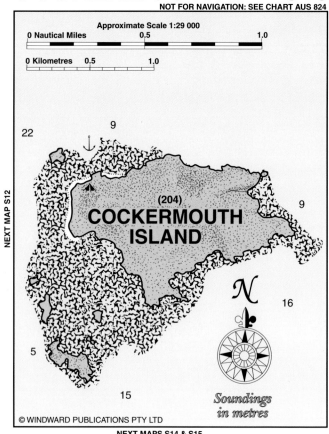

© WINDWARD PUBLICATIONS PTY LTD

NEXT MAPS S14 & S15

BRAMPTON ISLAND (S11)

Depth:	4–6 m
Bottom:	Sand

You can travel 'Brampton Roads' in the dinghy if the tide is high. Watch for swift current through the passage. This anchorage is not as protected as Anchorage No. 3.

COCKERMOUTH ISLAND (S13)

Depth:	6–9 m
Bottom:	Sand

Cockermouth has a national parks campsite on its beautiful sand beach at the western end. It is a lovely island with some casuarinas and coconut palms; it is also lonely, especially as there is really no comfortable anchorage for yachts and it is thus unlikely to be visited except by adventurers. If you are one, be careful of the reef on the north side, which makes off for some distance.

It is shallow enough to anchor, but it will be swelly in all conditions.

KESWICK ISLAND (S14)

Depth:	6–9 m
Bottom:	Sand & coral

KESWICK ISLAND (S14)

Depth:	4–7 m
Bottom:	Sand

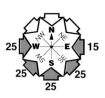

Keswick and St Bees islands are the southernmost of the Cumberland Islands to offer anchorage. They are not far from Mackay; the tides are just about as great as at Mackay. Strong streams are encountered in Egremont Pass (3-4 knots) and around Singapore Rock, on the western side of the island, where overfalls occur.

Anchorage No. 2 (and No. 4 on St Bees) are used by professional trawler fishermen, who use them to shelter. Anchorage No. 2 is opposite the airstrip. Keep as close in as practicable to get out of the stream; watch out for fringing reef.

KESWICK ISLAND

NEXT MAP S13

NOT FOR NAVIGATION SEE CHART AUS 824

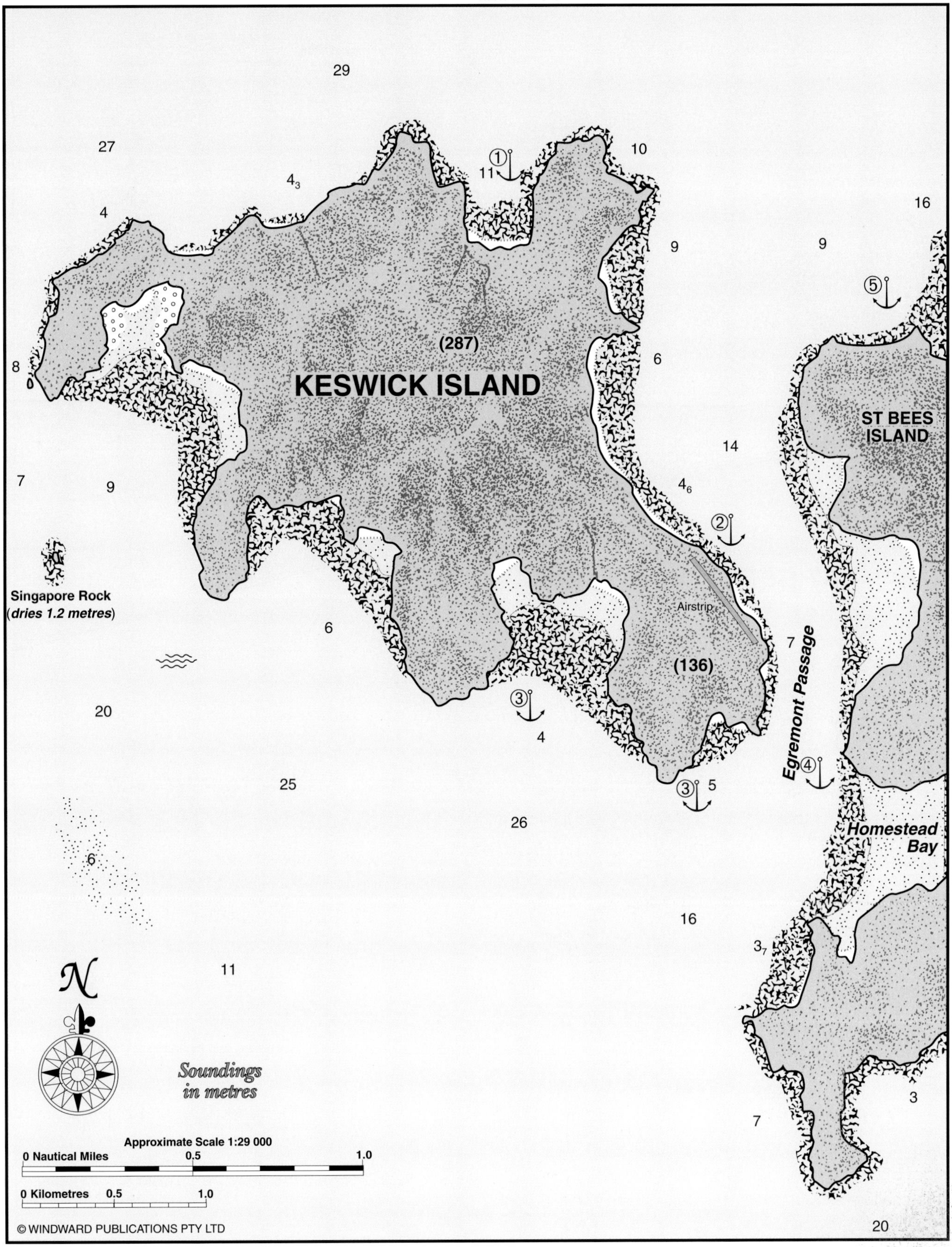

29

27

10

4_3

11 ①

16

4

9

9

⑤

8

(287)

6

KESWICK ISLAND

ST BEES
ISLAND

14

7

9

4_6

②

Singapore Rock
(*dries 1.2 metres*)

6

Airstrip

(136)

7

20

③

JOINS MAP S15

4

25

③ 5

26

④

Egremont Passage

*Homestead
Bay*

6

16

3_7

11

N

*Soundings
in metres*

7

3

Approximate Scale 1:29 000

0 Nautical Miles   0.5   1.0

0 Kilometres   0.5   1.0

© WINDWARD PUBLICATIONS PTY LTD

ST BEES ISLAND

NEXT MAP S13

NOT FOR NAVIGATION: SEE CHART AUS 824

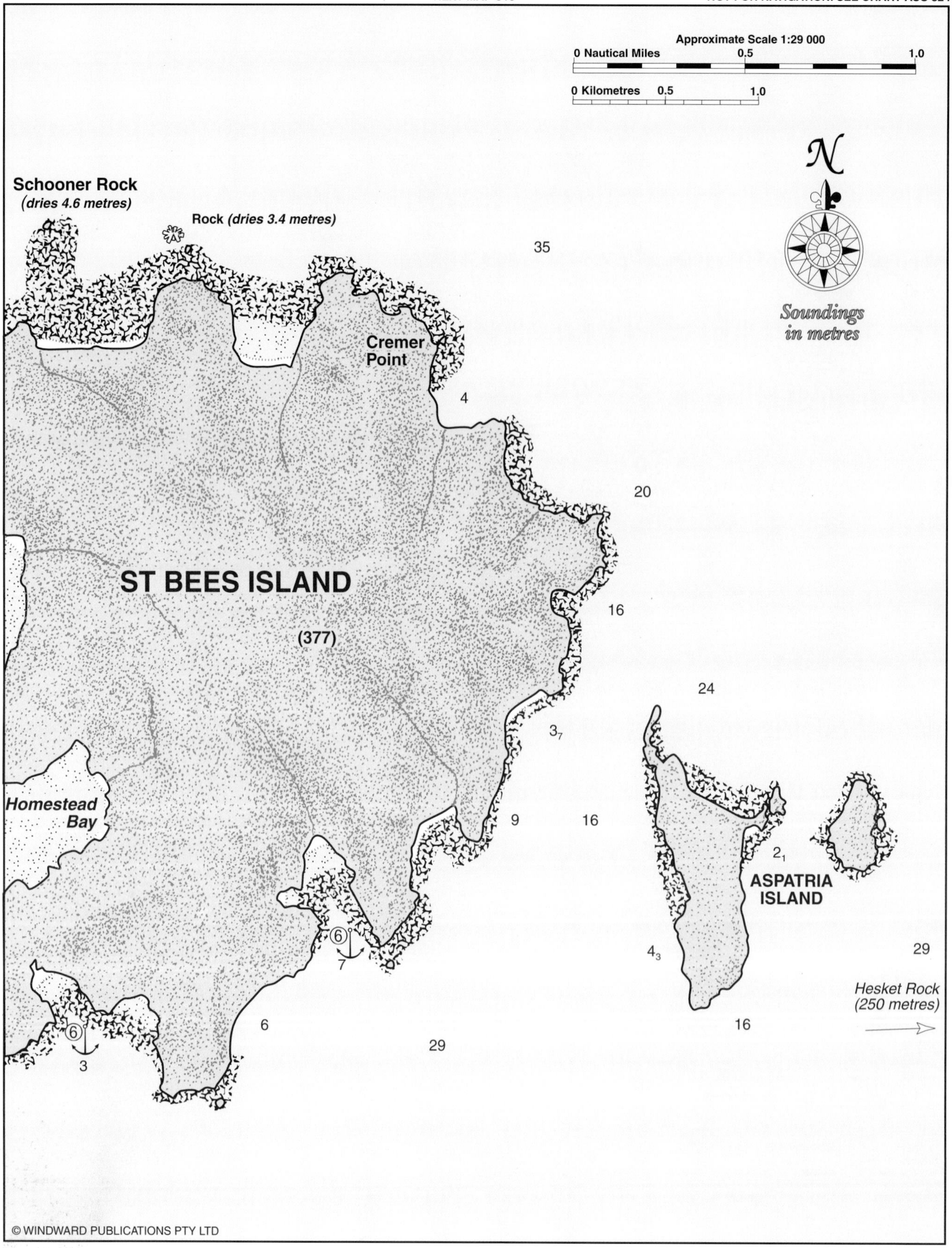

Approximate Scale 1:29 000

0 Nautical Miles   0.5   1.0

0 Kilometres   0.5   1.0

$\mathcal{N}$

Soundings in metres

Schooner Rock
(dries 4.6 metres)

Rock *(dries 3.4 metres)*

35

Cremer Point

4

20

ST BEES ISLAND

(377)

16

24

3_7

Homestead Bay

9

16

2_1

ASPATRIA ISLAND

29

4_3

⑥

7

⑥

6

16

Hesket Rock (250 metres)

29

⑥

3

NEXT MAP S14

NEXT MAP S16

SCAWFELL ISLAND

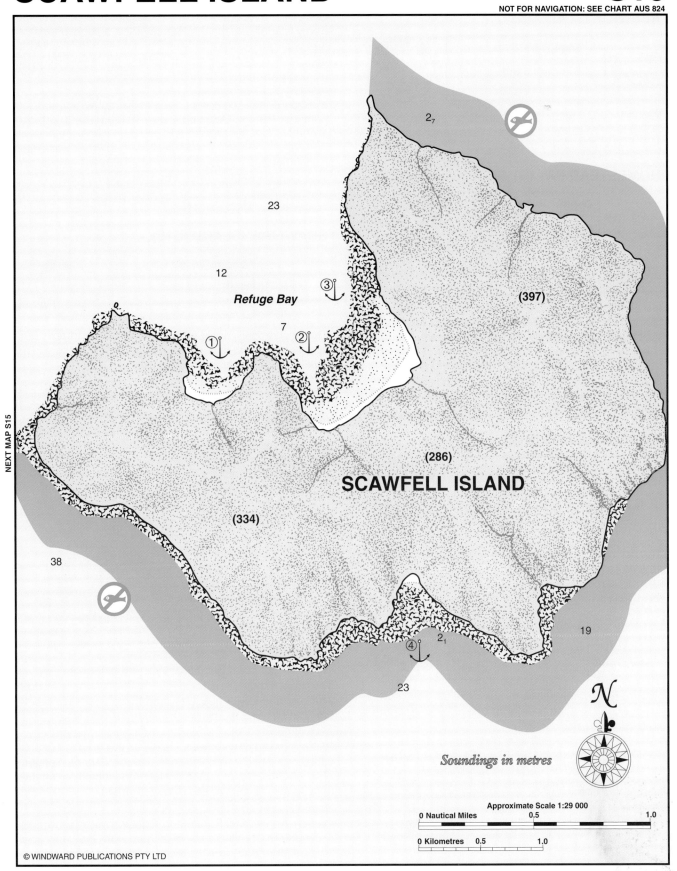

NEXT MAP S15

Refuge Bay

SCAWFELL ISLAND

(397)

(286)

(334)

23

12

7

38

23

19

2₇

2₁

Soundings in metres

N

Approximate Scale 1:29 000

0 Nautical Miles   0.5   1.0

0 Kilometres   0.5   1.0

KESWICK ISLAND (S14)

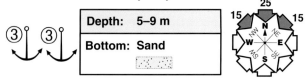

Depth:	5–9 m
Bottom:	Sand

Keswick Island offers several spots on the southern side to get out of northerly weather. These anchorages, however, have a tendency to be swelly.

HOMESTEAD BAY (ST BEES ISLAND) (S14)

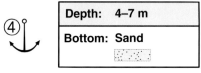

Depth:	4–7 m
Bottom:	Sand

Anchorage No. 4 is at the northern end of Homestead Bay; professional fishermen report having stayed in this anchorage comfortably in 30+ knots from the south-east.

Homestead Bay is where the pioneering Busuttin family built their homestead in 1907, one of the early island families. They began taking tourists to the island in 1926, and members of this family later established the resort on Brampton Island. The island is one of a handful that are not national parks, and plans are afoot for a resort development there.

ST BEES ISLAND (S14)

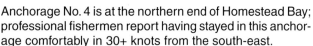

Depth:	5–9 m
Bottom:	Sand & coral

The northern bays of St Bees are not very deep and offer little protection from swell.

ST BEES ISLAND SOUTH (S15)

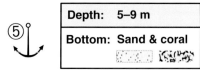

Depth:	6–9 m
Bottom:	Sand & coral

There are several places to seek shelter from northerly weather on the south side of St Bees. These anchorages tend to be swelly.

REFUGE BAY (SCAWFELL ISLAND) (S16)

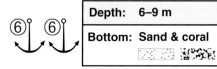

Depth:	6–9 m
Bottom:	Sand

Scawfell is a recognised convenient stopover between the Percy Islands and the Whitsundays. It is a popular anchorage with professional trawlers, and it is often possible to approach at night using their lights to guide you. Be alert, however, for those yachts that are oblivious to the requirement to show an anchor light.

In strong south-east weather swell reaches around the points of Refuge Bay, and it may be necessary to move around to find the best situation to deal with bullets, swell and tide. Normally, anchorage close to the rock walls near Anchorage No. 1 and Anchorage No. 3 will be best in strong south-east weather. Anchorage No. 1 is best in strong southerlies and is also good in south-westerlies. There may be current in Anchorage No. 3.

SCAWFELL ISLAND (S16)

Depth:	6–9 m
Bottom:	Sand

This anchorage is not ideal but does afford short-term protection from north to north-east winds provided there is no swell rolling in from the south-east.

Note: the following maps (S17–S19) were incorporated for the first time in the 5th Edition. They begin at Genesta Bay, on the mainland north of Cape Conway, and proceed to the Repulse Islands and then to Laguna Quays on the mainland opposite the Repulse Islands. Information on Mackay, at the far south of the area covered, is presented at the end of this section.

GENESTA BAY (S17)

Depth:	3–6 m
Bottom:	Mud & sand

Watch out for Long Shoal opposite the entrance.

The water in this bay is relatively shallow; anchor well out. The bay has lovely beaches, and there is a deep creek that can be explored by dinghy when the tide is up.

A lovely bay, Genesta was named by Lieutenant G.E. Richards, who conducted a survey of the area in 1885. It was a reference to the British America's Cup challenger, *Genesta*, which was sailing to New York at the time for the third America's Cup series against *Puritan*.

Round Head and Puritan Bay to the north are also associated by name. The Puritans in England were known as 'Roundheads' because some of them wore their hair very much shorter than was the style of the time (*source*: local historian Ray Blackwood).

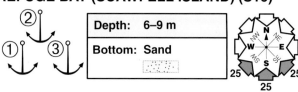

GENESTA BAY

NEXT MAP C7

NOT FOR NAVIGATION: SEE CHART AUS 252

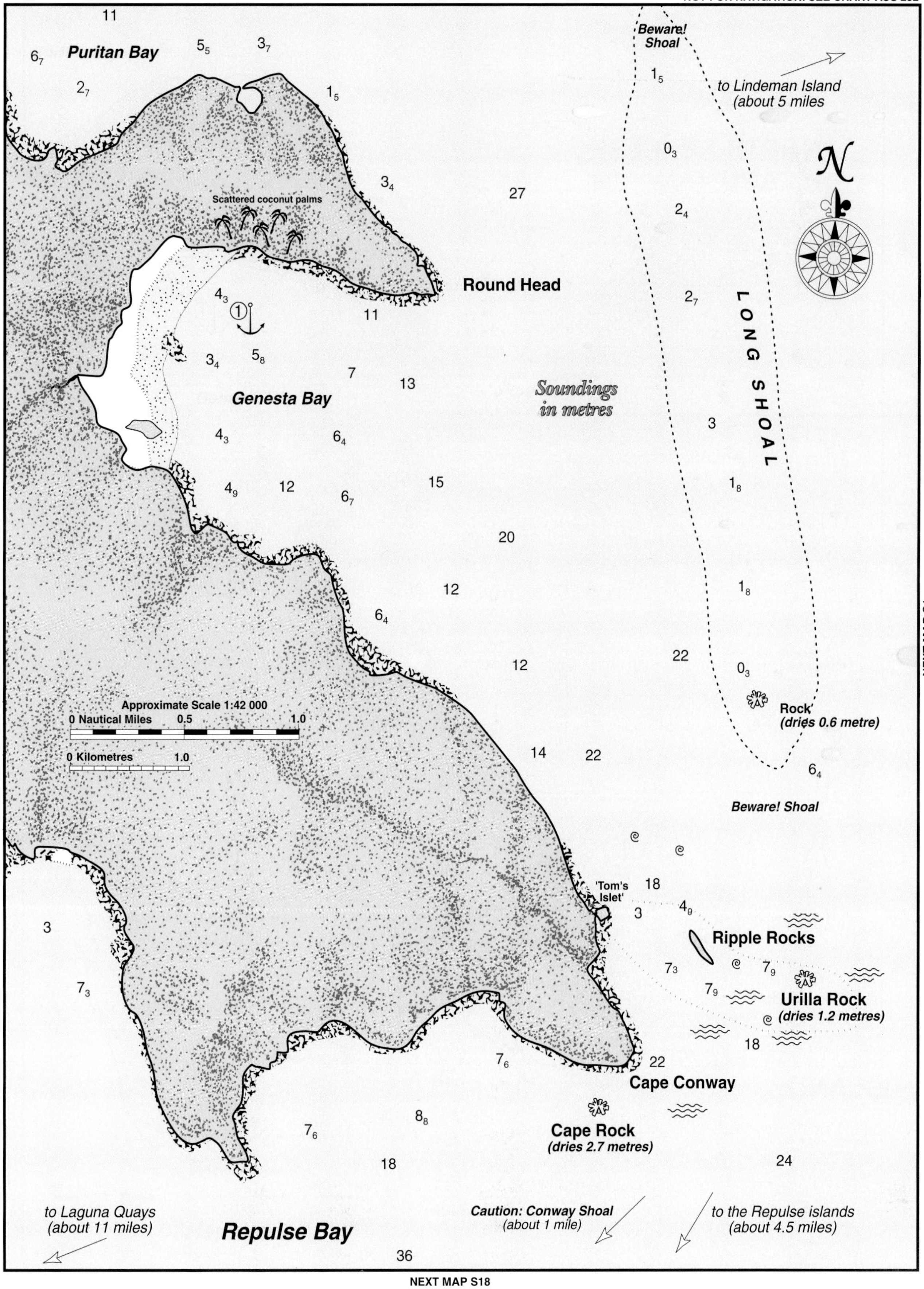

11

Puritan Bay

6_7

5_5 3_7

2_7

Beware!
Shoal

1_5

to Lindeman Island
(about 5 miles

1_5

0_3

2_4

3_4

27

2_7

N

Scattered coconut palms

Round Head

L O N G   S H O A L

4_3

① ⚓

11

3

3_4 5_8

1_8

7

13

Genesta Bay

Soundings
in metres

4_3 6_4

1_8

4_9 12

6_7

15

0_3

6_4 **Rock**
(dries 0.6 metre)

20

22

12

6_4

12

6_4

14   22

Beware! Shoal

Approximate Scale 1:42 000
0 Nautical Miles   0.5   1.0

0 Kilometres   1.0

18

'Tom's
Islet'

3   4_9

Ripple Rocks

3

7_3 7_9

7_9 **Urilla Rock**
(dries 1.2 metres)

7_3

18

7_6 22

Cape Conway

8_8 **Cape Rock**
(dries 2.7 metres)

24

7_6

18

to Laguna Quays
(about 11 miles)

Repulse Bay

Caution: Conway Shoal
(about 1 mile)

to the Repulse islands
(about 4.5 miles)

36

NEXT MAP S18

NEXT MAP S1

REPULSE GROUP

S18

NOT FOR NAVIGATION: SEE CHART AUS 252

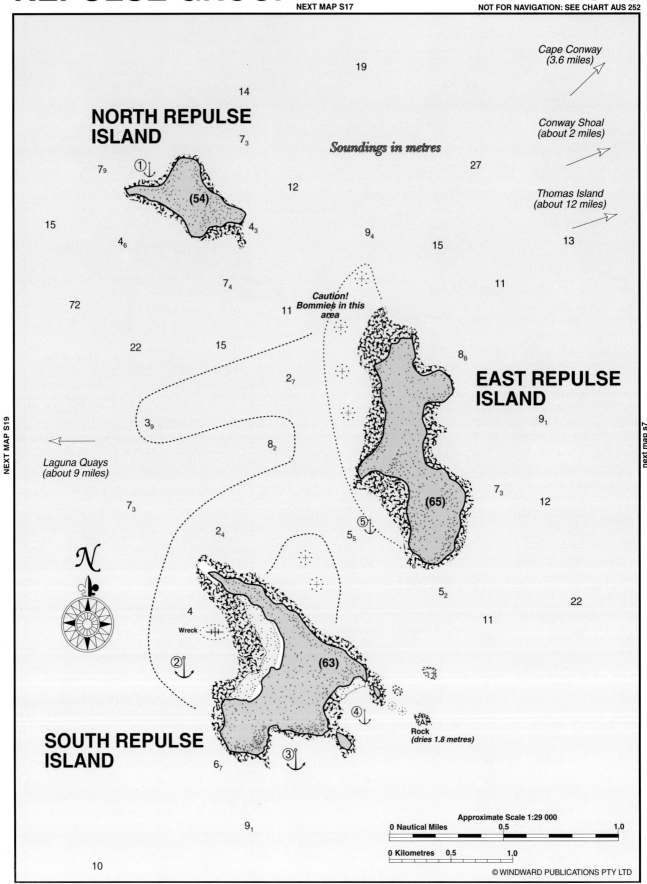

19

14

NORTH REPULSE ISLAND

7₃

Cape Conway
(3.6 miles)

Soundings in metres

7₉

①

(54)

27

Conway Shoal
(about 2 miles)

12

15

4₃

Thomas Island
(about 12 miles)

4₆

9₄

13

7₄

15

72

11

11

Caution!
Bommies in this
area

22

15

8₈

EAST REPULSE ISLAND

2₇

3₉

9₁

8₂

Laguna Quays
(about 9 miles)

7₃

(65)

7₃

12

⑤

7₃

5₅

4₆

2₄

N

5₂

22

4

11

Wreck

②

(63)

③

⑥₇

④

Rock
(dries 1.8 metres)

SOUTH REPULSE ISLAND

6₇

9₁

10

Approximate Scale 1:29 000

0 Nautical Miles   0.5   1.0

0 Kilometres   0.5   1.0

© WINDWARD PUBLICATIONS PTY LTD

Notes on Repulse Bay

Repulse Bay is a wide expanse of quite shallow water between Cape Conway (at its north-east) and Midge Island (at its south-west). The bay was named by James Cook, in 1770, because he was 'repulsed' by it, that is he was unable to find a passage north where he had thought there was one. This gives some clue to the size of the bay and the expanse of low-lying land at the head of it (west of the Conway Range) where the O'Connell and Proserpine rivers make their final tortuous journey to the sea. These rivers have a combined catchment of some 12 000 square kilometres, and each year they discharge millions upon millions of cubic metres of sediment-laden water into the sea, which has contributed to the shallowness of the bay. The combination of the south-east trade winds and the big tidal range in this area keeps the sediments stirred up so that the water is seldom clear. You cannot depend on a bow lookout to see submerged hazards.

Negotiating Cape Conway (map S17)

Coming around Cape Conway, beware of the following half-tide hazards in the vicinity of the Cape: Long Shoal, which runs parallel to the eastern shore of Conway Peninsula; Urilla Rock, which is about 0.4 mile south-east of Ripple Rocks; Cape Rock, which is about one mile south-west of Cape Conway. An underwater shallow ridge runs from 'Tom's Islet' (see map S17) south-east to Ripple Rocks and Urilla Rock. ('Tom's Islet' is attached to the mainland, but it stands proud and appears to be an island at high tide.)

When the tide is flooding against a south-east trade wind, or when the tide is ebbing and Repulse Bay is emptying and dumping masses of water into the main ebb stream travelling northwards, the whole area around Cape Conway can become very churned up and the sea conditions unpredictable, with eddies and large overfalls. In fact, the whole of Repulse Bay can be somewhat lumpy.

It is possible for small craft to go between Cape Conway and Ripple Rocks, but this will be a more pleasant trip in favourable conditions (moderate winds (<15 knots) and, preferably, when the tide is near high). South of Ripple Rocks the water is deeper towards the mainland (and therefore may be less disturbed). If conditions are active (caused by fresh winds and tides opposing each other, or if it's towards the time of low tide, particularly if there is a large tidal range), it's probably advisable to give the Cape and its hazards a good berth and go around to the outside (east of) Long Shoal, making a wide swing around this area. Then, watch out for Conway Shoal, which will be a very rough patch if winds and tides are jousting with each other.

NORTH REPULSE ISLAND (S18)

 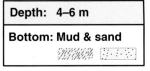

This is suitable as a daytime stopoff only in light weather. North Repulse has a surprising variety of vegetation, including a lush rain forest at the northern end. The shoreline is mainly rocky and inhospitable except at this anchorage, where a pebble beach provides a landing spot in calm conditions. Torresian imperial pigeons nest here from October to March; care should be taken not to disturb them at this time.

SOUTH REPULSE ISLAND (S18)

The water is quite shallow in this bay; anchor well out so that you are not in danger of swinging around into shoal water. The reef has many submerged coral heads. There is a wreck in the northern part of the bay which constitutes a hazard to navigation. This anchorage becomes swelly when the wind moves into the south.

There are several pleasant beaches.

SOUTH REPULSE ISLAND (S18)

This is not a particularly attractive bay, with a rocky foreshore, but it is a comfortable little anchorage in northerly conditions.

SOUTH REPULSE ISLAND (S18)

This is a more attractive anchorage than No. 3, with a pleasant beach, but it offers little protection from most winds. A daytime stopoff only.

Lieutenant Philip King and the botanist Allan Cunningham landed here in 1819 and climbed to the summit. They noted evidence of Aboriginal visitation.

EAST REPULSE ISLAND (S18)

This anchorage is right at the side of the channel between the islands and is subject to currents and swell. The rocky beach is not particularly attractive. On the southern tip of the island are the remains of a limestone mining venture commenced during World War I.

A light-weather, daytime stopoff only.

LAGUNA QUAYS

S19

NOT FOR NAVIGATION: SEE CHART AUS 252

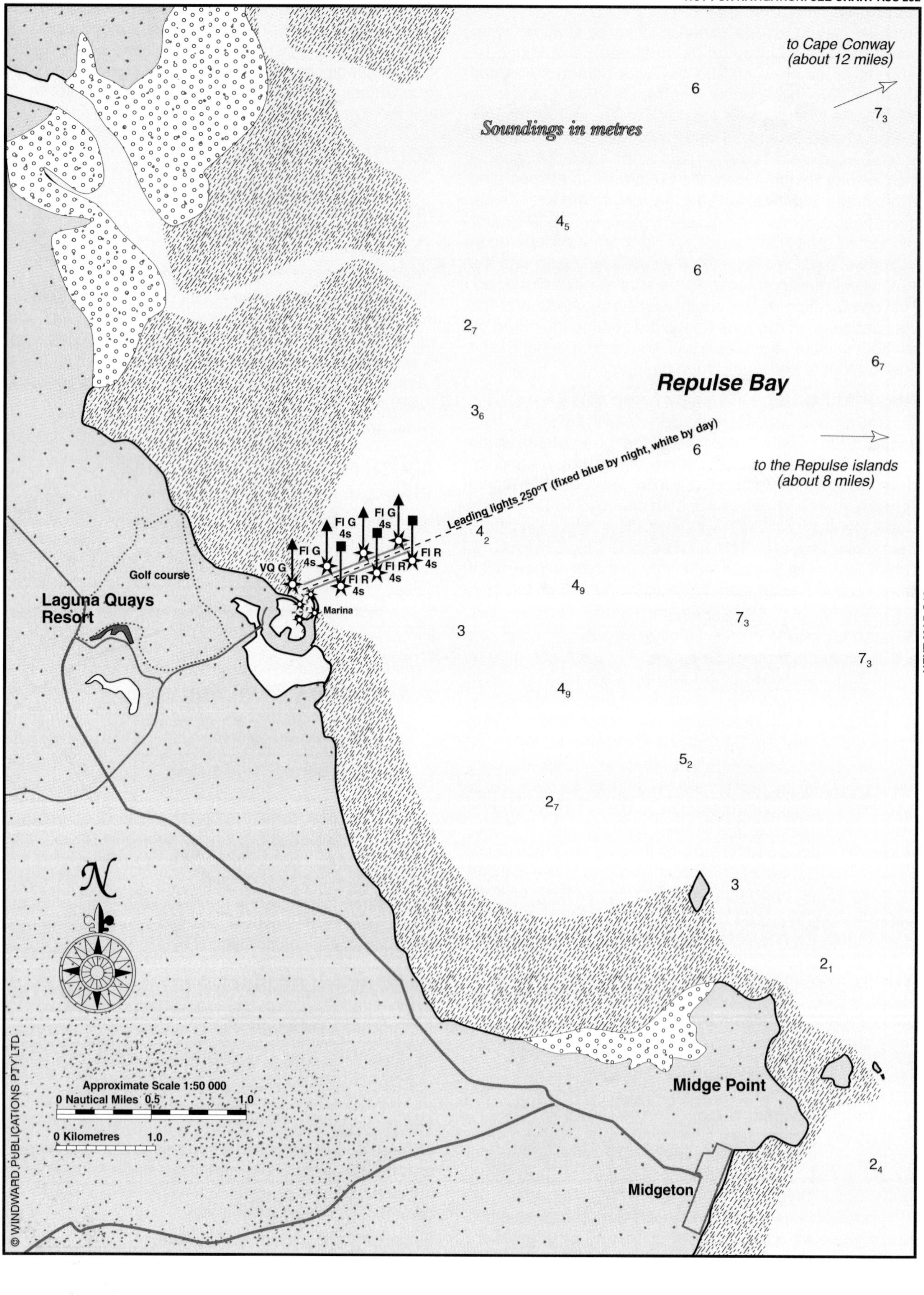

to Cape Conway
(about 12 miles)

6

7₃

Soundings in metres

4₅

6

2₇

6₇

Repulse Bay

3₆

6

Leading lights 250°T (fixed blue by night, white by day)

to the Repulse islands
(about 8 miles)

Fl G
4s

Fl G
4s

4₂

Fl G
4s

VQ G

Fl R
4s

Golf course

Fl R
4s

Fl R
4s

4₉

**Laguna Quays
Resort**

Marina

7₃

3

7₃

4₉

NEXT MAP S18

5₂

2₇

3

2₁

N

Midge Point

Approximate Scale 1:50 000
0 Nautical Miles 0.5   1.0

0 Kilometres   1.0

Midgeton

2₄

© WINDWARD PUBLICATIONS PTY LTD

LAGUNA QUAYS MARINA

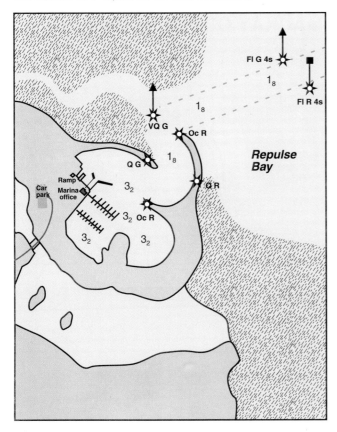

LAGUNA QUAYS MARINA (S17)

Depth:	1.8–3.2 m
Bottom:	Mud

White leading lights guide you into the centre of the channel to the harbour, which has three port and four starboard beacons marking the sides. The channel is dredged to 1.8 metres (lowest expected tide) with minor variations caused by silting. The depth in the harbour itself is 3.2 metres.

The marina accommodates vessels up to 40 metres length and has 70 floating berths each with water and power (single and three-phase). There are also 10 swing moorings. Fuel and water are available. Other services and facilities include sewage pump-out, a coin-operated laundry, a kiosk (open seven days a week, where basic groceries, newspapers and magazines may be purchased). There is a public launching ramp and ample car parking.

Laguna Quays resort

The Laguna Quays resort is quite a splendid five-star complex with a championship golf course (designed by David Graham). The resort is located 2 kilometres from the marina, a leisurely 15-minute stroll or a 5-minute ride in the complimentary resort shuttle bus. The bus can also be hired to go into Proserpine for shopping or to the airport. Proserpine is a 20-minute drive (27 kilometres to the north); Mackay is about 100 kilometres to the south (about one hour by car).

Payment of the marina fee entitles you to the same privileges as those enjoyed by resort guests. This includes: free entry to the beach club, including free use of non-motorised water sports equipment; use of three swimming pools; tennis; croquet; archery; and bush walks. You may also pay your green fees and play on the magnificent 18-hole Turtle Point Golf Course (while kangaroos stand tamely by – no doubt chuckling as you miss your putt). Golfers must be properly attired (including shirt with collar, and socks). Clubs and shoes are available for hire from the pro shop.

From Cape Conway the red roof tiles of Laguna Quays resort are visible at the right-hand end of the left-hand set of hills (bearing a little south of west). After rounding the Cape, proceed north of North Repulse Island. In a south-easterly you can look forward to an exhilarating reach to Laguna Quays. Approaching the harbour entrance the depth of water progressively falls to 3–4 metres at low tide. To avoid steering parallel to shorter and closer seas that will occur near the marina entrance, steer a little south from the outset and then bear away for the marina.

The mouth of the entrance channel to the man-made harbour is about two miles north of Midge Point at latitude 20°36' south, longitude 148°41.3' east, (the harbour itself is not visible on chart AUS 252, being just off its left margin). A river immediately north of the harbour causes some siltation around the entrance and in the channel. Tides for this area also vary. **It is therefore highly advisable to call the marina office for instructions for entering the channel well in advance of arriving at the entrance.** They keep a listening watch on VHF channels 16, 9 and 21, HF 2524 kHz and 27.88 MHz, from 8.00 am to 4.30 pm, seven days a week.

MACKAY

Mackay is a major commercial centre and the 'sugar capital' of Australia. It is smack in the middle of the Bowen Basin coal deposits, and the largest coal export terminal in the world is found at Hay Point, 45 kilometres south. The city itself is on the Pioneer River.

Cruising sailors visiting Mackay use Mackay Outer Harbour, another of Queensland's man-made harbours, the principal purpose of which is the storage and transhipment of massive quantities of sugar.

Berthing

There are 8 visitors' piles berths in the south-east harbour just north of the bend in the southern breakwater. The small boat harbour (south-west corner) has pile berths for yachts permanently resident. Temporary berthing is available at the tourist boat jetty on the south side of the harbour opposite the end of the main sugar wharf. All mooring arrangements must be made with the port officer, who is located in the middle of the south sugar wharf. The office can be contacted 24 hours a day on VHF channel 16.

If there is a vacant visitors' pile mooring when you arrive you may tie up there and make yourself known to the port officer later. If there are no visitors' berths available, you you may find an empty spot at the tourist boat jetty to tie up temporarily while you present yourself at the office to arrange a mooring in the small boat harbour or a formal berth at the tourist boat jetty. Someone is there at all times (even if it is a watchman in the middle of the night). You can tie up to a ladder near the office. A charge is made for moorings, slightly more for the jetty.

The harbour tends to be a bit active (swelly) in east to north-east conditions. Anchorage is not permitted in the north-western and north-eastern corners of the harbour (which are uncomfortable anchorages anyway). The best place to land in the dinghy is on the beach in the south-west corner of the harbour.

Fuel, water and cold showers are available at the tourist boat jetty. Chandlery and slipping service are available at the harbour. Taxis run regularly between the harbour and the city 3 kilometres away. A phone box is on the corner in the small boat harbour.

Just down the road from the small boat harbour is the Mackay Cruising Yacht Club, a very friendly club and one which welcomes visitors. Hot showers are available there.

MACKAY OUTER HARBOUR

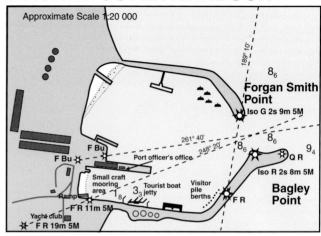

The main sugar wharf at Mackay Outer Harbour with the port officer's quarters on the pier just beyond it. The small boat anchorage with its pile berths is at the right, just out from the sand beach in the south-western corner of the harbour.

THE REEF GROUP

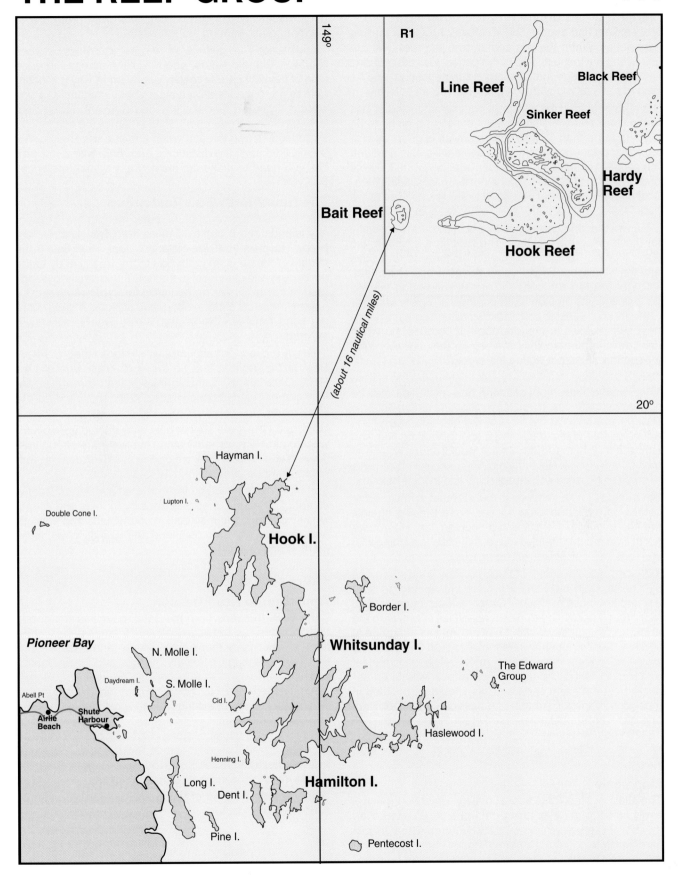

149°

R1

Line Reef

Black Reef

Sinker Reef

Hardy Reef

Bait Reef

Hook Reef

(about 16 nautical miles)

20°

Hayman I.

Double Cone I.

Lupton I.

Hook I.

Border I.

Pioneer Bay

N. Molle I.

Whitsunday I.

The Edward Group

Daydream I.

S. Molle I.

Abell Pt

Cid I.

Airlie Beach

Shute Harbour

Haslewood I.

Henning I.

Long I.

Hamilton I.

Dent I.

Pine I.

Pentecost I.

General notes on visiting the outer reefs

Most sailors find that visiting an offshore reef is a thrilling experience. When the tide comes over the reef, you are just sitting out in the middle of the ocean. Visit these areas with the knowledge that conditions can be testing, and it's best to have as many things going for you as possible.

It is recommended that skippers not attempt their first visit to the Hook/Hardy/Bait complex if the wind is going to be blowing more than 15 knots. That advice is given by professional skippers and cruising sailors alike. It is said that the experience of being trapped in a lagoon with 30 knots of wind and the tide rising is one not soon forgotten. (Bareboat charterers are not permitted to sail themselves to the outer reefs, but there are many other ways to get there.)

Light weather and good visibility are important, especially for those going the first time. The best time is after it has been blowing from the south-east for three to four days and the wind is starting to die off. A high pressure system, with gentle gradient, centred over Brisbane and moving very slowly, will provide good conditions – clear weather with light south-east to north-east winds and perhaps north-east sea breezes in the afternoon. If possible, go when low tide is in the middle of the day for best visibility (and for comfort at anchor during the night).

Depending upon your ultimate destination, the trip is from 17-25 nautical miles not counting how much tide may be flowing beneath you. If you leave Stonehaven or Butterfly Bay, for example, at the start of the ebb tide, everything will be going for you. If bucking a spring flooding tide, you can add 1–2 hours to the time it would normally take to travel the distance. Nevertheless, the principal objective is to arrive at the reefs with the sun high and the tide near low.

Set a course for No. 1 beacon. You will need to make some course correction to allow for set, more if going against the tide than with it. If bucking a flooding tide, steer more north than the rhumb-line course. If the tide is running with you, easterly correction will be needed.

Tidal currents are strong in the area; they flood south and ebb north. Both high and low tides are about one hour earlier than those at Mackay Outer Harbour (subtract one hour from Mackay times). The rise and fall is similar to the northern Whitsundays, about half as great as the range at Mackay. Tidal streams are seldom less than 2 knots. They may reach 8 knots in the deep channel between Hook Reef and Hardy Reef. Wind-against-tide effects should be observed carefully and certain areas should be avoided in these conditions; for example, the pass between Hook Reef and Bait Reef should not be used in south-east winds over 15–20 knots when the tide is flooding (setting south), because at such times you may encounter steep 3–4-metre waves.

Map scale

The scale of Map R1 is approximately 1:128 000 (necessarily small to get everything onto one page). Moreover, there is not very much more detailed information available from which to construct a more detailed chart. Most information exists solely in the heads of those who have acquired it by first-hand experience. Local knowledge is certainly useful, particularly in negotiating the entrance to Hardy Lagoon through the 'Waterfall'.

The distances are quite large - e.g. some 2 miles between Bait and Triangle Reefs, about 5 miles across the open side of Hook. It can be readily appreciated why it is desirable to go to the Reef on a clear sunny day and why you should arrive at, or near, low tide (but not earlier than 9.30 am in the winter and 7.30–8.00 am in the summer, to avoid looking into the sun when it is at a flat angle). With strong tidal sets, big distances, and reefs with a low profile, you need to make the most of any visual references that you have.

The Hook/Hardy/Bait Reef group

Bait Reef is the nearest of the outer reefs to the Whitsunday Islands and is some 17 miles from The Narrows, between Hayman and Hook islands. Hook Reef lies in the middle of the complex, with Bait to the west, Hardy to the north-east and Line Reef to the north. Two smaller associated reefs are Sinker, immediately north of Hardy, and Triangle Reef, west of the western end of Hook. A deep channel runs between Hook and Hardy Reefs, with swift currents.

There are overnight anchorages at Hook Reef, at Hardy Reef in the lagoon, and on the north-west side of Line Reef. Once again, it should be stressed that these are fairweather overnight anchorages. When the tide is up, the reefs cover.

Hook and Line reefs are not only unprotected from south-west to almost north-east winds but there are strong tidal flows in and around them which can cause discomfort with contrary winds of more than 10 knots.

The outer reefs provide a taste of what the Barrier Reef is all about. The area is heavily used by tourists and divers, who fly out from the mainland in amphibians and helicopters, or travel from the mainland and islands in fast catamarans and cruisers.

Excellent diving, snorkelling, fishing and reef exploring make it worth the trip.

Approach to No. 1 beacon

If the wind freshens from the south-east and the tide is flooding, don't go between Bait and Triangle reefs; conditions will be nasty there. Alter course and pass west of Bait Reef. Passage between Triangle and Hook Reef is possible, although locals do not recommend it to those without experience. No. 1 beacon is at the eastern end of Triangle and the reef extends a long way to the north-west and west. Watch out.

No. 1 beacon is usually visible as a 'black post' from some 6 to 8 miles off. Large limestone rocks and waves along the weather (south-east) side of Hook Reef are usually visible from 3 to 4 miles distance at half tide.

When approaching all of these anchorages, you should keep a lookout posted.

HOOK/HARDY/LINE/BAIT REEFS

R1

NOT FOR NAVIGATION: SEE CHART AUS 825

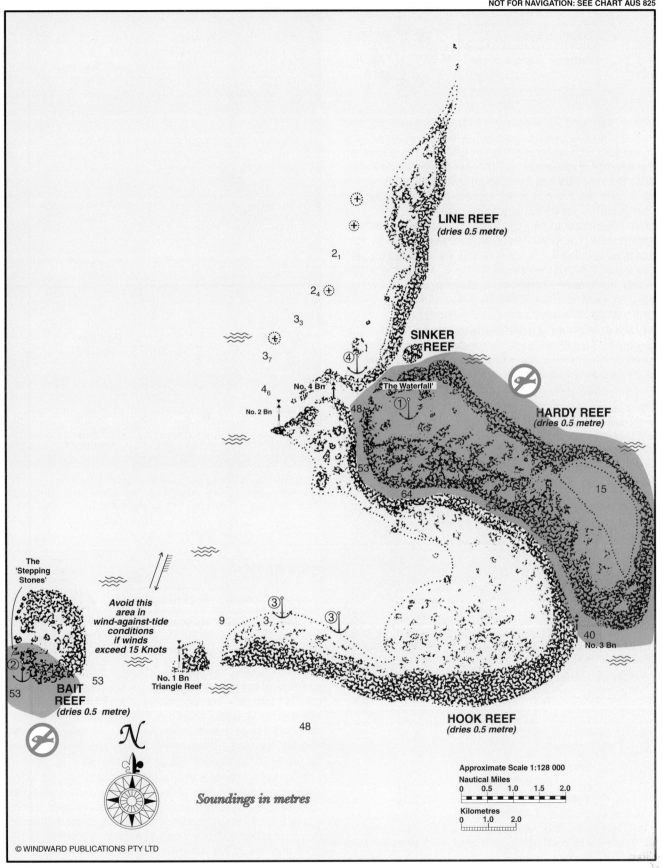

LINE REEF
(dries 0.5 metre)

2_1

2_4

3_3

SINKER
REEF

3_7

④

'The Waterfall'

No. 4 Bn

4_6

No. 2 Bn

①

48

HARDY REEF
(dries 0.5 metre)

53

64

54

15

53

The
'Stepping
Stones'

Avoid this
area in
wind-against-tide
conditions
if winds
exceed 15 Knots

③

③

9

3_7

③

②

53

53

BAIT
REEF
(dries 0.5 metre)

No. 1 Bn
Triangle Reef

48

40
No. 3 Bn

HOOK REEF
(dries 0.5 metre)

N

Soundings in metres

Approximate Scale 1:128 000
Nautical Miles
0   0.5   1.0   1.5   2.0

Kilometres
0   1.0   2.0

© WINDWARD PUBLICATIONS PTY LTD

HARDY LAGOON (R1)

Depth:	5–9 m
Bottom:	Sand & coral

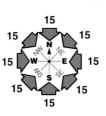

Leave No. 2 and No. 4 beacons to starboard and proceed to 'the Waterfall', which is actually the *third waterfall* (gap in the reef with water moving in/out). There is a pole on the left side of the entrance. Enter the lagoon immediately after the reef has just covered and is stabilised (water is no longer running out of the lagoon) or at high tide. The reef becomes stabilised about one hour after low water in neap tides or about two and a half hours after low water in spring tides. There is a depth of 2.2 metres (with '0' tide) just after stabilisation; coral is clearly visible close on both sides and the channel is unambiguous. The bommie just inside the lagoon entrance will also be sufficiently covered for vessels with 2.2 metres draught (although it may give you a momentary case of the jimjams).

Anchor as soon as you are inside and feel a comfortable distance from the reef. If you get too far in you may be frightened by amphibious aircraft that will be landing in the lagoon. The bottom is sand over coral; use plenty of chain.

The small waterfalls can be used for dinghy access at other times if you have a sufficiently powerful motor. The main waterfall in full ebb has such a volume of water pouring out that it produces a 'rooster tail'; only those with a death wish or seeking cheap thrills would attempt this one.

Hardy Reef is a Marine National Park 'B' Zone – a 'look-but-don't-take' zone (see pages 110–114).

Currents in the deep channel between Hardy Reef (right) and Hook Reef (left) can run swiftly. Hardy Reef is a Marine National Park 'B' Zone; fishing and shell collecting are prohibited.

'The Waterfall' entrance into Hardy Lagoon is a formidable sight when the ebb is in full swing. The reef becomes 'stabilised' about two hours after low water during neap tides and about two and a half hours after low water in spring tides.

BAIT REEF (R1)

Depth:	6–11 m
Bottom:	Sand & coral

This is a daytime, temporary anchorage only, and because it is one of the prime locations for scuba diving, special care is required when anchoring to avoid making contact with live coral. Boats should not be left unattended at anchor. It is infinitely preferable, for your own peace of mind and for the sake of the coral, to pick up one of the two public moorings for vessels up to 18 metres in length.

The western side of Bait Reef is lined with rows of bommies that uncover only at low water springs, called the 'Stepping Stones', with navigable gaps between them. There is a cluster of four bommies south of 'the entrance' (which should be entered only in a dinghy) and then bommies right on up the north-west side.

The bottom shelves fairly steeply from 3 to 18 metres. This spot is called the Manta Ray Dropoff by divers and is one of the best dives on the reef.

The Stepping Stones and bommies in the lagoon provide very good diving too. One tank of air will do you for one figure of eight around a couple of bommies.

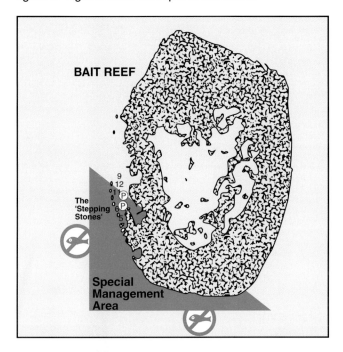

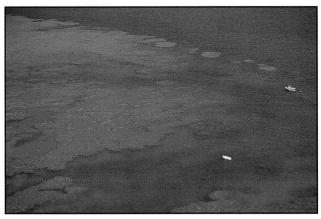

Looking south-west over Bait Reef and 'The Stepping Stones'.

HOOK REEF (R1)

Depth:	6–9 m
Bottom:	Sand & coral

There is quite a tidal sweep right across Hook Reef and if south-east winds exceed 15 knots with a flooding tide, it is very uncomfortable. It tends to be uncomfortable in winds other than south-east or east.

You can go between Triangle Reef and Hook Reef, although it is not recommended for those who are not familiar with the area. Go around Triangle if you are not sure.

LINE REEF (R1)

Depth:	3–9 m
Bottom:	Sand & coral

Coming from the south, after passing No. 2 and No. 4 beacons, there is a spot in Line Reef that has a minimum of 1.8 metres water over it which can be found by keeping No. 4 beacon in line with the gap between Hook and Hayman islands. You can go straight over the top of Line Reef until you get to a position where No. 2 and No. 4 beacons line up. Anchor there.

An easy way to remember the location of the anchorage is to have 'two and four in line behind Line'.

INDEX OF ANCHORAGES AND PLACENAMES

* Unofficial name not indicated on map

*Unofficial name not indicated on map

INDEX OF ANCHORAGES AND PLACENAMES

* Unofficial name not indicated on map

GENERAL INDEX

GENERAL INDEX (continued)